FORENSIC SCIENCE AND
THE ADMINISTRATION
OF JUSTICE

For my Mom and Dad, my children, Charlotte and Jack, and of course my wife, Amy. Thank you for your ongoing love and support (and for putting up with me).

—KJS

For Orit and Emerson, you are my love and my life.

—MJH

FORENSIC SCIENCE AND THE ADMINISTRATION OF JUSTICE

Critical Issues and Directions

Kevin J. Strom
RTI International

Matthew J. Hickman
Seattle University

Los Angeles | London | New Delhi
Singapore | Washington DC

Los Angeles | London | New Delhi
Singapore | Washington DC

FOR INFORMATION:

SAGE Publications, Inc.
2455 Teller Road
Thousand Oaks, California 91320
E-mail: order@sagepub.com

SAGE Publications Ltd.
1 Oliver's Yard
55 City Road
London EC1Y 1SP
United Kingdom

SAGE Publications India Pvt. Ltd.
B 1/I 1 Mohan Cooperative Industrial Area
Mathura Road, New Delhi 110 044
India

SAGE Publications Asia-Pacific Pte. Ltd.
3 Church Street
#10-04 Samsung Hub
Singapore 049483

Printed in the United States of America

A catalog record of this book is available from the Library of Congress.

ISBN: 978-1-4522-7688-5

Publisher: Jerry Westby
Publishing Associate: MaryAnn Vail
Production Editor: Melanie Birdsall
Copy Editor: Matt Sullivan
Typesetter: Hurix Systems Pvt. Ltd.
Proofreader: Annie Lubinsky
Indexer: Sylvia Coates
Cover Designer: Anthony Paular
Marketing Manager: Terra Schultz

This book is printed on acid-free paper.

Certified Chain of Custody
Promoting Sustainable Forestry
www.sfiprogram.org
SFI-01268

SFI label applies to text stock

14 15 16 17 18 10 9 8 7 6 5 4 3 2 1

Brief Contents

Detailed Contents

Preface

I t's an exciting time in the forensic sciences; we are in an era of unprecedented growth and fascination with the seemingly endless applications of science to law. But it is also a time of serious introspection about the history, current status, and future of the field. Fundamental questions about the underlying science of some mainstay areas of the forensic sciences have been raised, not for the first time, but with renewed vigor and determination. At the same time, there are larger questions about the role of forensic science in the justice process. We decided to put this book together because, within the context of criminal justice, we saw a substantial gap between the social and physical sciences despite a rapidly growing body of social science research on the forensic sciences. While it is certainly important to study technical issues related to crime scene processing and the accuracy of forensic analysis, understanding more broadly how forensic evidence is being used and how it is impacting the justice system is also critical. We decided it was time to try and compile this research and make sense of it all. But why social science research on the forensic sciences? Why should we pay attention to this area of research?

One of the central themes of this book is the idea that social science research can inform us about the utility of forensic science with respect to both criminal investigations and adjudication. For example, some research has shown that forensic evidence—including DNA evidence—appears to play little to no role in police investigations, which may in part be due to some investigators using DNA evidence as a "last resort" when all other forms of leads have been exhausted. Other studies have demonstrated the potential utility of forensic analysis for non-violent crimes such as burglary and motor vehicle theft, although there are questions about the cost of such practices given other forensic workload pressures. A related issue is the decision-making processes for using criminal justice resources for analyzing and storing growing amounts of forensic evidence. From a policy perspective, questions must be addressed with respect to the prioritization of resources for forensic analysis and improvements in efficiencies across each stage of criminal case processing.

A second theme of this book concerns questions about the scientific underpinnings of forensic services, including the accuracy and scientific methods of certain forensic disciplines as well as the influence of external factors (such as potential biases that can be presented by analysts). The 2009 National Academy of Sciences (NAS) report, *Strengthening Forensic Science in the United States: A Path Forward*, provided a thorough examination of the field of forensic science, the scientific methods applied to forensic practice, and the structure and operations of different components of the forensic system. The NAS report has served as a useful framework for social science research on the forensic sciences, and a number of scholars are pursuing research in these areas.

A final theme of the book is the role of the crime laboratory in the American justice system. We know that crime laboratories have evolved over the years, in concert with technological advancements as well as increasing demands for laboratory resources. The editors argue that we can now begin to think of the laboratory as a decision stage in the criminal justice process, with crime laboratory actors exercising discretion regarding what types of cases to prioritize, how to meet the growing requirements for staff training and laboratory accreditation, and how to manage increasing pressures on productivity, proficiency, and accuracy. As such, these actors influence decision making at other decision stages in the criminal justice process.

We have organized the book in five key sections: (1) essays exploring the *demand* for forensic services; (2) essays addressing the *quality* of forensic services; (3) essays on the *utility* of forensic services; (4) essays dealing with *post-conviction* forensic issues; and finally (5) essays exploring the *future* role of forensic science in the administration of justice. Within each section, we have recruited top-notch contributors including academic researchers, scientists, laboratory directors, and legal scholars, and those who have worn more than one of these hats at various times during their careers (be sure to read their biographies in the back of the book).

Joseph L. Peterson, professor of criminal justice and criminalistics at California State University, Los Angeles, starts us off with a historical overview of the demand for forensic services. Peterson might be aptly titled the "Dean" of social science research on the forensic sciences, having contributed to this body of research over the past 40+ years. Next, Rachel Dioso-Villa, professor of criminology and criminal justice at Griffith University, examines the research evidence bearing on a particularly interesting source of demand for forensics, the so-called "*CSI* Effect." Finally, the editors round out the *demand* section with a chapter exploring the current state of knowledge about forensic evidence backlogs.

Among the writers on the *quality* of forensic services, we have Barry A. J. Fisher, retired crime laboratory director for the Los Angeles County Sheriff's Office, writing on the prospects for a research culture in the forensic sciences; Reinoud D. Stoel, Charles E. H. Berger, Wim Kerkhoff, and Erwin J. A. T. Mattijssen of the Netherlands Forensic Institute, with Itiel E. Dror of University College London, writing on the sources and management of contextual bias; and Jay Siegel, emeritus professor of forensic science at Michigan State University, who takes the reader through a fascinating tour of various ethical issues in the forensic sciences.

Next, on the *utility* of forensic services, we have included Sally Kelty and Roberta Julian of the University of Tasmania, with Robert Hayes of the Victoria Police, writing on how criminal justice actors use forensic services, and providing a framework for understanding critical decision points in investigations and identifying "leakage" points where evidence is not being used effectively; Michael D. White, professor of criminal justice, and Andrea R. Borrego, doctoral student, at Arizona State University, with David A. Schroeder, professor of criminal justice at the University of New Haven, who examine the use of DNA in police investigations and, finding that DNA evidence was being used by detectives as a tool of last resort (after other investigative tools had been exhausted), offer an explanatory framework for understanding some of the barriers to more routine use of DNA evidence by investigators; and Nina W. Chernoff, professor at the CUNY School of Law, who examines how prosecutors use forensic evidence and, particularly, the potential implications of the 2009 NAS report for prosecutors' use of forensic evidence in the legal process and related decision making.

Some critical *post-conviction* issues are taken up by John M. Collins Jr., a forensic policy and management advisor with RTI International and former director of forensic science for the Michigan State Police, who writes about the problems and challenges of evidence retention; and Kristen Skogerboe, professor of chemistry at Seattle University, who discusses confidence in forensic DNA testing and writes about the types and sources of error, quality assurance programs, proficiency testing, and research on forensic DNA testing.

Finally, in the section dealing with the *future* role of forensic sciences in the administration of justice, Max M. Houck, director of the District of Columbia Consolidated Forensic Laboratories, and Paul J. Speaker, professor of finance and economics at West Virginia University, explore business models for the forensic sciences; the editors lay out their arguments that forensic laboratories and their personnel are properly recognized as criminal justice decision makers who influence decision making at other decision stages; and Walter F. Rowe, professor of forensic sciences at The George Washington University, examines some of the most pressing issues facing the forensic sciences that must be resolved in the next 20 years.

We hope that you enjoy these readings and that, although some difficult issues are presented that may challenge what you know or believe about the forensic sciences, you will leave with a sense of optimism. This optimism should derive from the fact that such a rich and diverse body of research on understanding the role of forensic sciences in the administration of justice demonstrates that, if nothing else, there is progress in tackling many of these difficult topics head-on. If we continue this momentum, the field will be much the better for it.

—Kevin J. Strom, Ph.D.   —Matthew J. Hickman, Ph.D.
Research Triangle Park, NC   *Seattle, WA*

Acknowledgments

SAGE gratefully acknowledges the contributions of the following reviewers:

John Edward Coratti, Lamar State College–Orange

Aman Gill, George Mason University

Mary Juno, San Jose State University

Mike Kusluski, Wayne State University

Virginia M. Maxwell, University of New Haven

Cynthia L. O'Donnell, Marymount University

Katherine A. Roberts, California State University, Los Angeles

Section I

The Demand for Forensic Services

No one seriously questions whether the demand for forensic services has increased over the past several decades. There is ample proof that over this period, more evidence has been submitted to crime laboratories, used in criminal investigations, and presented in judicial proceedings. What is commonly debated, however, are the sources of the increased demand and the role (and effect) of forensic evidence on the administration of justice. This section includes three readings that speak to the issue of demand. First, in "A Historical Review of the Demand for Forensic Evidence," Joseph L. Peterson begins by taking the reader through an important discussion of forensic evidence potential—that is, what physical evidence is and what it can tell us—and then provides a thorough history of the research bearing on the presence and use of physical evidence in criminal investigations. As the key producer of most of that research, there is perhaps no better person than Peterson to reflect on the past 50 years of research evidence on the demand for forensic services. Peterson shows that while general forensic resources have increased over time, they have not kept pace with submitted evidence, much less available evidence at scenes of crime. Yet, Peterson also shows that, despite the increased use of forensic evidence, still today only a relatively small fraction of available physical evidence at crime scenes is analyzed by laboratories.

Next, Rachel Dioso-Villa focuses on a specific source of public demand for forensic evidence, the so-called "*CSI* effect" in which popular media programs (The *CSI: Crime Scene Investigation* television program(s) in particular) are posited to generate an unrealistic expectation that forensic science is always available in every crime, and forensic science will save the day by delivering the truth to an otherwise fallible justice process. In Chapter 2, "Is There Evidence of a '*CSI* Effect'?" Dioso-Villa takes the reader through the all-too-familiar, idealized television version of forensic science, and draws on "cultivation theory" as a framework to help understand how such media can influence jurors' understandings of the nature and role of the scientific examination of physical evidence. Dioso-Villa reviews the available research evidence on the effect of forensic-based television programs on the justice process, and concludes that, while we can debate the existence of such an effect, there is no evidence in support of the most worrisome outcomes such as wrongful acquittals or convictions. However, the media, jurors, and legal actors nevertheless believe the "*CSI* effect" to be real, and, as a result, legal actors, forensic scientists, and law enforcement must deal with its consequences in practice.

Finally, the editors provide a chapter focusing on a specific side effect of increased demand for forensic services, namely, forensic evidence backlogs. In Chapter 3, "What We Know (and Don't Know) About Evidence Backlogs," Hickman and Strom present the available research on the nature and scope of forensic evidence backlogs in the United States, including those in crime laboratories and law enforcement agencies. Much debate has been focused on the extent to which evidence backlogs in crime laboratories might represent "justice delayed" (focused on the due process rights of the accused, as well as the safety of the public as offenders remain on the street free to commit additional crimes). Conversely, evidence backlogs in law enforcement agencies including police departments and sheriff's offices might represent "justice denied" (focused on the rights of crime victims). Hickman and Strom suggest that evidence backlogs might instead simply represent "justice satisficed" in that backlogs are possibly an expected consequence of imperfect information and communication about the utility and processing of forensic evidence. Yet, there is reason for optimism as some jurisdictions have experienced significant declines in evidence backlogs by improving internal processes and coordination with jurisdictional partners. The authors highlight steps that can be taken to reduce backlogs and successes made in some jurisdictions across the country.

1

A Historical Review of the Demand for Forensic Evidence

Joseph L. Peterson

Introduction

There have been many significant improvements and dramatic growth of forensic crime laboratories capabilities in the past half-century. The number of facilities, size of laboratory operations, and the sensitivity and precision of scientific tests have all increased (Durose, Walsh, & Burch, 2012). The ability of forensic examiners to characterize biological evidence using DNA testing methods has been the most notable of many scientific breakthroughs; the speed and sensitivity of laboratory techniques to examine traces of DNA have improved dramatically (National Institute of Justice, 2013). Computerized databases to store DNA profiles, fingerprints, and firearms- and ammunition-related information have been established and continue to expand daily, enabling investigators to solve cold cases and identify offenders leaving behind crime scene evidence. Growing approximately fourfold in the past 50 years, the more than 400 publicly funded forensic crime laboratories in the nation offer improved scientific services to law enforcement, and important contributions to the overall system of justice. The profession has also instituted many improvements to raise standards of education, training, operations, and quality-control steps within these laboratories (Bashinski & Peterson, 2003). In addition, the criminal justice system has grown to expect forensic science results in major criminal investigations and prosecutions that has, in turn, increased the demand for scientific evidence.

Estimating the Demand for Forensic Evidence

Although demand for scientific services has increased over the years, there are various factors that also limit the demand for forensic evidence and the ability of the profession to respond to it. The crime laboratory field continues to be hit with periodic controversies that cause concern over the scientific integrity of individual analysts, crime laboratories, and the profession itself (Balko, 2011; Clark, 2012). The 1993 U.S. Supreme Court decision *Daubert v. Merrell Dow Pharmaceuticals*, which set new minimum standards for the admissibility of scientific evidence, continues to challenge the forensic field (see also *Kumho Tire Co. v. Carmichael, General Electric Co. v. Joiner*). The 2009 National Research Council report, *Strengthening Forensic Science*, has also raised serious concerns over the scientific foundation of laboratory examination and data interpretation practices employed in many areas of forensic science testing.

While research shows that resources devoted to forensic scientific testing have increased, actual budgets have not increased at a pace to examine all submitted evidence, let alone all available physical evidence at crime scenes. Recent data will be presented in this chapter that show that use of scientific evidence still occurs in only a small percentage of criminal cases, and only a fraction of physical evidence available at crime scenes is actually collected and examined. Available scientific evidence may be filtered out at the crime scene itself or, if collected, remains in police evidence rooms unexamined because investigators do not request testing. Investigator failure to request an examination of submitted evidence is common and a reflection of various factors: long testing turnaround times, poor investigator training, a belief that testing would not be helpful in a given case, and concern about placing added demands on limited laboratory resources. This chapter will explore the critical interface between investigators and crime laboratories, and examine the reasons why much available physical evidence goes unexamined.

The demand for forensic evidence test results, and the ability of the system to respond, is a complex issue that depends on various factors, ranging from limited laboratory resources to a reluctance of investigators and prosecutors to request testing be done. At base, parent police organizations do not allocate sufficient resources to the crime scene investigation units and crime laboratories to capture and analyze available physical evidence. This chapter will begin with a discussion of forensic evidence potential, will proceed through a historical review of physical evidence utilization rates, and present recent research results that show most available physical clues are filtered by different personnel before completion of laboratory analysis. The chapter concludes with results of a recent study that shows physical evidence affects arrest, charging, and sentencing. and asks the question, "Why don't agencies capitalize on such findings and allocate needed resources to forensic crime laboratories?"

What Is Physical Evidence and What Can It Tell Us?

Much of the technical literature of forensic science over the decades, in academic texts and training manuals, has centered on the "theoretical" types of assistance that the scientific analysis of physical evidence can provide to investigators, prosecutors, and other legal fact-finders (Fisher & Fisher, 2012). This literature clearly delineates the potential that physical evidence can offer but does not consider how related information in active investigations may inflate or deflate that potential. Guidance present in most forensic training texts stresses that it is of the utmost importance to collect all available evidence at scenes because these physical traces are perishable, and one never knows early in an investigation if particular evidence might prove critical in solving a case. Forensic science practitioners and authors advise that scientific evidence examinations have the potential to offer investigators the following types of information (see Johnson et al., 2012; Peterson et al., 2010).

IDENTIFICATION

The great bulk of physical evidence that is examined in the forensic crime laboratory focuses (initially, at least) on the identification of various materials. This can range from the identification of confiscated drugs and other controlled substances, the identification of alcohol and poisons in toxicological samples, and the identification of volatile liquids that can be identified in the debris collected from scenes of suspicious fires. The identification of controlled substances such as marijuana, heroin, cocaine, and methamphetamines make up the great bulk (as high as 70% of total caseloads) of evidence analyzed by crime laboratories. This drug caseload has remained remarkably high for the past 40+ years as drugs and narcotics became a major law enforcement and social problem in the late 1960s, and where a chemical identification of the substance is essential for a successful prosecution. Identifying the specific type of substance can be the starting point for many examinations and move the process forward.

CLASSIFICATION

Forensic crime laboratories will not only identify the unknown substance (e.g., blood, paint, or a synthetic fiber) but also place it in a more restricted category such as human blood, acrylic blue paint, or rayon. This additional classification may aid in determining the possible origin of the unknown material and thereby show that it could or could not have originated from a particular person, object, or crime scene. The more narrowly defined the classification is, the greater the likelihood that questioned evidence could have shared a common origin with a known sample of comparable evidence. If an item's class characteristics are clearly different from a known sample, the examiner may definitively conclude they did not share a common source.

INDIVIDUALIZATION/DETERMINATION OF COMMON ORIGIN

Such a finding means the examiner is able to conclude an item of evidence of unknown source originated from a particular perpetrator, victim, or tool/firearm used during the course of a crime. Such evidence transfer between an offender and victim or physical scene helps to place persons at particular locations and can be highly incriminating. Examiners will compare evidence of unknown origin (such as a latent fingerprint, spent bullet, or biological stain) with a reference sample of known origin (a set of fingerprints taken from a suspect, a projectile test fired from a suspect's weapon, and blood or DNA sample taken from a particular person of known identity). These findings are termed "individualizations" and have the potential to link a person, weapon, or tool to a crime. In practice, such individualizations that connect a suspect to a scene or victim are quite unusual and largely limited to latent fingerprints, biological stains, and firearms-related evidence. Examinations of other mass-produced synthetics, construction materials, and even botanical evidence can usually only show they are indistinguishable or similar in all measurable characteristics with evidentiary materials. Typically, a forensic examiner may offer a partial or potential association, but not a true individualization.

Individuality may be the "holy grail" of criminalistics, but DNA testing of biological fluids is one of the few types of physical evidence where scientific data clearly support the individuality of the evidence. In fact, the recent 2009 NAS *Strengthening Forensic Science* report concluded that most other types of pattern physical evidence—from latent fingerprints, firearms/toolmarks, shoeprints, and handwriting to bitemarks—lack a solid scientific foundation to form such conclusions. The long biomedical history of DNA testing, and the collection of extensive data on the uniqueness of DNA characteristics from populations around the world, affords it the scientific basis to form such individuality conclusions. Even latent fingerprint examiners must use caution in concluding a partial latent fingerprint found at a crime scene originated from a particular suspect, because the field lacks empirical data on the number and type of fingerprint minutiae needed to form common origin conclusions. Computerized databases of DNA, fingerprints, and bullet and shell casings have enhanced the ability of criminalists to narrow their search and to link questioned evidence to a small group of possible suspects or firearms. After a review of candidate matches, follow-up examination by knowledgeable experts can confirm the match.

Automated Fingerprint Identification System (AFIS), National Integrated Ballistic Information Network (NIBIN), and Combined DNA Index System (CODIS) databases holding digital information on fingerprints, firearms ammunition, and known DNA profiles have enhanced the ability of forensic laboratories and identification bureaus to use evidence from a crime scene to solve "whodunit" and cold cases, and identify an otherwise unknown offender. Before such digital reference collections, investigators needed known standards from one or more suspects with whom they could compare crime scene evidence. This greatly restricted the use of physical evidence to aid in the solution of these challenging cases. Now, digital evidence collections have the ability to assist with these investigations and sort through this evidence. Cold "hits" exploiting such crime scene evidence when querying these databases have helped investigations tremendously.

Crime scene investigators still have the daunting task of locating evidence at a crime scene that will link the actual perpetrator to a crime. Finding such evidence at a scene can be very challenging as the investigator is required to assess large quantities of physical materials in the environment, much left by victims or other persons who had legitimate access to the crime scene. Most physical materials at a scene do not implicate the perpetrator or have little bearing on the investigation. Through training and experience, and by focusing on entry, exit, and "target areas" of the crime scene, the skilled investigator can select the most viable evidence. Investigators must be discriminating and not "scoop up" everything they see; crime laboratories do not have the resources to accept and evaluate all such materials and must rely on crime scene search officers to make discriminating choices.

In recent years, many agencies have focused on potentially available DNA evidence at scenes of crimes that may identify or confirm the identity of suspects. The National Institute of Justice (NIJ), in particular, has encouraged the use of DNA techniques and databases in cold and unsolved case investigations, and encouraged coordinated approaches among investigators, prosecutors, and crime laboratory personnel. NIJ has also been active in promoting the use of DNA in property and minor offenses (in particular, see Roman et al., 2009). The growth of the national CODIS database is enhancing these procedures (now reinforced by the recent U.S. Supreme Court *King v. Maryland* decision upholding the collection of DNA from arrestees). A brief summary of these DNA efforts is included in Peterson, Hickman, Strom, and Johnson (2013).

RECONSTRUCTION

One of Peterson, Mihajlovic, and Gilliland's (1984) earlier studies detailed how scientific results from the crime laboratory occasionally result in reconstruction findings. This study of five jurisdictions nationwide reported how crime laboratory results typically provided insight as to how crimes unfolded. Physical evidence may be useful in reconstructing the criminal incident, showing point(s) of entry, activities surrounding the target of the crime, and point(s) of exit (if different) from entry. It may indicate where the offender gained access to the crime scene (breaking and entering); the relative positions of offender, victim, or other participants when the crime was committed; the order of crucial events; or how the offender gained access to items stolen. Establishing such "ground truth" of how the offender committed the criminal act helps build a helpful narrative for investigators in developing the offender's modus operandi.

DIFFERENT ORIGIN/NEGATIVE IDENTIFICATION

A negative identification results when the criminalist determines the substance in question is not what the investigator suspected it to be (the reddish substance was paint, not blood, or the residue was baking soda, not cocaine). Such findings may serve to eliminate a suspect from suspicion, close an investigation, or turn it in a completely new direction. Where comparisons show an evidentiary item and a standard are of different origin, they serve to dissociate persons, objects, and locations. Examples include when a biological stain did not originate from a prime suspect, a projectile was not fired from a particular weapon, or a latent fingerprint does not belong to a particular suspect. Such findings can be significant in excluding or exonerating a particular suspect and redirecting an investigation.

INCONCLUSIVE FINDINGS

Many examinations are not conclusive, and the examiner is not able to form a clear conclusion (unlike on television!). The evidence may be badly damaged, contaminated, or compromised in some fashion, and the examiner is prevented from developing definitive information or answers to investigator questions. Searches of databases may not yield the identity of a particular individual because the owner's fingerprint or DNA is not in the database or the questioned evidence is contaminated or does not contain clear points of identity. Inconclusive results are different from exclusions in that examiners can only report that evidence failed to establish a connection between principals and the crime scene.

Physical Evidence Presence—Historical Indicators

There have been few studies over the years that have attempted to document the presence and utilization of physical evidence in criminal investigations. Brian Parker's (1963) survey of forensic laboratories was among the first to find that scientific evidence was used in a very small percentage of cases—in his survey, he found that evidence was used in only about 1% of criminal violations. Later, Parker was funded by the National Institute of Law Enforcement and Criminal Justice (the predecessor to the

National Institute of Justice) to empirically determine the presence of physical evidence at the scenes of serious crimes (Parker & Peterson, 1972). Teams of criminalistics graduate students responded to the scenes of crimes reported to the police and found physical evidence present at about 88% of locations. The physical materials varied by type of evidence and offense category. Multiple forms of evidence were commonly present at scenes. This is the only study reported in the literature that documented the various types of physical evidence at crime scenes that didn't rely on surveys or police reports cataloging evidence that was collected after the crime scene was investigated.

Parker and Peterson's early research also found that most of this evidence was neither collected nor routed to a forensic laboratory for examination. This original research found that only about 0.1% of the offenses in the sample resulted in evidence being examined in the laboratory. Peterson's (1974) subsequent monograph accounted for how and why this evidence was neither collected nor examined. He identified a series of police "filters" that accounted for the exclusion of this evidence. It began with a patrol officer's or investigator's decision not to request a specially trained crime scene technician to respond to the scene to locate, collect, and preserve the evidence. Evidence technicians responded to crime scenes but often did not gather evidence that was present. These decisions were not solely based on evidence being present/not present, but often resulted from judgments on the part of technicians and investigators that available evidence did not merit collection or examination. Most of these (negative) decisions were based on an assessment of the seriousness of the crime, an evaluation of the legitimacy of victims, as well as the condition and potential usefulness of the evidence. Subsequent filters led officers (and supervisors) not to forward collected evidence to the crime laboratory for analysis. Even if the evidence was submitted for analysis, it often remained unexamined unless the investigator in charge of the case requested the laboratory to examine it.

Peterson's 1974 monograph described various styles of evidence technicians for responding to different types of crime scenes, interacting with victims (usually in property crimes), and deciding if physical clues were to be collected. On numerous occasions, he reported that technicians found their primary mission to provide "service" to the victim that sometimes involved misrepresentation of their activities by collecting materials they had no intention of submitting for analysis. Occasionally, investigators were even found to deposit, dust, and lift their own fingerprints if they thought it would impress the victim. Even at this time, long before the modern *CSI* era, crime scene officers were observed taking actions or offering commentary to victims so as not to disappoint them, leaving them with the impression that they received professional service.

Almost 40 years later, Makin (2012) contributed an article that described "simulated evidence collection" where investigators might "swab, powder, or collect nonviable samples to demonstrate that the victim received the full resources of the agency" (p. 126). He described "bagging and tagging" practices of crime scene officers where evidence was collected, documented, and returned to police evidence storage rooms, never to be analyzed, and sometimes discarded. Makin found that about 30% of law enforcement officers in his study knew of officers or technicians who had engaged in collecting "simulated evidence." Officers thought that the television inspired *CSI* effect was in part responsible for driving such practices, and that the PR value of such steps on (property crime) victims was a prime explanation. Makin proposes an interesting theory that such practices might, in part, explain the sizeable fraction of physical evidence that is backlogged in evidence storage rooms and not examined (discussed elsewhere in this chapter).

More than 10 years elapsed after the Parker study before NIJ funded additional studies to investigate the role of physical evidence in criminal investigations and prosecutions. The first study, *Forensic Evidence and the Police* (Peterson et al., 1984), reviewed almost 2,700 randomly selected case files stratified by offense type (homicide, rape, robbery, aggravated assault, and burglary) and controlled for the presence or absence of physical evidence in the instant case. The utilization of physical evidence varied widely by crime type, ranging from almost 100% of homicides and drug cases and 75% of rapes, to only about 15% of attempted murders, 33% of burglaries, and 20% of robberies. On reviewing paper case files, these figures primarily estimated percentages of evidence collected *and* examined, but did not account for evidence collected but not examined.

Apart from suspected drug cases, which constitute upwards of three-quarters of crime laboratory caseloads, blood, hair, firearms, and fingerprints were the primary forms of physical evidence collected and examined in the laboratory. Very little trace evidence (fibers, glass, paint, soil, etc.) was collected and examined. Suspected semen was also a primary type of evidence collected in sexual assaults, primarily via sexual assault kits taken from the victim in post-assault medical examinations. Its analysis and eventual utility was largely a function of the prior relationship between the victim and the offender. Cases involving an offender previously known (identified) by the victim usually resulted in a lower percentage of examined evidence. Violent, personal criminal investigations typically involved greater collection and analysis of physical evidence, and it was usually done earlier in the investigation.

A recent study addressed collected physical evidence stored in police property rooms that remains unexamined nationwide (Strom et al., 2009; Strom & Hickman, 2010). In a survey of 2,000 law enforcement agencies covering the years 2002–2007, agencies reported that they had not submitted collected evidence for examination in 14% of unsolved homicides, 18% of unsolved rapes, and 23% of unsolved property crimes. The study concluded that there may be good reasons why such evidence is not examined, as where defendants pled guilty or charges were dropped, but there were also situations where untrained personnel did not appreciate the full potential of the unexamined evidence in cases without suspects, where prosecutors had not requested an analysis, or where lengthy crime laboratory backlogs discouraged police personnel from making such a request.

Attention has also been paid of late to the substantial percentage of sexual assault cases where physical evidence, though collected by medical personnel in sexual assault kits from victims, is never examined. Ritter (2011) was one of the first to highlight this issue in her NIJ report that looked at the types and quantities of untested evidence contained in these kits, and efforts to understand the reasons cited by law enforcement and crime laboratories for this situation. The Strom et al. (2009) study described above found evidence collected but not examined in almost one in five rape cases. Human Rights Watch (Tofte, 2009) published a study in 2009 investigating the problem of sexual violence in Los Angeles and brought attention to the volume of untested sexual assault kits in the hands of law enforcement agencies. A study followed (Peterson et al., 2011) of the almost 11,000 untested sexual assault kits stored in Los Angeles city and county law enforcement freezers over the past 10 or more years. DNA profiles were determined in a high percentage (~60%) of these ~2,000 cases sampled that were uploaded into CODIS, but exams did not result in any added arrests and only two additional convictions. Current "action research" studies in Detroit and Houston (Ritter, 2011) are reviewing thousands of untested kits in police and laboratory storage areas to discover the reasons for non-testing, whether these kits should still be tested, the results of real time testing, and proper testing policies and practices for the future.

One might consider this backlogged sexual assault evidence against the research by Makin on symbolic evidence collection. It may be that historically, the collection of this sexual assault kit evidence from victims was not always for its analysis, particularly in cases where the victim knew the suspect. Was it "symbolic" from an investigator's standpoint, where they never intended for it to be examined? What criteria should be used in the future by investigators and criminalists to decide if this evidence is to be examined? The reader should note, however, that the parent law enforcement agencies in the Peterson (2011) study have directed crime laboratories to examine *all* sexual assault kit evidence that is collected.

Macro Forces Influencing Utilization Patterns

Any treatment of factors influencing the growth of forensic science services and the demand for scientific evidence needs also to take a broad overview of legal, social, and political factors affecting the use of forensic evidence. Peterson and Leggett (2007) prepared a 40-year retrospective of criminal, legal, and professional issues affecting the growth and utilization of forensic evidence in the United States. In this article, their beginning point was the steep rise in violent crime and the drug abuse explosion occurring in the late 1960s. Violent crimes are the source of most physical/biological clues submitted to crime laboratories, and drug cases mandate a chemical analysis of the controlled substance in question for successful prosecution. These two forces started the first real surge of physical evidence and forensic laboratories in the modern era.

U.S. Supreme Court rulings in the 1960s (*Escobedo*, *Miranda*, etc.) provided more legal protections for criminal suspects and encouraged the police to place greater reliance on "extrinsic" physical evidence to link offenders to crime scenes and victims. The President's Commission on Law Enforcement and the Administration of Justice (Institute for Defense Analyses, 1967) forecast that the successful solution of crime depended on the discovery and analysis of physical clues. In the 1970s, the federally funded Law Enforcement Assistance Administration (LEAA) also injected billions of dollars into the nation's criminal justice system and supported the construction of many more regional crime laboratories that were in closer proximity to state and local law enforcement agencies, and that, presumably, would result in better use of physical evidence. NIJ launched its first round of research projects to document the educational, technical, and professional development needs in the field of forensic science, sponsored proficiency testing projects documenting testing deficiencies in the field, and underwrote programs to accredit laboratories and certify forensic examiners (Peterson, 1975).

The 1980s saw continued growth in and demand for forensic services, and efforts to upgrade the level of professionalism in the developing forensic field gained momentum. The introduction of DNA typing demonstrated the promise of enhanced forensic biological testing, but also the need for standardized methods of analysis and regulation of the field. Still, these voluntary professional efforts lagged and there were further legal challenges to the reliability of laboratory testing and the need for more rigorous ethical standards for examiners. Proficiency testing studies and legal critiques drew attention to areas like questioned document examination (Jonakait, 1991; Risinger, Denbeaux, & Saks, 1989), its reliability, and whether the courts should routinely admit such testimony. Clearly, the justice system's demand for expanded forensic services was also accompanied by scientific and legal demands that the forensic profession get its scientific house in order and address the quality and fairness with which laboratory services were practiced.

While the early 1990s saw scientific and legal acceptance of DNA testing as a forensic technique to individualize biological evidence, the field instituted DNA methods standardization (Technical Working Group on DNA Analysis Methods, or TWGDAM) and formation of a national database of DNA profiles of convicted offenders. The Innocence Project (InnocenceProject.org) also demonstrated that DNA was a technique that could remedy prior injustices, where old physical clues could be reexamined and exonerate convicted defendants who had been falsely imprisoned. The fact that DNA was a highly reliable testing technique that had both the power to link and to exclude suspects with a crime created great interest in the police and the legal communities, as well as the public, and stimulated greater demand for forensic DNA testing.

Legal efforts also continued to strengthen standards for evaluating the judicial admissibility of scientific and technical evidence and as a means to exclude "junk" science (Giannelli, 1993). The U.S. Supreme Court decision *Daubert v. Merrell Dow Pharmaceuticals* (1993), and its progeny (*Kumho Tire* and *Joiner*), outlined steps that judges could consider when assessing the admissibility of scientific evidence. Judges were tasked to think more like scientists in determining if the reasoning underlying expert testimony was "scientifically valid." In considering the admissibility of the technique, judges could evaluate if the theory had been subjected to peer review and publication, if there were known error rates and the maintenance of standards, as well as general acceptance of the technique. Twenty years later, many judges are still uncomfortable in applying *Daubert* standards to scientific evidence presented to the court. In spite of that reticence, some courts today are reconsidering the admissibility of such venerable techniques as latent fingerprint comparison, hair examination, and firearms and toolmark testing that make up a large part of forensic evidence collected and examined.

The 1990s were also significant in that there were several investigations of improper forensic crime laboratory practices in which substandard procedures led to questionable findings and testimony. The U.S. Department of Justice Inspector General Michael Bromwich's (2006) investigation of charges, leveled by a disgruntled FBI crime laboratory scientist about its explosives division, underscored the importance of the laboratory practicing good science and maintaining independence from criminal investigator influences (Office of the Inspector General, 1997). And, as forensic science grew in popular culture through such television programs as *CSI*, the general public and professionals questioned if crime laboratories could possibly live up to unrealistic television standards. Investigative journalists also began to target forensic laboratories and increasingly found crime laboratories to be in "crisis." Individual scientists like Fred Zain, Joyce Gilchrist, and Arnold Melnikoff were targeted for falsification of findings and reading far more into their examinations than the science allowed. Journalists have continued their investigations into crime laboratory operations, sometimes focusing on errant examiners and at other times questioning if laboratories had sufficient resources to respond to their caseloads. Laboratories have been found not to have adequate resources to respond to submitted evidence, which has led to high examiner caseloads and lengthy testing turnaround times.

Articles in major city newspapers during the past decade have continued this theme. The growth in DNA testing and public awareness of the potential of forensic science have resulted in the creation of new and expanded laboratory facilities (Hertzberg Davis Forensic Science Center, Los Angeles, CA, in 2007) and to more scientists, but the rise in evidence submissions and casework seems to have outdistanced laboratory capacity. While DNA capabilities have been greatly enhanced, the ability of laboratories to develop and meet scientific needs in other forensic testing areas have fallen short. The profession has failed to undertake the necessary studies to lay the proper scientific foundation to support the individualization conclusions of firearms, trace, latent fingerprints, and other pattern evidence (Giannelli, Imwinkelried, & Peterson, 2011). Some forensic examiners have ventured beyond proper scientific boundaries and have been too quick to support criminal investigator and prosecutor theories in their interpretation of evidence, and even taking shortcuts to achieve definitive results (Swecker & Wolf, 2010). The pressure on examiners to practice good scientific procedures and maintain high ethical standards has sometimes given way to pressures placed on crime laboratories to secure convictions and satisfy unrealistic public expectations.

Crime Laboratory Census Results

Over the past decade, the Bureau of Justice Statistics (BJS) of the U.S. Department of Justice has surveyed publicly funded forensic science crime laboratories in the United States, gathering data on their workload, staffing, budget, and operations. Three periodic surveys have been conducted and published thus far, with the most recent data published in 2012 (Durose, Walsh, & Burch, 2012). Survey results offer some insight into the growth of forensic sciences and the demand for forensic services. Between 2002 and 2009, the number of crime laboratories identified by BJS increased from 351 to 411. The number of responding crime laboratories rose from 305 in 2002 to 377 in 2009, almost a 26% increase. The total number of requests submitted to responding laboratories increased from about 2.7 million in 2002 to about 4.1 million in 2009, over a 50% increase. Forensic biology (DNA) made up about a third of all such requests. So, while the number of laboratories supplying data to the survey increased by more than 25%, the demand for services (DNA testing) grew even faster.

Because backlogs have been such a problem for crime labs in recent years, the surveys asked for the number of backlogged requests for testing that laboratories had at the end of the calendar year. Total backlogged requests grew from 0.5 million to 1.2 million over that seven-year time period. Forensic biology cases accounted for about three-quarters of this backlog, and most of these requests were for the analysis of convicted offenders' and arrestees' DNA samples. This is understandable, as forensic laboratories have been attempting to build the number of DNA profiles within CODIS. It is also interesting to note that budgets for all laboratories responding to the surveys had grown from about $1.0 billion in 2002 to about $1.6 billion in 2009, and the number of full-time equivalent (FTE) crime laboratory personnel grew from about 11,000 FTE personnel to over 13,000 personnel.

Clearly, the demand for forensic services has increased, and resources have increased, but backlogs have grown at an even faster pace.

Up-to-Date Utilization Patterns From the "Role and Impact" Study

The Role and Impact of Forensic Evidence in the Criminal Justice Process Project was funded in 2006 by the NIJ to enable researchers at California State University, Los Angeles to track the collection, examination, and value of physical evidence data represented in official police, laboratory, and prosecutor records in five jurisdictions (Los Angeles County; Indianapolis, IN; and the Indiana State Police Laboratory System: Evansville, Fort Wayne, and South Bend). The project had multiple objectives:

1. To estimate the percent of crime scenes where one or more types of physical evidence were collected and the types of forensic evidence collected

2. To track the use and attrition of physical evidence from crime scene through laboratory analysis, and then through subsequent stages of the criminal justice process

3. To assess the contribution of forensic evidence to case outcomes

This section will focus on the first two areas of the study to estimate the presence and demand for forensic evidence in various offense types (Peterson et al., 2010).

These sites were chosen to represent city, county, and state forensic crime laboratory service configurations in the United States. Collected physical evidence data were based on a random sample of the population of reported crime incidents for the year 2003, stratified by crime type and jurisdiction. Aggravated assault, burglary, homicide, rape, and robberies files were randomly selected to represent a range of serious personal and property crimes. Cases were primarily selected from the year 2003 so that case files would be closed and files would hopefully contain complete data, through to final court disposition. A total of 4,205 cases were sampled including 859 aggravated assaults, 1,263 burglaries, 400 homicides, 602 rapes, and 1,081 robberies.

Data were collected from three primary sources: police incident and investigation reports, crime laboratory reports, and prosecutor case files (primarily for case disposition and sentencing data). Various forensic variables were used for descriptive analyses: location and type of crime scene, presence of crime scene evidence (i.e., biological, latent prints, pattern evidence, firearms, natural and synthetic materials, generic objects, drugs), whether the evidence was submitted to the laboratory, and whether it was examined. Police incident and investigation reports yielded information on different forensic, offense, and disposition variables. Information from crime laboratory reports gave information on the type of evidence submitted and examined, and the results of laboratory examinations. Laboratory reports that resulted in unique identifications (individualizations) of evidence and those that linked one or more suspects to a crime scene or victim(s) were noted. The presence and type of physical evidence present, collected, and examined were determined exclusively from reports contained in police incident, crime scene technician, and investigator files.

AGGRAVATED ASSAULTS

Physical evidence/substrates were collected in about 30% of incidents, with firearms/weapons (e.g., guns, bullets, shell casings) the leading category of evidence gathered. In only about 12% of cases where evidence was collected was the evidence submitted to the crime laboratory, and most of it was firearms/weapons and latent print evidence. Examinations in 79 cases (9.2%) conducted across all crime laboratories yielded 34 cases with identifications of evidence, most of them (21) involving firearms-related evidence. In terms of individualizations, there were 18 cases with firearms individualities and four other individualities involving latent prints.

BURGLARY

Police collected physical evidence and substrates in almost one-fifth (19.6%) of burglaries. Latent prints made up a high percentage (84%) of the evidence collected. Most collected latent print evidence was submitted to the laboratories (75%), and crime labs examined approximately 72% of submitted prints. Laboratories produced 52 cases with individualized evidence—mostly latent prints.

HOMICIDE

A very high percentage (97%) of homicides resulted in physical evidence/substrates being collected, primarily firearms/weapons and natural/synthetic materials (mostly clothing). The next most frequently gathered physical clues were biological and latent print evidence. Unlike other crime types, a very high percentage (88.5%) of collected physical evidence was submitted to crime laboratories, and most was actually examined (81%).

RAPE

Approximately 64% of incidents had physical evidence or substrates collected. Biological and natural and synthetic materials were the two primary types of physical evidence collected. Sexual assault kits were employed to gather physical evidence in about half the cases. The kits held samples of suspected blood, semen, saliva, and DNA. The data revealed that there was a dramatic decline of collected evidence that was submitted to labs. More than two-thirds of sexual assault kits (68%) were not submitted to the laboratory for analysis. While some submitted evidence likely came from sexual assault kits, seldom were complete kits noted as submitted to the laboratories. A high percentage of cases with submitted semen evidence were examined (86.2%). Vaginal, blood, and latent print evidence also were examined in most submitted cases (87.5%, 59.0%, and 74.1%, respectively). In terms of establishing the uniqueness of evidence, 19 cases had individualized biological materials, and nine had individualized latent finger or palm prints.

ROBBERY

Physical evidence and substrates were collected in less than a quarter (24.8%) of the robbery incidents, but rates of collection varied greatly by jurisdiction. Latent prints, natural and synthetic materials, and firearms/weapons were collected most frequently. After latent prints, materials (clothing) was the next major category of evidence/substrates collected, followed by firearms/weapons. The evidence was submitted to crime laboratories in 44% of cases where it was collected (only 10.9% of all robbery incidents). A high percentage of the evidence submitted was actually examined (90.7%) but, overall, less than 10% of all robbery incidents had examined evidence. Latent print examinations yielded individualizations in almost half (44%) of the 41 cases where evidence was submitted to the respective crime laboratories.

Conclusion

The growth of forensic science has been steady over the past several decades. Agencies have devoted added resources to forensic laboratories, but there have been comparatively few efforts to ascertain the effects of such evidence. While there have been a handful of prior efforts, a recent article by Peterson et al. (2013) has made a renewed attempt. The authors examined data collected from a probability-based sample of 4,205 cases from five jurisdictions nationally that was described in the previous section. Cases were randomly selected from the crime categories of homicide (400 cases), rape (602), aggravated assault (850), robbery (1,081), and burglary (1,262).

Even though utilization rates were low, regression analyses showed that forensic evidence played a "consistent and robust role" in case-processing decisions across all crimes, but effects were time and examination dependent. The collection of evidence predicted arrest and case referral to prosecutors' decisions; the examination of evidence predicted case referral, charging, trial conviction, and the severity of sentences. While forensic evidence did not play a major role in plea bargains, interaction effects revealed that evidence that linked an offender with a victim or crime scene played a role in guilty pleas for stranger offenses. Interaction effects also indicated that collection of forensic evidence played a role in particular types of offenses: In robberies, collection of evidence from the scene increased the likelihood of arrest, and in homicides, evidence that linked the suspect to the victim/scene was a predictor of sentence length.

This is not the final word on the value of forensic evidence on criminal case processing. As those authors recommended, criminal justice and forensic science researchers should continue to examine the contributions of various types of evidence—including forensic—to criminal justice decisions. Quantitative and qualitative approaches are needed to understand how these processes work to advance the progress of cases through the justice process. Scientific evidence is a complex variable, and its value may shift depending on the presence or absence of other characteristics and evidence in a case. As one prosecutor observed when asked about the value of scientific evidence, "It depends!"

This review has detailed the following:

1. A high percentage of crime scenes have extensive varieties of physical evidence present. While collected evidence and substrates are not as high as the original Parker and Peterson (1972) study, a substantial percentage of crime scenes have evidence that is collected.

2. Evidence is collected from those scenes ranging from a higher percentage of serious personal crimes and a lower percentage of property crimes.

3. Only a fraction of that evidence is routed to forensic crime laboratories for analysis: A high percentage of homicide and burglary evidence is routed for analysis, but a lower percentage of rape and assault cases.

4. An even smaller percentage of evidence submitted to crime laboratories is actually examined. Less than 2% of cases result in scientific evidence associating a suspect with the crime scene or victim. Robberies had the highest percent of collected evidence that was actually individualized.

This study showed that despite low rates of evidence analysis and individualization, physical evidence still played a substantial role on case processing decisions. If agencies were to devote greater resources to the collection and analysis of evidence, and improve the training of investigative and prosecutorial personnel in wiser use of that evidence, they should be able to strengthen case solution, charging, conviction, and incarceration rates. It is doubtful, however, that single studies like this one will persuade agencies to make major reallocations of resources. Agencies will need to undertake similar studies in their own jurisdictions, with their own unique blends of personnel and resources, to determine how forensic evidence influences decisions in their respective jurisdictions. Heads of key agencies need to formulate their own research hypotheses and to be personally invested in such studies to determine the effects of scientific evidence in their communities.

The relative importance of increasing solution and conviction rates in specific jurisdictions also needs to be considered. Compared with reducing crime rates, maximizing case solution, conviction, and sentencing rates may not command the same attention. Arrest, prosecution, and sentencing practices are important from a justice system perspective, but the police executive (who holds the purse strings of most crime laboratories) may not be as concerned with these "secondary" measures. Prosecutors and judges typically don't wield great influence over laboratory resources. Build in the fact, also, that the primary measure of forensic science laboratories is to find the "scientific truth" of the evidence, and is not to achieve high arrest and conviction rates.

There are other important research and policy questions that need to be kept in mind, as well. *Daubert* and the National Research Council's recommendations in the 2009 *Strengthening Forensic Science* report concerning the scientific underpinnings of forensic science and the strength of individualization conclusions must be addressed. There are a range of other research studies that are needed to resolve other key questions and controversies, such as proper allocation of resources and decision criteria to be used in prioritizing evidence for evaluation in the laboratory. The newly impaneled National Commission of Forensic Science needs to rigorously evaluate studies like those described in this chapter, to improve on and replicate them, and to recommend new projects to answer other nagging questions. While this commission will be primarily concerned with enhancing "quality assurance" practices in forensic laboratories, matters of policy and allocation of resources will of necessity address questions of the value of scientific evidence on the process of justice. Hopefully, the data presented in this chapter will inform other researchers, policy makers, and practitioners to develop future studies to assess the continuing demand for and analysis of forensic evidence, and determine its effects on criminal justice case decision making.

References

American Society of Crime Laboratory Directors, Laboratory Accreditation Board. (n.d.). About ASCLD/LAB. http://www.ascld-lab.org/about-ascldlab/

Balko, R. (2011, June 14). Private crime labs could prevent errors, analyst bias: Report. *Huffington Post.* http://www.huffingtonpost.com/2011/06/14/the-case-for-private-crime-labs_n_876963.html

Bashinski, J., & Peterson, J. (2003) Forensic sciences. In W. Geller & D. Stephens (Eds.), *Local government and police management* (4th ed., pp. 559–597). Washington, DC: International City Management Association.

Bromwich, M. (2006) *Fifth report of the independent investigator for the Houston Police Department Crime Laboratory and Property room* (HBD Crime Lab Independent Investigation). Retrieved from http://hpdlabinvestigation.org/reports/060511report.pdf

Clark, M. (2012, November 26). Forensic science falls short of public image. *Stateline.* Retrieved from http://www.pewstates.org/projects/stateline/headlines/forensic-science-falls-short-of-public-image-first-of-two-parts-85899431908

Daubert v. Merrell Dow Pharmaceuticals, Inc., 509 U.S. 579 (1993).

Durose, M., Walsh, K., & Burch, A. (2012). *Census of publicly funded forensic crime laboratories, 2009.* Washington, DC: Bureau of Justice Statistics Bulletin.

Escobedo v. Illinois 378 U.S. 478 (1964).

Fisher, B. A. (2004). *Techniques of crime scene investigation* (7th ed.). Boca Raton, FL: CRC Press.

Fisher, B. A., & Fisher, D. R. (2012). *Techniques of crime scene investigation* (8th ed.). Boca Raton, FL: CRC Press.

General Electric Co. v. Joiner, 522 U.S. 136 (1997).

Giannelli, P. (1993). "Junk science": The criminal cases. *Journal of Criminal Law and Criminology, 84*(1), 105–128.

Giannelli, P., Imwinkelreid, E., & Peterson, J. (2011). Reference guide on forensic identification expertise. In National Research Council (Ed.), *Reference Manual on Scientific Evidence* (3d ed., Ch. 16). Washington, DC: National Academies Press.

Guillen, T., & Nalder, E. (1994, June 22). Overwhelming evidence: Crime labs in crisis. *Seattle Times,* p. A1.

Houck, M. (July 2006). CSI: Reality. *Scientific American, 295,* 84.

Huber, P. (1991). *Galileo's revenge: Junk science in the courtroom.* New York: Basic Books.

Institute for Defense Analyses. (1967). *Task force report: Science and technology: A report to the President's Commission on Law Enforcement and Administration of Justice.* Washington, DC: U.S. Government Printing Office.

Johnson, D., Peterson, J., Sommers, I., & Baskin, D. (2012). Use of forensic science in investigating crimes of sexual violence: Contrasting its theoretical potential with empirical realities. *Violence Against Women, 18*(2), 193–222.

Jonakait, R. (1991). Forensic science: The need for regulation. *Harvard Journal of Law and Technology, 4,* 109.

Kumho Tire Co. v. Carmichael, 526 U.S. 137 (1999).

Lassers, W. K. (1967). Proof of guilt in capital cases: An unscience. *Journal of Criminal Law, Criminology and Police Science, 58*(3), 310–316.

Makin, D. (2012). Symbolic evidence collection or "If all else fails, throw some dust around." *Forensic Science Policy & Management, 3,* 126–138.

McRoberts, F., Mills, S., & Possley, M. (2004, October 17). Forensics under the microscope: Unproven techniques sway courts, erode justice. *Chicago Tribune*, p. A1.

Miranda v. Arizona, 384 U.S. 436 (1966).

National Advisory Commission on Criminal Justice Standards and Goals. (1973). Standard 12.2: The crime laboratory. In *Task force report on the police* (pp. 299–304). Washington, DC: U.S. Government Printing Office.

National Institute of Justice (NIJ). (2013). *Forensic DNA*. Retrieved from http://www.nij. gov/topics/forensics/evidence/dna/pages/welcome.aspx

National Research Council (NRC). (2009). *Strengthening forensic science in the United States: A path forward*. Washington, DC: Author. Retrieved from http://www.nap .edu/catalog/12589.html

Office of the Inspector General. (1997). *The FBI laboratory: An investigation into laboratory practices and alleged misconduct in explosives related and other cases*. Washington, DC: U.S. Department of Justice. Retrieved from https://www.fas.org/irp/agency/doj/oig/ fbilab1/fbil1toc.htm

Parker, B. (1963). Scientific proof. *Revista Juridica de la Universidad de Puerto Rico, 32*(2), 201–213.

Parker, B., & Peterson, J. (1972). *Physical evidence utilization in the administration of criminal justice*. Washington, DC: U.S. Government Printing Office.

Peterson, J. (1974). *The utilization of criminalistics services by the police: An analysis of the physical evidence recovery process*. Washington, DC: U.S. Government Printing Office.

Peterson, J. (1975). LEAA's Forensic Science Research Program. In G. Davies (Ed.), *Forensic science* (pp. 43–57). Washington, DC: American Chemical Society.

Peterson, J., Hickman, M., Strom, K., & Johnson, D. (2013). Effect of forensic evidence on criminal case processing. *Journal of Forensic Sciences, 58*(S1), S78–S90.

Peterson, J., Johnson, D., Herz, D., Graziano, L., & Oehler, T. (2011). *Sexual assault kit backlog study: Final report*. Washington, DC: National Institute of Justice.

Peterson, J., & Leggett, A. S. (2007). The evolution of forensic science: Progress amid the pitfalls. *Stetson Law Review, 36*, 621–660.

Peterson, J., Mihajlovic, S., & Gilliland, M. (1984). *Forensic evidence and the police: The effects of scientific evidence on criminal investigations*. Washington, DC: U.S. Government Printing Office.

Peterson, J., Sommers, I., Baskin, D., & Johnson, D. (2010). *The role and impact of forensic evidence in the criminal justice process: Final report*. Washington, DC: National Institute of Justice.

Risinger, M., Denbeaux, M., & Saks, M. (1989). Exorcism of ignorance as a proxy for rational knowledge: The lessons of handwriting identification "expertise." *University of Pennsylvania Law Review, 137*, 731–788.

Ritter, N. (2011). Solving the problem of untested evidence in sexual assaults. *NIJ Journal, 267*, 18–20.

Roman, J., Reid, S., Reid, J., Chalfin, A., Adams, W., & Knight, C. (2009). *The DNA field experiment: Cost-effectiveness analysis of the use of DNA in the investigation of high-volume crimes*. Washington, DC: Urban Institute.

Strom, K., & Hickman, M. J. (2010). Unanalyzed evidence in law-enforcement agencies: A national examination of forensic processing in police departments. *Criminology & Public Policy, 9*(2), 381–405.

Strom, K., Ropero-Miller, J., Jones, S., Sikes, N., Pope, M. W., & Horstmann, N. (2009). *The 2007 survey of law enforcement forensic evidence processing: Final report*. Prepared for the National Institute of Justice.

Swecker, C., & Wolf, M. (2010, August 18). *An independent review of the SBI forensic laboratory*. Retrieved from http://www.ncids.com/forensic/sbi/Swecker_Report.pdf

Tofte, S. (2009). *Testing justice: The rape kit backlog in Los Angeles city and county*. New York: Human Rights Watch.

U.S. Department of Justice. (2003, March 11). *Advancing justice through DNA technology*: Executive summary. Retrieved from http://www.justice.gov/ag/dnapolicybook_exsum.htm

2

Is There Evidence of a "*CSI* Effect"?

Rachel Dioso-Villa

Introduction

Crime show dramas, such as *CSI: Crime Scene Investigation*, are among the top-rated programs on television amassing millions of viewers each year. Unlike other law- or police-based television programs, in these shows, forensic science and its scientists take center stage. The protagonists are crime scene investigators who tirelessly examine the physical evidence to solve gruesome and often graphic crimes using the latest scientific technology to identify perpetrators. The investigations are often carried out without assistance from the police and entirely outside of the courtroom, as science becomes law's truth-telling tool to resolve disputes without ambiguity and all within the hour program. This fascination with the capacity and role of forensic science in the criminal justice system would not necessarily be problematic, except the portrayals of forensic science and its examiners are exaggerated and distorted, and do not reflect reality (Houck, 2006), which begs the question, is the criminal justice system affected by *CSI*-type programs?

This chapter assesses whether or not there is a "*CSI* effect" and what effects forensic-based television programs have on jurors and on the activities of prosecutors, defense attorneys, and judges in the legal system. When jurors watch these programs, do they take what they see on television into the courtroom? Are they convicting or acquitting defendants based on their expectations and understanding of forensic science as portrayed on programs like *CSI*? If they are, then the responsibility to prevent and correct these expectations may fall on the justice system, which makes this particular topic important to address. For example, judges and attorneys may question television-viewing habits at *voir dire* prior to the start of the trial to identify potential jurors who believe the portrayals of forensic science on *CSI*-type programs. Prosecutors may seek forensic evidence in cases where it is irrelevant or unnecessary to satisfy a conviction if *CSI* had never aired. As a consequence, on the front end of the justice system, this may create a strain on police personnel to collect additional evidence at crime scenes, and on the back end, it may exacerbate the backlog of evidence requiring analysis by crime laboratories. Defense attorneys may seek counter-experts to contest the forensic evidence presented by the prosecution or highlight the lack of forensic evidence based on the assumption that *CSI*-viewing jurors have an exaggerated faith in the capabilities and reliability of forensic science.

In this chapter, I first review the popular depictions of forensic science in television programs, then propose a plausible theory from media and communication studies that might explain how *CSI* might come to influence jurors' perceptions of forensic science. I define the various definitions of the *CSI* effect based on earlier work with Simon Cole that analyzed news stories and media accounts of the term (Cole & Dioso-Villa, 2007). This is followed by an analysis of the empirical research that tests whether forensic-based television programs impact the criminal justice system to determine if the *CSI* effect is, in fact, real. Whether there is evidence of a *CSI* effect or not, legal actors, expert witnesses, and jury members are faced with the possibility that it is real and therefore must acknowledge it as a potential factor influencing criminal cases. If necessary, they may also adopt practices to limit the possibility of *CSI* expectations effecting jury verdicts and case outcomes.

CSI's Depictions of Forensic Science

Since the debut airing of *CSI* in 2000, various iterations and spin-offs have featured police dramas that focus on forensic science to solve crimes, such as *CSI: Miami*, *CSI: New York*, *Bones*, *Crossing Jordan*, and *Cold Case*, just to name a few. Similarly, reality television programs have also experienced an influx of new shows that focus on the role and use of forensic science in the investigation or legal process, such as *Solved: Extreme Forensics*, *Forensic Files*, *Body of Evidence*, and *Dr. G.: Medical Examiner*. Movies such as *Murder by Numbers* (2002), *Angels Don't Sleep Here* (2002), and *Pathology* (2008) all featured forensic examiners as the lead protagonists or the necessity of forensic evidence to solve crimes and overstated the role and capabilities of forensic science in the criminal justice system. The presence of forensic science in the popular media has no doubt contributed to common misperceptions about the availability and use of forensic evidence and the *CSI* effect.

CSI is the archetypal program to this genre of media, and considerable academic scholarship has been devoted to deconstructing the portrayals of forensic science depicted on this program. For example, academics have assessed the accuracy of the roles of forensic examiners and their methods (Deutsch & Cavender, 2008; Houck, 2006; Kruse, 2010; Nolan, 2007) and reviewed its impact on the public's understanding of science (Cole, 2013; Ley, Jankowski, & Brewer, 2010). Some academics have gone so far as to examine the program through different theoretical lenses such as actor network theory (Mopas, 2007), criminological theories of race and class (Bonnycastle, 2009), and applying the works of French philosopher Jacques Derrida (Gere, 2007). Consistent throughout these articles is the premise that the forensic science and the examiners depicted in the program do not reflect the reality of the science or the job of forensic scientists, and portray to the public a distorted view of what forensic science can and cannot do.

In a typical *CSI* episode, the crimes are violent in nature, but little information is available with regard to a motive or known suspects and forensic science is needed to solve the "whodunit" mystery (Deutsch & Cavender, 2008). Unlike other crime show dramas, such as *Law & Order*, the police take the backseat in the investigation and defer to the authority of the forensic examiner (Nolan, 2007). In the investigation, they "follow the evidence," a common statement made by its characters, to find the "truth" in the evidence left behind at the crime scene (Nolan, 2007). There is often no need for witnesses or victim statements, since forensic science and the evidence are active parties in the program that lead CSI investigators to the perpetrator and allow for a reenactment of the crime in the absence of witnesses. For example, in an episode on *CSI: Las Vegas*, Chief CSI Investigator Gil Grissom says to the known suspect, "You have anything to say?" [Suspect does not respond.] "You don't have to talk to us." [Grissom shines flashlight on the dead body.] "He'll talk to us." (Cannon, 2001). Forensic science is depicted as absolute and certain, and viewers are given the visual tools throughout the show to solve the crime alongside the investigator by following the evidence (Kruse, 2010). However, the technology and methods on *CSI* are not real, and it is estimated that 40% of the science depicted on *CSI* is fiction (Cole & Dioso, 2005).

On *CSI* and similar programs, the laboratories feature high-tech equipment and all analyses are carried out on demand by one laboratory that produces indisputable results. This is an inaccurate depiction of the capabilities of forensic science on several levels. First, not all crimes leave forensic evidence, and not all forensic evidence is recoverable from crime scenes. Laboratories frequently do not perform all tests required for an investigation, due to inadequate resources, a lack of equipment, or the lack of expertise; rather, evidence may be processed by different laboratories for any given case (Houck, 2006). Moreover, results are far from immediate given the backlog of cases most laboratories experience. For example, in 2002 to 2003, state and local laboratories across the country reported an estimated 57,000 backlogged rape and homicide cases (Pratt et al., 2006). Additionally, law enforcement officials collect evidence during an investigation, but do not submit it to forensic laboratories for testing. In a national study of over 3,500 law enforcement agencies, Kevin Strom and Matthew Hickman (2010) found that 14% of all unsolved homicides (approximately 4,000 cases) over a five-year period contained unanalyzed evidence due to the lack of a suspect and the fact that the case has remained unresolved.

The forensic investigators on the show are "scientists" who are part of an elite group who work in the top laboratory in the nation (Kruse, 2010). They wear white lab coats and use scientific jargon that gives its characters the air of scientific knowledge and expertise (Deutsch & Cavender, 2008). They act independently of the police and the courts and are portrayed as absent of social pressures or cultural biases to draw their conclusions (Kruse, 2010). In reality, there are no "forensic investigators"; instead, what is portrayed on television is a combination of several personnel including police officers, detectives, and criminalists/forensic technicians (Houck, 2006). Criminalists and technicians do not work on a single case, nor do they collect evidence from the crime scene; rather, they process samples from a multitude of cases (Houck, 2006). Moreover, their techniques and the equipment available to them are rare or fictional in their capabilities to produce conclusive evidence, when in reality forensic tests may be fraught with inconclusive results (Thompson & Dioso-Villa,

2008). *CSI*'s forensic science delivers absolute truths that are the basis of indisputable justice; real forensic science has no absolute truths, since it is carried out by individuals who are subject to human fallibility, and bias can occur at a subconscious level absent of a person's ill will or malicious intent (Dror, Charlton, & Peron, 2006; Risinger et al., 2002; Thompson, 2011).

Cultivation Theory

The television depictions of the capabilities of forensic science and its scientists are more fiction than reality, but is it possible that what jurors watch on television affects the verdicts they draw at trial in real cases? The fact that television may influence people's behaviors is not a novel concept; media and communications theory explains this relationship as a process of cultivation whereby heavy television viewing impacts viewers' perception of reality (Gerbner, 1998; Gerbner & Gross, 1976; Morgan & Shanahan, 2010). The cultivation hypothesis states that people who watch more television are more likely to perceive the world in ways that reflect depictions of the world as portrayed on television than those who watch little or no television (Gerbner, 1998; Gerbner & Gross, 1976). According to Michael Morgan and James Shanahan (2010), the core of this theory relies on the notion that "living in a symbolic environment in which certain types of institutions with certain types of objectives create certain types of messages, tends to cultivate (support, sustain, and nourish) certain types of collective consciousness" (p. 339). Therefore, according to cultivation theory, our actions are based on our social reality that is in part influenced and created by what we see on television. For example, early research demonstrated that compared to those who watched little to no television, heavy television viewers were more likely to see the world as a mean and dangerous place and believed that most people cannot be trusted (Gerbner & Gross, 1976; Gerbner et al., 2002). They also reported fears of victimization, danger, and crime (Gerbner & Gross, 1976; Morgan & Shanahan, 2010). For these heavy viewers, because of these beliefs and perceptions, they may be inclined to carry a weapon as a means of self-defense, install home alarm systems, or find other ways to protect themselves from potential victimization.

The pioneer studies that tested cultivation theory based their findings on television viewing habits of any and all types of programs; however, recent studies have narrowed viewing habits to specific television genres. With over 400 channels available that cover a wide a range of television genres, it is quite possible that a heavy television viewer may watch exclusively programs within a particular genre of interest (Podlas, 2007). For example, heavy viewers of beauty makeover programs reported lower levels of self-esteem and higher levels of dissatisfaction with their bodies than those that were exposed to all types of television programs (Kubic & Chory, 2007). As an extension of this notion, forensic crime dramas, including shows like *CSI*, may cultivate perceptions of forensic science as infallible and ever present as it is portrayed on the programs. In turn, heavy viewers who sit on juries may have certain expectations of forensic evidence in actual cases based on what they see on television. Cultivation theory offers a plausible theory that television programs can affect our perceptions of reality and may shape how we react to our world, making the *CSI* effect possible.

Typology of *CSI* Effects Found in Media Accounts

One can surmise that shows like *CSI* impact the criminal justice system based on *CSI*'s unrealistic portrayals of the role and capabilities of forensic science and cultivation theory's notion that television can influence viewers' perceptions of the world. Media outlets have coined the term "*CSI* effect" to refer to any impact of *CSI*-type program viewership on the criminal justice system and in society. The term first appeared in 2002 on the *CBS Early Show* and the *Oregonian* newspaper to describe the prosecutor's fear that *CSI* shows have increased jurors' expectations of the presence and capabilities of forensic science in criminal cases (Franzen, 2002). However, the media has used the term loosely to describe very different impacts of the show on various aspects of the criminal justice system and in society. In an earlier work with colleague Simon Cole, we identified a typology of several "effects" based on how the media has defined the *CSI* effect and named them after the actor that articulated the effect in the media (Cole & Dioso-Villa, 2007). Table 2.1, presented at the end of this section, summarizes the various "effects" and supporting evidence taken from the literature.

STRONG AND WEAK PROSECUTOR'S EFFECT

The most common use of the term *CSI* effect in the media and in academic papers refers to the fear that *CSI* and similar television programs are creating increased jury expectations for "slam-dunk evidence and quick convictions" (Roane & Morrison, 2005). Prosecutors claim that *CSI* has altered the standard of proof and created a scientific standard of proof that is higher than proof beyond a reasonable doubt (Cole & Dioso-Villa, 2009). As the "strong prosecutor's effect," they claim that because of these television programs, jurors expect forensic evidence in criminal cases, and when it is not present, they alter their verdicts and acquit defendants who would otherwise be convicted were it not for *CSI*.

The "weak prosecutor's effect" assumes that wrongful acquittals occur (or there is a fear of their occurrence), and in response or as a preventative measure, prosecutors alter their behaviors at trial and adopt remedial measures to counter this effect (Cole & Dioso-Villa, 2007). Prosecutors may question potential jurors' television viewing habits at *voir dire*, present "negative evidence" in which experts testify as to why forensic evidence was not collected or found to be inconclusive, or may offer explanations for the lack of forensic evidence in their opening and closing arguments (Cole & Dioso-Villa, 2011; Ley et al., 2010). In this effect, prosecutors do not necessarily claim that jurors are wrongly acquitting defendants; rather, they claim that the program forces them to address jurors' heightened expectations of forensic evidence in their case preparation and at trial. Here, the "weak prosecutor's effect" is a preventative measure or a tactical change, without evidence of actual proof that *CSI* produces more acquittals than prior to the airing of the show.

DEFENDANT'S EFFECT

Although less commonly covered in the media, defense attorneys posit the opposite effect. They claim that *CSI* programs produce extremely positive portrayals of forensic science and the capabilities of forensic scientists, and that the show enhances the cred-ibility of forensic scientists who testify as expert witnesses. In cases where the prosecu-tion presents forensic evidence, defense attorneys claim that jurors who watch *CSI*-type programs give this evidence more weight than it deserves, because they associate it with the forensic science that they see on the show that is infallible and extremely pro-bative. The program depicts forensic scientists as heroic, acting independently from the police, and the science they perform is infallible. This may create an unwarranted trust in the prosecution's forensic expert witnesses at trial; therefore, defense attorneys claim that jurors in actual cases wrongly convict criminal defendants who would oth-erwise be acquitted were it not for *CSI*.

PRODUCER'S EFFECT

Media coverage has produced other versions of the *CSI* effect that do not directly impact the criminal justice system, but impact society. The "producer's effect" is one such effect where the media claim that *CSI* and similar programs have had a positive influence on juror understanding of forensic science by educating them on science and creating greater public awareness on the topic (Weaver et al., 2012). This may have indirect consequences on the justice system, since if jurors' understanding of forensic science improves, they may in turn better understand or be more receptive to the util-ity of forensic evidence when presented in court.

EDUCATOR'S EFFECT

The "educator's effect" describes the surge of interest in forensic programs in col-leges and universities as a result of the show. The glamorous life of *CSI*'s forensic inves-tigators have attracted students to careers in forensic science, much like *L.A. Law* was said to draw students to study law and *E.R.* to medicine. Student enrollment in forensic programs has grown since the show's inception, and colleges and universities are hav-ing to accommodate for the increased demand (Bergslien, 2006; Colgan, 2002; Derksen & Harvey, 2009; Jackson, 2009; McManus, 2010; Mennell, 2006; VanLaerhoven & Anderson, 2009). An unexpected consequence is that students who watch *CSI* pro-grams may have unrealistic expectations of the field and are disillusioned when they discover that what they learn in their classes is not what is depicted on television (Durnal, 2010; McManus, 2010; Weaver et al., 2012).

POLICE CHIEF'S EFFECT

Media sources also claim that *CSI* programs serve to educate existing or potential criminals on how to evade detection when committing crimes. The "police chief's effect" is the claim that criminals adopt countermeasures to prevent detection from forensic evidence, such as using bleach to clean up any biological evidence left at a crime scene or wearing gloves to avoid leaving fingerprints (Durnal, 2010; Machado, 2012).

VICTIM'S EFFECT

The "victim's effect" claims that programs like *CSI* produce the expectation that the police can collect and examine forensic evidence from all crime scenes, and as a

Table 2.1 Typology of *CSI* Effects in Media Accounts and Supporting Research

CSI *Effect Name*	*Definition*	*Evidence for (+), Against (–) and Mixed Review (+/–) of Effect*
Strong prosecutor's effect	Acquit cases in which they would have convicted if *CSI* never existed	(+): Roane & Morrison, 2005; Robbers, 2008; Thomas, 2005
		(–): Cole & Dioso-Villa, 2007; Ferris, 2011; Kim, Barak, & Shelton, 2009; Okita, 2007; Podlas, 2006, 2007; Schweitzer & Saks, 2007
		(+/–): Brewer & Ley, 2010; Cole & Dioso-Villa, 2009; Shelton, 2009
Weak prosecutor's effect	Alter practices to compensate for the absence/weaknesses of forensic evidence	(+)*: Cole & Dioso-Villa, 2011; Hughes & Magers, 2007; Lawson, 2009; Ley et al., 2010; Roane & Morrison, 2005; Robbers, 2008; Smith, Patry, & Stinson, 2007; Stevens, 2008; Thomas, 2005; Watkins, 2004
Defendant's effect	Afford more weight and credibility to forensic evidence	(–): Brewer & Ley, 2010; Ferris, 2011; Okita, 2007; Schweitzer & Saks, 2007
Producer's effect	Know more science	(+): Holmgren & Fordham, 2010; Smith et al., 2007; Weaver et al., 2012
		(–): Brewer & Ley, 2010; Ferris, 2011; Okita, 2007
Educator's effect	Attract students to forensic science programs and careers	(+): Bergslien, 2006; Colgan, 2002; Derksen & Harvey, 2009; Durnal, 2010; Jackson, 2009; McManus, 2010; Mennell, 2006; VanLaerhoven & Anderson, 2009; Weaver et al., 2012
Police chief's effect	Criminals who learn and adopt countermeasures from *CSI* programs to prevent police detection by forensic evidence	(+): Durnal, 2010; Machado, 2012
Victim's effect	Expect forensic testing for all crimes	(+): Makin, 2012
Tech effect	Hold higher expectations of forensic evidence due to actual advancements in forensic technology	(+): Okita, 2007; Shelton, 2009, 2010; Shelton, Kim, & Barak, 2006, 2009

*Includes evidence of legal actors altering practices to compensate for the absence/weaknesses in forensic evidence and evidence of increased jury expectations of forensic evidence.

result, crime victims expect forensic testing for all crimes. Police officers have responded to this by collecting non-viable forensic evidence from crime scenes to satisfy anticipated victim demands (Makin, 2012). This serves to satisfy victim expectations of the police officers conducting the investigation and maintains their credibility; however, it is balanced by the fact that the evidence is redundant and a waste of police resources (Makin, 2012). This simulated or symbolic evidence collection may contribute to the backlog of forensic testing in laboratories that has increased since the first airing of *CSI* in 2000 (Nelson, 2011) and to the backlog in evidence rooms in police stations across the country whose evidence may remain unanalyzed (Strom & Hickman, 2010).

Evidence of the *CSI* Effect

Based on media accounts, the *CSI* effect in its many forms is affecting the criminal justice system and altering verdicts in criminal cases; however, these accounts are largely based on interviews with prosecutors, judges, and police officers, rather than on empirical research. For example, one of the most highly cited cases as evidence of the *CSI* effect is a Peoria rape case, where there was positive eyewitness identification of the defendant, incriminating testimony by the emergency room nurse and police officer, and DNA from the rapist's saliva found on the victim's breast. The jury acquitted the defendant, and based on interviews after the trial, one juror told media sources that the jury wanted more forensic evidence, such as testing a soil sample from the victim's cervix to match a soil sample found at the crime scene (Roane & Morrison, 2005). There is no way to confirm that the jury required this forensic testing to convict the defendant or if this was simply the view of one outspoken juror. Before concluding that this is a case of the *CSI* effect, there could be a multitude of reasons that the jury, when all the evidence was taken into consideration, could not find the defendant guilty beyond a reasonable doubt. Since the law prohibits jurors from questioning to disclose the rationale for their verdicts, we may never know whether the Peoria acquittal was in fact due to the failure to test the alleged soil sample in the rape victim's cervix and an example of the *CSI* effect affecting jury verdicts.

In contrast, in surveying the socio-legal research on the topic, there is little evidence of an effect. If the *CSI* effect referred to the impact of the program on *actual* cases and *actual* verdicts, then the discussion is limited to the strong prosecutor's effect (wrongful acquittals) and the defendant's effect (wrongful convictions). The police chief's effect would also impact actual cases and would have a deleterious effect on the criminal justice system, since it purports that existing criminals are now more knowledgeable of forensic science thanks to *CSI* and apply the methods learned on the program to evade detection by police. As another potential consequence of the police chief's effect, crime may increase due to otherwise law-abiding individuals who now elect to commit crimes without fear of getting caught. The other *CSI* effects do not produce any major problem to society or the criminal justice system, although the "weak prosecutor's effect" may create a bigger workload for prosecutors, defense attorneys and judges who elect to change their practices to combat or prevent a *CSI* effect. This section reviews the evidence to support these claims that there is a *CSI* effect as measured by its actual and potential effects on cases (essentially measuring the strong prosecutor's effect and the defendant's effect) by looking at empirical research that studies acquittal rates and jury verdicts in mock trials.

ACQUITTALS

Before concluding that there is or is not a *CSI* effect that impacts actual trials, one would expect to find changes in the rate of jury acquittals before and after the airing of *CSI*. This would amount to an *increase* in jury acquittals post-*CSI* as evidence of the strong prosecutor's effect or a *decrease* in jury acquittals post-*CSI* as evidence of the defendant's effect. In a series of studies, Simon Cole and I examined acquittal rates for jury trials in federal and state courts that occurred before and after *CSI* first aired on television to determine whether there has been a change in jury behavior since the advent of the show (Cole & Dioso-Villa, 2007, 2009). If jurors altered their behaviors in favor of the strong prosecutor's effect, this would mean that they would acquit defendants whom they would have otherwise convicted had *CSI* not existed. Therefore, we would expect an increase in the number of acquittals either immediately after the airing of *CSI* in 2000 or after its peak in popularity a few years later.

When we looked at acquittal rates of federal cases over the period before and after the first airing of *CSI*, we found no discernable increase in jury acquittal rates following *CSI* (Cole & Dioso-Villa, 2007). In fact, there was an 11% drop in the federal acquittal rate in 2005, and it remained at this rate for the three years that followed. In a follow-up study, we attempted to collect jury acquittal rate data from all 50 states in the United States by contacting state court administrators and searching court websites (Cole & Dioso-Villa, 2009). At the end of our search, we collected acquittal rate data for 11 jurisdictions: California, Florida, Hawaii, Illinois, Kentucky, Missouri, New York, North Carolina, South Dakota, and Vermont, and the federal data. We restricted the data to felony jury trials, since this composed the majority of cases included in the datasets and removed any misdemeanor offenses when possible. We restricted the analysis to jurisdictions that provided acquittal rates between 1986 and 2008, since this would account for a pre- and post-*CSI* analysis. In the end, we excluded Kentucky, Missouri, and South Dakota, since they did not meet all inclusion criteria (Cole & Dioso-Villa, 2009, p. 1360).

When we performed a pooled time-series cross-section analysis by jurisdiction, the data showed that although there was variability in the jury acquittal rate between jurisdictions, within each state the rate was stable over time (with the exception of the two smallest states). We conducted linear regressions of acquittal rates before and after 2000, 2001, 2002, and 2003 to take into account the possibility of a lag effect where *CSI* did not have an immediate effect on acquittal rates until a few years later; however, we did not find any statistically significant differences before and after these years.

When we treated each trial as an observation irrespective of its jurisdiction, we found a statistically significant difference in acquittal rates post-2001 and post-2002, but not post-2003. This may indicate a short-lived, two-year strong prosecutor's effect; however, there are also alternative explanations. For instance, we also found statistically significant increases in acquittal rates prior to *CSI* between 1997 and 2000, which may indicate that the increase is part of a larger trend of acquittal rates on the rise. Also, since there were 207,274 trials from 1997 to 2006 included in the total sample of data, the statistical power of the analysis was very high, and statistically significant findings are more likely in any direction. Overall, considering all three analyses, the relatively small and short-lived differences, and the equivocal nature of acquittal rate data, there does not appear to be a *CSI* effect according to our findings.

JURY VERDICTS

Another means to examine whether a *CSI* effect exists is to investigate how juries respond to mock cases. Kimberlianne Podlas is one of the first researchers to investigate the *CSI* effect by conducting jury simulations where mock jurors deliberated on crime scenarios and mock trials (Podlas, 2006). Podlas surveyed 306 college students and asked them about their television viewing habits and also had them answer questions and provide a verdict on a crime scenario that recounted an alleged rape. The vignette was designed so that a decision as to whether the act was consensual could not be determined through forensic evidence, rather through weighing the credibility of the victim against the defendant. Therefore, in this scenario the legally correct verdict should be "not guilty," and forensic tests would not produce relevant results to the guilt or innocence of the defendant. Of the viewers that gave not guilty verdicts, Podlas did not find any significant difference between frequent viewers of *CSI* and infrequent/non-viewers. Based on these results, she concluded that there was no evidence of a *CSI* effect.

In a set of follow-up studies designed to test the *CSI* effect, Podlas gave 538 mock jurors crime scenarios on which they had to deliberate to reach a verdict (Podlas, 2007). The crime scenarios included "balanced" evidence scenarios where guilt was not obvious, since the evidence included two possible stories that were equally viable; and "complete" and "incomplete" scenarios where she either kept or removed the key evidence that was necessary to prove guilt. Mock jurors completed surveys on their television viewing habits, their verdicts for the crime scenario, and factors that may have influenced their verdict, if they found the defendant not guilty. The factors that tested for the *CSI* effect included reasons for not guilty verdicts due to the evidence not tested for fingerprints; the fact that the prosecution did not perform forensic tests to prove the defendant's innocence, or forensic tests that the defendant was in the bedroom; and the fact that there was no DNA evidence. Again, she found no evidence of the strong prosecutor's effect, or wrongful acquittals. *CSI* viewing did not appear to influence jurors' decisions to acquit or convict the defendants. They did not appear to rely on *CSI* factors in their decision-making process, nor did *CSI*-viewers rely on forensic evidence to a greater degree than their non-*CSI* viewing counterparts.

Neil Schweitzer and Michael Saks (2007) conducted a small study of 48 mock jurors that tested whether *CSI* viewers are more skeptical of forensic evidence (due to heightened expectations of forensic science) than non-*CSI* viewers to test the strong prosecutor's effect. They also tested whether *CSI* viewers give forensic evidence more weight than it deserves to test the "defendant's effect" that argues that *CSI*-type programs create an exaggerated faith in forensic science that can translate to wrongful convictions. They asked respondents about their television viewing habits and they presented them with trial transcripts of a mock case where a guilty verdict was unlikely unless the forensic expert testimony was given significant weight. The forensic scientist in the crime scenario testified about microscopic hair evidence and overstated the probative value of the evidence. *CSI* viewers perceived themselves as having a better understanding of forensic evidence and were more critical of the forensic evidence presented in the scenario than their non-*CSI* viewing counterparts, but this did not translate to differences in convictions or acquittals; hence, no evidence of the strong prosecutor effect or defendant's effect. *CSI* viewers on the whole expected more advanced technology than what is often presented in courts; however, this expectation does not appear to alter their final verdicts.

The Perceived *CSI* Effect

If acquittal rates have not changed as a response to *CSI*, and psychological experiments of potential jurors have found that verdicts by *CSI*-viewers are no different than non-*CSI* viewers, then this would indicate that there is little to no research to support a *CSI* effect in its harshest forms. That is, to date, there is no empirical evidence to show that jurors who watch *CSI* are wrongfully acquitting in cases that lack forensic evidence or wrongfully convicting in cases that have forensic evidence, because of their belief in its infallibility. In light of the lack of empirical evidence, the *CSI* effect may be nothing more than a media phenomenon, or the basis for alternative explanations provided by prosecutors or defense attorneys in cases that have not had their desired outcome (Cole & Dioso-Villa, 2007; Tyler, 2006). This section assesses the weak prosecutor's effect and the evidence that legal actors are altering their practices because of forensic television programs like *CSI*.

As mentioned earlier, the term "*CSI* effect" originated in the news media that claimed that jurors had changed their verdicts in actual cases based on the shows they watch on television. After a review of the news coverage, we found that the stories were repetitive and appeared to include the same elements in a local context, such that you can create the *CSI* effect story in any given location by interviewing a forensic investigator, prosecutor, and judge or defense attorney (Cole & Dioso-Villa, 2007). Forensic investigators tend to discover the problem; prosecutors then blame *CSI*-type shows for raising juror expectations of forensic science and cite their own experience in dealing with questions on *CSI* at trial or during *voir dire*; and when defense attorneys are interviewed, they tend to express their skepticism or claim that jurors can distinguish the difference from television and reality, or they admit to exploiting the effect in their own cases. The media portrays the *CSI* effect as a serious problem, and the danger of this media hype lies in the undue stress this may cause or the promotion of unnecessary changes in the legal system.

The news media is not the only source to claim that the *CSI* effect is real; this is bolstered by personal accounts and opinion surveys of legal actors in the criminal justice system. Prosecutors, defense attorneys, and judges were surveyed on their perceptions of the impact of forensic television programs on pre-trial preparations, the trial, and jury verdicts. Overall, the results of these surveys overwhelmingly suggest that the *CSI* effect is a serious problem in need of precautionary actions and solutions. However, this is simply what criminal justice actors *perceive* to impact cases without any empirical evidence to show that jurors are altering their behaviors because of *CSI* and forensic-based programs.

One such study carried out by the Maricopa County Attorney's Office (MCAO) surveyed 102 prosecutors who reported speaking to jurors after their trials (Thomas, 2005). They found that 38% of prosecutors reported that they had at least one trial in which they believed there was sufficient evidence to warrant a conviction without forensic evidence, but the cases resulted in either acquittals or hung juries. However, in the same report, the MCAO admitted that the conviction rate had remained stable in the county since *CSI* first aired and that there was no noticeable change in jury verdicts that were due to jurors watching programs like *CSI*.

While jury verdicts had not reportedly changed despite the personal anecdotes, the MCAO found that prosecutors reported having altered their behaviors to account for increased juror expectations of forensic science based on *CSI*-type television programs (Thomas, 2005). More than half (61%) of prosecutors reported asking jurors of their forensic television viewing habits during *voir dire*, nearly all prosecutors (90%) explained to jurors why there was a lack of forensic evidence in cases, and three-quarters of them called on counter experts to combat juror expectations of forensic evidence. The study also found that defense attorneys were reportedly altering their behaviors as well, and found that 80% of prosecutors surveyed reported that defense attorneys use jurors' heightened expectations of forensic science as a trial tactic to undermine the prosecution's evidence.

In Florida, Michael Watkins (2004) found similar results when he surveyed 53 prosecutors and defense attorneys to determine whether or not they altered their pre-trial preparation or trial strategies in response to the popularity of forensic crime dramas. Of the 23 prosecutors surveyed, half of them (49%) claimed to have observed actual acquittals in cases that had sufficient circumstantial evidence to warrant a conviction; 55% reported that they asked questions about forensic television viewing habits during the selection of jurors at *voir dire*; and 17% requested forensic testing when they otherwise would not have prior to *CSI*. Similarly, Dennis Stevens (2008) surveyed 444 prosecutors, and approximately three-quarters of the prosecutors reported that defense attorneys presented unrealistic portrayals of forensic analysis as a trial tactic to gain favor from the jury or judges.

Monica Robbers (2008) surveyed 290 prosecutors, defense attorneys, and judges to investigate whether they reported specific instances in which they believed that *CSI*'s depictions of forensic science impacted jury verdicts and whether the program had affected their activities. Her results indicated that, overall, prosecutors, defense attorneys, and judges held similar opinions that jurors have increased expectations of forensic evidence due to forensic television programs affecting their own trial behavior and jury verdicts in actual cases. Of the total sample, 79% reported that they could cite specific instances in which they believed case outcomes were influenced by increased expectations of forensic science based on forensic programs, especially in murder trials, drug cases, and sexual assault cases. Over half of the respondents (53%) reported that jurors discounted eyewitness testimony in preference for forensic evidence, and half of the respondents reported that juries interpreted a lack of forensic testing as a critique of the police even though testing may have been unnecessary for the case. One third of all respondents reported an increased use of negative evidence to explain why forensic evidence was not collected or tested, and 45% of judges reported this to be the case.

Robbers (2008) also found that forensic television programs had affected the ways in which judges, prosecutors, and defense attorneys perform their jobs; 85% of the total sample reported that their job had changed in some way. Two-thirds of all judges, prosecutors, and defense attorneys surveyed reported that additional time was spent discussing forensic evidence due to *CSI*-type television programs. Judges reported spending more time clarifying the role of forensic evidence for jurors; prosecutors spent more time explaining the forensic evidence after the expert testimony; and defense counsel spent more time discussing how the forensic evidence could cast doubt on the prosecution's case. In general, respondents felt that they spent more time in *voir dire* (38%), learning about specific forensic testing and procedures (36%), and mentioned or deferred to television programs and the differences between programs and actual trials (31%) as part of their work.

In a survey of 58 circuit court judges in Kentucky, Thomas Hughes and Megan Magers (2007) found that 60% of them reported that shows like *CSI* have impacted their courtroom proceedings; however, 80% reported not having had to change their personal behavior to administer justice in their courts. Over half of the judges surveyed (53%) believed that the show has made it harder to convict defendants. Three-quarters (79%) reported that they have observed an increase in jury expectations of forensic evidence in their courts, but this did not necessarily translate to an increased use of forensic evidence, since two-thirds (67%) did not report seeing an increase in the use of forensic science in court since the shows became popular. The majority of judges surveyed found that since *CSI*, they have witnessed changes in the way cases are presented by the prosecution (48%) and defense counsel (60%), and in *voir dire* jury selection (62%).

Surveys of legal actors indicate that prosecutors, judges, and even defense attorneys have observed changes in the legal system as a consequence of jurors watching programs that feature forensic evidence, like the archetype for the genre, *CSI*. Their accounts support the weak prosecutor's effect that says that legal actors are altering their jobs to combat or prevent the *CSI* effect in its strongest form. Nevertheless, these opinions do not necessarily translate into wrongful acquittals or convictions as described in the strong prosecutor's effect or defendant's effect, rather they are only *perceived* wrongful verdicts. These surveys illustrate how legal actors are altering their trial preparation and courtroom behaviors, which amounts to actual changes in the criminal justice system. Taken together, these studies provide empirical evidence that *CSI* is affecting the daily workings of the criminal justice system especially in criminal litigation. Regardless of whether or not the effect is changing verdicts, courtroom actors (prosecutors, defense attorneys, and judges) must deal with it in their cases heard before juries.

Juror Expectations and Their Understanding of Forensic Science

Prosecutors, defense attorneys, and judges reported that they have had to change their court strategies to account for jurors' increased expectations for and of forensic evidence. Whether juries hold different views or expectations of forensic evidence is an important question that has been the topic of several studies that attempt to shed light on what jurors take into account when making their verdicts. What jurors understand about forensic science as presented on *CSI*-type programs is important to survey and measure, since this may affect their interpretation of real forensic evidence presented to them in court, which in turn may impact verdicts in actual cases.

In a series of studies, the Honorable Donald Shelton, Young Kim, and Gregg Barak (2006) surveyed 1,027 jury-eligible persons called to jury duty and measured their television viewing habits. They asked them what evidence they might expect to find a defendant guilty for a selection of crimes. They found that jurors expected scientific evidence in every criminal case regardless of how many *CSI* television programs they watched. Those who frequently watched *CSI* programs had slightly higher expectations for forensic and non-forensic evidence than their non-*CSI* viewing counterparts, and *CSI* viewers were more likely to give a guilty verdict without scientific evidence when eyewitness evidence was present than non-*CSI* viewers. Despite increased expectations of evidence, *CSI* viewers were not more or less likely to acquit defendants based on a lack of forensic evidence, and therefore Shelton and colleagues found no support for the strong prosecutor's effect that would produce wrongful acquittals. Rather than the increase in juror expectations due to the influence of forensic television programs, the authors suggested that this increase can be explained by an increased awareness of technological advances that they called the "tech effect." The tech effect suggests that any effect on jurors' perceptions of the capabilities of forensic science is due to the actual increased capabilities of forensic science through technological advancements. According to Shelton and colleagues, the tech effect is due to actual scientific and technological advancements that have changed popular culture and in turn may increase juror expectations of and for scientific evidence (Shelton, Kim, & Barak, 2009).

In a follow-up study, they surveyed respondents' exposure to a broader range of changes in popular culture that exposed the public to scientific and technological advancements to account for any increases in expectations of forensic and scientific evidence (Shelton et al., 2009). Again, Shelton and colleagues found that jurors held higher expectations for scientific evidence, but would not necessarily acquit defendants without forensic evidence, regardless of their television viewing habits. However, they found some support that the increased expectations for forensic evidence could, in part, be accounted for by respondents' level of familiarity with the use of technology and exposure to various popular media as suggested in the tech effect.

In Amber Ferris' (2011) doctoral dissertation, she examined the relationship between *CSI* television viewing and viewers' expectations and understanding of forensic science, and their favorability toward forensic scientists. She surveyed 188 individuals taken from a college student snowball sample. She found that *CSI* viewers did not differ from non-*CSI* viewers in their expectations or favorability of forensic evidence across different types of crimes, nor did they hold differing views of science's perceived infallibility. In another thesis, Kiara Okita (2007) conducted a telephone survey of 1,200 Canadians about their television viewing habits and their attitudes toward forensic science. She also did not find any differences between *CSI* viewers and non-*CSI* viewers regarding their expectations for forensic evidence in criminal cases or the perceived accuracy of the science.

Although general questions regarding jurors' expectations about forensic evidence do not appear to be different between *CSI* and non-*CSI* viewers, perhaps not all forensic evidence is treated the same. Steven Smith, Marc Patry, and Veronica Stinson (2007) tested whether and how *CSI* television programs influence jurors' perceptions of forensic evidence by giving participants different types of forensic evidence (e.g., fingerprint, DNA, ballistics evidence) to evaluate its reliability, accuracy, and the fairness of a guilty verdict that relied on this evidence as the key evidence against the defendant.

They found that watching *CSI* programs was associated with judgments of reliability, accuracy, and fairness for some forensic types (e.g., DNA, ballistics and arson evidence), but not to others. When they forced participants to watch episodes of *CSI* in a second study, they found evidence that *CSI* viewing can influence viewers' perceptions of evidence such as fingerprint and DNA evidence, and these participants see them as more reliable techniques than non-*CSI* viewers.

Paul Brewer and Barbara Ley (2010) also found no evidence that watching *CSI*-type programs was related to whether jurors put weight toward the presence or absence of DNA evidence in their telephone survey of 908 individuals. They found that heavy viewers of *CSI*-type programs reported that they had a clear understanding of DNA, despite scoring low on their actual understanding of DNA according to the researchers' measures. Also, compared with the lightest viewers, the heaviest viewers were more likely to see the evidence as reliable and were more favorable of national DNA databanks.

In another study that examined jurors' understanding of forensic evidence, Janne Holmgren and Judith Fordham (2010) conducted two studies of 605 Canadian jury-eligible persons to test whether *CSI* programs affected jurors' understanding of forensic concepts. They asked participants about their *CSI*-viewing habits, their understanding of forensic concepts portrayed in *CSI*, and their experience as a juror in actual cases. Holmgren and Fordham found that *CSI* viewers were more likely than their non-viewing counterparts to rely on their understanding of the criminal justice system and forensic evidence based on the portrayals depicted on *CSI* programs.

Taken together, the empirical evidence shows that jurors hold high expectations for the capability and presence of forensic evidence in criminal cases, and that the perceived accuracy and reliability may depend on specific types of forensic evidence. The studies concur that these heightened expectations of forensic evidence are not necessarily associated with jurors watching *CSI*, and may be attributed to other factors, such as advancements and the availability of technology in society, in general. *CSI* viewing may instead impact jurors' self-perceived understanding of forensic evidence, though this has not been shown to affect their final verdicts.

What Can Be Done?

In a surprisingly short period of time since the coining of the term "*CSI* effect," there has been an abundance of research dedicated to measuring and testing its existence. As research and interest continues in this area, there are several ways in which research can build on existing studies. For example, future attempts can be made to collect longitudinal data for acquittal rates in additional states and other countries to make it more representative of national rates and to test for the potential effect of *CSI* on acquittal rates around the world. Another avenue into this line of research is to investigate specific cases before and after the airing of *CSI* where forensic evidence is presented or where jurors might expect forensic evidence and examine the verdicts. Once the cases are identified, one could look at the transcripts of the cases to determine whether or how the judges and attorneys adjusted their behaviors to accommodate or prevent the *CSI* effect.

Another possible avenue to extend research in this area is to investigate juror perceptions of different types of forensic evidence. Do jurors hold the same expectations of all forensic evidence, or are they different for DNA evidence, gunshot residue, or fingerprint evidence? Are jurors' expectations of and for forensic evidence increased in all cases, or are there certain cases or crimes where this is true? Also, what level of exposure to *CSI*-type programs creates these heightened expectations, and is there a saturation point? Or does the type of exposure matter? For example, how closely they follow mainstream media and crime-related news may affect their perceptions or level of exposure to forensic science, as may their interest in or exposure to movies, documentaries, fiction and non-fiction books in which forensic analysts are the protagonists, and their capabilities or the availability or capability of the evidence is exaggerated. Studies on jurors could also test the effects of deliberation on final verdicts by having subjects give individual verdicts after all evidence is presented, followed by a simulated jury deliberation with other participants and a group verdict. Perhaps if there is a *CSI* effect, it may be neutralized, diminished, or enhanced with deliberation.

Surveys of legal actors can measure how a perceived *CSI* effect or increased jury expectations have altered the behaviors of judges, prosecutors, and defense attorneys; however, they are not good measures of whether actual cases have been affected, since the accounts are anecdotal and cannot be verified or tested. There may also be alternate explanations for legal actors' portrayals and accounts that the effect is real. It may be a matter of "sour grapes" where prosecutors use the *CSI* effect to explain why they might have lost cases they felt they should have won, or referring to the *CSI* effect may be a form of strategic gamesmanship for defense attorneys who plan to argue for the presence or absence of forensic evidence in individual cases. Research in this area could look retrospectively at cases identified as wrongful acquittals or convictions due to the *CSI* effect, and collect the trial transcripts to contextually analyze whether and where *CSI* or the accompanied inflated expectations of forensic science were raised in the courtroom. If possible, in these cases where the *CSI* effect is claimed to have occurred, researchers could survey and interview the specific prosecutors and defense attorneys about their motivations to select, present, or challenge the forensic evidence at trial. The same could be done with cases where judges feel it necessary to provide instructions before or after the presentation of evidence to the effect that what they may see on television does not necessarily reflect reality.

Whether or not the *CSI* effect is real, the media, prosecutors, defense attorneys, judges, expert witnesses, and jurors are faced with the possibility that it is, and legal actors must address this in their practices to limit, prevent, or counter the possibility of *CSI* expectations impacting jury verdicts. There are several ways in which this can happen and several of which already take place according to the surveys from judges and prosecutors previously discussed, mainly during *voir dire*, open and closing arguments, jury instruction, or the presentation of negative evidence (Cole & Dioso-Villa, 2011).

Prior to the start of the trial, prosecutors and defense attorneys may ask jurors about whether they watch *CSI* or *CSI*-type programs during *voir dire* in an attempt to combat the *CSI* effect. However, judges should ensure that the questioning of jurors remains with the purpose of detecting prejudice, rather than creating bias. For example, it is one thing for an attorney to ask questions about whether jurors believe what they see on television or what their thoughts are about the capabilities of forensic science, and quite another thing for them to make declarative statements about the "true" capabilities of forensic science compared to those depicted on television that can unduly bias the jurors unnecessarily before the trial (Cole & Dioso-Villa, 2011).

At trial, judges may issue a jury instruction either before or after the presentation of expert evidence. Tamara Lawson (2009) proposes that to combat any potential *CSI* effect, the standard jury instruction should be amended to include a statement that reminds jurors that what they see on television programs cannot be used in the assessment of the case. At the close of the evidence, jury instruction may also be given prior to jury deliberation to remind the jury that their task is to only use evidence presented at trial and to not base their decisions on information outside of the courtroom, such as from television sources. Or jury instructions may deal specifically with scientific evidence to remind jurors that the prosecution is not required to present scientific evidence to establish their burden of proof (Cole & Dioso-Villa, 2011). Similarly, attorneys may reiterate these sentiments during opening and closing arguments, so long as they do not attempt to alter the burden of proof from "beyond a reasonable doubt" to any television standard of proof (Cole & Dioso-Villa, 2009).

At trial, attorneys may elect to present "negative evidence" to either counter forensic experts presented by the opposition or to explain why they did not find forensic evidence or did not present a forensic expert at trial (Robbers, 2008). This form of evidence typically does not inform jurors of the defendant's guilt, and it is the attorney's prerogative as to whether they feel this is necessary to bolster their case. For example, if DNA forensic testing is not performed in a case, a prosecutor may elect to present a forensic expert or police officer to explain that biological specimens are not available at every crime scene. The increased use of negative experts may pose financial burdens on the justice system and also increase time spent at trial.

Conclusion

To date, the empirical research suggests that there is no evidence of the *CSI* effect in its harshest forms of wrongful acquittals or wrongful convictions due to the expectations that jurors hold of forensic science and its examiners. However, this is not to say that juries are unaffected by what they watch on television. Cultivation theory offers an explanation for how television media may influence our beliefs and ultimately our actions, by creating messages that become part of our collective consciousness, permeate our lives and how we perceive our world. In fact, there seems to be a consensus among academics that jurors have increased expectations of forensic science whether this is as a result of watching *CSI* or due to general advancements in technology that become part of society's general knowledge. Even though this may not materialize into changes in verdicts, it has altered the legal landscape as prosecutors, defense attorneys and judges attempt to accommodate or counter these expectations at trial.

New areas of research could stand to look at the effects of increased expectations of forensic evidence and how it impacts the work of criminal justice actors *outside* of the courtroom. For example, as mentioned with reference to the victim's effect, there is a backlog of evidence either logged in police stations or awaiting analysis in crime laboratories (Strom & Hickman, 2010). Investigations could be made into whether such a backlog is the result of increased expectations for forensic evidence by measuring the rates before and after the airing of *CSI* and other forensic shows.

Another new avenue of research that extends beyond the courtroom is to examine whether police perceive that a *CSI* effect exists and to investigate whether this has had an impact on their jobs and performance. While this has not been the focus of the bulk of research on the *CSI* effect, Laura Huey (2010) interviewed investigative police personnel in Canada and found that they experienced role strain and some frustration from the unrealistic portrayals of police work on television programs such as *CSI*. They reported that during investigations, citizens questioned the way in which they conducted an investigation, offered suggestions for alternative methods based on what they have seen on television, or attempted to assist the investigation by interviewing witnesses or identifying evidence. Since police officers attributed this behavior to the public's consumption of *CSI*-type shows, this can be another avenue of research and can be identified as another *CSI* effect.

A final area, and arguably the most crucial area for the criminal justice system on this topic, is the potential impact on forensic examiners and how they testify as expert witnesses in court. In 2009, the National Academy of Sciences published a report evaluating each forensic discipline and the presentation of such evidence in court (National Research Council, 2009). They recommended an overhaul of the forensic sciences to increase their research and validation of their methods and to standardize the terminology forensic examiners used to present their findings to prevent the overselling of claims made in interpreting evidence. Future research could target forensic examiners to investigate whether and how increased juror expectations of forensic science or the suggested infallibility of forensic science in shows like *CSI* have impacted their procedures and duties. For example, when forensic examiners testify as expert witnesses, do they liken their role in an investigation to the criminalists on television to bolster their credibility or the capabilities of the forensic techniques? Or do they distance themselves from *CSI* and take steps to correct inflated juror expectations of forensic evidence?

With the recent announcement of the National Commission on Forensic Sciences headed by the National Institute of Justice and the National Institute of Standards and Technology, there is the hope that significant improvements can be made to enhance the forensic sciences. Since the commission will comprise forensic practitioners, academics, prosecutors, defense attorneys, judges, and community stakeholders, there is also the potential to develop policy recommendations that apply to federal, state, and local agencies. The litany of studies testing for a *CSI* effect and the threat of a *CSI* effect or its perceived pervasiveness may, at the very least, pressure the commission to prioritize the creation of standardized terminology that forensic examiners can use when they testify as expert witnesses to address, counter or prevent further misrepresentations of forensic evidence in the justice system.

Author's Note: This chapter expands on earlier work with coauthor Simon Cole on the *CSI* effect. For detailed descriptions of the data and analyses, please see Cole and Dioso-Villa (2007, 2009).

References

Bergslien, E. (2006). Teaching to avoid the "CSI effect": Keeping the science in forensic science. *Chemical Education Today, 83*(5), 690–691.

Bonnycastle, K. D. (2009). Not the usual suspects: The obfuscation of political economy and race in CSI. In M. Byers & V. M. Johnson (Eds.), *The CSI effect: Television, crime and governance* (pp. 149–176). Toronto: Lexington Books.

Brewer, P. R., & Ley, B. L. (2010). Media use and public perceptions of DNA evidence. *Science Communication, 32*(1), 93–117.

Cannon, D. (Writer). (2001). Alter boys [Television series episode]. In J. Bruckheimer & C. Mendelsohn (Producers), *CSI: Crime Scene Investigation*. Las Vegas, NV: CBS Productions.

Cole, S. A. (2013, April 11). A surfeit of science: The "CSI effect" and the media appropriation of the public understanding of science. *Public Understanding of Science.* doi:10.1177/0963662513481294

Cole, S. A., & Dioso, R. (2005, May 13). Law in the lab, opinion editorial. *Wall Street Journal,* p. W13.

Cole, S. A., & Dioso-Villa, R. (2007). CSI and its effects: Media, juries and the burden of proof. *New England Law Review, 41*(3), 435–469.

Cole, S. A., & Dioso-Villa, R. (2009). Investigating the "CSI effect" effect: Media and litigation crisis in criminal law. *Stanford Law Review, 61*(6), 1335–1374.

Cole, S. A., & Dioso-Villa, R. (2011). Should judges worry about the "CSI effect"? *Court Review, 47,* 16–27.

Colgan, C. (2002). Teaching forensics, then and now. *The Education Digest, 68*(1), 59–61.

Derksen, L., & Harvey, E. (2009). Science fiction or social fact? An exploratory content analysis of popular press reports on the CSI effect. In M. Byers & V. M. Johnson (Eds.), *The CSI effect: Television, crime, and governance* (pp. 3–28). Toronto: Lexington Books.

Deutsch, S. K., & Cavender, G. (2008). CSI and forensic realism. *Journal of Criminal Justice and Popular Culture, 15*(1), 34–53.

Dror, I. E., Charlton, D., & Peron, A. E. (2006). Contextual information renders experts vulnerable to making erroneous identifications. *Forensic Science International, 156,* 74–78.

Durnal, E. W. (2010). Crime scene investigation (as seen on TV). *Forensic Science International, 199,* 1–5.

Ferris, A. L. (2011). *Examining the "CSI effect": The impact of crime drama viewership on perceptions of forensics and science* (Doctoral dissertation). Kent, OH, Kent State University.

Franzen, R. (2002, December 10). TV's "CSI" crime drama makes it look too easy. *Portland Oregonian,* p. A1.

Gerbner, G. (1998). Cultivation analysis: An overview. *Mass Communication and Society, 1*(3–4), 175–194.

Gerbner, G., & Gross, L. (1976). Living with television: The violence profile. *Journal of Communication, 26*(2), 172–199.

Gerbner, G., Gross, L., Morgan, M., Signorielli, N., & Shanahan, J. (2002). Growing up with television: Cultivation processes. In B. Jennings & D. Zillmann (Eds.), *Media effects: Advances in theory and research* (pp. 43–68). Mahwah, NJ: Lawrence Erlbaum Associates.

Gere, C. (2007). Reading the traces. In M. Allen (Ed.), *Reading CSI: Crime TV under the microscope* (pp. 129–139). London: I.B. Tauris.

Holmgren, J. A., & Fordham, J. (2010). The CSI effect and the Canadian and the Australian jury. *Journal of Forensic Sciences, 56*(S1), 63–71.

Houck, M. M. (2006). CSI: Reality. *Scientific American, 295*(1), 84–89.

Huey, L. (2010). "I've seen this on CSI": Criminal investigators' perceptions about the management of public expectations in the field. *Crime, Media, Culture, 6*(1), 49–68.

Hughes, T., & Magers, M. (2007). The perceived impact of crime scene investigation shows on the administration of justice. *Journal of Criminal Justice and Popular Culture, 14*(3), 259–276.

Jackson, G. P. (2009). The status of forensic science degree programs in the United States. *Forensic Science Policy and Management, 1*, 2–9.

Kim, Y. S., Barak, G., & Shelton, D. E. (2009). Examining the "CSI-effect" in the cases of circumstantial evidence and eyewitness testimony: Multivariate and path analyses. *Journal of Criminal Justice, 37*, 452–460.

Kruse, C. (2010). Producing absolute truth: CSI science as wishful thinking. *American Anthropologist, 112*(1), 79–91.

Kubic, K. N., & Chory, R. M. (2007). Exposure to television makeover programs and perceptions of self. *Communication Research Reports, 24*(4), 283–291.

Lawson, T. F. (2009). Before the verdict and beyond the verdict: The CSI infection within modern criminal jury trials. *Loyola University Chicago Law Journal, 41*, 119–173.

Ley, B. L., Jankowski, N., & Brewer, P. R. (2010). Investigating CSI: Portrayals of DNA testing on a forensic crime show and their potential effects. *Public Understanding of Science, 21*(1), 51–67.

Machado, H. (2012). Prisoners' views of CSI's portrayal of forensic identification technologies: A grounded assessment. *New Genetics and Society, 31*(3), 271–284.

Makin, D. A. (2012). Symbolic evidence collection or "if all else fails, throw some dust around." *Forensic Science Policy & Management: An International Journal, 3*(3), 126–138.

McManus, S. E. (2010). *Influence of the CSI effect on education and mass media* (Master's thesis). University of Central Florida, Orlando.

Mennell, J. (2006). The Future of Forensic and Crime Scene Science Part II. A UK Perspective on Forensic Science Education. *Forensic Science International, 157* (S13-S20), S13.

Mopas, M. (2007). Examining the "CSI effect" through an ANT Lens. *Crime Media Culture, 3*(1), 110–117.

Morgan, M., & Shanahan, J. (2010). The state of cultivation. *Journal of Broadcasting & Electronic Media, 54*(2), 337–355.

National Research Council. (2009). Strengthening forensic science in the United States. Washington, DC: National Academy of Sciences.

Nelson, M. (2011, February). *Making sense of DNA backlogs, 2010—myths vs. reality* (NIJ Special Reports). Washington, DC: National Institute of Justice.

Nolan, T. W. (2007). Depictions of the "CSI effect" in popular culture: Portrait in domination and effective affectation. *New England Law Review, 41*, 575–590.

Okita, K. (2007). *The CSI effect: Examining CSI's effects upon public perceptions of forensic science* (Master's thesis). Alberta, Canada, University of Alberta.

Podlas, K. (2006). "The CSI effect": Exposing the media myth. *Fordham Intellectual Property, Media and Entertainment Law Journal, 16*, 430–465.

Podlas, K. (2007). The CSI effect and other forensic fictions. *Loyola of Los Angeles Entertainment Law Review, 27*, 87–125.

Pratt, T. C., Gaffney, M. J., Lovrich, N. P., & Johnson, C. L. (2006). This isn't CSI: Estimating the national backlog of forensic DNA cases and the barriers associated with case processing. *Criminal Justice Policy Review, 17*(1), 32–47.

Risinger, D. M., Saks, M. J., Thompson, W. C., & Rosenthal, R. (2002). The Daubert/Kumho implications of observer effects in forensic science: Hidden problems of expectation and suggestion. *California Law Review, 90*(1), 1–56.

Roane, K. R., & Morrison, D. (2005, April 25, 2005). The CSI effect. *U.S. News & World Report,* 48.

Robbers, M. L. P. (2008). Blinded by science: The social construction of reality in forensic television shows and its effect on criminal jury trials. *Criminal Justice Policy Review, 19*(1), 84–102.

Schweitzer, N. J., & Saks, M. J. (2007). The CSI effect: Popular fiction about forensic science affects the public's expectations about real forensic science. *Jurimetrics, 47,* 357–364.

Shelton, D. E. (2009). The "CSI effect": Does it really exist? *National Institute of Justice, 259,* 1–7.

Shelton, D. E. (2010). Juror expectations for scientific evidence in criminal cases: Perceptions and reality about the "CSI effect" myth. *Thomas M. Cooley Law Review, 27*(1), 1–35.

Shelton, D. E., Kim, Y. S., & Barak, G. (2006). A study of juror expectations and demands concerning scientific evidence: Does the "CSI effect" exist? *Vanderbilt Journal of Entertainment and Technology Law, 9*(2), 331–368.

Shelton, D. E., Kim, Y. S., & Barak, G. (2009). An indirect-effects model of mediated adjudication: The CSI myth, the tech effect and metropolitan jurors' expectations for scientific evidence. *Vanderbilt Journal of Entertainment and Technology Law, 12*(1), 1–43.

Smith, S. M., Patry, M. W., & Stinson, V. (2007). But what is the CSI effect? How crime dramas influence people's beliefs about forensic evidence. *The Canadian Journal of Police and Security Services, 5*(3–4), 187–195.

Stevens, D. J. (2008). Forensic science, wrongful convictions, and American prosecutor discretion. *The Howard Journal, 47*(1), 31–51.

Strom, K. J., & Hickman, M. J. (2010). Unanalyzed evidence in lawenforcement agencies: A national examination of forensic processing in police departments. *Criminology & Public Policy, 9*(2), 381–404.

Thomas, A. (2005). *The CSI effect and its real-life impact on justice.* Phoenix: Maricopa County Attorney's Office.

Thompson, W. C. (2011). What role should investigative facts play in the evaluation of scientific evidence? *Australian Journal of Forensic Sciences, 43*(2), 123–134.

Thompson, W. C., & Dioso-Villa, R. (2008). Turning a blind eye to misleading scientific testimony: Failure of procedural safeguards in a capital case. *Albany Law Journal of Science and Technology, 18,* 151–204.

Tyler, T. R. (2006). Viewing CSI and the threshold of guilt: Managing truth and justice in reality and fiction. *Yale Law Journal, 115,* 1050–1085.

VanLaerhoven, S., & Anderson, G. (2009). The science and careers of CSI. In M. Byers & V. M. Johnson (Eds.), *The CSI effect: Television, crime and governance* (pp. 29–59). Toronto: Lexington Books.

Watkins, M. J. (2004). *Forensics in the media: Have attorneys reacted to the growing popularity of forensic crime dramas?* (Master's thesis). Florida State University, Tallahassee.

Weaver, R., Salamonson, Y., Koch, J., & Porter, G. (2012). The CSI effect at university: Forensic science students' television viewing and perceptions of ethical issues. *Australian Journal of Forensic Sciences, 44*(2), 1–11. doi:10.1080/00450618.2012.691547

3

What We Know (and Don't Know) About Evidence Backlogs

Matthew J. Hickman and Kevin J. Strom

Introduction

It is widely accepted that forensic evidence can play an important role in convicting the guilty, exonerating the innocent, and ensuring that justice is served. But when backlogs prevent the timely processing of evidence and reporting of analytic results, concerns emerge about how such problems might translate to systemic impacts on due process rights of the accused (i.e., "justice delayed"), as well as victim rights in the case of evidence that goes unanalyzed (i.e., "justice denied"). These are very real concerns in a democratic system of justice.

The forensic community has experienced tremendous growth along with its share of growing pains and challenges over the past 40 years. The 1970s saw a sharp increase in the application of forensic evidence along with growth in the number of crime laboratories. During the 1980s, there were new scientific and technological developments, particularly in DNA testing, while in the 1990s, questions were raised about the reliability of forensic testing and increasing DNA backlogs in crime laboratories (Peterson & Leggett, 2007). In the decade that followed, backlog reduction was a primary focus in all forensic areas—not only in the area of DNA analysis. The 2009 National Academy of Sciences report *Strengthening Forensic Science in the United States* was widely regarded as a critical moment for the forensic sciences, revealing the (somewhat lacking) scientific underpinnings in some areas of forensic science but also discussing other problems of the forensic community, including evidence backlog. Backlog remains a significant issue, and to this day, we expend many federal dollars in support of backlog reduction and backlog elimination in the nation's crime laboratories. Research has shown that the funding targeted toward backlog reduction has resulted

43

in greater efficiencies in crime laboratory processing and the analysis of more cases than ever before (Lothridge, 2009; Nelson, 2011). However, as more and more evidence is submitted to laboratories for analysis, backlogs continue to rise in many jurisdictions.

Forensic backlogs are a reality that require serious attention and action, but we must also be intellectually honest and admit that we really don't know everything there is to know about the true nature and scope of forensic backlog, the underlying causes of backlog, and the possible remedies, nor do we have a complete understanding of the impact of forensic backlog on the administration of justice. This chapter will begin by discussing the varied definitions of forensic backlog, then move to the sources of backlog and what we really know about the nature and scope of forensic backlog. The chapter then looks at a particularly troublesome area of "artificial" backlog. Finally, the chapter ends with a discussion of what backlogs really mean for the administration of justice in the United States.

What Is a "Backlog"?

The question "What is a backlog?" might sound somewhat self-explanatory or elementary, but it's actually a very serious, complicated, and important question. It is a central question to understanding the workload and workload pressures with which forensic laboratories must deal. It is also important for gauging the performance of laboratories (and in a larger sense, the performance of the broader forensic system in the United States), particularly in the context of federal funding to eliminate or alleviate backlog.

The term *backlog* refers to physical evidence that has been submitted to a laboratory for analysis, but is waiting processing. A conservative interpretation of backlog might include all evidence awaiting the initiation of processing, while a more liberal view might consider evidence backlogged up until the point at which the results of the analyses are reported to the entity that requested them (i.e., under this view, any "current" case is considered part of the backlog). Backlog can also refer to the individual items of evidence and requested analyses (commonly referred to as *requests* within particular forensic areas, such as latent prints, drug chemistry, trace evidence, toxicology, and DNA) that are performed within *cases*. Or, backlog can refer to the cases as a whole (including several constituent items of evidence or analytic requests). It is important to note that backlog can apply to delays in analyzing evidence received within a forensic laboratory (items or cases submitted to a laboratory, but awaiting processing) as well as to evidence within a law enforcement agency that has been delayed extensively in going to the lab (items or cases awaiting submission to laboratories).

The definition of backlog also varies with regard to time components, and there is little consensus on what amount of time, if any, might be reasonable before a request or case is considered part of a backlog. A laboratory might consider a case backlogged from the point of submission until the actual processing begins (implying a desire for minimal "wait time") or until the analysis is completed and reported (implying a desire for minimal "turnaround time"). Suffice to say, forensic laboratories are not 60-minute, drop-off photo labs, and some amount of time will be required before a newly submitted case and its constituent evidence can make its way up the queue and through the decision tree of various sequential, analytic procedures.

The National Institute of Justice (NIJ) has, for its purposes, defined a *backlogged case* as one that has not been tested for 30 days after submission to a laboratory. This definition emerged, in part, out of consensus achieved among a group of American Society of Crime Laboratory Directors (ASCLD) advisors to the Bureau of Justice Statistics (BJS) crime laboratory census projects as well as to NIJ on related projects. However, some laboratories do not subscribe to the 30-day benchmark, instead using some other timeframe, such as 60 days. In some instances, this is a matter of a laboratory defining its backlog based on its existing workload rather than some industry standard to be achieved. It is noteworthy that many Laboratory Information Management Systems (LIMS) automatically generate backlog reports based on the 30-day benchmark, implying some degree of consensus among the LIMS consumers (who are also a source of LIMS modifications and improvements).

An additional twist in defining backlog is that evidence backlogs are not unique to forensic laboratories. As previously mentioned, law enforcement agencies are also a source of backlog, insofar as evidence collected is being held in storage/lockup and not submitted to a laboratory for analysis. Two recent studies have examined law enforcement agency backlogs, and found them to be quite substantial in scope (Lovrich et al., 2004; Strom et al., 2009). These studies also documented some of the reasons for not submitting evidence for analysis, and found them to be varied (and even somewhat disturbing), particularly where they demonstrate a misunderstanding of the utility of forensic analysis for investigative purposes. Related to this is the concern over untested rape kits (better known as *Sexual Assault Kits*, or *SAKs*) in some jurisdictions, which is where much of the concern over "justice denied" emerged following revelations about evidence that sat untested beyond relevant statutes of limitations (e.g., Los Angeles, CA; see Peterson et al., 2011; Chapter 1, this volume; see also Ritter, 2013).

What Are the Sources of Backlog?

There are many possible sources of laboratory backlog, but the major sources seem to relate to general increased demand from drug evidence over a long period of time and in the DNA area since the 1990s (see Chapter 1, this volume), general laboratory capacity issues (including equipment, personnel, etc.), popular media effects (such as the *CSI* effect; see Chapter 2, this volume), and a related misperception that the absence of scientific evidence somehow equates to reasonable doubt, and that forensics can (and should) be used in criminal cases without regard to the very real opportunity costs (Collins, 2012).

Drug evidence has been a consistent source of workload for the nation's crime laboratories, comprising roughly half[1] of the total volume of forensic requests annually (Peterson & Hickman, 2005; Durose, 2008; Durose, Walsh, & Burch, 2012). This translates to about 1.3 million drug-related requests per year to be handled by approximately 400 laboratories. The identification of controlled substances is often not as time consuming as the procedures in other forensic areas, so laboratories actually have

---

[1]Excluding CODIS samples; with CODIS samples included, controlled substance requests account for about a third of all requests as of 2009 (Durose et al., 2012).

a fairly high processing capacity for controlled substances. Laboratories are typically able to process about 80–85% of the total accumulated controlled substances analysis requests in a year (i.e., any prior backlog, plus new requests), but this still results in a net backlog of requests (amounting to about half of the total backlog across all forensic areas). From a historical perspective, this is not really news as drugs have comprised a substantial share of laboratory work for the past 40 or more years (Benson, Stacy, & Worley, 1970; Parker & Gurgin, 1972; Peterson, Mihajlovic, & Gilliland, 1984; Peterson, Mihajlovic, & Bedrosian, 1985). Yet, during the 1980s and 1990s, drug submissions increased about 180% while the number of laboratories increased 10%, and forensics employment increased 88% (see Peterson et al., 1985; Peterson & Hickman, 2005). As a result, drug evidence increased substantially on both per laboratory and per examiner bases. Further complicating the problem is the emergence of synthetic drugs, including synthetic cannabinoids, cathinones (bath salts), and hallucinogens. Because of the rapidly changing nature of the designer drug market, analyzing and characterizing these often unknown compounds can be time-consuming and expensive. As such, these drugs are contributing to larger proportions of laboratory backlogs in some jurisdictions.

This problem points to the broader issue of laboratory capacity. Capacity concerns encompass both human resources as well as equipment and infrastructure needs. In simple terms, during any given year, more cases are coming in the door (and added to any existing backlog) than can be processed given current laboratory resources, resulting in net yearend backlog. In the 2002 BJS crime laboratory census (Peterson & Hickman, 2005), examiner workloads were contrasted with performance expectations, and it was reported that examiners processed requests at or above 90% of the expected examiner averages in eight of 10 categories of forensic services (the two areas that lagged were firearms/toolmark analysis and computer crimes). When laboratory directors were asked what they needed in order to achieve a 30-day turnaround on all requests for forensic services, they indicated a need for about 1,900 additional full-time equivalent (FTE) examiners. In addition, more than three-quarters of laboratories indicated additional needs, including: new and renovated laboratory space and facilities; additional and updated equipment; instrumentation, robotics, and computers; basic and advanced training opportunities; and improved LIMS.

Another potential reason for the increased number of requests for forensic analysis is the so-called "*CSI* effect" (see Chapter 2, this volume, for detailed treatment). The constant presentation of forensic evidence on television has led to an expectation that all cases contain forensic evidence (Caruso, 2006). Juries—and, to a degree, prosecutors and judges—have come to expect almost instantaneous scientific analysis. Some laboratory directors have reported that the law enforcement agencies they serve are submitting a range of evidence to forensic laboratories that they have no intention of ever using in court.

Related to this is a condition of unreasonable expectations wherein the absence of scientific evidence is taken as reasonable doubt (Collins, 2012). Recognizing that backlogs are a very real phenomenon, and the typical reaction is to focus on increasing laboratory processing capacity, Collins (2012) asks, "But for what exactly are we building capacity?" (p. 37). As an example, Collins offers the common request to confirm that a suspect's fingerprints are on a firearm, even though the police collected the firearm directly from the suspect. Why, he reasons, do we need to expend the resources to confirm what is already known? Unfortunately, jurors have expectations (perhaps derived from popular media), and prosecutors must deal with them; thus, the chance of a juror concluding that the prosecutor did not rule out the possibility that the gun was planted, even when the defense has made no such claim, is very real and places a great burden on the laboratory. Too, the range of forensic applications is seemingly endless, and these requests delay testing in other cases where the need for scientific analysis is much greater.

These various pressures (popular media, juror expectations, police, and prosecutors) create a set of demands that cannot be met with existing resources. Out of necessity, laboratories must make decisions about what types of cases to accept, what types of evidence to process, and how to prioritize their workload. And these decisions necessarily impact the administration of justice at other stages (see Chapter 13, this volume). Some of this pressure may impact decisions about whether to submit evidence to the laboratory, contributing to backlogs elsewhere (such as in law enforcement agencies), and while knowledge among police about the investigative utility of evidence may be expected to increase (though see Chapter 8, this volume, on the utility of DNA in police investigations), laboratories may also de-prioritize investigative requests as a means of handling backlog.

Finally, it is important to acknowledge the potential problem of "simulated" or "symbolic" evidence collection (Makin, 2012), which refers to a practice where investigators or forensic technicians collect samples of evidence so that it appears that the agency is being responsive to the victim and to the case; however, there is no intention of processing or analyzing the evidence to benefit the investigation. While the overall impact of this practice on evidence backlogs is not known, the phenomena will be discussed in greater detail later in this chapter.

What Do We "Know" About the Nature and Scope of Forensic Backlog?

Our knowledge about the nature and scope of forensic backlog really starts with concerns about DNA backlogs emerging in the 1990s. The BJS has played an important role in supporting this line of research. Two BJS studies in particular mark the beginning of systematic social science research on the nature and scope of backlog (Steadman, 2000, 2002). Sizeable backlogs were documented in these national surveys of DNA crime laboratories, with reference years of 1997 and 2000. In 1997, about 70% of the laboratories reported backlogs totaling about 6,800 subject cases and 287,000 CODIS samples; in 2000, the percentage of laboratories reporting backlogs increased to 80%, with about 16,000 subject cases and more than 265,000 CODIS samples. CODIS backlogs decreased by about 7%, but subject case backlogs increased 135% during the three year period anchored by the two surveys.

The forensic community greatly appreciated this research on DNA processing (especially insofar as it documented "the problem" and led to the availability of additional resources), but quickly pointed out that backlogs also existed in other areas of forensic science, not just DNA analysis. In response, the 2002 national census of public crime laboratories documented evidence processing across a wide range of forensic services and reported more than 262,000 backlogged cases and approximately 500,000 backlogged requests (Peterson & Hickman, 2005). The "big three" backlog areas included controlled substance processing, which accounted for the bulk of the backlog, followed by latent print requests and DNA analysis. However, backlogs were observed in all areas of forensic services. In a 2005 update of the census, a 34% increase in backlogged cases was reported for laboratories that provided data in both years (Durose, 2008). Another update in 2009 did not report comparisons with prior years due to methodological concerns, but it appears that the backlog continues to grow and the category of forensic biology, including requests for DNA analysis (both casework and CODIS) and biology screening, is now the largest portion of forensic backlog in the United States (Durose et al., 2012).

Importantly, Congress has generally been responsive to this body of research. The BJS laboratory census, along with NIJ's growing research portfolio on backlog, led directly to additional and expanded funding for backlog reduction from Congress. This can be seen in continued Paul Coverdell funding for backlog reduction, as well as the DNA Backlog Reduction Program, and the Convicted Offender/Arrestee Backlog Reduction and Outsourcing programs. However, it remains to be determined whether this funding has had any actual effect on backlogs. Lothridge (2009; see also NFSTC, 2010) reported that state and local laboratories had increased their productivity in processing DNA cases, enabling laboratories to keep pace with increasing requests from law enforcement, but that these laboratories still cannot make significant reductions in their existing backlogs.

LAW ENFORCEMENT AGENCY BACKLOGS

Law enforcement agency backlogs were brought to light in two NIJ-funded studies. Lovrich et al. (2004) surveyed a nationally representative sample survey of both law enforcement agencies and crime laboratories to estimate the number of unsolved criminal cases that could benefit from DNA analyses. The survey covered a 20-year period and resulted in an estimated 169,000 unsolved rape cases and 52,000 unsolved homicide cases that contained biological evidence that could potentially be submitted for DNA analysis. In addition, more than half a million other unsolved cases (including about a quarter million property crimes) had biological evidence that had not been submitted to laboratories.

Respondents from state and local law enforcement agencies also provided information about the reasons for not submitting DNA evidence to laboratories. Somewhat surprisingly, 31% reported that there was no suspect in the case (surprising, given that this is certainly much of the purpose for the CODIS system). Another 10% reported that a suspect had been identified but not charged, and 9% reported a prosecutor had not requested testing. Funding was identified as a constraint to submitting DNA evidence to laboratories in about a quarter of agencies. Lovrich et al. (2004) discussed crime laboratory workload, personnel, and funding issues as key factors in the generation of law enforcement agency backlogs.

Building upon the work of Lovrich et al. (2004), a second study (Strom et al., 2009; see also Strom & Hickman, 2010) sought to provide more recent estimates of the backlog problem in law enforcement agencies, and to include a broader range of forensic evidence beyond DNA, such as trace evidence, latent prints, and firearm/toolmark evidence. In addition, the recall period was shortened (five years as compared to 20), and improved estimation and non-response strategies were employed. The study found that, during the five-year period, about 14% of all unsolved homicides (about 4,000 cases), 18% of all unsolved rapes (about 27,500 cases), and 23% of all unsolved property offenses (about 5 million cases) contained forensic evidence that had not been submitted to a forensic crime laboratory for analysis. In addition, about 40% of the unanalyzed homicide and rape cases were reported to have contained DNA evidence, and 26% were reported to have contained latent print evidence. Similar to Lovrich et al. (2004), the lack of a suspect in the case was a commonly cited reason for not submitting evidence to laboratories. Just 6% of agencies cited laboratory backlogs as a reason for not submitting evidence. Strom and Hickman (2010) concluded that the investigative capabilities of forensic science were not being fully exploited by law enforcement. Training on the utility of forensic science for developing investigative leads as well as the creation of departmental policies that prioritize and streamline the analysis of forensic evidence for homicide and rape cases, even in "no suspect" cases, were identified as important directions.

In addition, to provide more detail on the estimated 18% of all unsolved rapes containing forensic evidence that had not been submitted to a laboratory (cited above), it is important to mention research focused specifically on the backlogs associated with SAKs. SAK backlogs have been the subject of recent media scrutiny (particularly in Los Angeles, CA, but also in other jurisdictions), perhaps due to the very personal nature of the underlying crimes and the strong sense of injustice when it is perceived that this type of evidence is not being given due attention. Current research in this area is working to document the scope of the problem, identify reasons why SAKs are not being tested and what should be done, and identify sound policies for SAK processing. Most recently, the NIJ-sponsored New Orleans SAK project, which emerged out of a DOJ civil rights division investigation into the New Orleans Police Department, documented 830 untested "old" SAKs and 178 current SAKs that were in need of testing (Nelson, 2013). The project supported testing of all 1,008 cases, which resulted in 256 DNA profiles being uploaded to CODIS, with 139 CODIS hits. Other research in this vein includes Peterson et al.'s (2011) examination of about 2,000 untested SAKs sampled from nearly 11,000 held in evidence storage by Los Angeles city and county; as noted by Peterson (Chapter 1, this volume), DNA profiles were determined in a high percentage of the sampled cases and uploaded to CODIS, but exams did not result in any added arrests and only two additional convictions. Ongoing NIJ-sponsored action research in Detroit has documented about 8,500 untested SAKs, and similar research in Houston has documented about 4,200 untested SAKs.

The Problem of "Artificial" Backlog

One substantial limitation in our understanding of backlog is what one might term the problem of "artificial" backlog. That is, some unknown portion of laboratory backlog is artificial in the sense that the evidence unquestionably exists, and it is accounted for and awaiting analysis, but the analysis is unnecessary for the purposes of investigating or adjudicating a case. This category of backlog includes three distinct types of evidence submitted to laboratories:

1. Evidence for which there is no intent to use or rely upon a laboratory analysis

2. Evidence for which analysis is no longer necessary (due to settlement or other disposition) but the laboratory was not informed

3. So-called simulated or symbolic evidence collection

The first category, evidence submitted for which there is no intention to use or rely on a laboratory analysis, is primarily an artifact of prosecutors who may choose to request that each item or exhibit in a case be analyzed even though the particular exhibit in question may not be essential, or even when the case is not necessarily trial bound. Some of this behavior by prosecutors may stem from a blanket desire to be prepared for all contingencies in the case including unpredictable requests from defense lawyers or juries. Past studies that involved stakeholder interviews in multiple U.S. jurisdictions documented that some prosecutors want all evidence submitted and analyzed in all cases regardless of their intention to use each piece of evidence in court (Strom et al., 2011; see also Chapter 2, this volume). Concerns about preparing for "what if" scenarios and the expectations of juries and defense counsel were often driving prosecutors to make these requests.

The second category is evidence submitted and in the queue for laboratory analysis but for which analysis is no longer necessary because the case has already been settled (i.e., pled out) or otherwise dismissed or disposed of, rendering analysis unnecessary. The main influences driving these so-called artificial backlogs are poor communications and ineffective information tracking systems between police, laboratories, and prosecutors. This leaves some proportion of cases (and exhibits) in the backlog that do not need analysis because the cases have been resolved but the laboratory staff has not been notified of these developments. For instance, some laboratories have estimated that as much as 50% to 75% of their drug case "backlog" represented cases that had already been pled out or dismissed (Strom et al., 2011). Frequent and routine communication between submitting law enforcement agencies, laboratories, and prosecutors, and information systems that allow these entities to update and share information in real-time on case outcomes, are essential toward promoting both the efficient and effective use of all forms of evidence (Strom & Hickman, 2010, Strom et al., 2011).

The third category, simulated or symbolic evidence collection (Makin, 2012), is particularly disturbing from laboratory management and evidence storage perspectives. As Peterson (Chapter 1, this volume) points out, this is not a new phenomenon, having observed it in field study some 40 years ago (Peterson, 1974). However, Makin's (2012) work is an attempt to move this into the realm of more systematic investigation by exploring its prevalence, varied justifications, and theoretical linkage to backlogs. His research emerged from a focus group discussion in which forensic technicians in a law enforcement agency described a practice where investigators somewhat gratuitously "swab, powder, or collect nonviable samples to demonstrate that the victim received the full resources of the agency" (p. 126). In short, evidence would be collected and processed into evidence storage, but never analyzed.

Makin (2012) conducted a survey of police officers, buttressed with interviews and focus groups, to estimate how widespread knowledge of the practice might be. Although the study suffers from a low response rate, it is the only study of its kind and thus offers important, if not generalizable, information about this behavior. Makin reported that 30% of the officers in the study reported they have engaged with or knew of other officers or forensic technicians who had engaged in simulated evidence collection (p. 131). Focus group data revealed that officers thought the *CSI* effect (see Chapter 2, this volume), public relations, organizational pressure, and community pressure were sources of influence on the decision to simulate evidence collection. Although Makin's study goes farther than any prior study in shedding light on this curious practice, it remains unclear to what extent such simulated evidence contributes to backlog. This is a critical area for further investigation.

Do Backlogs Represent Justice Delayed and Justice Denied, or Simply Justice "Satisficed"?

What do backlogs mean for the administration of justice? We have already suggested, as have many others, that laboratory evidence backlogs represent a potential threat to the due process rights of the accused in that the justice process is being delayed while evidence awaits analysis and reporting. This is not a trivial matter; in many cases, the accused has been incarcerated by the state pending the outcome of the state's case against them. We should seek to minimize such delays, to the extent possible. We have also suggested that the backlogs attributable to law enforcement agencies represent a potential threat to victim rights in that they may never receive justice and restoration in seeing the perpetrator of the crime held accountable. Both forms of backlog also can impact public safety, in the form of offenders who remain free to commit subsequent crimes as the evidence that could potentially be used to identify, apprehend, and prosecute them remains unanalyzed. Although our system of justice is weighted heavily toward protecting the due process rights of the accused (and we wouldn't suggest changing that), it would seem that some balance might be sought between due process rights and victim rights. We should seek to minimize the denial of justice, to the extent possible.

We argue here that, in reality, rather than justice delayed and justice denied, these backlogs probably represent justice "satisficed." In other words, backlogs could be thought of as an expected and reasonable consequence of imperfect information and communication about the utility and processing of forensic evidence. That is, the present state of affairs does not reflect an optimal situation for the justice process, but rather reflects the satisfaction of some criteria and the sacrifice of others, in the presence of imperfect information.

Herbert Simon (1957) is generally credited with the notion of satisficing. The concept emerges from the idea that decision making with perfect information (i.e., pure rationality) is not realistic, and that individuals more realistically operate under conditions of "bounded rationality" (i.e., decision making with less than perfect information). Rather than seeking rational-optimal solutions to problems, satisficing individuals look for solutions (or accept solutions) that are *adequate* for their purposes. It may still be *possible* to optimize, but the process of optimizing may have resource costs that exceed optimization benefits. As such, it may be more rational to satisfice. Laboratory policies and practices may well reflect what is believed to work to get the job done to a reasonably high probability of satisfaction. As such, laboratories may be doing what is necessary to satisfy the minimum requirements to achieve goals, but not necessarily in the "best" (i.e., pure rational-optimal) way of accomplishing the work. What is missing is an efficient and effective means of determining how optimally laboratories are performing and whether or how it may be desirable to seek greater optimization.

Max Houck and Paul Speaker (Chapter 12, this volume) discuss how forensic service providers must develop a balanced approach that weighs the sometimes competing goals of accuracy, timeliness, and cost. Focusing too much on creating a high-volume, high-processing efficiency in crime laboratories can potentially have a negative impact on "longer-term issues, such as quality and value." As such, they argue that crime laboratories should identify business models that take into account outcomes related to both efficiency and effectiveness. As part of this dynamic analysis, a number of questions still need to be answered regarding the true impact of forensic backlogs on the administration of justice. For example, do backlogs for certain types of crimes and certain types of evidence have a greater impact on victims, public safety, and confidence in the justice system than others? Given the tremendous emotional, physical, and economic toll of crimes such as homicide and sexual assault, we would certainly expect the answer to be affirmative. However, significant delays in investigating and prosecuting property and drug crimes can also have negative effects, including serious delays in justice and, in some instances, cases being dropped.

Moving forward, there is not a single "magic bullet" solution to ending forensic evidence backlogs. While funding is certainly helpful in addressing the problem, funding alone cannot be the solution. Following a theme from other chapters in this book, the evidence backlog problem can only be solved if all criminal justice actors recognize that they have important and necessary roles in solving this problem. As we have seen time and time again, the inability to develop common goals, to communicate effectively, and to coordinate resources can have system-wide effects.

References

Benson, W., Stacy, J., & Worley, M. (1970). *Systems analysis of criminalistics operations.* Kansas City, MO: Midwest Research Institute.

Caruso, J. (2006). Forensic laboratories feel the impact of the CSI effect. *Clinical and Forensic Toxicology News* (June), 1, 3–5.

Collins, J. (2012). A reality check on crime lab backlogs. *Michigan Bar Journal* (October), 36–38.

Durose, M. (2008). *Census of publicly funded forensic crime laboratories, 2005.* Washington, DC: Bureau of Justice Statistics.

Durose, M., Walsh, K., & Burch, A. (2012). *Census of publicly funded forensic crime laboratories, 2009.* Washington, DC: Bureau of Justice Statistics.

Lothridge, K. (2009). Presentation as part of the "Making Sense of the DNA Backlog" panel at the annual National Institute of Justice Research and Evaluation Conference, June 16, 2009, Arlington, VA.

Lovrich, N., Pratt, T., Gaffney, M., Johnson, C., Asplen, C., Hurst, L., et al. (2004). *National forensic DNA study report, final report* (Report No. 203970). U.S. Department of Justice.

Makin, D. (2012). Symbolic evidence collection or "If all else fails, throw some dust around." *Forensic Science Policy & Management, 3,* 126–138.

National Forensic Science Technology Center (NFSTC). (2010). *2007 DNA evidence and offender analysis measurement: DNA backlogs, capacity and funding.* Final Report to the National Institute of Justice.

National Research Council, Committee on Identifying the Needs of the Forensic Science Community. (2009). *Strengthening forensic science in the United States: A path forward.* Washington, DC: The National Academies Press.

Nelson, M. (2011). *Making sense of DNA backlogs, 2010—Myths vs. reality*. Washington, DC: National Institute of Justice.

Nelson, M. (2013). *Analysis of untested sexual assault kits in New Orleans*. Washington, DC: National Institute of Justice.

Parker, B., & Gurgin, V. (1972). *Criminalistics in the world of the future*. Menlo Park, CA: Stanford Research Institute.

Peterson, J. (1974). *The utilization of criminalistics services by the police: An analysis of the physical evidence recovery process*. Washington, DC: U.S. Government Printing Office.

Peterson, J., & Hickman, M. (2005). *Census of publicly funded forensic crime laboratories, 2002*. Washington, DC: U.S. Department of Justice.

Peterson, J., Johnson, D., Herz, D., Graziano, L., & Oehler, T. (2011). *Sexual assault kit backlog study: Final report*. Washington, DC: National Institute of Justice.

Peterson, J., & Leggett, A. (2007). The evolution of forensic science: Progress amid the pitfalls. *Stetson Law Review, 36*, 621–660.

Peterson, J., Mihajlovic, S., & Bedrosian, J. (1985). The capabilities, uses, and effects of the nation's criminalistics laboratories. *Journal of Forensic Sciences, 30*(1), 10–23.

Peterson, J., Mihajlovic, S., & Gilliland, M. (1984). *Forensic evidence and the police: The effects of scientific evidence on criminal investigations*. Washington, DC: National Institute of Justice.

Ritter, N. (2013). Untested evidence in sexual assault cases: Using research to guide policy and practice. *Sexual Assault Report, 16*, 33–43.

Simon, H. (1957). *Models of man—social and rational*. New York: Wiley and Sons.

Steadman, G. (2000). *Survey of DNA crime laboratories, 1998*. Washington, DC: Bureau of Justice Statistics.

Steadman, G. (2002). *Survey of DNA crime laboratories, 2001*. Washington, DC: Bureau of Justice Statistics.

Strom, K., & Hickman, M. (2010). Unanalyzed evidence in law enforcement agencies: A national examination of forensic processing in police departments. *Criminology & Public Policy, 9*(2), 381–404.

Strom, K., Hickman, M., Smiley-MacDonald, H., Ropero-Miller, J., & Stout, P. (2011). Crime laboratory personnel as criminal justice decision makers: A study of controlled substance processing in ten jurisdictions. *Forensic Science Policy & Management, 2*(2), 57–69.

Strom, K., Ropero-Miller, J., Jones, S., Sikes, N., Pope, M. W., Horstmann, N. (2009). *The 2007 survey of law enforcement forensic evidence processing: Final report*. Washington, DC: National Institute of Justice.

Section II

The Quality of Forensic Services

The 2009 National Academy of Sciences report *Strengthening Forensic Science in the United States: A Path Forward* was in many ways a seminal event for the forensic community and perhaps more so in the eyes of the public who have tended to view the forensic sciences as relatively infallible. Important questions were raised in the NAS report about the underlying *science* of many mainstay areas of forensic science, particularly in the area of pattern evidence. The report also addressed such matters as cognitive bias, and the need for a national code of ethics in forensics. In this section, we have included three readings that speak to issues related to the quality of forensic services. First, in "Adopting a Research Culture in the Forensic Sciences," Barry A. J. Fisher discusses the call for more research on the scientific foundation of forensic science (both in the NAS report and in an influential law review article that Fisher coauthored) and the implied need for forensic science to become more "mainstream" with the academic scientific establishment. Fisher makes the interesting point that one should not necessarily fault the forensic science establishment for the lack of research. Crime laboratories and their personnel do not generally engage in the type of scientific research called for in the NAS report, but they are the parties most easily associated with the lack of research. The point concerning laboratories generally not engaging in research is supported by earlier BJS crime laboratory censuses that found very few, if any, laboratory resources were available for research.

Next, Reinoud D. Stoel and colleagues (including renowned researcher Itiel E. Dror) discuss a concerning topic taken up in the NAS report, namely, the problem of contextual biases in the forensic sciences. In "Minimizing Contextual Bias in Forensic Casework," Stoel et al. emphasize the importance of maximizing forensic examiners' exposure to domain-relevant information and minimizing exposure to domain-irrelevant information—that is, providing examiners with only the information about a case that is necessary for them to perform scientific analyses and report results. An example from their chapter is the forensic document examiner who must examine the hand-writing on a questioned document, compare it to reference samples, and try to determine the authorship of a document. The fact that the document is an apparent suicide note and that the reference samples are from the deceased and his twin brother (who has a criminal history, financial troubles, and a potential financial gain from his brother's death) are not relevant to the examiner's task. Knowledge that it is a suicide note creates a context for the analysis, and a potentially biasing one at that. Preventing these potentially biasing situations can be accomplished through what Stoel et al. describe as a process of multi-level "context management" in forensic casework. Context management is designed to optimize the use of available information and minimize the potential for bias.

Finally, in "A Survey of Ethical Issues in the Forensic Sciences," Jay Siegel provides a very helpful taxonomy of ethical violations in forensic science ranging from fabricating (or "dry-labbing") to achieve desirable results, to improper use of terminology, to excessive testimonial fees, to dishonest continuing education practices, and much more. Given some of the "headline" cases, such as Annie Dookhan and Fred Zain—discredited chemists from the Massachusetts and West Virginia state crime laboratories, respectively—and others, the realization that extreme behavior such as dry-labbing does in fact occur could be eye-opening for some readers. Yet, one could take some comfort in the notion that we might at least expect such behavior to be rare in the full context of all forensic services in the United States. The problem is we really don't know the full extent to which these behaviors take place. In discussing movements toward a national code of ethics for forensic scientists, Siegel notes that for it to work, a licensure process for forensic scientists would need to be instituted; ethical violations could then result in loss of licensure, and this would help to eliminate unethical practice. Siegel points out that the national forensic science institute called for in the NAS report may help to coordinate national efforts toward these goals.

4

Adopting a Research Culture in the Forensic Sciences

Barry A. J. Fisher

Introduction

Forensic science arose out of a need by the police, prosecution, and the courts to assist criminal investigations through the use of science, medicine, and technology. Long before crime laboratories were established, police often relied on university scientists and physicians for assistance (Thorwald, 1965, 1967). Forensic practices were commonly validated by trial and error. For example, the identification of criminals became a vexing problem by the 19th century, particularly in large metropolitan areas. Alphonse Bertillon, the French police investigator, was an early practitioner to use anthropometry to identify individuals by taking measurements of various anatomic features on the subjects' bodies (see "Alphonse Bertillon," n.d.). Eventually, the cumbersome technique proved to be unable to identify persons with similar measurements and, ultimately, fingerprinting became the generally accepted practice by which to identify individuals. Over time, forensic science techniques were generally developed along two different tracks. Some techniques were derived through the application of applied physical and natural sciences: chemistry, biochemistry, biology, and medicine. These disciplines include forensic toxicology; forensic chemistry, including the testing of controlled substances and arson samples; forensic DNA testing; and forensic pathology. Their predecessors were developed from academic-based science programs found within universities. Other branches of forensic science that have been used in criminal cases for decades were established outside of academia and a research-oriented framework. These branches fall outside what some might call "traditional" scientific disciplines, such as chemistry, biology, and physics. One grouping of forensic evidence that falls outside traditional scientific areas has been referred to as *pattern evidence*. Some of these disciplines include fingerprint identification, firearms identification, shoe print and tire impression analysis, bitemark identification, and toolmark examination. Such disciplines did not arise from university science fields but had their start in applied police science. Law enforcement, when faced with a technical problem, brings physical evidence associated with a crime to forensic science labs, universities, hospitals, or anyone who might be able to help associate evidence with a particular person or crime scene. Police rely on chemists, biologists, physicians, engineers, and others to help solve their cases. Sometimes, new and novel techniques might be used to bring light on a case.

As an example for how some disciplines such as pattern evidence have evolved, consider a major case in the history of American crime: the Saint Valentine's Day murders of 1929 in Chicago. The Chicago Police Department was faced with the murders of several bootleggers allegedly committed by a rival gang who were dressed as Chicago police officers. One could imagine the public outcry and media attention to solve this heinous crime. The police turned to Col. Calvin Goddard, a U.S. Army physician by training and a firearms examiner by avocation. Through Goddard's observations of marks made on fired bullets and shell casings, he was able to conclude that bullets were fired from firearms recovered from the crime and associated with the rival gang's members. Goddard's medical training and expertise in firearms allowed him to make observations and associations between guns and fired bullets. No university programs existed that conducted research into this methodology of firearms testing. Nevertheless the courts accepted the premise that this type of association could be done even without academic research into the efficacy of forensic firearms identification.

The rise of forensic DNA testing, growth in case law bearing on the admissibility of evidence and expert testimony, and more recently, the National Academy of Science (NAS) report released in 2009, combined to raise a call for more research in forensic science as a means to demonstrate reliability. In 2011, I coauthored an article titled "The Need for a Research Culture in the Forensic Sciences" (Mnookin et al., 2011). The principal author of the article was Prof. Jennifer Mnookin of UCLA Law School. The focus of that review was to highlight the need for forensic science to become more "mainstream" within the greater academic scientific establishment. The article was in response to the NAS report on forensic science, which raised a number of questions on the state of forensic science today. The article focused on a number of disciplines within forensic science developed outside of traditional academic science (chemistry, biology, medicine, etc.) and the importance of research to demonstrate the reliability of these areas.

A casual reader of the law review article or of the NAS report might come away with the notion that the responsibility for the insufficiency of university-backed research is somehow the fault of the forensic science establishment. In reality, professional organizations—such as the American Society of Crime Laboratory Directors, the American Academy of Forensic Sciences (AAFS), the National Association of Medical Examiners, and the International Association for Identification (National Institute of Justice, 2006; American Academy of Forensic Sciences, 2006), and, subsequently, beginning around 2000, the Consortium of Forensic Science Organizations (CFSO)—have been pressing Congress for more funding for forensic science research and other needs. The CFSO successfully petitioned Congress to fund the National Science Foundation to review and report on the status and needs of forensic science in the United States (Edwards, 2010).

Why a Research Culture Does Not Currently Exist in the Forensic Sciences

In discussing the need for a research culture in the forensic sciences, it is important to start by exploring some of the reasons why such a research culture presently does not exist. One of the primary reasons is the lack of funding. Those responsible for delivering public forensic science services to the criminal justice system do not typically engage in the sort of scientific research discussed in either the *UCLA Law Review* article or the NAS report (exceptions include the FBI, Department of Defense, and several other federal agencies involved in forensic science who do engage in research and development in forensic science). Crime laboratories and those who work in government-supported laboratories understand the strengths and limitations of their field, and have a good idea of the types of research that would help to strengthen their disciplines. They would certainly support such research.

Unfortunately, some of the stakeholders within our adversarial legal system often challenge the seeming lack of research in some areas of forensic science. Such arguments are good strategy in criminal trials, because issues of reliability and limited research may be used to argue to judges and juries about the lack of research and, by extension, the inadmissibility of the evidence. For research into forensic science to be conducted, Congress needs to fund that research. Regrettably, funds for such activities are not very great. A historical examination of the level of funds earmarked for forensic science research and development is a clear indicator why the situation continues unabated.

The report of the President's Commission on Law Enforcement and Administration of Justice (1967), initiated by President Johnson, made the following statement about the need for science and technology in support of the criminal justice system:

> The Federal Government should take the initiative in organizing and sustaining a science and technology research and development program. Whether it be equipment development, field experimentation, data collection, or analytical studies, the limited budgets of individual State and local criminal justice agencies cannot provide the necessary investment. Furthermore, the results will be of nationwide benefit. Thus, the Federal Government should support a major scientific and technology research and development program relating to all areas of criminal justice.
>
> The program should introduce science and technology to criminal justice. The Federal Government should sponsor research, development, test, and evaluation supporting those widely useful projects that no single agency could support alone. The Government should help criminal justice agencies get the technical support they need. (pp. 269–270)

Sadly, in my opinion, the report has only collected dust, but the needs are still present. This chapter discusses some recent developments in forensic science, how the justice system understands scientific expertise proffered in criminal cases, the challenges and factors that have inhibited a stronger research foundation in forensics, and how orienting the field of forensics within a research-based culture can improve the use of science in the criminal justice system.

Recent Developments in the Forensic Sciences

In the early 1990s, three events took place and had a significant influence on forensic science: (1) the growth and widespread use of DNA testing in criminal trials; (2) the *Daubert* decision; and (3) the start of the Innocence Project. In addition, the O.J. Simpson trial offered the general public an unprecedented view of modern forensic science in the courtroom and attracted the public's interest.

THE IMPACT OF DNA

Forensic DNA testing was a "game changer." Heretofore, only fingerprint evidence was able to conclusively place a suspect in contact with a crime scene or victim. DNA, found in blood, semen, or other biological evidence, connected a suspect and victim with near certainty. Bloodstain evidence, seminal fluid, and saliva are present in many murder and rape investigations as well as in other crimes. DNA evidence became the key to proving the perpetrator's involvement.

DNA evidence presents a challenge to defense attorneys as it points with virtual certainty to a defendant in a crime. As the technology was relatively new to criminal cases, it raised issues about its admissibility in court, and it was only natural that the defense bar would seek to keep the evidence out by means of evidentiary hearings. Raising *Daubert* challenges was a reasonable extension to other types of evidence by questioning the reliability of the evidence proffered.

FRYE, RULE 702, AND DAUBERT

None of the current issues surrounding the admissibility of scientific or expert evidence might have arisen had it not been for the *Daubert* decision (and its subsequent cases) and the advent of forensic DNA testing with its use of statistics to describe the likelihood of biological evidence being associated with a person, object, or location. It is curious, however, that most of the initial cases dealing with scientific reliability of expert evidence are related to civil litigation rather than criminal cases.

There is a divide between law and science, and courts have to reconcile what is legitimate science and what is not. Just because many believe that astrology is reliable, for example, does not mean that it ought to be accepted in a trial. The admissibility of technical information has been considered by the courts for some time. The question of admissibility of scientific evidence in court was addressed in 1923 by the Court in *Frye v. United States* 293 F. 1013 (D.C. Cir 1923). The court stated,

> Just when a scientific principle or discovery crosses the line between the experimental and demonstrable stages is difficult to define. Somewhere in this twilight zone the evidential force of the principle must be recognized, and while the courts will go a long way in admitting experimental testimony deduced from a well-recognized scientific principle or discovery, the thing from which the deduction is made must be sufficiently established to have gained general acceptance in the particular field in which it belongs.

The Frye Rule, also referred to as the *General Acceptance rule*, defined how courts could deal with scientific evidence for nearly 90 years. Today, the rule has changed to reflect the notion of reliability and is codified in the Federal Rules of Evidence, 702, which states, in part, that

> an expert witness, professional witness or judicial expert is a witness, who by virtue of education, training, skill, or experience, is believed to have expertise and specialized knowledge in a particular subject beyond that of the average person, sufficient that others may officially and legally rely upon the witness's specialized (scientific, technical or other) opinion about an evidence or fact issue within the scope of his expertise, referred to as the expert opinion, as an assistance to the fact-finder.

Daubert marked a turning point in how the court viewed scientific evidence. The notion of reliability was added to the mix beyond general acceptance. Experts were asked to demonstrate that the procedures used were reliable for the material to be presented to the court. Reliability could be shown in a number of ways: published reports in peer-reviewed journals, known error rates, and so on. The focus on the need to prove reliability of scientific, and expert opinion evidence marked a change from the earlier general acceptance test (*Frye*). Experts could be asked in *Daubert* jurisdictions to demonstrate reliability (*Daubert* admissibility requirements are followed in federal court and some state courts. Many states still follow the *Frye* standard).

THE INNOCENCE PROJECT

The Innocence Project, started at Cardozo Law School by Barry Scheck and Peter Neufeld in 1992, and subsequently spread to similar law clinics across the country as part of the Innocence Network, has demonstrated how DNA evidence in particular can shed light on the reliability of many mainstay areas of forensic science, flawed eyewitness testimony, and misconduct by actors within the criminal justice system. As of January 2014, the Innocence Project website indicates 312 exonerations.

Factors Affecting the Admissibility of Forensic Science

THE USE OF STATISTICS TO EXPRESS THE RELATIONSHIP BETWEEN EVIDENTIARY AND KNOWN SAMPLES

A significant factor influencing the admissibility of scientific or expert evidence in court is the use of statistics to indicate the likelihood of an item of evidence being connected to a reference sample. In the past, statistics only played a minor role in forensic science. For instance, chemical analysis may involve statistics, such as when quantitative analyses are reported out. If a drug test measures the concentration of a controlled substance or a sample is weighed, there is a statistic that is part of a measurement. Measurements are not absolute. There is a range wherein the actual number is. Thus, 1.000 grams of methamphetamine might actually be 1.000 plus or minus 0.050 grams. Similarly, the concentration of a sample, such as a blood alcohol test, might be within 10% of the reported number.

Statistics to connect a person with another person or location are important in criminal investigations. In the past, statistics were used to a limited extent in forensic serology cases. The likelihood of ABO blood groups, A, B, AB and O types, were well known. ABO type AB is the least common and happens in about 4% of the population. But in the most common cases (type O or type A), the expert could only report that the blood or semen sample came from about two of five people in the population. As forensic biology became more discriminating, the chance of connecting a person with a biological evidence sample got better. When polymorphic enzymes became widely used in criminal cases, the statistical occurrence of enzymes, such as phosphogluco-mutase or PGM, could limit the odds further.

Yet the use of DNA in forensic science elevated how statistics were used in forensic science and, in turn, how other forensic disciplines were viewed from a statistical perspective. DNA evidence provided the ability to quantify the likelihood that a given sample came from one person. As a result, the use of forensic evidence changed in profound ways. Juries were being given information that for practical purposes placed the defendant in contact with the victim with near absolute certainty. DNA evidence, with its use of statistics to describe the significance between evidence samples and a known sample, has been a driving force in how we express conclusions about the commonality of evidence sources.

Prior to the use of statistics in DNA evidence, conclusions presented from forensic analysis could be vague. The use of terms such as *consistent, similar to, same as,* and so on, were rarely challenged to ascertain what the expert meant or how he came to that conclusion (see Chapter 6, this volume). Before the rise of DNA testing and the use of statistics to describe the likelihood of a match, expert testimony was general expressed using terms such as *similar to, consistent with,* and, in some cases, *unique* (used to convey that the evidence came from a specific source). The reason for using these somewhat ambiguous declarations was simple. Expert witnesses did not have precise ways to express the connection between one item of evidence collected at a crime scence and the reference specimen. The conclusions used were a means to express a level of uncertainty. As a result, experts resorted in subjective terms. These were simply efforts on the part of the examiner to express the relationship between the item of interest and the reference. Statistics do not exist at the moment to express the likelihood of a connection between two specimens.

Unlike DNA evidence, which uses statistics to convey the likelihood that two specimens are from a common source, statistics are not readily available in pattern evidence cases. We do not have any way to explain to a jury that a latent print came from a specific person (Kaye, 2010). An expert might say something like the opinion is "based on my knowledge, training and experience; it is my opinion that this print came from the defendant." If pressed on the certainty of his opinion, the expert could opine, "While I haven't looked at every fingerprint in existence, I am of a very strong opinion that the print came from the defendant." That conclusion is far different from a conclusion that the print came from the defendant, to the exclusion of every other person on the planet—a conclusion that has far less cachet than it once had.

Historically, it has been a tenet in criminalistics that certain types of physical evidence may be individualized (shown to have come from a unique or sole source). Thus, an expert might contend that, with sufficient data, bullets can be shown to have been fired from single gun, latent fingerprints came from a single person, shoe prints and tire impressions from a single source, and so on. The notion made in this assertion of uniqueness or individuality is that given a sufficiency of comparative data, a conclusion can be drawn that the sample in question came from a sole source, to the exclusion of anything or anyone else. This assertion of uniqueness or individuality has come under fire in recent years (Saks & Koehler, 2007).

Another criminalistics concept is the term *identification*. That term is used to describe the forensic examination of mass-produced items, such as clothing. No matter how much testing is conducted, source attribution can only be to a common source, perhaps thousands or tens of thousands of garments made from identical material. Other examples are building materials, paint, glass, fibers, and textiles.

There is an overlap between the concepts of identification and individualization. Take, for example, a pair of running shoes with a particular tread pattern. Initially, a pair of shoes would have the same pattern as any other new pair. Shoes exhibit marks that are the same as any other shoe of the same size and model. They have class characteristics and may be identified as coming from a common source. With usage and wear, the sole pattern will change. With careful examination the tread may take on unique characteristics, and after a time these changes may become unique to a shoe impression left at a crime scene. The challenge is that opinions about similarity and uniqueness are subjective. Different experts may see different markings that allow them to conclude the shoe and the crime scene mark are the same or perhaps unique.

Examiners have opined that inductive reasoning (i.e., observing items of evidence over and over again) allows the expert to conclude that two items are identical. Statistically, this assertion has yet to be proven. There is research ongoing to determine the statistical likelihood of some types of pattern evidence (e.g., fingerprints), but such numerical representations have yet to be used widely (see Ulerya et al., 2011). Over a career, an examiner may conduct thousands of examinations on impression evidence cases. Over time, he may convince himself of the uniqueness of individual items because of those observations. For the present, suggesting that one item is identical to another, to the exclusion of any other, has yet to be supported by the larger scientific community (i.e., those outside of forensic science).

On a similar topic, the notion of uniqueness is compounded by other concerns. Observations, which lead an examiner to conclude that evidentiary items are the same, may be erroneous. What if the characteristics we are viewing are not significant for some reason? Consider, for example, the analysis of trace elements in bullet lead. This procedure was used to link bullets found at a crime scene to bullets found in possession of a suspect because of a belief that these similarities in the composition of lead used in the manufacture of bullets could be used to prove a common source. The National Research Council (2004) concluded that the statistics behind an assertion of a common source could not be made. The result was that hundreds and perhaps thousands of cases were undermined.

Class characteristics or identification presents a further issue not often discussed. Assume a person alleged to have broken into a house is apprehended in the neighborhood of the crime. His shoes are taken and sent to a crime laboratory. The examiner finds a small glass fragment imbedded in the sole. The glass matches the glass from the broken window at the crime scene. The trace evidence examiner reports this fact and states that the class was the same as the crime scene glass and could have come from any similarly manufactured glass. However, one important piece of information is missing: How often is this type of glass found in people's shoes? If it is commonplace, the jury might conclude that such information has less probative value than if it were a rare occurrence. The problem in this example is that there is way to convey that kind of information to a trier of fact.

More research is needed into the reliability of the various types of physical evidence used in criminal investigations. Studies to test the reliability of testing procedures and to determine the statistical likelihood of a questioned item of evidence matching a known sample would clarify many of the issues now facing the admissibility of certain forms of physical evidence examined in crime laboratories.

Contemporary Challenges Facing Forensic Science

Public forensic science laboratories and their scientific staffs are under fire, perhaps more today than at any point in recent history. In the time following the landmark NAS report, *Strengthening Forensic Science in the United States: A Path Forward*, forensic science has been under a microscope. Congress, the White House, the press, and, in a few cases, the courts have raised some difficult questions for forensic science practitioners. Questions focus on topics such as reliability of forensic science, ethics, oversight, and administrative control over labs, to name a few.

In the Mnookin et al. (2011) article, we highlighted improvements in forensic science education, improving the quality of forensic science journals, using scientific standards to guide casework, improving access to data, and managing the tension between the adversarial culture and research culture as necessary conditions for change. While I allude to some of these at various points in this chapter, I have chosen to focus on a topic we also raised in that article—an area that I feel is the most acute challenge to developing a research culture in the forensic sciences, namely the availability of funding.

The subject of the reliability of forensic science continues to be a topic of discussion by critics. The reliability issue is often focused on pattern evidence disciplines: fingerprint evidence, firearms and toolmark evidence, tire impression evidence, bitemark evidence, handwriting evidence, and so forth. Research is the key to addressing the question of reliability. While it is true that pattern evidence has been studied, most studies have been done by forensic scientists and published in forensic science journals. The scientific establishment housed within universities has not done very much in these areas, mainly because the amount of federal funding from entities like the National Institute of Justice and National Science Foundation has been relatively small. There have been some changes in recent years, but the amount is still limited.

Demonstrating reliability in these specialties is not an impossible matter. Research is needed and should be conducted at research universities with experts in a wide variety of research areas, including forensic scientists. Some areas may be unfamiliar to researchers, but models can be developed to understand the problem.

What is missing here is sustained and focused government funding to conduct the research and defining the nature of the research. Without these efforts, the reliability issue will continue to be raised by the defense bar, the Innocence Project, and the press. It is unlikely to go away on its own accord. Compounding the funding challenge is the present budget problem(s) faced by the U.S. government. It is uncertain how seriously Congress and the Administration view these matters. Certainly, it could be argued that limited progress has been made since the publication of the NAS report. Legislation has moved at a glacial pace in Congress, and the administration has done little. The Department of Justice and NIST have announced the creation of a National

Commission on Forensic Science within the U.S. Department of Justice. The selection of 30 commissioners was completed as this chapter went to press. At the moment, there is no word of funding.

The NAS report should have been a watershed event. Unfortunately, it wasn't. Neither was the many exonerations resulting from the work of the Innocence Project. Attempts to improve how the public forensic science delivery system operates have had limited success. Congress and the White House have been slow to act. State governments, when they have done so, initiate tepid programs to oversee forensic science laboratories. What, then, is the answer?

Ultimately, ongoing pressure from the defense bar will result in progress. If cases are lost or overturned, the result will be more robust forensic sciences. This is not to say that the current state of forensic sciences is all bad. But clearly, it can do better, and concerns about reliability and quality can be reduced. Hopefully, criticism will result in change through legislation and ultimately funding to address the presumed shortcomings.

For the moment, courts have not fully addressed forensic science criticism. Yet they certainly have a role to play and at some point decide if opinion evidence proffered by the prosecution is reliable and competent work. The courts have yet to take significant action in managing these issues.

Yet, if the funds were to become available and the kinds of research needed to put to rest the reliability issues started immediately, a significant time period will be needed to conduct these studies—easily five years or more will be necessary. What can be done in the meantime? Some have suggested that some types of pattern evidence should not be admitted. Others suggest that expert opinions should limited. Perhaps there is a middle ground that can be advanced where experts more completely explain both the strengths and shortcomings of their conclusions.

We are at an interesting time period. The U.S. Department of Justice in cooperation with the National Institute of Science and Technology has just empaneled a National Forensic Science Commission. Many of the issues raised in this chapter will likely be reviewed and perhaps even resolved. Certainly, the prospects for funding for research and development stand a far better chance than at any time in the past. I choose to be optimistic for a successful outcome.

References

Alphonse Bertillon. (n.d.) *Wikipedia*. Retrieved January 15, 2014 from http://en .wikipedia.org/wiki/Alphonse_Bertillon

American Academy of Forensic Sciences. (2006). *Report prepared by the American Academy of Forensic Sciences*. Retrieved from https://www.ncjrs.gov/pdffiles1/nij/grants/213424 .pdf

Daubert v. Merrell Dow Pharmaceuticals, Inc. 509 U.S. 579, 113 S.Ct. 2786 (1992)

Edwards, H. T. (2010). *The National Academy of Sciences Report on Forensic Sciences: What it means for the bench and bar*. Paper presented at the Conference on the Role of the Court in an Age of Developing Science and Technology, Washington, DC, May 6, 2010. Retrieved from http://www.law.yale.edu/documents/pdf/Alumni_Affairs/Stith_ Edwards_NAS_Report_Forensic_Science.pdf

Kaye, D. (2010). Probability, individualization, and uniqueness in forensic science evidence: Listening to the academies. *Brooklyn Law Review, 75*(4), 1163–1185.

Mnookin, J., Cole, S., Dror, I., Fisher, B., Houck, M., Inman, K., et al. (2011). The need for a research culture in the forensic sciences. *UCLA Law Review, 58,* 725–779.

National Institute of Justice. (2006). *Status and needs of forensic science service providers: A report to Congress.* Retrieved from https://www.ncjrs.gov/pdffiles1/nij/213420.pdf

National Research Council, Committee on Scientific Assessment of Bullet Lead Elemental Composition Comparison. (2004). *Forensic analysis: Weighing bullet lead evidence.* Washington, DC: National Academies Press.

President's Commission on Law Enforcement and the Administration of Justice. (1967). *The challenge of crime in a free society.* New York: Dutton. Retrieved from https://www.ncjrs.gov/pdffiles1/nij/42.pdf

Saks, M. J., & Koehler, J. J. (2007). The individualization fallacy in forensic science evidence. *Vanderbilt Law Review, 61*(1), 199–219.

Thorwald, J. (1965). *The century of the detective* (Richard and Clara Winston, Trans.). New York: Harcourt, Brace and World.

Thorwald, J. (1967). *Crime and science* (Richard and Clara Winston, Trans.). New York: Harcourt Brace and World.

Ulerya, B., Hicklina, R., Buscaglia, J., & Roberts, M. (2011, May 10). Accuracy and reliability of forensic latent fingerprint decisions. *Proceedings of the National Academy of Sciences, 108*(19), 7733–7738.

5

Minimizing Contextual Bias in Forensic Casework

Reinoud D. Stoel,
Charles E. H. Berger, Wim Kerkhoff,
Erwin J. A. T. Mattijssen, and Itiel E. Dror

Introduction

Criticism has been raised by several scholars on the subjective nature of expert opinion in forensic casework and the absence of sufficient precautions to reduce the risk of the possible biasing effect of contextual information (e.g., Dror & Cole, 2010; Dror & Rosenthal, 2008; Risinger et al., 2002; Saks et al., 2003). There have also been a number of official inquiries that focused explicitly on this issue. For example, the U.S. National Academy of Science inquiry (NAS, 2009) concluded that

> a body of research is required to establish the limits and measures of performance and to address the impact of sources of variability and potential bias. Such research is sorely needed, but it seems to be lacking in most of the forensic disciplines that rely on subjective assessments of matching characteristics. These disciplines need to develop rigorous protocols to guide these subjective interpretations and pursue equally rigorous research and evaluation programs. The development of such research programs can benefit significantly from other areas, notably from the large body of research on the evaluation of observer performance in diagnostic medicine and from the findings of cognitive psychology on the potential for bias and error in human observers. (p. 8)

Furthermore, a number of professional working groups have been established to examine these issues. The U.S. National Institute of Standards and Technology (NIST) and the U.S. National Institute of Justice (NIJ) have jointly formed a working group consisting of scientists and practitioners to examine these issues (NIST, 2012).

The notion that expert opinions may be biased by irrelevant factors is not at all new, and was raised more than a century ago. Hagan (1894), with reference to questioned document examination, addresses the problem, and provides an implicit solution when he wrote, "Where the expert has no knowledge of the moral evidence or aspects of the case in which signatures are a matter of context, there is nothing to mislead him, or to influence the forming of an opinion" (p. 82). Hagan was already aware back in 1894 that expert opinions may be influenced by factors that should not do so, and implicitly suggests withholding such information from the expert doing the examination.

While "subjective" does not imply "unreliable," or "not valid," the risk of being affected by external factors increases with increasing subjectivity (Dror, 2013). If a judgment is affected by impertinent factors that should not contribute, then that judgment is said to be biased. In this chapter, we deal with bias in the judgment of forensic experts that provide evidence in criminal cases. That evidence most often consists of written reports that describe the examination and present the conclusions of this examination. The reports usually focus on one specific type of evidence (i.e., a finger-mark found on the crime scene or the handwriting in a questioned document) and its correspondence with some reference material (i.e., a fingerprint or the handwriting of a suspect, respectively). They are written by experts from different forensic disciplines, and in many cases, more than one report is being sent to the trier of fact. The trier of fact should combine the reports with all other information in the case.

The logic of the interpretation of forensic evidence (Aitken & Taroni, 2005; Evett, 1998; Robertson & Vignaux, 1995) tells the forensic experts (i.e., the persons performing the analyses, comparison, and evaluation of the evidence) to consider the probability of their observations, given the appropriate propositions in the case. If the experts would consider the probability of those propositions, they would have to consider much more (if not all) of the other information in the case. That would take them well outside their own area of expertise. By considering the probability of the observations, they have no need to know about information that influences the probability of the propositions. They are to report only on the evidential value of their own observations, and confined to their own area of expertise. For those not familiar with the principles of evidence interpretation, we will return to these issues in the examples in the remainder of this chapter.

In the 20th century, psychological studies showed cognitive processes to play a major role in human behavior and in (expert) judgments (Nisbett & Ross, 1980; Nisbett & Wilson, 1977; Tversky & Kahneman, 1974). These cognitive processes enable us to prioritize and group large amounts of information, and draw conclusions, despite often ambiguous and incomplete information (see Dror, 2009b, for a discussion in the forensic context). While these cognitive processes form the very basis of human intelligence and expertise (allowing us, for example, to distinguish our next-door neighbor from a burglar in the dark, or to cross a busy street), they also entail cognitive bias in terms of selectivity and biased information processing. We will use the term *contextual bias* here to make explicit that we focus on the human tendency to draw conclusions in certain situations based on (irrelevant) contextual factors, other than the results of the examination (i.e., the evidence). This is generally a good thing to do; it is just not part of the role of the forensic expert, who is there to aid the trier of fact in drawing conclusions, not draw them himself. Forensic science should acknowledge the existence of contextual bias and minimize its effects by proper training and the development of appropriate methods and procedures.

Consider the following examples:

1. Forensic handwriting examiners can be biased by the meaning of the very words written in a questioned document they are asked to examine to find evidence concerning authorship based on a comparison of the characteristics of the questioned document with some reference material. If the words in the document reveal information with respect to the person that committed the crime, the examiner could be selectively looking for features that correspond to the expectation created by this information. While the information contained in the written text itself may be very important for the trier of fact to consider, it is not within the province of the document examiner.

2. Pathologists may be biased by the information that a human body has been found in an illegal grave, when they are asked whether their observations provide evidence for murder. The fact that the body has been found in an illegal grave may indeed have probative value (i.e., illegal graves are much more common for murdered people than for people that died of natural causes), but one may question whether that belongs to the expertise of the pathologist. If it does not belong to the expertise of the pathologist, it may well create a bias toward a conclusion of murder, but what are the consequences if the pathologist does not know?

3. Forensic firearms examiners, asked to assess evidence for whether two cartridge cases have been fired by a suspect's gun, may be biased by the fact that two cartridges are missing from the magazine. The observation of two missing cartridges may provide some evidence, especially if the only other gun under consideration is not missing any of its cartridges. But the forensic firearms examiner should look at corresponding class characteristics and striations between cartridge cases and test fires from the two guns.

4. Another illustrative, but hypothetical, example is given by Risinger et al. (2002) where an odontologist investigates an incomplete bitemark on human skin. The bitemark gives only little information, and suppose the odontologist concludes that "the bitemark was probably from a human adult, but there was insufficient detail to identify any particular adult as the source of the bite." Unfortunately, when the odontologist receives information that the victim was raped, and that the DNA profile of the sperm recovered matches that of the defendant, the odontologist concludes "the source of the bitemark can be assigned to the defendant to a very high degree of probability." While the suggested source may very well be the true one, the assignment seems to be based on information that does not belong to the domain of odontology. When the DNA evidence is implicitly included in the odontology evidence the DNA evidence will be counted twice by the trier of fact.

Please note that we do not propose to disregard all case information. Such information is important and should be weighed by someone, and could be used to phrase the appropriate propositions and interpret the results of the examination. But it is important that the expert judgment is based on the domain-relevant information only, and not more than that. With respect to the odontologist example, the information that is not related to the teeth is indeed important for the case since it will impact the probability that it was the suspect that bit the victim, but it is not part of—or even at all relevant for—the bitemark evidence, and should not be used by the odontologist. Odontologists cannot properly weigh such information as it is outside their area of expertise; if they use it implicitly, it will likely be weighed again by the trier of fact. It is easy for evidence to get counted multiple times.

An important question is whether these biasing effects do actually occur in practice. The answer to this question is not as easy as it might seem. If one would base it on the existing psychological research, the answer would certainly be affirmative. However, as noted by Dror, Charlton, and Peron (2006), an important weakness in forensic science is the lack of research on and attention for cognitive aspects that could play a key role in the task of the forensic expert concerned with the analysis and interpretation of the evidence: Empirical research is scarce.

Dror and Cole (2010), Risinger (2009), and Kassin, Dror, and Kukucka (2013) provide overviews of studies related to the existence of contextual bias in the forensic sciences. However, the few studies in the literature do not give a clear answer. Kersholt et al. (2007; 2010), as well as Hall and Player (2008), come to the conclusion that contextual bias in forensic science is not such a big issue (for criticisms of these findings, see Dror, 2009b). In contrast, other studies find biasing effects. Thompson (2009) showed in an *ad hoc* experiment that knowledge of the DNA profile of the suspect by forensic DNA experts may affect the interpretation of the trace (partial and complex) DNA profile.

An experiment by Dror et al. (2006) provides evidence for contextual bias in forensic fingerprint casework. Five experts were given a fingermark and fingerprint that they had previously evaluated in a real case as left by the same finger. But this time, fingermark and fingerprint were presented in a context that very strongly pointed to different sources. The participating experts were not aware of the fact that they had analyzed them before. Three experts who participated in this experiment concluded that the fingermark and fingerprint did not come from the same finger, and one expert concluded that there was insufficient information. Four out of five experts thus drew a different conclusion than they had previously drawn based on exactly the same mark and print. These findings were replicated and subjected to meta-analytic examination (see Dror & Rosenthal, 2008).

One could argue that the findings by Dror and Thompson are based on fairly limited experiments (e.g., small sample sizes; non-randomized experiments; experts' awareness of participating in an experiment), and that the few studies performed have not presented consistent findings. On the other hand, one might argue that forensic science cannot ignore the vast amount of findings from cognitive research outside of forensic science, which provides clear evidence for contextual influences.

Furthermore, if there is at least a chance that contextual bias exists, it would be prudent to perform forensic examinations in such a way that the risk of contextual bias is minimized. Risinger (2009) argues it is unwise to await more research with respect to whether, when, and how forensic examinations may be biased: "What is needed is not more research, but a simple analytic reflection on what kinds of information are clearly not called for by virtue of the claims of the area, and which are relevant, under what conditions, and in which order" (p. 33). Indeed, the question *whether* contextual bias plays a role in forensic examinations should not be the focal point of further research. Knowing more about this "whether, when, and how" might help, though, in finding and improving ways to minimize contextual bias.

The aim of this chapter is to present different levels of contextual information that lay the foundation for a structural approach for what we will call *context management* in forensic casework. Context management aims to optimize the flow of information to and from a forensic expert in a case. This means minimizing as much as possible the effects of domain-irrelevant information, and maximizing the role of domain-relevant information. We will first provide some more historical background and overview of the literature on bias in forensic science. Then we briefly address the psychological background of contextual bias, and end with a detailed description of a classification model of contextual information that may guide the development of appropriate methods to minimize contextual bias.

Historical Background

One of the first to apply psychological principles in the practice of forensic casework in an attempt to control contextual bias was Miller (1984) working in the area of questioned document examination. Miller realized that questioned document examination "lends itself readily to unintended bias on the part of the examiner" and "depends primarily on a subjective analysis by the examiner," and that "there are no specific tests for identification that . . . limit the amount of subjectivity in an analysis" (p. 407). He proposed to reduce the amount of case information given to the expert, and to present the evidence together with other items in a line-up. In a later publication, Miller (1987) extended his lineup approach to the field of human hair analysis.

Stoel et al. (2010) have argued that the constructed lineup approach is not feasible due to the simultaneous effects of the expert, the evidence, and the choice of foil specimens on the outcome of the analysis. Still, Miller did address, as one of the first in forensic science, the vulnerability to bias due to contextual factors. His ideas were, however, not developed any further in the years following the publications, nor were they applied in practice until the late 1990s.[1]

In the past decade, much has been written on contextual bias in forensic science, often with reference to the highly visible error by the FBI's fingerprint identification unit in the Madrid bombing case (see e.g., Stacey, 2004; Thompson & Cole, 2005). The largest part of this literature focuses on the existence of contextual bias among forensic experts (e.g., Dror, Charlton, & Peron, 2006; Dror & Hampikian, 2011; Hall & Player, 2008; Kerstholt et al. 2010; Kerstholt, Paashuis, & Sjerps, 2007; Langenburg, Champod, & Wertheim, 2009; Schiffer & Champod, 2007; Thompson, 2009) and on criticizing the field for not adopting appropriate precautions (e.g., Risinger, Saks), and on blind procedures like the evidence line-up and the "case managers model" (Risinger et al., 2002; Kassin et al., 2013). The case managers model distinguishes a case manager who is fully informed of the facts of the case, and an analyst who is "blind" to irrelevant information (Risinger et al., 2002; Thompson, 2009, 2011).

Only few scholars provided practical and sufficiently detailed guidelines as to what to do in practice. One of these exceptions may be Krane et al. (2008; see also

---

[1]An early discussion on the absence of—and need for—good procedures to manage the information in forensic casework was initiated by Turvey (1998) in reaction to a study by Wells and Bradfield (1998).

Thompson, 2009) who developed the concept of "sequential unmasking" designed to minimize observer effects in the interpretation of DNA profiles. Sequential unmasking is now the standard procedure in some forensic laboratories, such as the Netherlands Forensic Institute (Meulenbroek, de Blaeij, & Kloosterman, 2009). Recently, Page, Taylor, and Blenkin (2012) proposed to apply a combination of the case managers model and sequential unmasking in forensic odontology.

Case Assessment and Interpretation (CAI, Cook et al., 1998b) is an approach developed in the 1990s to guide and maximize the utilization of forensic science in the criminal justice process. It stresses the importance of the application of the logical principles of evidence interpretation, and the communication of case information between case investigators and forensic scientists. The fact that often not enough information is obtained adds to the urgency of identifying what information should be used and what information should be disregarded. It is not simply a matter of leaving out as much information as possible, which would do more harm than good.

Another very important part of CAI which takes into account cognitive aspects is pre-assessment: The scientist should make his expectations explicit before the examination is carried out, to avoid *post hoc* rationalization once the results are known. In this chapter, we will focus mostly on how to avoid exposure to extraneous and potentially biasing information, and not on how to obtain more relevant information (which is just as important).

Psychological Background

As noted in the introduction, many psychological studies in the 20th century have demonstrated time and again that context plays a major role in human judgment. In this section, we will briefly address some of the psychological background relating to contextual bias in forensic casework.

Broadly speaking, information can be processed "bottom-up" or "top-down." Data-driven processing of information that reaches our cognitive system through our senses is processed bottom-up. Often, there is far too much information, and it is too demanding for the brain to fully process this amount of information. The brain therefore uses a variety of cognitive mechanisms that enable the brain to effectively handle the large amounts of incoming bottom-up information (such as selective attention, chunking, and automaticity; see Dror, 2011). These mechanisms draw from past experience, knowledge, and expectation, and they influence how incoming information is processed. Such "conceptually driven" processing is top-down and widespread, and takes part in most cognitive operations.

Top-down processing stands at the core of human intelligence and expertise. It results, generally, in better performance (i.e., better decisions and actions). There is, however, a downside to this way of processing information. With the selection of certain information, other information is disregarded and ignored. As we gain experience and knowledge, the top-down cognitive mechanisms become increasingly powerful, until we eventually become experts. Expertise thus entails top-down cognitive mechanisms that improve performance and result in superior abilities. Experts have abilities that allow them to perform at a high level, much higher than non-experts. To achieve such performance levels, experts need to have well-organized knowledge, use sophisticated and specific mental representations and cognitive processing, and be able to deal with very large or small amounts of information, in the presence of noise, or to deal with ambiguous information and many other challenging tasks (see, e.g., Patel, Arocha, & Kaufman, 1999; Wood, 1999).

When cognitive mechanisms increasingly rely on top-down information processing, human performance often increases. Nevertheless, although expertise and top-down processes lead to superior overall performance, it also brings about potential weaknesses and vulnerabilities that degrade performance and can result in error, such as

- restricted flexibility;
- limited control;
- overlooking of important information;
- tunnel vision; and
- bias.

Therefore, paradoxically, the very underpinning of expertise can also result in degradation of performance in specific cases (Dror, 2011).

These phenomena are inherent cognitive side effects of expertise and are a professional challenge in the medical domain, the military, policing, and other highly skilled expert domains (Dror, 2011), including forensic science. It is important to emphasize that these cognitive side effects occur without explicit intention, so experts are not aware of these effects. This is critical, because not understanding the underlying cognitive mechanisms involved in these phenomena often results in ineffective ways to counter-measure their effects. For example, contextual biases have sometimes been categorized as an ethical issue. Such misunderstandings attribute the problem of cognitive bias to forensic examiners who violate ethical codes and intentionally engage in unethical practices. This misunderstanding suggests (incorrectly) that cognitive bias can be dealt with by ethical training and following ethical codes. This is not only an ineffective way of combating them but it is also unfair to the forensic experts because it suggests that they are doing something wrong intentionally and that they can stop doing it by mere willpower—a misunderstanding of the very nature and mechanisms of contextual bias (see, e.g., Page et al., 2012).

The type of bias we deal with here affects perception, cognition, and decision making unintentionally, often without awareness. If the problems of bias and error were caused by experts' intentional misconduct, then it would be a minor problem. First, it would only pertain to a very small number of examiners, and not be as widespread and general a problem as cognitive bias; second, it would be relatively easy to identify and show the misconduct (Dror, Kassin, & Kukucka, 2013). Byrd (2006), in an attempt to understand (contextual) bias, identifies the three general types of errors in forensic science: (1) Ethics violations, such as fabricated prints, dry benching (estimating results without completing an examination), intentional erroneous results, and covering up mistakes; (2) honest errors, such as lack of training and mentoring, feeling pressure to complete work or being overwhelmed with work, and administrative errors or complacency in one's work; and (3) biased oversight. Byrd states that bias and honest mistakes can sometimes overlap (e.g., the wrong interpretation of a distorted latent fingermark because of the lack of training, and the fact that the officer informed the fingerprint examiner that the suspect had already been visually identified by the victim as the perpetrator).

Since the forensic expert is the main instrument in most forensic disciplines, cognitive factors play an important role in forensic casework, stressing the need for what has been termed elsewhere *cognitive forensics* (Dror & Stoel, 2014)—a field that addresses a range of cognitive issues that relate to forensic casework. Nowadays, with the growing acceptance that these issues are real and significant, it seems appropriate to take steps to deal with and countermeasure them. With increased implementation of such steps, they should become the accepted norm, and forensic evidence from laboratories that do not take such steps should be treated with extra reservation.

Levels of Contextual Information

Contextual information in a criminal case exists in several different forms. Consider the examples mentioned in the introduction. These examples described contextual information of different kinds. The first example described contextual information obtained from the meaning of the words in a written questioned document. The second example described contextual information obtained from the case information, that is, that the body was found in an illegal grave. In the third example, the contextual information that two cartridges are missing comes from the reference gun, and in the last example, the contextual information comes from other incriminating forensic evidence. Again, while such information may be very important for the trier of fact to consider, it should not be used by the expert during the examination. In the words of Thompson (2011),

> By considering contextual information, analysts may well become more likely . . . to reach conclusions that correspond to what actually happened. Yet by doing so, they also (paradoxically) undermine the ability of the trier-of-fact to determine the truth, and thereby reduce the likelihood the legal system will reach a just outcome. (p. 130)

Thompson terms this the *criminalist paradox*: "By helping themselves be 'right' such analysts make it more likely that the justice system will go wrong. By trying to give the 'right' answer, they prevent themselves from providing the best evidence" (p. 130).

In this section, we will describe a classification of contextual information into four different levels.[2] This classification into separate levels is instructive since the approach for minimizing the potential biasing effect of this information will differ for each level. It may also serve as the basis for the development of appropriate standards for how best to deal with contextual information in forensic casework (cf. Risinger et al., 2002).

The levels of contextual information are based on the "distance" of the information from the evidential material under consideration, with a lower level denoting a closer and more intimate relation to the "trace" at hand (see Figure 5.1).

---

[2]Dror (2009a) used Francis Bacon's doctrine of idols to find ways to improve forensic science by identifying potential vulnerabilities. One can make a connection between the levels of contextual information and Bacon's idols, although there is not a one-to-one correspondence.

Figure 5.1   Levels of Contextual Information

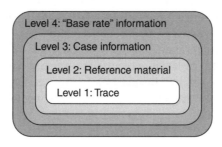

LEVEL 1: THE TRACE

Level 1 contains contextual information that is inherent to the examined trace and cannot easily be separated from it. This information is coming from (physical) features of the trace that are (at least for that moment) irrelevant to the expert. The forensic handwriting examiner, for instance, who has been asked to provide evidence regarding the authorship of questioned handwriting in a threatening letter, should only look at the handwriting itself. Features such as the used ink, paper, and stamps that are surrounding the handwriting, however, should not influence the handwriting comparison. Although these features may be of great importance for the case at hand (and should be considered by the specific experts), they should be treated as impertinent contextual information for the handwriting comparison.[3]

Furthermore, even if these aspects do not play a role in the case, a handwriting examiner is usually able to read the actual words written in the questioned document. These words have a meaning, and the examiner will interpret these words, thereby creating a context for the handwriting comparison. But the meaning of these words is possibly biasing for the task to be performed by the handwriting examiner.

LEVEL 2: THE REFERENCE MATERIAL

Whenever a crime scene trace is analyzed simultaneously with reference material of a known, suspected source (be it a suspect, a gun, etc.), the perception and choice of the features of the questioned material may become partly dependent on what the expert has seen in the reference material. But, normally, the very question is whether the reference material has any connection with the case. The comparison should depend on both questioned and reference items, but the perception of the features of the questioned item should not. The reference material can thus be regarded as contextual information when analyzing the trace.

The study of Thompson (2009) focused on exactly this issue. DNA analysts in the *ad hoc* experiment tended to overestimate the value of DNA evidence by shifting the purported criteria for a "match" or "inclusion" after the profile of a suspect becomes known. Depending on whether the suspect's profile had a "peak" at a certain locus, the

---

[3]We are aware of the fact that in most English-speaking countries, document examination includes handwriting as well as technical document examination, but this example considers them as separate disciplines, or at least as separate activities.

peak in the trace evidence was interpreted as a true allele or an artefact. Knowledge of the profile of the suspect thus affected the assignment of peaks in the profile from the trace. But the reference profile should only play a role in the comparison part and not in the assignment of peaks in the trace profile.

Similarly, in fingerprint examination, the process of ACE (analysis, comparison, and evaluation) allows one to (re-)analyze the crime scene fingermark after analyzing the reference print, with the risk that the expert starts to "see" features that he would not have seen otherwise, and that might not be there (see Dror, 2009a).

LEVEL 3: THE CASE INFORMATION

The third level contains case information in the broadest sense. That is, all information (oral, written, and nonverbal) that surrounds the case. In many cases, it is necessary to contact the police or prosecutor prior to the forensic examination. There are many good reasons for doing so. For example, to obtain appropriate propositions concerning the main issues in the case, to make sure that the right items are sent to the laboratory, or to agree on an examination strategy. Furthermore, in most cases, the evidence is sent to the forensic laboratory accompanied by a more or less detailed police report. Some of the information in this police report is indeed important to know for the forensic expert, some for an expert working on the same case in another discipline, and another part of this information is very important for the case and the trier of fact. Nevertheless, some of the information is completely irrelevant for any forensic examination (e.g., whether the suspect confessed to the crime or not; see Dror et al., 2013).

As an example, let us look at a fictitious case where the main question for a forensic handwriting examiner is whether a suicide note has been written by the deceased person, or by his twin brother. The police sent in the suicide note for forensic examination due to a serious suspicion that the deceased has not committed suicide, but was murdered by his twin brother with whom he shared a household. The twin brother was in serious financial trouble, and their recently deceased father had left them an unexpectedly large inheritance. The full inheritance would be sufficient to rid the surviving twin brother of his debts. He was widely known for his irascible behavior and has been convicted twice of a violent crime. This information is summarized in the police report that accompanies the request to examine the questioned suicide note. Furthermore, DNA and a fingerprint matching that of the living twin brother were found on the suicide note. The suicide note was sent in together with some natural handwriting from both brothers, and a writing test of the suspected twin. The handwriting of the deceased consisted of several shopping lists and a diary covering writings from the past four weeks.

The main request to the handwriting expert is to provide evidence for whether the deceased or the surviving twin wrote the note, based on a comparison of the suicide note with reference handwriting from the deceased and the suspect. For this task, all the written information in the case report mentioned above is irrelevant to the forensic examiner (except for the information that the reference material is recent). Let us again make clear that all the information is potentially very important case information to be used by the police and the trier of fact, and may even be used by the lab at a later stage. At the stage of the comparison of the handwriting per se, it is all domain-irrelevant information.

LEVEL 4: THE BASE RATE INFORMATION

Level 4 contains the "base rate" information. Base rate information is organization and discipline-specific information that can create an expectation about the outcome prior to any examination. For example, due to the work of the police investigators, most evidence presented for forensic evaluation is incriminating: There is a high base rate of inculpation (Risinger et al., 2002).

The expert thus may have an expectation that the evidence under consideration is inculpatory, which could result in unconsciously looking for information that supports the more likely scenario. The possible influence of such base rate information is undesirable because it should have no effect on the probative value of the examination itself. It is important to note the base rate information is present from the start of the investigation, even before any casework has been done. Thus, this is "information" that is independent of the particular case at hand, but may nevertheless have an effect on the casework.[4]

How to Deal With Contextual Information

In the previous sections, it was explained that contextual information in a case may be of different kinds, and four levels of contextual information have been described. To decide how to deal with contextual information and to develop procedures, the next step is to decide which contextual information is relevant for the case and for the examination, and which information may be relevant for the case but is irrelevant for the examination. We examine this question at each of the four levels. This may not be an easy task, though, and the answer may depend on the discipline and on the case. In the "suicide note" example in the previous section, there is obviously a lot of information in the description of the case that is not relevant for the forensic handwriting examination. Moreover, it is potentially biasing information. The effect of the bias depends on the quality of the evidence. The impact of bias is larger when the evidence is more difficult to assess, as in a fingerprint examination where a partial fingermark is of poor quality due to noise or distortion (Dror et al., 2006). In these cases, we expect a greater susceptibility of the expert opinion to contextual cues.

The distinction between domain-relevant and domain-irrelevant contextual information is important (Risinger et al., 2002; see also Table 5.1). The aim of any forensic investigation should be to provide an accurate assessment of the evidential value of some evidence. This implies that it should be based on the available domain-relevant information only. Any influence of domain-irrelevant contextual information results in bias, and it is important to make sure the expert comparing the items is not affected by it. Assessing the relevance of contextual information may not be a trivial task, though.

---

[4]Apart from the base-rate information, there are other factors that are independent from the case at hand that can play a role. Since contextual bias is the main topic of this paper, we will not go into this in detail.

Table 5.1   Overview of the General Actions That Can Be Taken

	Domain-Relevant Information	*Domain-Irrelevant Information*
Biasing	Keep, but take measures	Remove
Not Biasing	Use	No action needed

Information that is neither domain relevant nor biasing is not needed for reaching a conclusion. An important question is whether one can reliably assess if information is biasing or not, so in practice, it may be best to remove such information anyway. Domain-relevant information is all information an expert should use to reach conclusions, either biasing or not. An example of non-biasing domain-relevant information is the condition under which reference handwriting was obtained. Differences between handwritten texts from the same person could be explained when a considerable amount of time has passed between writing the questioned document and the reference material. The same goes when this person obtains a disease that affects his or her motor skills.

Another example of domain-relevant contextual information is knowledge about whether the reference material forms a so-called "open" or "closed" set. Consider a case were a firearms examiner receives one questioned bullet and four reference firearms. If the four guns form a closed set (i.e., one of them must have been the source of the questioned bullet), reporting which guns can be excluded can be as important as reporting the amount of agreement between the questioned bullet and the reference bullets fired from one of the four guns. This may occur, for instance, in a shooting incident that involved four police officers. If limited agreement is found with bullets fired from gun #1, but a lot of disagreement with bullets fired from guns #2, #3, and #4, the evidence points strongly toward gun #1. This is, of course, not the case if the guns form an open set, and most of the candidate guns and even their number are unknown.

A more difficult situation occurs when domain-relevant information can be biasing, such as with Level 2 contextual information. In such a case measures should be taken, and we will return to this issue in a later section.

It is clear that a forensic expert should not reach a conclusion based (at least) in part on domain-irrelevant contextual information. But disagreement is more likely to exist as to what should be done with domain-irrelevant contextual information. It is sometimes claimed that intensive training programs could give forensic experts some sort of immunity to bias, but this claim is likely to be false. The large amount of evidence from cognitive psychological studies of the last century points in another direction. While forensic experts were not often included as research subjects, it seems reasonable to assume "they are no more successful in guarding against such distortions by willing them away than any other group ever studied" (Risinger, 2009, p. 24).

Apart from the question of whether information is biasing and to what degree, it is also important to know how, when, and to whom it is biasing, and to be able to decide what measures to take, if any.

LEVEL 1 CONTEXT MANAGEMENT

Level 1 contextual information is generally difficult to manage since it is inherent to the evidential material and cannot easily be separated from it. Approaches do exist to minimize bias originating from Level 1 contextual information. Domain-irrelevant features from the trace (i.e., the questioned material) can be removed. In the suicide note example from the prior sections, for instance, an effort can be made to remove the meaning of the handwriting, to such an extent that it is not clear to the examiner what is the nature of the questioned handwriting and the reference material. Words can be removed digitally or reshuffled (leaving out the words that carry the highest risk of bias). If one prefers to work with the original material, an overlay can be placed such that only "meaningless" words are visible to the examiner, or maybe even individual characters. Such an overlay may be especially useful in the examination of questioned signatures, where the type of document and other information around the questioned signature are immaterial for the examination of the questioned signature.

An objection that can be made against such Level 1 context management is that too much information may be lost. Many handwriting examiners, for instance, do not favor using digital scans of questioned documents, or only using part of the available handwriting. These may be legitimate concerns, and research should focus on such procedures, testing whether the expectation of a decrease in performance (in the eyes of the examiners) due to the absence of "holistic" information is justified.

LEVEL 2 CONTEXT MANAGEMENT

Reference material can have a strong biasing effect on the perception of the features of the questioned material, and should consequently not be given to the expert before or during the analysis of the questioned material. This sequential analysis of the questioned material, the reference material, and the comparison of the two has been termed *sequential unmasking*. Sequential unmasking is an important topic in the DNA literature (Krane et al. 2008; Thompson, 2009, 2011; Budowle et al., 2009; Meulenbroek et al., 2009). With respect to DNA, Krane et al. state that sequential unmasking minimizes bias by "preventing analysts from knowing the profile of submitted references (i.e., known samples) when interpreting testing results from evidentiary (i.e., unknown or questioned) samples" (p. 1006).

The idea of sequential unmasking already exists since more than 50 years ago when, for example, Böttcher (1954) stressed the importance of such an approach in forensic handwriting analysis. In a 54-page paper titled "Theory and Practice of Forensic Handwriting Comparison," Böttcher describes a detailed approach for minimizing bias due to contextual information, including ideas similar to sequential unmasking. Sequential unmasking is in line with the (linear) ACE-V methodology,[5] the widely used procedure for latent fingerprint examination (friction ridge analysis), which comprises the following steps: analysis, comparison, evaluation, and verification.

Sequential unmasking is now part of the standard working procedures of some forensic institutes for DNA and fingerprint evidence, among which are the Netherlands Forensic Institute and the Dutch National Police. For other types of evidence, sequential unmasking may not be easy to implement (see below). Sequential unmasking helps to prevent or minimize bias due to knowledge of the reference material. The reason is simply that if reference material has not been given to the expert, it cannot influence the analysis of the questioned material (i.e., the crime scene trace). Krane et al. (2008) write with respect to sequential unmasking,

---

[5]See Scientific Working Group on Friction Ridge Analysis, Study and Technology (2013). See also Dror (2009b). Please note that ACE was first discussed by Huber (1959, in Triplett & Cooney, 2006).

With advances in technology, DNA testing has increasingly been used to analyze marginal samples that are likely to produce ambiguous results, such as older samples, samples exposed to environmental insult, and limited samples resulting from incidental contact. Consequently, the need for measures to minimize the consequences of observer effects in forensic DNA testing is growing. (p. 1006)

While sequential unmasking is a very powerful procedure in the minimization of bias in forensic examinations, it can only be implemented for specific types of evidence: evidence for which it is possible to analyze the questioned material without knowledge of the reference material. This implies that at least the features can be defined (and measured). Unfortunately, for some types of evidence, this requirement cannot be fulfilled. For such evidence features cannot be defined prior to seeing the reference material and prior to the comparison. This is the case, for example, in cartridge case and bullet comparisons. When the caliber and the class characteristics are compatible, the expert will proceed to compare the striations on the questioned bullet and on the reference bullets with a comparison microscope, explicitly looking for agreement in the form of matching striations and for disagreement. It is, consequently, not possible to analyze the features of the questioned material before looking at the reference material, because it is not clear what to look for. In DNA and fingermark examinations, it is clear what to look for, and where, and a sequential unmasking procedure can be applied. In areas like toolmark examination, firearm examination, and handwriting analysis, which strongly rely on subjective judgment, it is more complicated but also more important to apply a form of sequential unmasking. If sequential unmasking cannot be applied, it becomes especially important to remove domain-irrelevant information by means of Level 3 context management.

To deal with domain-relevant potentially biasing contextual information, sequential procedures may be of use as well. For instance, in the discipline of forensic hair examination, the place where a hair is found may have probative value with respect to the question of what type of hair it is, and one would certainly want to use this information in the report. However, the first task of the forensic hair examiner is to answer that question based on the characteristics of the questioned hair. In a sequential procedure, the forensic hair examiner would first base his conclusion only on the characteristics of the hair, and later combine that with the evidential value of the place the hair was found.

LEVEL 3 CONTEXT MANAGEMENT

Level 3 information is from the case at hand, and reaches the expert through communication with colleagues, the police, or the prosecutor, via written reports, oral discussion and exchanges, or even nonverbal communication. The general description of Level 3 context management is straightforward: optimizing the information flow to minimize the risks of the forensic expert getting any domain-irrelevant information, or too little domain-relevant case information.

The solution to minimize bias due to exposure to this type of contextual information is not to expose the expert to it in the first place, by carefully distinguishing between the domain-relevant and domain-irrelevant case information. Level 3 context management parallels the approach mentioned by Risinger et al. (2002) to control the information flow in forensic casework. Found and Ganas (2013) describe a similar approach for questioned document examination. The solution implies that the expert doing the analysis and subsequent comparison is not the person who decides what is domain-relevant information, and what is not. To decide what is the domain-relevant information, another expert who is knowledgeable in the relevant forensic discipline is required.

We realize that the decision on what is domain-relevant information may not be straightforward, and it may depend on the specific discipline and particular case. Consequently, development and implementation of context management in practice requires quite some effort. In the suicide note example, the examiner doing the comparison of the handwriting of the suicide note with the reference material from both twins should not be aware of the suspicion, the financial troubles, the inheritance, and the violent behavior, or of the DNA and fingerprint evidence. This information is very relevant for the case, very relevant for the trier of fact, but completely irrelevant for the handwriting examiner, and since this information is of a biasing nature, it should be removed. The domain-relevant information is (1) the suicide note, (2) the reference material from both twins,[6] (3) the fact that it is recent reference material, and (4) the question put to the examiner in the form of two mutually exclusive propositions (including the information that the writers considered are twins[7]).

By means of Level 3 context management, we can minimize the risk of the handwriting examiner being biased by managing the information flow. The important aspect is putting all effort in making sure only (and all!) the domain-relevant information reaches the examiner that compares the questioned and reference material.

The Netherlands Forensic Institute has implemented Level 3 context management for cartridge case and bullet comparisons. As the pilot project with these examiners was very promising, it is currently being implemented for handwriting examinations, and plans are to structurally implement context management throughout the institute, wherever applicable. Found and colleagues from the Document Examination Unit of Victoria Police Forensic Services Department in Australia have undertaken a similar effort. Found and Ganas (2013) provide a detailed description of how procedures were modified such that all handwriting cases are stripped of all but domain-relevant information for carrying out handwriting comparisons.

LEVEL 4 CONTEXT MANAGEMENT

Base-rate information may result in a continuing expectation that the evidence under consideration is inculpatory. While this expectation may be valid in general, it remains the question in a specific case, and the examiner's opinion should be based on the evidence only. Adding fake cases to the case flow could be a solution to control the effect of base rate information. Although effective in theory, it is clear that this is not always a very practical solution given the difficulty of creating realistic cases, with the experts not being aware that they are fake cases. Furthermore, the proportion of fake cases that can be added to the existing flow of real cases is necessarily small, in view of efficiency. The

---

[6]Note that even this evidence may contain possibly biasing information in the meaning of these written texts.

[7]If the fact that the considered writers are twin brothers influences the probability that their handwriting is similar, that makes it domain-relevant information.

direct numerical effect of these fake cases on the base rate may consequently be relatively small. The psychological effect of the presence of fake cases may, however, be larger.

Studies employing fake cases may give valuable information with respect to this effect. Over a certain period of time, cases may be sent to the lab that will later be revealed as fake cases. The results of such a study will give some insight in the effect of adding fake cases in changing expectations, and will allow an estimate of how feasible the addition of fake cases is, and whether the study succeeds in creating fake cases that are perceived as real.

Outlook and Conclusion

The human expert is the main "instrument" of analysis in many forensic domains. Conclusions drawn by forensic experts in casework are intrinsically subjective, where cognitive processes play an important role in their work, and information from the context surrounding a case creates a risk of bias. Consequently, after many years of not taking these issues on board, forensic laboratories are starting to realize that just as we take steps to minimize physical contamination of evidence, we must also make an effort and take active steps to minimize cognitive and psychological contamination. Not exposing examiners to irrelevant contextual information, making the examiners preferably work linearly from the questioned material to the reference material as with sequential unmasking, and other types of context management should become part of the regular workflow. Once such steps have been taken, all the usual methods of quality assurance[8] can be applied, such as best practices, accreditation (e.g., ISO/IEC-17025), and training. Currently, some forensic laboratories are making steps in this direction, for example, in the United States the FBI and New York State and Los Angeles crime laboratories have started to provide training in this area and are considering best practices. Similar actions are being taken in Europe (e.g., the Netherlands Forensic Institute, and labs in the United Kingdom and Finland), as well as the Victoria Police in Australia.

An important step is the development of more objective analysis and evaluation methods. Conclusions must be logically correct (Aitken & Taroni, 2005; Evett, 1998; Robertson & Vignaux, 1995), and based on quantitative data as much as possible. Many forensic institutes are putting a lot of effort in research and development of objective, evidence-based methods. Subjectivity and personal factors will, however, remain important in many disciplines. Even with more quantitative and objective methods, human judgment will continue to play a role. The answers to questions like "How representative are the data used for the population as defined by the case?" and sampling decisions, and so on, will still require subjective human judgment.

Forensic scientists are also increasingly trying to answer questions at the activity level (Cook et al. 1998a), and not only at the source level. Evidence that is powerful in pointing to a specific source might not tell you much about the (possibly innocent) activity that led to the trace ending up at the crime scene. Answering questions at the

---

[8]See, e.g., Forensic Science Regulator (2011a). See also the European Union Council Framework Decision 2009/905/JHA on accreditation of forensic service providers carrying out laboratory activities: http://eurlex.europa.eu/LexUriServ/LexUriServ.do?uri=OJ:L:2009:322:0014:0016:EN:PDF

activity level generally requires more information and expertise but is usually of greater relevance to the trier of fact. Inferences at the activity level generally also require a lot more contextual information and human judgment. As a consequence, the risk of contextual bias may be even greater than for source level conclusions.

These developments are important and positive, but also stress the need for context management and other procedures to minimize contextual bias in forensic casework. In this chapter, we presented a categorization of contextual information consisting of four levels, and we have argued that different methods need to be implemented to minimize the risk of contextual bias for each level. We propose context management as a general approach for minimizing as much as possible the impact of domain-irrelevant information, and maximizing the role of domain-relevant information.

In general, more research is needed to understand what factors determine the effects of bias (e.g., the experts, difficulty of the case, types of bias, etc.) and how they interact. Through better understanding of these cognitive aspects, it can be determined how forensic science can best deal with their effects.

The Forensic Science Regulator (2011b) in the United Kingdom recently concluded that "cognitive bias (also referred to as contextual bias or observer effects) is an issue that is relevant to forensic science" and that "organizations who undertake fingerprint examination should demonstrate within their accredited quality management system that they understand the potential for cognitive bias and build into their technical procedures safeguards to minimize the risk of bias and peer pressure" (p. 12). We believe that the context management approach we described in this chapter should eventually become part of quality management systems of forensic laboratories around the world. Even though the risk of bias may never be reduced to zero, including context management in the standard operating procedure would improve on current practice and show that the risk of bias is taken seriously.

Acknowledgment: The contribution of Itiel E. Dror was supported in part by a research grant by the National Institute of Standards and Technology (NIST) and the Federal Bureau of Investigation (FBI) (DoD/CTTSO/TSWG), #N41756–10-C-3382, awarded to Itiel E. Dror.

References

Aitken, C., & Taroni, F. (2005). *Statistics and the evaluation of evidence for forensic scientists.* New York: Wiley.

Böttcher, C. J. F. (1954). Theory and practice of forensic handwriting comparison. *Tijdschift voor Strafrecht, 63,* 77–131.

Budowle, B., Bottrell, M. C., Bunch, S. G., Fram, R., Harrison, D., Meagher, S., et al. (2009). A perspective on errors, bias, and interpretation in the forensic sciences and direction for continuing advancement. *Journal of Forensic Sciences, 54,* 798–809.

Byrd, J. S. (2006). Confirmation bias, ethics, and mistakes in forensics. *Journal of Forensic Identification, 56,* 511–525.

Cook, R., Evett, I. W., Jackson, G., Jones, P. J., & Lambert, J. A. (1998a). A hierarchy of propositions: Deciding which level to address in casework. *Science and Justice, 38,* 231–239.

Cook, R., Evett, I. W., Jackson, G., Jones, P. J., & Lambert, J. A. (1998b). A model for case assessment and interpretation. *Science and Justice, 38*, 151–156.

Dror, I. E. (2009a). How can Francis Bacon help forensic science? The four idols of human biases. *Jurimetrics: The Journal of Law Science and Technology, 50*, 93–110.

Dror, I. E. (2009b). On proper research and understanding of the interplay between bias and decision outcomes. *Forensic Science International, 191*, 17–18.

Dror, I. E. (2011). The paradox of human expertise: Why experts can get it wrong. In N. Kapur (Ed.) *The paradoxical brain* (pp. 177–188). Cambridge: Cambridge University Press.

Dror, I. E. (2013). The ambition to be scientific: Human expert performance and objectivity. *Science and Justice, 53*(2), 81–82.

Dror, I. E., Charlton D., & Peron, A. (2006). Contextual information renders experts vulnerable to making erroneous identifications. *Forensic Science International, 156*, 74–78.

Dror, I. E., & Cole, S. (2010). The vision in "blind" justice: Expert perception, judgment and visual cognition in forensic pattern recognition. *Psychonomic Bulletin & Review, 17*, 161–167.

Dror, I. E., & Hampikian, G. (2011). Subjectivity and bias in forensic DNA mixture interpretation. *Science and Justice, 51*, 204–208.

Dror, I. E., Kassin, S. M., & Kukucka, J. (2013). New application of psychology to law: Improving forensic evidence and expert witness contributions. *Journal of Applied Research in Memory and Cognition, 2*, 78–81.

Dror, I. E., & Rosenthal, R. (2008). Meta-analytically quantifying the reliability and biasability of forensic experts. *Journal of Forensic Sciences, 53*, 900–903.

Dror, I. E., & Stoel, R. D. (2014). Cognitive forensics: Human cognition, contextual information and bias. In G. Bruinsma & D. Weisburg (Eds.), *Encyclopedia of criminology and criminal justice* (pp. 353–363). Dordrecht: Springer.

Evett, I. W. (1998). Toward a uniform framework for reporting opinions in forensic science case work. *Science and Justice, 38*, 198–202.

Forensic Science Regulator. (2011a). *Codes of practice and conduct for forensic science providers and practitioners in the Criminal Justice System.* Fingerprint Quality Standards Specialist Group, United Kingdom. Retrieved from https://www.gov.uk/government/uploads/system/uploads/attachment_data/file/118949/codes-practice-conduct.pdf

Forensic Science Regulator. (2011b). *Developing a quality standard for fingerprint examination.* Fingerprint Quality Standards Specialist Group, United Kingdom.

Found, B., & Ganas, J. (2013). The management of domain irrelevant context information in forensic handwriting examination casework. *Science & Justice, 53*, 154–158.

Hagan, W. E. (1894). *A treatise on disputed handwriting and the determination of genuine from forged signatures.* New York: Banks & Brothers.

Hall, L. J., & Player, E. (2008). Will the instruction of an emotional context affect fingerprint analysis and decision making? *Forensic Science International, 181*, 36–39.

Huber, R. (1959). Expert witness. *The Criminal Law Quarterly, 2*, 276–295.

Kassin, S. M., Dror, I. E., & Kukucka, J. (2013). The forensic confirmation bias: Problems, perspectives, and proposed solutions. *Journal of Applied Research in Memory and Cognition, 2*, 42–52.

Kersholt, J. H., Eikelboom, A., Dijkman, T., Stoel, R. D., Hermsen, H., & van Leuven, M. (2010). Does suggestive information cause a confirmation bias in bullet comparisons? *Forensic Science International, 198*, 138–142.

Kerstholt, J. H., Paashuis, R., & Sjerps, M. (2007). Shoe print examinations: effects of expectation, complexity and experience. *Forensic Science International, 195,* 30–34.

Krane, D. E., Ford, S., Gilder, J., Inman, K., Jamieson, A., Koppl, R., et al. (2008). Sequential unmasking: A means of minimizing observer effects in forensic DNA interpretation. *Journal of Forensic Science, 53,* 1006–1007.

Langenburg, G., Champod, C., & Wertheim, P. (2009). Testing for potential contextual bias effects during the verification stage of the ACE-V methodology when conducting fingerprint comparisons. *Journal of Forensic Science, 54,* 571–582.

Meulenbroek, A. J., de Blaeij, T. J. P., & Kloosterman, A. D. (2009). Richtlijnen borgen onbevooroordeeld DNA-onderzoek Stapsgewijze benadering voorkomt "post hoc target shifting." *Expertise en Recht, 6,* 119–129.

Miller, L. (1984). Bias among forensic document examiners: A need for procedural change. *Journal of Police Science and Administration, 12,* 407–410.

Miller, L. (1987) Procedural bias in forensic examination of hair. *Law and Human Behavior, 11,* 157–163.

National Academy of Sciences. (2009). *Strengthening forensic science in the United States: A path forward.* Washington, DC: Author.

National Institute of Standards and Technology. (2012). Expert working group on human factors in latent print analysis. *Latent print examination and human factors: Improving the practice through a systems approach.* Washington, DC: U.S. Department of Commerce, Author.

Nisbett, R. E., & Ross, L. (1980). *Human inference: Strategies and shortcomings of social judgment.* Englewood Cliffs, NJ: Prentice Hall.

Nisbett, R. E., & Wilson, T. D. (1977). Telling more than we can know: Verbal reports on mental processes. *Psychological Review, 84,* 231–259.

Page, M., Taylor, J., & Blenkin, M. (2012). Context effects and observer bias—implications for forensic odontology. *Journal of Forensic Sciences, 57,* 108–112.

Patel, V. L., Arocha, J. F., & Kaufman, D. R. (1999). Expertise and tacit knowledge in medicine. In R. J. Sternberg & J. A. Horvath (Eds.), *Tacit knowledge in professional practice: Researcher and practitioner perspectives* (pp. 75–99). Mahwah, NJ: Basic Books.

Risinger, M. D. (2009). The NAS Report on forensic science: A glass nine-tenths full (this is about the other tenth). *Jurimetrics, 50,* 21–34.

Risinger, M. D, Saks, M., Thompson, W., & Rosenthal, R. (2002). The Daubert/Kumho implications of observer effects in forensic science: Hidden problems of expectation and suggestion. *California Law Review, 90,* 1–56.

Robertson, B., & Vignaux, G. A. (1995). *Interpreting evidence: Evaluating forensic science in the courtroom.* Chichester, NY: John Wiley & Sons.

Saks, M. J., Risinger, D. M., Rosenthal, R., & Thompson, W. C. (2003). Context effects in forensic science. *Science and Justice, 43,* 77–90.

Schiffer, B., & Champod, C. (2007). The potential (negative) influence of observational biases at the analysis stage of finger mark individualization. *Forensic Science International, 167,* 116–120.

Scientific Working Group on Friction Ridge Analysis, Study and Teaching. (2013, March 13). *Document #10: Standards for examining friction ridge impressions and resulting conclusions (latent/tenprint).* Retrieved from http://www.swgfast.org/documents/examinations-conclusions/130427_Examinations-Conclusions_2.1.pdf

Stacey R. B. (2004). Report on the erroneous fingerprint individualization bombing case. *Journal of Forensic Identification, 54,* 706–718.

Stoel, R. D., Berger, C. E. H., Van den Heuvel, E., & Fagel, W. (2010). De Wankele Kritiek op de forensische handschriftkunde [The shaky criticism on forensic handwriting analyses]. *Nederlands Juristenblad, 39,* 2537–2541.

Thompson, W. C. (2009). Painting the target around the matching profile: The Texas sharpshooter fallacy in forensic DNA interpretation. *Law, Probability and Risk, 8,* 257–276.

Thompson, W. C. (2011). What role should investigative facts play in the evaluation of scientific evidence? *Australian Journal of Forensic Sciences, 43,* 123–134.

Thompson, W. C., & Cole, S. A. (2005). Lessons from the Brandon Mayfield case. *The Champion, 29,* 42–44.

Triplett, M., & Cooney, L. (2006). The etiology of ACE-V and its proper use: An exploration of the relationship between ACE-V and the scientific method of hypothesis testing. *Journal of Forensic Identification, 56,* 345–355.

Turvey, B. (1998). The need for "blind" procedures in forensic science: An internet discussion. *Scientific Testimony: An Online Journal.* Retrieved December 18, 2013 from http://www.scientific.org/open-forum/articles/blind.html

Tversky, A., & Kahneman, D. (1974). Judgment under uncertainty: Heuristics and biases. *Science, 185,* 1124–1131.

Wells, G.L., & Bradfield, A.L. (1998). "Good, you identified the suspect": Feedback to eyewitnesses distorts their reports of the witnessing experience. *Journal of Applied Psychology, 3,* 360–376.

Wood, B. P. (1999). Visual expertise. *Radiology, 211,* 1–3.

6

A Survey of Ethical Issues in the Forensic Sciences

Jay Siegel

Introduction

Proper attention to ethical behavior is as much a part of being a good scientist as are the use of best practices, maintaining currency in one's field, and responsible conduct of research and analysis. This is all the more important when science is involved in the administration of justice. This is the essence of forensic science—*the applications of scientific methods to matters involving the justice system.* Ideally, forensic scientists analyze evidence in criminal or civil cases using the latest, validated scientific methods; write comprehensive scientific laboratory reports of their findings; and then, when called by the court, offer effective, lucid expert testimony to the trier of fact (judge or jury), which consists of people who are largely untrained and ignorant in the ways and language of science. Yet, these reports and testimony must be delivered in a manner that helps inform the trier of fact in determining the guilt or innocence of the accused in a criminal case or the culpable party in a civil suit. Forensic scientists may also be called on to help with the collection of evidence at a crime scene, help craft legislation, and help train police officers, crime scene investigators, attorneys, and judges in their area(s) of expertise.

Forensic scientists are responsible for applying the principles of science to the analysis of evidence in criminal and civil cases. In carrying out their responsibilities as scientists, they will encounter ethical questions that are common to all scientists who perform some sort of analysis. However, in addition to being scientists, forensic scientists interact with crime investigators, crime scene investigators, and detectives on a regular basis, and with attorneys, judges, and the public (usually juries) during a trial or other judicial processes. All of the duties and interactions of forensic scientists with other actors in the justice system will, at times, present ethical questions and dilemmas. Thus, forensic scientists face two types of ethics: (1) those driven by the natural or physical sciences, and (2) those that arise from justice system interactions. These can be very different and require that the forensic scientist pay heed to a variety of behaviors and interactions. This can be a challenge to someone who sees herself as a scientist, is interested in being an ethical scientist, and has less appreciation for the "forensic" part of her job.

In recent years, there have been a number of instances where forensic scientists have strayed from proper ethical behavior because they become caught up in the justice system. Instead of analyzing the evidence using validated, reliable scientific methods and reporting their results without regard to the consequences to the justice process, they permit bias to creep in, or they seek wealth and notoriety, or they become jaded or burned out, and they are no longer neutral, unbiased scientists. Instead, they become advocates, and the value of what they are doing in the laboratory and in the court room is diminished as a result.

This chapter is concerned with the major ethical considerations faced by forensic scientists that arise from their position as scientists as well as those that are a result of the justice system environment within which they practice their science. In the end, two things will be clear: (1) Many or most of the ethical problems that have occurred in recent years are the result of ethical lapses in the justice context,

A Taxonomy of Ethical Violations in Forensic Science

1. Scientific Issues
   a. Misrepresentation of professional credentials including formal education, continuing education, and training
   b. Insufficient or indiscriminant analysis, dry-labbing
   c. Tailoring scientific analysis to fit the law

2. Bias
   a. Bias toward or against a party
   b. Contextual bias
   c. Confirmational bias

3. Presentation of Testimony in Court
   a. Sufficiency of laboratory reports
   b. Use of associative and scientific terminology
   c. Deceptive or confusing testimony or outright lies
   d. Overselling or underselling the value of evidence

4. Status of Employment: Public v. Private
   a. Fees
   b. Hired gun
   c. Always testifying for prosecution (or defense)

5. Obligations to the Profession
   a. Failure to maintain currency in field
   b. Faulty proficiency tests
   c. Dishonest continuing education practices

and (2) ethical considerations in the scientific context are much easier to interpret and recognize than those that arise from justice system interactions. The chapter closes with a discussion of movements toward a national code of ethics in forensic science.

Discussion of Ethical Issues

SCIENTIFIC ISSUES

Credentials

Some of the most difficult ethical issues in forensic science involve scientific procedures and methods of analysis and demonstration of one's competence to the trier of fact. This is, in part, because scientific issues are poorly understood by nonscientists, especially attorneys, judges, and juries. This makes the issues difficult to understand and interpret. Often, scientific ethical violations may be uncovered only through the involvement of other scientists. First among these are the scientific credentials that a forensic scientist describes to establish her competency and expertise in the field(s) of forensic science in which she is working and testifying. There are, of course, the formal educational credentials of the analyst, including the level of college degree(s) and the major. These seem to be straightforward but are, in fact, fraught with pitfalls. It may be difficult for the layperson to determine whether or not the scientist even possesses the degree(s) that she claims. Verification takes effort, and, in many cases, it is difficult to pry such information out of a college registrar. It may be surprising to see the number of people that misrepresent their qualifications. Even if it can be verified that a scientist possesses a degree from a particular institution, it is much harder to determine what courses she took that are relevant to her expertise and what grades she achieved. For example, there can be a major difference in rigor and coursework between a BA and a BS in chemistry, and there is a huge variety in the quality of forensic science degree programs.

Beyond the formal educational degrees, there are other scientific credentials that are at least as important in evaluating the expertise possessed by the forensic scientist. These fall into two major categories: training and continuing education. Many forensic scientists do not list their training credentials on their resumes, or at least not in sufficient detail such that an interested party can determine the depth, breadth, and quality of the training received by the scientist that enabled her to become proficient in her field(s). This information must usually be obtained by discovery or by *voir dire* of the expert in court. Even then, it is very difficult to assess the quality of the training and to determine if the scientist is being truthful about her training credentials. Statements about the length, intensity, breadth, depth, and assessment of training are subject to obfuscation by unethical scientists and can only be verified by testimony from the trainers, a difficult and cumbersome process.

In addition to formal training on entry to the laboratory, scientists have the responsibility to maintain currency in their field. This is often accomplished through continuing education opportunities. The ethical considerations concerning this area will be discussed in the "Obligations to the Profession" section below.

Analysis

The heart of forensic science is the scientific analysis of evidence. It is the common currency of all of forensic science. Forensic scientists analyze evidence and testify in court. It is not surprising, therefore, that a significant number and type of ethical violations involve the analysis of evidence. Some areas of forensic science have well-developed, scientifically validated methods of analysis of evidence that are generally accepted by the global forensic science community as proper procedure and best practices. In many if not most cases, such methods and protocols are not mandatory. In some fields, validated sets of procedures and processes don't exist or aren't agreed on. Laboratory accreditation and scientific working groups and organizations, such as the American Society for Testing and Materials (ASTM), have made great progress in establishing standard methods of analysis, but there is not yet a mechanism for imposing this on all analysts. Not only are there issues with standards, but scientific and administrative reviews of forensic science laboratory analyses and reports also vary widely, rendering oversight a questionable proposition. This can lead to a number of ethical issues.

How does one know when sufficient tests have been done on evidence to support the conclusions reached by the examiner, if standards do not exist for sufficiency? It is essentially up to the discretion of the individual examiner. If ethical violations exist, the courtroom is not the place to discover them—few judges or attorneys are scientifically literate enough to determine if the analysis of evidence has been done sufficiently to support the scientist's conclusions, and the process of cross-examination will not usually uncover them. For example, there is no agreed-on number of features in known and unknown fingerprints being compared that must be present to establish that the prints came from the same finger. It is up to the examiner, and there is no mandatory, legislated process for comparing the prints.

Related to the sufficiency of analysis issue is one of indiscriminate analysis. This occurs when inappropriate or needlessly repetitive or cumulative tests are done to pad the time spent on the analysis or create the illusion that the scientist has done so much testing that the conclusions reached are indisputable. Buried in all of this may be the prospect that sufficient testing was actually accomplished, but it may be difficult to tell. In public laboratories, this is unduly consumptive of the public's resources and is unethical.

The most egregious of all of the analytical issues is so-called "dry-labbing." This is defined as the process of writing a laboratory report expressing conclusions about the identity or association of forensic evidence without the benefit of *any* analysis. Serious, committed dry-labbers will open the evidence but will not perform any scientific analysis although they may do some perfunctory sensory testing (e.g., smelling an exhibit of green-brown plant material for the odor of marijuana may be pseudo-scientific but is not recognized as a scientific examination). The scientist will then seal the evidence back up, using all of the chain of custody and security trappings (tamper evident tape, initials and signatures, etc.). Notes will be taken and even graphs, charts, spectra, or chromatograms could be produced (using results from other cases or standard materials) to bolster the conclusions. Without reanalysis of the evidence, it would be impossible to determine if the evidence had actually been analyzed. There are a number of cases where dry-labbing was suspected and eventually proven by reanalysis of evidence. Probably the most notorious example was Fred Zain, a West Virginia forensic scientist who for many years issued results of laboratory examinations of evidence that were seldom exculpatory (see, e.g., http://truthinjustice.org/expertslie.htm).

His case work was never questioned by prosecutors or courts. His transgressions were only discovered when a determined defense attorney questioned Zain's findings in the analysis of evidence against the attorney's client. Extensive reanalysis of Zain's cases revealed apparent dry-labbing. No amount of administrative review of his cases would have uncovered the ethical problems here.

Analyzing to the Law

In some jurisdictions, the legislature has written laws that prohibit specific behaviors that bear heavily on forensic science. This is most commonly seen in the area of illicit drugs. Many states have threshold weights or purities of drug exhibits that trigger mandatory minimum penalties. Ethical issues can arise when, for example, the weight of an exhibit of a drug is very near the weight that triggers a higher penalty for possession or distribution. Perhaps because of pressure from a prosecutor or revulsion toward drug users or dealers, a scientist might "put the thumb on the scale" to increase the weight of the exhibit over the threshold. Once again, this is extremely difficult to detect without reanalysis of the exhibit. One might expect that this would only occur if the suspect or his attorney suspected that there was a problem with the weighing—an unlikely occurrence indeed.

BIAS

For or Against a Party

In those countries, such as the United States, where the adversarial judicial system is employed, witnesses are retained or called by either the prosecutor (or plaintiff in civil cases) or the defense. Presumably, a witness is called by one side or the other because that party believes that the witness will be able to provide conclusions or testimony that favors that side of the case. This is of course true in the case of lay witnesses, who can generally only testify as to what their five senses reveal and are usually not permitted to render opinions. In the case of forensic scientists, or, indeed, scientists in general, they are often called on to render expert opinions on matters within their expertise. Strictly speaking, a scientific opinion would be value free and would not purposefully favor one side or the other, but in actuality, opinions, even rigorous scientific ones, can do more harm than good to one party or the other and can often be shaded so that the opinions more explicitly favor one side. This is where ethical dilemmas arise. Expert witnesses may be pressured by the side for whom they have been retained, to color their opinions and conclusions so that they favor that party at the expense of the other party. It is an ethical violation to shade a scientific opinion so that it is taken out of the scientific realm, to favor one party over another, but this is highly subjective and often difficult to discern. It often can lead to battles of the experts in court.

Contextual Bias

The issue of contextual bias and the related confirmational bias have come to be recognized in recent years as serious problems in forensic science, mainly through the research efforts of Itiel E. Dror and his colleagues (see Chapter 5, this volume). Contextual bias refers to the all-too-familiar situation in a crime laboratory where a forensic scientist is given a great deal of information about the incident that gives rise to the evidence being analyzed. This information can include the circumstances about the case, the identity of the suspect and why that person is the focus of the investigation, and what other evidence there is that links this suspect to the incident. This can, and often does, cause the scientist to focus on that suspect consciously or subconsciously, and can color her analysis of the evidence and interpretation of her findings in light of her knowledge of the incident. If this is done knowingly, it is clearly a violation of ethics. It may also be unethical to fail to take whatever steps are necessary to mitigate the contamination of the scientist even if it has not been demonstrated. The issue of contextual bias has long been recognized by law enforcement in the case of eye witnesses who are asked to identify a suspect seen at a crime scene. The suspect is placed among other similar looking people behind a one-way mirror so that the witness doesn't focus only on the suspect. Similarly, with photographic lineups, the witness is shown a series of pictures rather than just the picture of the suspect.

Confirmational Bias

In 2004, a terrorist bombed the subway system in Madrid, Spain. Police investigators discovered a partial fingerprint at the scene. To help narrow the search for the perpetrator(s), they sent a photograph of the print to the FBI and asked them to run the print through their automated fingerprint identification system to see if anyone of interest surfaced. The search yielded the print of Brandon Mayfield, an attorney in Oregon who had recently converted to Islam and whose wife was from the Middle East. His prints were examined along with the one sent from Madrid, and the FBI examiner determined that there was a match. Subsequently, two other FBI examiners, who both had knowledge of the results of the previous examiner, confirmed the match, and Mayfield was arrested and charged with the bombing. In an attempt to secure his freedom, he hired an independent examiner who also knew of the FBI examiners' results, and he confirmed the match. Eventually, the Madrid Police uncovered the real perpetrator of the bombing. The FBI sent a team to Madrid to examine the evidence and agreed with the Madrid police that Mayfield was not the one who deposited the print, and he was eventually released. This provides a textbook example of confirmational bias, the tendency to confirm a previous finding in an examination or event when the circumstances of the event are known.

The process of verification of forensic examinations is fairly common in crime laboratories in the United States, and often, the second or subsequent examiner knows what the first examiner found. Confirmational bias is a well-known phenomenon, and there are a number of steps that can be taken to mitigate it. Misidentification of evidence is always an ethical problem and needs to be minimized in any way possible.

PRESENTATION OF TESTIMONY IN COURT

Laboratory Reports

Only a very small percentage of criminal or civil cases ever make it into a courtroom. The vast majority are settled out of court. In criminal cases, this usually means that some sort of plea bargain has been reached. Plea bargains and other settlements rely in part on the evidence that has been gathered for both parties in the case. This will often include laboratory reports issued by forensic scientists working in public or private laboratories. In civil cases, these reports tend to be very comprehensive and lay out all of the details of the analysis. This is, in part, because discovery rules are very liberal in civil cases. The situation is different, however, in criminal cases where discovery is generally restricted. Many laboratory reports are little more than certificates of analysis. They contain a description of the evidence and the results of the analysis but little else—no methods and procedures, no explanation of findings, no estimates of errors. A research study currently being carried out by the author of this chapter confirms this finding.

Having only bare bones laboratory reports makes it difficult for attorneys and other experts to evaluate the quality and accuracy of the analysis. Decisions about guilt or innocence or monetary payments may be dependent on the findings described in these laboratory reports. Incomplete or insufficient laboratory reporting is an ethical violation because it does not provide full disclosure of the laboratory examinations to the parties. There are a number of comprehensive laboratory templates that have been put forth by organizations inside and outside of forensic science that can be used to format laboratory reports. The National Academy of Sciences Forensic Science Committee saw this as a sufficiently serious problem that they devoted a major recommendation to it.

Terminology

One of the most difficult problems in forensic science has been gaining consensus on the meanings of terms used to associate items of evidence to a known source. Most types of evidence are not subject to any type of statistical evaluation, and so it is not possible to relate an unknown piece of evidence to a known with a quantitative degree of certainty. The nearly lone exception is DNA typing, where there are well-established databases that can supply data concerning the frequency of a particular DNA type. In the absence of quantitative data on associations, terminology has been developed to express qualitative relationships. Such terms include *individualized, similar to, consistent with, identical, unable to eliminate,* and *indistinguishable.* One of the major problems with these terms is that there is a lack of agreement in the testifying forensic science community on their exact meanings. In some cases, forensic scientists themselves don't have a clear idea of what they mean when they use a term. This means that jurors may not have an idea of what is meant by the term and will impart their own understanding to the term. The danger here is that a juror or even a judge may impart a degree of certainty to the association of evidence that is not justified by the analysis that was done. Another problem is that sometimes terms are used that are not justified by the science. For example, sometimes pattern evidence examiners (fingerprints, firearms and toolmarks, handwriting) may offer a conclusion of individuality, for example, that the unknown fingerprint was made by one and only one finger to the exclusion of all other fingers in the world. This conclusion is not supportable by current scientific research yet it is commonly used today in courts of law. These terms are thrown about willingly and knowingly and this could be viewed as an ethical violation.

Deceptive Testimony

Whereas the use of associative terminology is a difficult problem with few solutions, the practice of offering deceptive or confusing testimony, or even outright lies, is never justified and is always a serious violation of ethics. It is hard to conceive of a situation where this would be done accidently or unavoidably. It is always a considered, deliberate act. The main reason that people get away with these practices is that there is most often no one in the courtroom to challenge the testimony; the attorneys and judges are too ignorant of the science to know when testimony is faulty. Unless the adverse party has retained their own scientific expertise, a practice which is seldom done in the United States, the testimony will go unchallenged.

Over- or Underselling Evidence

A related issue is to oversell or undersell the value of the evidence. To oversell evidence is to ascribe a degree of association with known evidence that is not justified by the state of the science or by analytical considerations. For example, if a fiber examiner indicates that fiber strands found at a crime scene came from a particular garment, that would be overselling the evidence. Fiber evidence cannot be associated with one particular garment. On the other hand, if the examiner found that there were a large number of similarities between the fiber strands and the garment and no unexplainable differences, and then concluded that the results were inconclusive, that would be underselling. A proper conclusion would be that the suspect fibers *could* have arisen from that garment.

ETHICAL CONSIDERATIONS THAT ARISE FROM EMPLOYMENT STATUS

Fees

Of course, everyone who works in a crime laboratory, private or public, presumably gets paid for their work. In the case of those scientists who work for a public laboratory that is administered by a branch of government, the scientists are paid by the government. For scientists who are privately employed, their paycheck comes from the party that retains them. There really isn't an ethical issue here *per se*, but accusations of bias are sometimes made by the adverse party in the case. This happens most often to privately employed experts who are accused of being paid to testify. The implication is that the expert is being paid to offer testimony that is favorable to the client, regardless of its scientific merit. This charge is most often, but not always, disingenuous—while it is true that the expert probably wouldn't be testifying if her testimony were not in some way favorable to the client, most scientists would not slant their testimony to one side of a case because they are getting paid. That would of course be a violation of ethics. The "playing for pay" issue is much more open in civil cases where expert witnesses are hired solely because they can provide testimony that benefits their client. Seldom is there an issue made of this in court because it applies equally to both sides.

The fee problem doesn't happen very often with government scientists, at least not openly. There are, of course, examples of forensic scientists (e.g., Fred Zain and the like) who apparently heavily slanted their analyses and testimony toward the prosecution in criminal cases, but this is because they are biased against what they perceive as criminals, not because their paycheck comes from a state or city.

The "Hired Gun" and Working Only on One Side

Related to the employment status issue of ethics is the "hired gun" situation. Again, this most commonly occurs with privately employed forensic scientists in the civil arena. Many of them will build a practice working only for plaintiffs or only for defendants. Examples would be medical malpractice experts who only testify against physicians who are accused of malpractice, or chemists who testify only for insurance companies in arson cases. They develop a (sometimes deserved) reputation for favoring one side of the case in a particular issue, and they are therefore always biased towards that side. Working for only one side of an issue is not necessarily a violation of ethics, unless clear bias against the interests of good scientific practice can be shown. Even though government forensic scientists always testify "for" the prosecution, they are not usually subject to the "hired gun" accusation because that is the nature of the system that they can only work for the prosecution in criminal cases.

OBLIGATIONS TO THE PROFESSION

Currency in the Field

At first glance, one would think that the obligation of a scientist to maintain currency in her field is a required trait of all scientists and shouldn't be an issue. On the other hand, perhaps it should be the decision of the individual scientist as to whether this needs to be done. While it is true that some forensic science methods and practices haven't changed for many years (e.g., illicit drug analysis, fingerprint comparisons), that doesn't mean that they won't change in the future. The fact is that there are always new illicit drugs coming on the market (e.g., bath salts, steroids, synthetic marijuana), and there have been recent calls for development of better methods and analytical tools for comparing items of pattern evidence. Failure to maintain currency in one's field(s) of expertise means that a scientist will not possess the modern tools to engage in best scientific practices. Evidence may be neglected or misidentified. Failure to maintain currency in the field of DNA analysis means that a forensic biologist may not be able to do mitochondrial DNA analysis or Y-chromosome determinations, or may have problems with mixed DNA types. This can easily result in miscarriages of justice which would be a clear ethical violation.

Proficiency Testing

This brings up the issue of how one maintains currency in one's field. There are a number of ways of doing this. This is, or should be, a shared responsibility between the scientist and the employer. The laboratory should pay for subscriptions to the major journals in forensic science and keep them current so that the scientists have ready access to them in the laboratory. The laboratory should also maintain a library with current reference and textbooks in forensic science and related areas. Again, these are needed for ready access by the scientists in the laboratory. It is the scientists' responsibility to read the journals and books, but this is very hard to monitor and verify.

Another method of maintaining and demonstrating currency is through the use of proficiency testing. This has been done in one form or another in forensic science laboratories for more than 40 years, but the procedures have been controversial from the start. There were, and still are, problems with outside vendors who market and administer proficiency tests to laboratories, and one reaction has been to use internal tests. For proficiency testing to be an effective measure, the tests must be anonymous and should be external. The test should look exactly like a typical case to the examiner. Ideally, they would be double-blind: Neither the examiner nor the personnel in the laboratory who are in charge of the testing should be aware of the presence of a proficiency test. Unfortunately, this has not been common practice in forensic science laboratories in the United States. In a typical case, an outside vendor supplies the tests without the answers. The laboratory administration issues the tests to the scientists. Both are aware of the tests. The scientists respond by pulling out all the stops and sometimes collaborating with others in the laboratory to make sure that they get the correct answers. The result is that this form of testing doesn't say much about the competency of the scientists to handle routine casework. Responsibility to do proficiency testing correctly lies with the laboratory and the scientist. Failure to do so is a violation of ethics, especially if the scientists testify in court that they regularly take proficiency tests to measure their competence. It is worth noting that the American Society of Crime Laboratory Directors / Laboratory Accreditation Board (ASCLD/LAB) requires external proficiency testing as part of the accreditation process, but does not require anonymity. It should also be pointed out that creating a procedure that would make the proficiency tests look like a real case is extremely difficult and expensive. There would have to be a cooperating law enforcement agency that would slip the test in as a real case and create a dummy scenario. This can be cumbersome to say the least.

Continuing Education

Continuing education, the practice of taking short courses, seminars, online modules, reading books, and so on, to keep current with one's profession, is a long-standing process in the sciences and other endeavors, such as the legal profession. Many states require, for example, that all lawyers complete a certain number of hours of continuing legal education each year to keep their license to practice law. This practice of mandatory continuing education has not, for the most part, been imposed on forensic scientists largely because there is normally no license to maintain and because forensic science does not have this process in its background or culture. Nonetheless, there are many opportunities for continuing education in forensic science including national and regional professional meetings, short courses offered by national and regional laboratories, college classes, and, increasingly, online offerings. As these educational development activities are not usually mandated, one wonders where the ethical problems lie. The answer is that there is very little in the way of evaluation of continuing education activities in forensic science. It is feasible, for example, for a scientist to register for a national forensic science meeting and spend the entire time on the golf course. It is difficult to verify that the scientist actually attended any paper sessions, workshops, lectures, or other educational sessions. To claim that continuing education hours have been completed without actually doing so is a serious violation of ethics, but is also extremely difficult to prove.

Toward a National Code of Ethics in Forensic Science

There are a large number of forensic science organizations that have a code of ethics. These include national and regional associations as well as discipline-specific groups. Although there is some overlap between these organizations with respect to the types of behaviors that constitute ethical violations, there are also significant differences. The main problem is that these disparate ethical codes lack consequence. There are very few certifications in forensic science, and virtually none of these are required for someone to maintain a practice in that field. The only consequence of violating an organizational code of ethics is that the individual can be removed from membership in that organization. Even major ethical violations do not prevent a forensic scientist from practicing forensic science. This makes it extremely problematic to prevent a bad scientist from causing significant damage to the justice system. The eleventh recommendation of the NAS Committee report on forensic science is that there be a consensus national code of ethics that is tied to certification. For this to have any real effect on the miscreants, however, there must be real consequences for serious ethical violations, up to and including loss of the right to practice forensic science and offer expert testimony in court. Other vocations including medicine and law have national, consensus codes of ethics and a mechanism for denying a miscreant the right to practice in that field. In such cases, there is a licensure process in place that requires practitioners to possess a license. In the case of medical practice, a physician must possess a medical license to practice medicine. In the law profession, a lawyer cannot practice law without a state license, which, in many cases, is attached to passage of the state bar exam and maintenance of continuing education credits. There is no licensure process in place for forensic scientists, thus making enforcement of ethical codes difficult since there is no mechanism for removing a forensic science from practice.

Since the NAS report has come out, there has been some discussion about the development of a national code of ethics. At the 2010 meeting of the American Academy of Forensic Sciences, the California Association of Criminalists, a regional forensic science organization with a very strong code of ethics, presented a possible blueprint for development of a national code of ethics for forensic science. Since that meeting, however, little has been accomplished. The major reason for the failure to develop a national code of ethics for forensic science and for the failure to develop a licensure or certification process that is tied to an ethical code is a lack of leadership. There is no organization in forensic science that speaks for all forensic scientists with one voice, analogous to the American Bar Association or the American Medical Association. There is no network of state forensic science boards to supervise the practice of forensic science in that state, analogous to state bar associations or medical societies. The American Academy of Forensic Sciences is more of a professional and trade association and was not set up to supervise and coordinate all forensic science activities on a nationwide scale, including developing and enforcing a national code of ethics. This is a major reason why the NAS report called for the formation of an independent Forensic

Science Institute at the federal level that would coordinate a suite of activities on a national scale. These would presumably include development of a national code of ethics and a linked mechanism for enforcement that would tie ethics and practice together, although the report never mentioned licensure specifically as this mechanism. The two bills that emerged from the last Congress, both in the Senate, called for the formation of a forensic science entity within the Justice and Commerce Departments that would perform some of the functions of the recommended Forensic Science Institute. There were some hearings associated with these bills, but neither was subject to a committee vote, and both died with the adjournment of the Congress at the end of 2012. Many people inside and outside of forensic science hope that a federal forensic science entity will eventually be created that will, among other things, oversee the development of a national, consensus code of ethics that has a necessary system of sanctions that can, in the most serious of cases, result in the loss of a violator's ability to practice forensic science and testify in court.

Section III

The Utility of Forensic Services

Following the demonstration about increases in the demand for forensic services but unresolved questions about the quality of forensic services a logical inquiry is whether or not forensic evidence "matters." Not only *whether* forensic evidence matters, but *how* it matters, or perhaps more accurately, how it gets used in the justice system. In this section, we have included three readings that speak to issues related to the utility of forensic services. First, in "The Impact of Forensic Evidence on Criminal Justice: Evidence From Case Processing Studies," Sally Kelty, Roberta Julian, and Robert Hayes provide a review of research from the United States, United Kingdom, and Australasia on the utility of forensic evidence in understanding criminal justice outcomes at different decision stages. Following this review, Kelty et al. discuss a five-year Australian project, "The Effectiveness of Forensic Science in the Criminal Justice System," designed to understand how criminal justice actors use forensic services and with what degree of effectiveness. The authors present a conceptual framework for understanding critical decision points in the investigative stages (identification, collection, analysis, and eventual use of forensic evidence) in Australian cases, with an eye toward identifying "leakage" points where evidence is not being used effectively (e.g., "actions or omissions of people, or agency policies that result in evidence contamination, destruction or blurring of scientific or medical experts' knowledge boundaries or prevention of expertise contributing to an investigation"). As Kelty et al. point out, this is important because if forensic evidence is not being used effectively, attempts to measure the impact of the forensic sciences on the administration of justice may prove fruitless. Their call for mixed methods research designs in this area of study is compelling.

Next, Michael D. White, Andrea R. Borrego, and David A. Schroeder ask some difficult questions about the effectiveness of DNA evidence in particular on criminal investigations. They point out that while DNA evidence has achieved popular status as an indispensable tool for solving crimes, there is very little research on the actual use of DNA evidence in police investigations. In "Assessing the Utility of DNA Evidence in Criminal Investigations," White et al. review the current evidence bearing on the use of DNA evidence by police, and note the great potential of DNA evidence to help solve crimes. However, in an earlier study of homicide cases in New York City, Schroeder and White found that DNA evidence (and results) was only available to investigators in a small percentage of cases, and those cases also had the lowest clearance rates. This led Schroder and White to conclude that DNA evidence was being used by detectives as a tool of last resort, after other investigative tools had been exhausted. In this chapter, White et al. offer an explanatory framework ("Diffusion of Innovation") for understanding some of the barriers to more routine use of DNA evidence by criminal investigators.

The third reading in this section focuses on how prosecutors use forensic evidence, and particularly the potential implications of the National Academy of Sciences report, *Strengthening Forensic Science in the United States: A Path Forward*, for prosecutors' use of forensic evidence in the legal process and related decision making. In "Forensic Science: The Prosecutor's Role," Nina W. Chernoff uses the pseudonymous "Daniel Green" case to illustrate how current rules governing the prosecutor's conduct might seem to require candidness about the reliability of forensic disciplines, but that vagueness, narrowly defined requirements, and weak enforcement limit the effectiveness of the rules to help ensure that forensic evidence plays an appropriate role in the adjudication process. Chernoff argues that these problems contribute to the potential unjust exercise of prosecutorial discretion, and that judges and defense attorneys alone are an inadequate check. In discussing various proposals for reform, Chernoff highlights the need for "Accuracy Advocates"—proactive members of the scientific community who will "facilitate the transfer of scientific knowledge into the legal system" by making their research more accessible to wider audiences, participate in conferences that bring scientists and legal actors together, conduct training for legal professionals, and, perhaps most important, provide expert testimony in such a way that one is not an advocate for the state or the defense, but an advocate for accuracy.

7

The Impact of Forensic Evidence on Criminal Justice

Evidence From Case Processing Studies

Sally Kelty, Roberta Julian,
and Robert Hayes

Introduction

Reliance on forensic evidence (FE) in police investigations and court trials has increased rapidly over the past 20 years. Traditionally, FE was used mainly to corroborate evidence (Bradbury & Feist, 2005); however, FE is increasingly becoming influential in focusing the direction of police investigations (Julian, Kelty, & Robertson, 2012) and in exonerating the innocent (Sangha, Roach, & Moles, 2010). The increased use of FE in investigations and the courts is evident in the fourfold increase over 40 years in the number of forensic laboratories and the rapid growth in more sophisticated techniques to analyze FE (Peterson et al., 2012).

Coinciding with the rise in the use of FE is a widespread belief that recent developments in forensic science, especially DNA, have "revolutionized" the ability of law enforcement to identify and prosecute offenders (Dunsmuir, Tran, & Wetherburn, 2008). Despite this belief, what evidence is there that forensic science has in fact revolutionized law enforcement's ability to process criminal cases more effectively? Recently, a growing number of studies have assessed the impact of FE in the criminal justice system (CJS), but there is still limited empirical research on how effective FE can be on the solvability of serious crime (crimes against the person, such as homicide, rape, and assault) and volume crime (crimes against property, such as burglary and criminal damage) (Julian et al., 2011).

In this chapter, the impact of FE on criminal justice outcomes is explored. The first part is a review of the current state of knowledge in this area from the United States,

United Kingdom, and Australasia. In the second part, we present the conceptual framework and case-processing flowchart that map out critical decisions and leakage (attrition) points in the use of FE in homicide cases from a large Australian project. In the final part, we conclude with a brief discussion of the impact of FE on criminal justice outcomes based on some of the findings from this research project.

The Impact of Forensic Evidence (FE) on Solvability and Case-Processing Outcomes: Evidence From the Literature

In this section, we review current knowledge on the impact of FE on solvability and case-processing outcomes of criminal cases. In the studies that we review, various terms are used that relate to measures of success for the use of FE; for example, the terms *case clearance/clearance rate* are not the same as *conviction*. Case clearance refers to arrest/s made and suspect/s charged with an offense. Conviction is where a charged suspect is eventually convicted in court. Further, the types of FE assessed vary by study. Overall, the most commonly assessed types of FE have been fingerprints and DNA; however, some studies have assessed a wider range of FE, such as hairs, fibers, and firearm-related evidence. The type of evidence assessed is noted below in each study reviewed. It is noteworthy that one problem encountered with conducting research that requires crime data is that many police and court databases have not historically stored the range of variables that researchers need to assess the value of FE on justice outcomes. Police and court databases were established to assist in administrative tasks (such as tracking clearance rates and recording court outcomes); they were not designed to provide data for research purposes such as evaluating the impact of FE on justice outcomes. Consequently, researchers have worked with the data that has been available, and often this has set limits on the types of questions that can be asked.[1] The review that follows is international in scope, presenting a comprehensive coverage of empirical research conducted to date in the United States, the United Kingdom, and Australasia.

U.S. RESEARCH

One of the most comprehensive studies assessing the impact of FE on CJS outcomes was by Peterson et al. (2010). This project, funded by the National Institute of Justice, used a random sample of incidents during 2003 stratified by crime type (assault, burglary, homicide, rape, robbery) and jurisdiction (Los Angeles, Indianapolis, Evansville, Fort Wayne, and South Bend). The study estimated the impact and attrition of FE collected at crime scenes as it progressed through the laboratory and into the courts. Variables assessed included the types of evidence collected at crime scenes, submitted to the laboratories, and examined in the laboratories, as well as the results of FE

---

[1]It is possible that the results from research presented in this chapter may have occurred due to the different ways that forensic science is organized, measured, and practiced in different police jurisdictions, states, even countries. It is beyond the scope of this chapter to overview the differences in the forensic sciences in the United States, United Kingdom, and Australasia. For an overview of this topic, the interested reader is referred to Houck et al. (2011) and Ross (2012).

analyses, database hits, and the linking of suspects to crimes. The results showed that FE collected from homicide crime scenes was extensive, whereas FE collected for assault, burglary, and robbery was more limited. FE was submitted to laboratories in 89% of homicide cases, in 32% of rape cases, and under 15% of burglaries, assaults, and robberies. The most frequently collected types of FE were fingerprints, firearms, and biological traces (blood and semen). Once submitted to the laboratories, 70% of FE was analyzed. The results showed that while FE can have an impact on case processing, the impact is not uniform across all crime types. FE was a consistent predictor of *arrest* for homicide, rape, assault, burglary, and robbery; however, just as consistent were non-FE variables, including victim statements, victim/suspect relationships, victim medical treatment, and arrest methods. FE was not a significant predictor of *conviction* for any crime type (Peterson et al., 2010).

Several studies have utilized the Peterson et al. (2010) dataset (as above). Baskin and Sommers (2012) assessed the impact of FE on assault ($n = 851$) and robbery ($n = 1081$) case outcomes. FE types assessed in the study included fingerprints, pattern evidence, firearms/weapons, natural/synthetic materials, genetic traces, electronic/printed data, trace evidence, and drugs. The results showed that the role of FE in case processing for assault and robbery cases was minimal. Regression analyses showed that FE did not impact on arrests made, referrals, charges, or convictions for these cases. Instead, good police work and witness or victim statements predicted movement through the case processing of these types of crimes (Baskin & Sommers, 2012). Similar results were obtained by this research team in homicide cases (Baskin & Sommers, 2010) and rape cases (Johnson et al., 2012).

More positive results for both serious and volume crime were obtained from a recent analysis of the extensive Peterson et al. (2010) data set. This analysis was carried out to assess the relative impact of FE on case processing on 4,205 cases of homicide, rape, assault, and burglary cases across five U.S. jurisdictions (Peterson et al., 2012). A three-stage method was adopted using descriptive statistics, bivariate analysis, and multivariate model predictions. The dependent variables were arrest, referral, charges, guilty pleas, conviction, and sentence length. Criminal justice decision variables were offense seriousness, stranger relationship, and prior criminal conviction. Extra-legal and case characteristics were suspect gender, suspect race, victim gender, victim race, witness reports to police, victim reports to police, suspect apprehended, and guilty plea. This research showed that FE could play a significant role in most of the criminal case decision variables measured. Collection of FE from the crime scene was predictive of arrest. Collection and examination of FE was predictive of referral to prosecutor. Examination of FE predicted filing of charges, conviction, and sentence length. Collection and examination of FE, however, was not predictive of guilty pleas. Further findings included that conviction rates were higher when two or more types of FE were present, especially biological FE. Peterson et al. concluded that although FE appeared to have a positive impact, it would be beneficial to analyze separately the decisions made at the crime scene about sample collections and decisions by detectives and lawyers about the use of FE in determining how cases proceed.

Brown and Keppel (2012) explored the impact of FE in solving child abduction homicides. Data was collected through interviews and analyses of case files of 733 omicide cases across 44 states from 1968 to 2002. Solvability referred to cases where an arrest occurred or probable cause existed. Cases without an arrest or probable cause were considered unsolved. Variables assessed were age, gender, victim–offender relationship, time, and distance. FE collected at the crime scene included hair, weapons, prints, semen, fibers, blood, firearms, bitemarks, tire tracks, trace evidence, vehicle, clothing, bedding, bindings, plants and dirt, and other evidence. The most important predictor of solvability was victim–offender relationship, followed by distance from murder site to the deceased location. FE had a significant impact on solvability when two or more items were examined. One limitation of this study was the time span for the cases being considered (1968 to 2002). It could be argued that the results reflect what forensic science was able to do in the 1960s, 1970s, and 1980s rather than the current capacity of the forensic sciences to assist in solving cases. It would be useful if important research such as this was carried out using contemporary cases that had utilized modern advanced scientific procedures and techniques.

In 2007, Schroeder released his work investigating homicide detectives' use of DNA in investigations and the impact on case clearance rates (persons arrested). Data were located from 593 homicide case files in New York (1996–2003). Using regression and survival analysis to identify predictors of case clearance and time to clearance, the results showed that police work was a better predictor of clearance than the use of FE. Significant predictors were a detective's follow-up with witnesses resulting in new leads and more checks on suspects. The researchers found that FE, especially DNA, was rarely used and had no discernible impact on clearance rates. Fingerprints and DNA were not significant predictors of clearance even when they were collected. From this research, the authors concluded that detectives used fingerprints and DNA as a last resort for their investigations, preferring to first exhaust other investigative techniques. It was possible that this occurred as a result of costs (around $1,000 per sample tested) and laboratory backlogs. It also appeared that the testing was done at the prosecution stage rather than during the earlier investigative stage (Schroeder, 2007; Schroeder & White 2009).

With the exception of the Peterson et al. (2012) findings, the remainder of the studies reviewed above suggest that FE has limited impact on solvability or how cases proceed through the criminal justice system. Research by Strom and Hickman (2010) identified a key reason that FE may have limited impact, namely, that in many cases, collected crime scene samples are not taken to laboratories for analysis. They aimed to provide an accurate national estimate of the extent of evidence backlogs for cases from 2003 to 2007. They found that in 23% of unsolved volume/property crimes, there was unanalyzed FE. In 40% of unsolved rape and murder cases, there was unanalyzed DNA, and in 10% unanalyzed fingerprints. Of note was that approximately 80% of backlogged murder cases, 59% of backlogged rape cases, and 65% of backlogged property cases were from the larger organizations explored. Finally, of the law enforcement agencies surveyed, 43% reported they may not submit evidence to the laboratory if a suspect had not been identified. This research suggests that police often use evidence to confirm the suspect's identity rather than using FE to guide the direction of the investigation (Strom & Hickman 2010; Strom et al. 2009).

In contrast to assessing the impact of FE on serious crime, Roman et al. (2009) investigated both the impact and cost-effectiveness of FE (DNA) in residential burglary. They assigned cases to two groups (DNA analyzed/DNA unanalyzed) to give an indication of the success of traditional investigative/police work alone compared with police work and FE, and examined the associated costs of this. Data were collected from 500 cases across five U.S. cities from 2005 to 2007. They hypothesized that police work together with analyzed DNA would result in more suspects identified, arrested, and prosecuted. Over 1,000 samples were analyzed to assist in identifying offenders through DNA database matches. Of the samples analyzed, a DNA profile was generated in 70.3% of cases. In 23.3% of cases, a hit occurred from the database, with a suspect being identified in 19.4% of cases. This led to arrests in 14.4% of cases. The results showed that for residential burglary, police work/DNA evidence combined had significantly better outcomes for suspect identification (31.0% vs. 12.8%), suspect arrest (21.9% vs. 10.1%), and acceptance of case for prosecution (19.3% vs. 8.1%), than did traditional police work alone. Traditional methods of suspect identification were used in 11.6% of treatment group cases compared with 12.8% of control cases. The conclusions were that DNA can be more effective than fingerprints in identifying suspects in volume crimes, but is associated with much higher costs.

Whether training in the collection of FE can make a difference to how cases proceed was assessed by Campbell, Patterson, and Bybee (2012). This research focused on whether taking part in a senior forensic nursing program in a large Midwestern county improved the likelihood of investigation and prosecution of sexual assault cases. Between-groups comparisons were used to assess efficacy of collection of FE by forensic personnel pre- ($n = 156$) and post-training ($n = 137$). The following criteria had to be met for case inclusion in both groups. The victim was aged 18 years or over, the case was investigated by a large police department, a complete medical forensic examination was completed, and the results were analyzed by a state crime laboratory for DNA evidence. Forensic nurses who had participated in the training program collected evidence that resulted in significantly higher case progression; positive DNA evidence was also a significant predictor of higher case progression. These results suggest that the utility of FE is as much about the skill and training of the person collecting the evidence as it is about the FE itself.

Alderden and Ullman (2012) assessed decision making at four stages of sexual assault case processing, including case founding, arrest, presentation to prosecution, and prosecution approval of felony charges. The sample was 465 sexual assault cases of adult women reported to the Midwestern Police Department in 2003. Incident variables collected included whether a rape kit was completed, the victim sustained physical injuries, the assault resulted in penetration, a weapon was used, witnesses to the incident were present, there was a discrepancy in the victim statement, and the victim reported actively resisting the assault. The results showed the only significant variable was whether there was a discrepancy in the victim's statement at the case-founding stage. Police officers were significantly more likely to present cases to the prosecution when the victim was willing to pursue the case. Victim preference to pursue the matter was the only significant variable in the decision to arrest. At the felony approval stage, the predictive variables were whether the victim was injured, the victim–suspect relationship, and discrepancy in the victim statement. In this study, the presence of a completed rape kit was not predictive of a case proceeding. Overall, the study concluded that decisions at each stage were not related to FE but were more influenced by extralegal decision making.

UK RESEARCH

The increased ability to store DNA results saw an increase in the establishment of national DNA databases. An evaluation of English DNA databases between 1995 and 1998 found the number of matches was between 300 and 500 per week, including 28,128 matches of suspects to crime scenes (Werrett & Sparkes 1998). The results of more recent analyses also confirm the positive impact of FE, including DNA evidence, on case clearance rates (A. Smith, 2004). Annual reports from the UK's Forensic Science Service in 2004 were positive, reporting that a burglary reduction initiative within the West Midlands saw a reduction in crime of 10% with the use of FE compared to a national increase of 1%. In 2005, a comprehensive review estimated that for directly detected volume crimes, the main variable securing detection was FE in more than one quarter of cases (Bradbury & Feist 2005). In contrast, Briody and Prenzler (2005) analysed the impact of DNA on burglary convictions in Britain, finding that the average conviction rate achieved from reported burglaries was close to 1%, and concluded that the impact of an expanding UK database on convictions for volume crime was likely to be minimal.

The most comprehensive end-to-end project carried out in the United Kingdom was the 2004 Scientific Work Improvement Model (SWIM) (Adderley, Townsley, & Bond 2007). The SWIM project built on an earlier pilot conducted in the Derbyshire Constabulary, in which a direct correlation between the time taken from crime occurrence to FE led detection (lead time) was assessed. The pilot found that reducing the lead time from crime scene attendance, through analysis and investigation could reduce the level of volume crime. The SWIM project was carried out over two years across the 41 police forces in England and Wales. SWIM focused on lead times from incident to arrest in burglaries and car thefts using DNA and fingerprints. Four case processing phases were extensively analyzed using data-mining software (attendance, submission, identification, and detection). Attrition points and lag times between each phase were assessed, and for each crime report, the lead time was calculated based on the earliest activity date at each forensic process phase. The success rate was calculated as the percentage of cases that successfully moved to the next phase. The SWIM Report made a large number of recommendations for improvement at all phases of the forensic process. In particular, it demonstrated the need to identify significant leakage points. Most of the findings mirror those of U.S. research showing that the impact of FE was affected by the people who collect and use FE, including police and forensic officers. For example, the SWIM project found that 25% of crime scene personnel clearly outperformed their peers by arriving at crime scenes faster, and by collecting higher quality evidence that was significantly more likely to lead to database hits, and then led on to more identifications and arrests.[2]

AUSTRALASIAN RESEARCH

Briody (2002) assessed how biological FE was used in 200 Australian sexual offense cases with reference to decisions to prosecute, guilty pleas, and convictions. Of the 200 cases, 102 had DNA evidence. The results showed that the impact of biological FE at various stages depended on other aspects of the case. DNA evidence did not significantly predict guilty pleas. However, with DNA present, cases were more likely to result in decisions to prosecute, to reach court, and to attract slight increases in sentence length. Rape cases were less likely to reach court when the defendant refused to make a statement. The most important variable for explaining convictions was a confession to police. Juries

---

[2]It is beyond the scope of this review to detail the complete research carried out in the United Kingdom, especially by the British Home Office. The interested reader is referred to the following seminal works: Blakey (2000, 2002), Burrows et al. (2005), Tilley and Townsley (2009).

were more likely to convict if tangible evidence was present. The prosecution was weakened, even with DNA, if the complainant had used alcohol or drugs prior to the incident.

Briody (2004) found similar results in a later study assessing the impact of DNA on 150 homicide cases in Queensland, Australia from 1996 to 1999. Of these cases, 75 had DNA present. Collected FE included fingerprints and DNA. Defendant variables were age, employment status, race, gender, plea, prior convictions, and offender–victim relationship. Outcomes measured were case reached court, plea entered, and jury outcome. The results showed that significant predictors of reaching court were DNA evidence, the defendant's gender, and a confession. Predictors of jury convictions were both fingerprint and DNA evidence and defendant confessed. Length of sentence was predicted by presence of FE and prior record of violence.

In 2010, the Waikato Police District in New Zealand (NZ), in collaboration with the forensic branch of the Institute of Environmental Science and Research (ESR Forensic, i.e., the main government forensic science laboratory), undertook an end-to-end project to assess and implement quicker turnaround times for FE submitted in the course of police investigations of volume crimes. The trial led to a significant improvement in turnaround times by NZ forensic scientists that in turn increased the value of FE for NZ Police. The reduction in turnaround time made a significant contribution to volume crime reduction through better prioritization of volume crime DNA collection, submission, and analysis. It was found that ESR Forensic Volume Crime Laboratory reduced turnaround times from 20 days to an average of 5.4 days in approximately 78% of all sample submissions to the laboratory over a three-month period. By ensuring that Scenes of Crime Officers (SOCOs) attended volume crime scenes on the day of the incident, they were able to see the added value of their forensic results and the effect of their timely response on the current crime environment. Further, investigators identified the benefits of working with rapid identifications on the potential to recover property, to prevent future offending and to assist in identifying current "hot" offenders, which in turn allowed the police to apply a targeted approach disrupting and influencing current crime patterns (Roux et al., 2014).

In 2011, the Australia New Zealand Policing Advisory Agency National Institute of Forensic Science (ANZPA-NIFS) carried out a nationwide project called the "End-To-End Forensic Identification Process." This project reviewed current end-to-end processes and developed a national framework and recommendations for more efficient FE collection and analysis. End-to-end processing was defined as the time from the report of a crime through to the arrest of an offender. The process was broken into five stages (attendance, submission, analysis, identification, and investigation). The study benchmarked performance in the use of fingerprints and DNA in burglary cases. In partnership with all eight Australian police agencies and a number of relevant DNA laboratories, 17 sites in total were selected for data analysis (consisting of metropolitan centers and regional cities/towns) across Australia. Over 8,000 burglaries reported over a five-month period were included. Overall, this project provided an indicative evaluation of the current lead time and success rates in relation to the performance of burglary investigations in Australia. Results are currently being reported to participants and stakeholders with a view to developing recommendations for change; a further study is envisioned that would assess the impact of any recommended changes (Brown, Ross, & Slater 2012).

These rare end-to-end studies provide a more holistic view than do some of the earlier studies that examine the impact of FE on the criminal justice system because they adopt a more comprehensive case processing approach. Nevertheless, it is difficult to make any generalizations about the contributions of FE to the criminal justice system as a whole as practices vary for serious and volume crime, and, in most jurisdictions, forensic science is not explicitly integrated into policing strategies (Roux et al., 2014).

FINDINGS FROM THE LITERATURE: AN OVERVIEW

The research detailed above indicates that there are many factors that contribute to the effective and efficient use of forensic science other than the amount of FE evidence collected (whether it be DNA, hairs and fibers, accelerants, etc.). It is clear that there are many aspects of the forensic process that can enhance or undermine effectiveness of the FE—for example, the time taken by police detectives/investigators to respond to positive hits, the lag time between evidence collected and when it is submitted to the laboratory, whether the evidence submitted is then analyzed, the quality of the fingerprint/DNA lifts themselves, and whether a DNA sample produces a complex mixed profile, or a single but weak partial profile. The reviews also show that increasing the amount of DNA evidence collected from crime scenes may not necessarily lead to a higher proportion of finalized cases and convictions. This is because there are numerous factors that influence case progression including the knowledge and awareness of the benefits of forensic science among police officers, and the existence or management of backlogs. Previous research in the United States and the United Kingdom has identified deficiencies in the police use of forensic science in criminal investigations (McCulloch, 1996; Tilley & Ford, 1996). The studies reviewed here suggest these deficiencies still exist, and, significantly, there is little evidence of the proactive use of FE by police. Equally, the existence of extensive backlogs should be noted. Funding has not kept pace with the demand for testing such that substantial backlogs documented at the beginning of the most recent decade (e.g., ASCLD, 2004; Peterson & Hickman, 2005), have continued to increase across subsequent measurements (Durose, 2008; Durose, Walsh, & Burch, 2012). Such backlogs cause significant delays in evidence being analyzed, resulting in delays in the courts as well as in the investigation of crimes. In short, when the forensic *process* is not effective and efficient, it is not surprising that studies find FE has a limited impact on case outcomes. Recent moves to address issues of police training and to prioritize the analysis of FE (e.g., through triage) have improved the collection and use of FE by police officers, enhanced processing efficiency, and reduced backlogs, resulting in the more effective and efficient use of FE in case processing (Tjin-A-Tsoi, 2013).

Conceptual Framework and Case-Processing Model of Critical Decisions and Leakage Points in Homicide Cases: Findings From the Effectiveness of Forensic Science in the Criminal Justice System (EFS) Project

CONCEPTUAL FRAMEWORK FOR THE RESEARCH PROJECT

"The Effectiveness of Forensic Science in the Criminal Justice System" is a five-year Australian Research Council (ARC) Linkage Project examining the value of forensic science in criminal investigations and court outcomes (Julian et al., 2011).

This project brings together, possibly for the first time in Australia, a multi-disciplinary approach involving social scientists, legal and economic researchers, state and federal police agencies, forensic science practitioners, forensic researchers, and intelligence experts from both Australian and international universities.[3] This project does not aim to assess the reliability or validity of the science itself (e.g., test the reliability of analytical techniques) but rather to explore how people within the criminal justice system use forensic services and whether these services are used as effectively as possible.

The project involves a comprehensive analysis of the role of forensic science in the criminal justice system that focuses on processes and outcomes from the crime scene through to the courts. Fundamental to the project's conceptual framework is the recognition that the criminal justice process involves a number of successive phases that may involve the use of FE (e.g., crime scene examination, police investigation, elimination or determination of suspects, arrest, charges laid, preparation of a prosecution brief, court outcome). As noted in our review of international research, decisions made about the use of FE during each of these phases may have a significant impact on case progression. This forensic-led case processing framework therefore offers opportunities for operationalizing a number of key decision-making points that have been missed in past studies and assists in identifying "leakage" points in the criminal justice process (i.e., where FE is not used effectively). In particular, the project has highlighted the significance of a number of decisions made during the crime scene examination phase. Our research design has enabled a detailed analysis of these decision-making points to be undertaken, and we have been able to demonstrate how these decisions impact on the effective use of FE. A primary aim of the EFS project is to identify the processes involved in police investigations and court trials and to investigate the phases in which forensic science is typically employed (specifically, to identify the objective and subjective factors that impact on the effective and efficient use of forensic science). Our focus is on serious crime because these investigations are costly and resource intensive requiring a range of specialist personnel (e.g., ballistics, fingerprints, hair and fibers) to attend most scenes and with a number of specimens examined by different disciplines. In such investigations, it is crucial that resources be used as effectively as possible throughout the forensic process.

We adopted a case study approach to track the forensic process so that we can identify key decision-making points—from the collection of traces at the crime scene through to the court—and to understand the effect of FE at each critical point as well as on the final outcome of the case in court. The analysis of case studies is a method particularly suited to exploratory research of this type. The richness of the data available in in-depth case studies "enables the researcher to understand and unpack the intricately woven parts of complex social processes" (Mason, 1998) while allowing the investigation "to retain the holistic and meaningful characteristics of real-life events" (Yin, 1998). In the analysis of case processing in volume crime, it is useful to examine a large number of cases to identify systemic issues in relation to resource inputs and outputs. In contrast, it has been suggested that one of the best ways to analyze case processing in serious crime is to identify the factors affecting critical

---

[3]Please refer to author's notes for an overview of the research team, industry partners, and universities involved.

decisions made at various phases as the case progresses (Barclay, 2009; Peterson et al., 2012). This conceptual framework (the forensic-led case processing model) and methodological approach (case studies) provides the foundation for the following analysis.

THE EFFECTIVENESS OF FORENSIC SCIENCE (EFS) FORENSIC-LED CASE PROCESSING MODEL

The essence of the EFS forensic-led case processing model presented below is to highlight critical decision points in the investigative phase of homicide/fatal arson cases. At each of the critical points, a decision made can result in either the effective or ineffective use of forensic science/medical expertise or services. The term *ineffective* in this model refers to actions or omissions of people, or agency policies that result in evidence contamination, destruction, or blurring of scientific or medical experts' knowledge boundaries, or prevention of expertise contributing to an investigation.[4] The EFS model was developed through the in-depth analysis of 11 case studies that covered the range of the most common forms of homicide and fatal/arson occurring in different states throughout Australia (murder/arson between family members or persons known to each other/acquaintances). None of the cases used involved police shootings, deaths in custody, serial offenders/offenses, or deaths occurring during arson bush fires.

The data used to develop the EFS model came from a number of sources, including court transcripts, judicial sentencing remarks, newspaper and media reports, police journal reports, and 26 in-depth interviews with personnel who had been directly involved in one or more of the 11 cases analyzed. Additional data came from 103 participants who were police officers, detectives, forensic scientists, lawyers, judges, coroners, pathologists, and forensic physicians practicing in Australia. These participants took part in interviews or focus groups to talk through interagency and interdisciplinary issues occurring during the investigative and adjudicative stages of homicide cases. The insights from these 103 participants further enriched the data set and helped us to develop insight into where and how FE adds value to serious criminal cases. All participants in this research freely gave their consent, and no rewards were offered or provided. All procedures adhered to the National Health and Medical Research Council (NHMRC) guidelines for ethical research carried out in Australia. The data (transcripts, media, or interview narrative) were subjected to content analysis using a sequential idiographic approach (J. Smith, 1995). Each document or transcript was read in full and themes running through the data were highlighted.

Figure 7.1 shows the EFS model charting the effective and ineffective use of FE in a forensic-led criminal investigation. Effective use of FE can be seen on the left following a vertical path. Ineffective use of FE, as represented in the flow chart, can be seen in the process boxes to the right. Whether FE is used effectively or ineffectively stems from a number of critical decision points made by various personnel as the investigation gains momentum. The EFS model starts when police or other emergency

---

[4]In the EFS case processing model the terms expert and expertise refer to police, science or medical practitioners who have specialized knowledge, training, and qualifications in an area (such as fire and explosives investigation) and who are recognized by legal practitioners and the courts as being able to present expert opinion in criminal trials.

Figure 7.1   EFS Forensic-Led Case Processing Model for the Investigation of Homicide/Fatal Arson

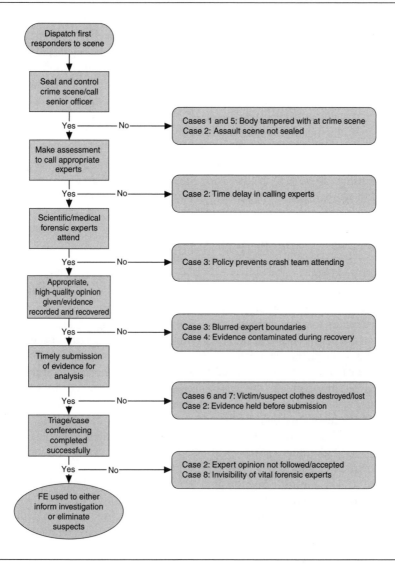

NOTES: To cases 1 to 8:

Case 1. *R v. Adam Emilio Mocenigo* (domestic homicide; deceased weighted down in a lake)

Case 2. *R v. Rebecca Massey* (assault with a weapon/homicide between two female associates)

Case 3. *R v. Vandergulik* (domestic homicide/arson; deceased died in a staged motor vehicle accident)

Case 4. *R v. Stafford* (domestic homicide family-in-law member; contaminated evidence and incorrect analysis used for time of death; conviction now overturned).

Case 5. *R v. Hillier* (domestic homicide/arson; conviction now overturned)

Case 6. *R v. Griffin* (assault with a weapon/homicide between two male associates)

Case 7. *R v. Gatto* (homicide between male associates)

Case 8. *R v. Scott Alexander McDougall* (double homicide/arson by a male on a male and female associate)

management personnel are called to an incident scene. The EFS model ends at the point where accurate and high-quality FE is used either to eliminate suspects or to further an investigation.

The first critical decision made is whether and when to seal an incident scene (such as set up command and control procedures, e.g., place a guard at the entry of a scene). The crime scene has not always been conceptualized as an integral part of forensic science. In the past, activities at the crime scene were viewed as "police work," and managing a crime scene was seen as a technical rather than a scientific process (Crispino, 2008). Over the past few years, maintaining the integrity of the crime scene and the management of personnel in attendance has come to be seen as crucial. If the front end of a criminal investigation is not handled effectively and reliably, then there are significant flow-on effects in the forensic process and, potentially, in justice outcomes (Brown & Willis, 2009; Julian et al., 2012; Sangha et al., 2010). Ineffective practices at the crime scene can be seen in the EFS model and are reflected in Case 1 (*R v. Adam Emilio Mocenigo*), where the crime scene was not sealed immediately, allowing the suspect to return to the scene and tamper with the deceased. In contrast, effective use of forensic services was apparent in *R v. Ian Edward Hirst*, where a homicide scene occurring within a city apartment block was sealed as soon as the first responders arrived therefore maintaining the integrity of the FE.

The next two critical decisions made by police are whether to call forensic experts and determining which forensic experts can assist in the investigation. It may seem obvious that in certain situations, forensic experts need to be called. However, it does not always follow that the right expertise is called at the right time, or whether the experts can attend. As shown in the model, in Case 2 (*R v. Rebecca Massey*), an assault took place, and the victim was taken to a hospital and later died. Blood pattern analysts/ crime scene examiners were not called to the incident scene until several hours later, leading to a time delay in the collection of valuable evidence. In Case 3 (*R v. Vandergulik*), a deceased was found in a burnt-out vehicle that had collided into a tree. The incident occurred in a regional area 2.5 hours from a capital city. Policy within this jurisdiction held that specialist crash investigators only attend scenes given certain conditions (a single motor vehicle with single occupant is one condition where the policy provides that special permission must be granted for the crash team to attend). These cases can be contrasted by the process in *R v. Walker, De Bono & Conci* and *R v. Morgan & Tamme* where detectives were advised and assisted by experts in blood pattern analysis, DNA experts, and forensic chemists early on in the investigations.

Having experts attend scenes can be vital for effective investigations. It is also imperative that experts remain within their boundaries of knowledge and that the collection of FE is not contaminated through flawed or outdated practices. The next critical decision is whether the experts attending the scene do or do not blur their boundaries of expertise. What counts for expert opinion has been under scrutiny in recent years in relation to what the criminal courts regard as "having expertise" (Edmond & Roberts, 2011; McClellan, 2009).[5] According to McClellan, with the increased reliance on specialized knowledge in society, the role of experts in the criminal justice system has expanded so that they now play a crucial role in many civil and criminal trials. One danger of relying on expertise is when experts act outside their

---

[5]Also see *HG v. The Queen* [1999] 197 CLR 414 and *F v. The Queen* [1995] 83 A Crim R 502.

area of knowledge and legitimate expertise. A number of factors are relevant here. First, whether the police at the scene have the level of forensic awareness, knowledge, and training to determine the necessary and actual expertise of the person they rely on. A number of studies have noted the low level of forensic awareness among frontline police officers (McCulloch, 1996). Furthermore, although frontline officers may have been exposed to critical incidents, they may not have regular exposure to homicide scenes or forensic experts, especially in smaller non-metropolitan areas. When a low-level of forensic knowledge combines with low exposure to suspicious/crime scenes, less experienced frontline responders may be heavily reliant on "expert advice" to assist them in determining what has occurred. Regardless of the motive for why people act beyond their area of expertise (whether it be self-interest or wishing to assist the police investigation), the outcomes for justice can be less than optimal. There is significant flow-on effects of not having the "right" expert at the scene. This was exemplified in Case 3 (*R v. Vandergulik*) where the fire investigator who attended the accident scene went beyond his of expertise (fires) to provide the police with an estimated speed of impact of 50 to 60 kilometers per hour. At this speed, the fire investigator suggested the vehicle could have self-ignited. The police report recorded this as "not suspicious." Later, it was discovered that the widow of the deceased staged the accident. Tests later performed on the vehicle by two independent crash experts found the speed to be 25 to 30 kilometers per hour (not fast enough for a vehicle to self-ignite when colliding into a tree).

The next critical decision is the timely submission of clothing and other FE to the laboratory for analysis. This can be crucial for certain analyses where time can erode forensic traces. The work of Strom and Hickman (2010) showed that police are not always timely in their submission of evidence to the laboratory in serious criminal matters. This was also apparent in our interviews with detectives where items were often collected from serious crime scenes but not submitted. Loss and destruction of FE was evident in our interviews and in three of the case studies. In Cases 2 (*R v. Rebecca Massey*), 6 (*R v. Griffin*), and 7 (*R v. Gatto*), the clothing of the deceased or homicide suspect was lost or destroyed, and was therefore unable to be examined for the presence of hair, DNA, glass, or other trace evidence (e.g., cut off the body and then destroyed at autopsy, incinerated at the hospital, or lost by the police officers who collected clothing from a suspect).

After the evidence is submitted or before it is analyzed, the next critical decision is whether to hold a case conference (sometimes called *investigative meetings/briefings* or *triage*). Holding case conferences in homicide matters is routine (Kelty, Julian, & Ross, 2012); however, what can be problematic is which experts are asked to attend these meetings. When there is an absence of meaningful and regular communication between experts in the forensic sciences, forensic medicine, law, and police, this can be described as the *justice silo effect*. Justice silos mean that practitioners, even within their own organizations, operate in isolation, unaware of the role and responsibilities of other justice personnel. It is commonplace to think about the criminal justice system as a combined entity with agencies working together toward a single purpose. However, a recent commentary painted a different picture within Australia of siloed agencies with a fragmented approach to collaboration (Ross, 2012). Within the United States, similar fragmented interactions between forensic practitioners, police, and lawyers and siloed agencies have been noted (Carter, 2006; National Academy of Sciences [NAS], 2009). A clear example of the detrimental effect of justice silos occurred in *R v. Jama*

(FJ: imprisoned in 2008 in Australia for a rape he did not commit) (Rayment, 2010). FJ was convicted solely on the basis of DNA evidence, with no other evidence presented at trial. In 2009, it became apparent that the original DNA swabs had been contaminated in the rape crisis centre. FJ was acquitted. It is noteworthy that during the FJ investigation, when the possibility of DNA contamination was very briefly raised by a police officer to a superior officer, neither the police officers nor the forensic scientists who discussed this issue contacted the forensic physician who had undertaken the examination of the alleged victim (Vincent, 2010).

In the EFS model, agency silos and semi-invisibility of some forensic experts represents an ineffective use of forensic science when vital expertise is not called on or acted on when police make decisions about how to proceed with their investigations. Recent research showed the practitioners most likely to be siloed were forensic physicians and nurses[6] during both the investigative and pre-trial/adjudication process. The invisibility (not asked to investigative or pre-trial cases meetings) of these practitioners was not deliberate (Kelty et al., 2012). In many instances, it was an omission by the police, forensic science, and lawyers who did not invite them to meetings. This was exemplified in Case 8 (*R v. Scott Alexander McDougall*), a double homicide/arson where the police, crime scene examiners, and forensic scientists involved in the investigative and briefing case meetings of this complex homicide did not realize/consider that the forensic physician who had examined the injuries sustained by the homicide suspect could have added valuable information to the investigation.

The final ineffective use of forensic expertise to guide investigations in the EFS model occurred when forensic scientists or medical practitioners give police advice or information about FE that was not considered or followed. This can lead to inefficient practices in the laboratory as well as creating conflict and acrimonious working relationships between practitioners and different agencies. This was exemplified in Case 2 (*R v. Rebecca Massey*) where the advice of the forensic scientists that trace evidence (hair samples and DNA) would not be found on certain items was not accepted by the detectives. Pressure was placed on the laboratory and the DNA biologists and chemists to carry out the analysis despite advice the analyses would be fruitless. In line with what the scientists had advised, a useful DNA profile or useful hair analysis could not be produced.

Conclusion

The review of research on case-processing in the United States, United Kingdom, and Australasia presented in the first part of this chapter showed mixed results in terms of the impact of FE on criminal justice. Early studies concluded that the impact of FE on case outcomes was limited, while some of the more sophisticated current research identified positive impacts of FE on the solvability of crimes. These findings should be considered in the context of major reviews of forensic science and criminal justice agencies such as *Under the Microscope* in the United Kingdom (Blakey, 2000, 2002) and *Strengthening Forensic Science in the United States* (NAS, 2009) that identify systematic

---

[6]Medical practitioners who carry out examinations on homicide suspects, rape and physical assault victims, and assist in the autopsy of victims of sexual homicides and child deaths.

weaknesses in the application of forensic sciences in the criminal justice system. If forensic science is not being *used* effectively, it is not surprising to find that attempts to measure the impact of FE do not necessarily lead to positive findings. These discrepancies may also be symptomatic of the fact that assessing the contribution of forensic science is not straightforward because it occurs on a number of different dimensions or levels depending on the context of the judicial response or police activity. In addition, the judicial response itself is neither linear nor continuous, but can be seen as successive phases with different aims, distinct reasoning, and distinct ways of using information (Roux, Crispino, & Ribaux, 2012). It is important, therefore, to identify relevant (and possibly different) measures of "success" at discrete phases of the forensic case process. We argue that measures of success could be varied; examples include the ability of FE to eliminate suspects from police investigations, to be associated with changes in pleas during investigations, and to allow police to effectively link multiple crime scenes, ultimately leading to a recidivist effect by the disruption of prolific volume crime offending.

The Australian research presented in the second part of this chapter, "Conceptual Framework and Case-Processing Model of Critical Decisions and Leakage Points in Homicide Cases," built on the evidence base overviewed earlier and has explored in depth different phases of the forensic case process. The case-processing model presented identified a number of critical decisions at distinct phases during the investigative phase of homicide/fatal arson cases. The model showed that at each critical point, the types of decision made, or the types of policies in place in law enforcement agencies, lead either to effective or ineffective use of FE/scientific expertise. The emphasis in the second part of this chapter has been on case processing during the investigative stage of serious criminal matters.

The model presented was developed using in depth analysis of 11 Australian cases and interviews with Australian scientists, medical practitioners, lawyers, and police. However, it is likely that the critical decision points presented in this model are not specific to Australia with many of these same issues influencing criminal investigations in the United States, United Kingdom, and Europe. For example, the reliance on unreliable evidence by police and lawyers (UK: *R v. Suzanne Holdsworth [2008] EWCA Crim 971*); reliance on un-validated science by police and lawyers (US: *Willingham v. Johnson [N.D.Tex. 2001]*); blurred expert boundaries (UK: *R v. Sally Clarke, Court of Appeal [Criminal Division] 11 April 2003*); lost clothing by police and forensic agencies (US: *State v. Joe Gentz, Wayne County, 19 February 2013*); evidence held by police and not submitted or disclosed to the defense (US: *State v. Gregory F. Taylor and Law Enforcement Misconduct in the NCSBI Crime Laboratory*); evidence contaminated at crime scene by forensic scientists (Italy: *The Hellmann-Zanetti Report, acquittal of Amanda Knox, Corte di Assise di Appello in Perugia, 2011*).

We conclude this chapter by suggesting that the optimal way forward for future case-processing research is to adopt mixed-methods approaches. This will enable researchers to develop a deeper understanding of the impact that FE can have on justice outcomes and will indicate ways forward in enhancing the use of forensic science in the criminal justice system. Quantitative studies, with good datasets, can assess overall case clearance but cannot identify the subtle critical points in criminal justice decision making that undermine the effective use of FE. Qualitative research using case studies or interviews can identify a range of critical points and critical decisions but cannot show overall effectiveness in terms of case clearance. This suggests that measuring effectiveness at a single point, or one or two points, underestimates the different impact that decisions can have regarding the use of FE at various points in the investigation. Mixed-method research designs are more rigorous and demanding in terms of data collection; however, the findings can be more robust because they satisfy the principle of triangulation. The seminal work on triangulation by Denzin (1970) noted that optimal research satisfies four types of triangulation. First, data triangulation is achieved when similar data is collected from similar populations; for example, data is collected in focus groups or surveys from a range of different participants with different perspectives, such as serving police officers, forensic scientists, forensic medical practitioners, lawyers, or social workers. Second, investigator triangulation is achieved when the data is collected by experienced researchers in the field. Third, theoretical triangulation is achieved thorough interdisciplinary analysis, such as industrial sociology, organizational psychology, police studies, and business management. Last, methodology triangulation is achieved through mixed-method approaches, such as observation, case studies, surveys, interviews, job analytical techniques, psychometric assessment, document analysis, and database searches.

Finally, it is notable, as discussed in the first part, that one of the problems associated with doing quantitative research in this area is that researchers are often provided with datasets that police and law agencies extract from their administrative databases. The types of information stored on police databases vary considerably from country to country and within police jurisdictions. Often, the databases have been established to monitor case clearance (arrests) and court outcomes (convictions) and hold limited data on the range of FE used or the outcomes of FE analyses for each criminal case that proceeds through an investigation and into court. This means that evaluation questions are limited by the datasets. This makes assessing research findings difficult and could ultimately explain why much of the quantitative research reviewed showed limited impact. It is possible that the police and courts at the present time do not collect or record the type of data needed to answer the question of how does FE impact on justice outcomes. We argue that mixed-methods research designs will be further enhanced when complimented with more robust information management systems capable of providing case and business intelligence (Bell, 2006; Ribaux, Baylon, Lock, et al., 2010; Ribaux Baylon, Roux, et al., 2010). This type of model may enable "whole-of-business" improvement through supply of advanced intelligence products to investigators, real-time reporting of operational performance leading to improved effectiveness and efficiency, and a platform for the introduction of contemporary integrated Total Quality Management. Research using a mixed-methods model to investigate the prediction of erroneous convictions provides further support for the methodology (Gould et al., 2012). Further collaborative benchmarking initiatives such as the FORESIGHT program using the LabRAT benchmarking tool could be envisaged as a method to improve evaluations of efficiency and effectiveness in the forensic sciences (Houck et al., 2009; Kobus et al., 2011).

Acknowledgments: We would like to acknowledge the support provided in two research grants that allowed us to carry out this work. We acknowledge the Australian Research Council (LP0882797) and our industry partners—Victoria Police, ACT Policing, Australian Federal Police Forensic and Data Centres, and the National Institute of Forensic Science and Forensic Foundations—for funding this collaborative research project "The Effectiveness of Forensic Science in the Criminal Justice System." This five-year project is a comprehensive investigation into the effectiveness of forensic science in police investigations and court trials. It aims to identify when, where, and how forensic services can add value to police investigations, court trials, and justice outcomes while ensuring the efficient use of available resources. The research team for this project includes social science researchers from the Tasmanian Institute of Law Enforcement Studies (TILES) and the University of Tasmania, together with forensic science researchers from University of Technology, Sydney; University of Canberra; and the University of Lausanne, Switzerland.

We acknowledge the support of the Australian and New Zealand Policing Advisory Agency-National Institute of Forensic Science (ANZPAA-NIFS) for funding the Interfaces Project, which assessed the interface between forensic science, medicine, law, and police during the investigation and adjudication into homicide and adult sexual assault matters. We thank the Interfaces project team, especially Mr. Alastair Ross; Associate Professor David Wells; the Hon. Frank Vincent, AO QC; and our research associates Mrs. Katherine Cashman and Ms. Loene Howes.

Thanks also to Professor Pierre Margot, Dr. Simon Walsh, and Ms. Loene Howes for their valuable comments and suggestions on earlier drafts of this chapter.

Cases

(Used in the Development of the EFS Model; Refer to the Second Part of This Chapter, "Conceptual Framework and Case-Processing Model of Critical Decisions and Leakage Points in Homicide Cases")

R v. Adam Emilio Mocenigo [2012] VIC
R v. Gatto [2005] VIC
R v. Griffin [2006] ACTSC 77
R v. Hillier [2007] HCA 13; (2007) 233 ALR 634; 81 ALJR 886
R v. Ian Edward Hirst [2008] ACT
R v. Jama. Supreme Court of Victoria. Court of Appeal, Warren, Redlich & Bongiorno, 7 December 2009.
R v. Morgan & Tamme [2002] VSC 574
R v. Rebecca Massey [2009] ACTSC 70
R v. Scott Alexander McDougall [2011] ACTSC 51
R v. Stafford [2009] QCA 407
R v. Vandergulik [2009] VSC 0003
R v. Walker, De Bono and Conci [2003] VSC 155

References

Adderley, R., Townsley, M., & Bond, J. (2007). Use of data mining techniques to model crime scene investigator performance. *Knowledge-Based Systems, 20*(2), 170–176.

Alderden, M. A., & Ullman, S. E. (2012). Creating a more complete and current picture: Examining police and prosecution decision-making when processing sexual assault cases. *Violence Against Women, 18*(5), 525–551.

American Society of Crime Laboratory Directors (ASCLD). (2004, May 28). *180-day study report: Status and needs of United States crime laboratories.* Largo, FL: American Society of Crime Laboratory Directors.

Barclay, D. (2009). Using forensic science in major crime inquiries. In J. Fraser & R. Williams (Eds.), *Handbook of forensic science* (pp. 337–358). Cullompton, UK: Willan Publishing.

Baskin, D., & Sommers, I. (2010). The influence of forensic evidence on the case outcomes of homicide incidents. *Journal of Criminal Justice, 38,* 1141–1149.

Baskin, D., & Sommers, I. (2012). The influence of forensic evidence on the case outcomes of assault and robbery incidents. *Criminal Justice Policy Review, 23*(2), 186–207.

Bell, C. (2006). Concepts and possibilities in forensic intelligence. *Forensic Science International, 162*(1–3), 38–43.

Blakey, D. (2000). *Under the microscope: Thematic inspection report on scientific and technical support.* London: Her Majesty's Inspector of Constabulary.

Blakey, D. (2002). *Under the microscope: Refocused.* London: Her Majesty's Inspector of Constabulary.

Bradbury, S., & Feist, A. (2005). *The use of forensic science in volume crime investigations: A review of the research literature* (Home Office Online Report 43/05). London: Home Office.

Briody, M. (2002). The effects of DNA evidence on sexual offence cases in court. *Current Issues in Criminal Justice, 14*(3), 162–181.

Briody, M. (2004). The effects of DNA evidence on homicide cases in court. *Australian and New Zealand Journal of Criminology, 37,* 231–253.

Briody, M., & Prenzler, T. (2005). D.N.A. databases and property crime: A false promise? *Australian Journal of Forensic Sciences, 37*(2), 73–86.

Brown, C., Ross, A., & Slater, J. (2012). The end-to-end forensic identification process project. Paper presented at the 6th European Academy of Forensic Science Conference, Netherlands Forensic Institute, The Hague, Netherlands, August 20–24, 2012.

Brown, K. M., & Keppel, R. D. (2012). Child abduction murder: The impact of forensic evidence of solvability. *Journal of Forensic Sciences, 57*(2), 353–363.

Brown, S., & Willis, S. (2009). Complexity in forensic science. *Forensic Science Policy and Management: An International Journal, 1*(4), 192–198.

Burrows, J., Hopkins, M., Robinson, A., Speed, M., & Tilley, N. (2005). *Understanding the attrition process in volume crime investigation* (Home Office Research Study 295). London: Home Office.

Campbell, R., Patterson, D., & Bybee, D. (2012). Prosecution of adult sexual assault cases: A longitudinal analysis of the impact of sexual assault nurse examiner program. *Violence Against Women, 18*(2), 223–244.

Carter, M. (2006). *The importance of collaborative leadership in achieving effective criminal justice outcomes.* Silver Spring, MD: Centre for Effective Public Policy.

Crispino, F. (2008). Nature and place of crime scene management within forensic science. *Science & Justice, 48,* 24–28.

Denzin, N. K. (1970). *The research act in sociology.* Chicago: Aldine.

Dunsmuir, W., Tran, C., & Wetherburn, D. (2008). *Assessing the impact of mandatory DNA testing of prison inmates in NSW on clearance, charge and conviction rates for selected crime categories.* Sydney, NSW: Attorney General's Department, NSW Bureau of Crime Statistics and Research.

Durose, M. (2008). *Census of publicly funded forensic crime laboratories, 2005.* Washington, DC: Bureau of Justice Statistics.

Durose, M., Walsh, K., & Burch, A. (2012). *Census of publicly funded forensic crime laboratories, 2009.* Washington, DC: Bureau of Justice Statistics.

Edmond, G., & Roberts, A. (2011). The Law Commission's Report on expert evidence in criminal proceedings: Sufficiently reliable? *Criminal Law Review, 11,* 844–862.

Gould, J. B., Carrano, J., Leo, R., & Young, J. (2012). *Predicting erroneous convictions: A social science approach to miscarriages of justice.* Washington, DC: National Institute of Justice.

Houck, M. M., Riley, R. A., Speaker, P. J., & Witt, T. S. (2009). FORESIGHT: A business approach to improving forensic science services. *Forensic Science Policy & Management: An International Journal, 1*(2), 85–95.

Houck, M. M., Robertson, J., Found, B., Kobus, H., Lewis, S., Raymond, M., et al. (2011). A round table discussion on forensic science in Australia. *Forensic Science Policy and Management: An International Journal, 2*(1), 44–54.

Johnson, D., Peterson, J., Sommers, I., & Baskin, D. (2012). Use of forensic science in investigating crimes of sexual violence: Contrasting its theoretical potential with empirical realities. *Violence Against Women, 18*(2), 193–222.

Julian, R., Kelty, S. F., & Robertson, J. (2012). Get it right the first time: Critical issues at the crime scene. *Current Issues in Criminal Justice, 24*(1), 25–38.

Julian, R., Kelty, S. F., Roux, C., Woodman, P., Robertson, J., Davey, A., et al. (2011). What is the value of forensic science? An overview of the effectiveness of forensic science in the Australian criminal justice system project. *Australian Journal of Forensic Sciences, 43*(4), 217–229.

Kelty, S. F., Julian, R., & Ross, A. (2012, November 16). Dismantling the Justice Silos: Avoiding the pitfalls and reaping the benefits of information-sharing between forensic science, medicine and law. *Forensic Science International.* doi:10.1016/j.forsciint.2012.10.032

Kobus, H., Houck, M., Speaker, P., Riley, R., & Witt, T. (2011). Managing performance in the forensic sciences: Expectations in light of limited budgets. *Forensic Science Policy and Management: An International Journal, 2*(1), 36–43.

Mason, J. (1998). *Qualitative researching.* Thousand Oaks, CA: Sage.

McClellan, P. (2009). Admissibility of expert evidence under the Uniform Evidence Act. Paper presented at the Emerging Issues in Expert Evidence Workshop, Judicial College of Victoria, Melbourne, October 2, 2009.

McCulloch, H. (1996). *Police use of forensic science.* London: Home Office Police Research Group.

National Academy of Sciences. (2009). *Strengthening forensic science in the United States: A path forward.* Washington, DC: National Academies Press.

Peterson, J., & Hickman, M. (2005). *Census of publicly funded forensic crime laboratories, 2002.* Washington, DC: U.S. Department of Justice.

Peterson, J. L, Hickman, M. J., Strom, K. J., & Johnson, D. J. (2012). Effect of forensic evidence on criminal justice case processing. *Journal of Forensic Sciences.* doi: 10.1111/1556–4029.12020

Peterson, J. L., Sommers, I., Baskin, D., & Johnson, D. (2010). *The role and impact of forensic evidence in the criminal justice process.* Washington, DC: National Institute of Justice.

Rayment, K. (2010). Faith in DNA: The Vincent Report. *Journal of Law, Information and Science, 20*(1), 214–219.

Ribaux, O., Baylon, A., Lock, E., Delémont, O., Roux, C., Zingg, C., et al. (2010). Intelligence-led crime scene processing. Part II: Intelligence and crime scene examination. *Forensic Science International, 199*(1–3), 63–71.

Ribaux, O., Baylon, A., Roux, C., Delémont, O., Lock, E., Zingg, C., et al. (2010). Intelligence-led crime scene processing. Part I: Forensic intelligence. *Forensic Science International, 195*(1–3), 10–16.

Roman, J. K., Reid, S. E., Chalfin, A. J., & Knight, C. R. (2009). The DNA field experiment: A randomised trial of the cost-effectiveness of using DNA to solve property crimes. *Journal of Experimental Criminology, 5*, 345–369.

Ross, A. (2012). Forensic science in Australia: Where does Australia sit in relation to trends and issues in the international context? *Current Issues in Criminal Justice, 24*(1), 121–130.

Roux, C., Crispino, F., & Ribaux, O. (2012). From forensics to forensic science. *Current Issues in Criminal Justice, 24*(1), 7–25.

Roux, C., Julian, R., Kelty, S. F., & Ribaux, O. (2014). Forensic science effectiveness. In G. Bruinsma & D. Weisburd (Eds.), *Encyclopedia of criminology and criminal justice* (pp. 1795–1805). New York: Springer Science & Business Media.

Sangha, B., Roach, K., & Moles, R. (2010). *Forensic investigations and miscarriages of justice: The rhetoric meets the reality.* Toronto, ON: Irwin Law.

Schroeder, A. (2007). DNA and homicide clearance: What's really going on? Paper presented to the "Miscarriages of Justice: Current Perspectives" conference, Warrensburg, MO, February 19–21, 2007.

Schroeder, A., & White, M. D. (2009). Exploring the use of DNA evidence in homicide investigations: Implications for detective work and case clearance. *Police Quarterly, 12*(3), 319–342.

Smith, A. (2004). Programme delivery and the impact on combating crime and practical implementation issues. Paper presented to "Beyond DNA in the UK: Integration and Harmonisation" conference, Newport, South Wales, May 17–19, 2004.

Smith, J. A. (1995). Semi-structured interviewing and qualitative analysis. In J. A. Smith, R. Harré, & L. Van Langenhove (Eds.), *Rethinking methods in psychology* (pp. 9–27). Thousand Oaks, CA: Sage.

Strom, K. J., & Hickman, M. (2010). Unanalyzed evidence in law-enforcement agencies: A national examination of forensic processing in police departments. *Criminology and Public Policy, 9*(2), 381–404.

Strom, K. J., Ropero-Miller, J., Shelton, J., Sikes, N., Pope, M., & Horstmann, N. (2009). *The 2007 survey of law enforcement forensic evidence processing, final report.* Washington, DC: National Institute of Justice.

Tilley, N., & Ford, A. (1996). *Forensic science and crime investigation.* London: Home Office Police Research Group.

Tilley, N., & Townsley, M. (2009). Forensic science in UK policing: Strategies, tactics and effectiveness. In J. Fraser & R. Williams (Eds.), *Handbook of forensic science* (pp. 359–383). Cullompton, UK: Willan Publishing, Cullompton.

Tjin-A-Tsoi, T. (2013). *Trends, challenges and strategy in the forensic science sector.* Netherlands Forensic Institute White Paper. Retrieved from www.forensicinstitute.nl/about_nfi/news/2013/white-paper-on-trends-challenges-and-strategy-in-forensic-science.aspx

Vincent, F. H. R. (2010). *Inquiry into the circumstances that led to the conviction of Mr Farah Abdulkadir Jama.* Melbourne, Australia: Victorian Government Printer.

Werrett, D. J., & Sparkes, R. (Eds.). (1998). *Proceedings of Ninth International Symposium on Human Identification.* Madison, WI: Promega Corporation.

Yin, R. (1998). *Case study research: Design and methods.* Thousand Oaks, Sage.

8

Assessing the Utility of DNA Evidence in Criminal Investigations

Michael D. White, Andrea R. Borrego, and David A. Schroeder

Introduction

Supreme Court of California, County of Los Angeles in the matter of the State of California versus Orenthal James Simpson, case number BA 097211. We the jury, in the above-entitled action, find the defendant, Orenthal James Simpson, *not guilty* of the crime of murder.

Property crime cases where DNA evidence is processed have more than twice as many suspects identified, twice as many suspects arrested, and more than twice as many cases accepted for prosecution compared with traditional investigation . . . [O]ur research suggests that large numbers of offenders not currently identified by traditional investigations could be identified via DNA. (Roman et al., 2008, pp. 3, 6)

Over the past two decades, the development of techniques to analyze DNA evidence has garnered significant public attention and raised questions about its potential impact on the clearance and prosecution of certain crimes. Conventional wisdom suggests that DNA evidence helps investigators solve crimes, particularly homicides (Fisher, 2000; Gaines & Kappeler, 2005; Geberth, 1996; Gilbert, 1983; Inman & Rudin, 2001; Lyman, 1999; Schroeder, 2007). Media portrayals support this notion, with more than a dozen television shows detailing how DNA evidence is used as an investigative "super weapon" to routinely arrest offenders in criminal cases. However, there have been few empirical studies examining this issue, and as a result, little is known about how evidence likely to yield DNA (hereafter referred to as DNA evidence) is utilized by police during criminal investigations, as well as how its use has, over time, influenced clearance rates.

The two quotes above serve as anchors to the development and examination of DNA evidence as a tool for detectives. The O.J. Simpson murder investigation and prosecution in 1995 represented a watershed moment for DNA, as blood evidence collected both at the crime scene and in Simpson's house tied him to the crime. Of course, Simpson was acquitted of all criminal charges in that case, in large part because of questions raised about DNA evidence and the chain of custody.[1] The second quote is from Roman et al.'s (2008) study examining the impact of DNA evidence in high-volume crimes including burglary. Though the researchers note the value of DNA evidence in providing workable leads for investigators (e.g., suspect identification), they go on to note that the collection and processing of the evidence is costly, resource intensive, and complex.

In this chapter, the authors explore the approximately 15 years between these two anchors, and offer an assessment of the current state of evidence regarding the utility of DNA for criminal investigations conducted by law enforcement agencies. The chapter is divided into two sections. The first section provides a review of the available empirical evidence to date on the use of DNA evidence in criminal investigations, particularly in homicide cases. This section includes a description of the authors' own study of DNA evidence in homicide investigations conducted by the New York Police Department (NYPD), as well as a brief overview of a current project led by one of the authors in the state of Connecticut. The second section focuses on explanatory perspectives for understanding the use of DNA by law enforcement, and the authors highlight the Diffusion of Innovation perspective as a useful framework. Comparisons are drawn between DNA evidence—a slowly diffusing technology—and the TASER—a rapidly diffusing technology—to highlight the utility of the framework for understanding current use of DNA evidence in criminal investigations.

Empirical Evidence on the Utility of DNA Evidence in Criminal Investigations

THE EMERGENCE OF DNA EVIDENCE

The *Locard exchange principle* asserts that "whenever two objects come into contact, a mutual exchange of matter will take place between them" (Miller, 2003, pp. 116–117). This principle is at the foundation of crime scene investigation, as it maintains that offenders leave behind trace physical evidence at the scene of a crime, typically through contact with the victim. The presence of trace physical evidence represents a workable lead for detectives as they seek to identify and arrest the offender who committed the crime. One potential source of physical evidence is deoxyribonucleic acid—DNA. DNA

---

[1]Blood evidence and DNA testing represented a key component of the prosecution's case, but additional evidence was presented. For more detail on the trial and the evidence presented, see http://usatoday30.usatoday.com/news/index/nns25.htm.

is essentially a genetic fingerprint that can be extracted from any human cell that contains a nucleus—most commonly from blood, hair, semen, or saliva. DNA testing was first used in the mid-1980s (Morton, 2001), but it gained worldwide attention as part of the O.J. Simpson murder trial in the early 1990s (e.g., see the quote at the beginning of the chapter). By 1996, DNA evidence from 15,000 criminal cases was referred to publicly operated DNA labs for analysis, and by 2000, that number was up to 25,000 (BJS, 2002a, 2002b).

Forensic evidence, particularly DNA, has been a tremendously popular topic in the media. Television shows such as the *CSI* series depict police investigators and prosecutors routinely using DNA in their daily activities. For example, in a typical *CSI* episode, the investigators collect evidence from the crime scene, take it back to the lab for analysis, and, within minutes, have the results to narrow (or broaden) their search for the killer. By the end of the episode (and apparently before the end of their work shift), the murderer is confronted with the DNA evidence and he/she gives a complete confession that includes motive and method. This highly unrealistic depiction of detectives' use of DNA evidence has led some to posit a "*CSI* effect," whereby real-life attitudes are affected by these media portrayals (Dowler, Fleming, & Muzzatti 2006; Goodman-Delahunty & Tait, 2006; see Chapter 2, this volume). However, until recently, there has been very little empirical research on the role and influence of DNA in the criminal justice process, particularly at the pre-arrest stage.

DNA EVIDENCE AND CRIMINAL INVESTIGATIONS

Available research suggests that there is a substantial divide between the potential utility of DNA evidence in criminal investigations and its actual use by detectives. On the one hand, the potential impact of DNA evidence on police work is profound. DNA evidence has the potential to create new investigative leads and accurately identify criminal offenders (or rule out potential offenders), which should lead to increases in arrests and prosecutions (Strom & Hickman, 2010). It can also aid in the release of wrongfully convicted individuals (Geisser, 2000; Weir, 2000; Wilson, McClure, & Weisburd, 2010). On the other hand, there are numerous barriers to the widespread use of DNA evidence in criminal investigations. Researchers have identified two problems, in particular, that have limited its utility: the time it takes to process DNA samples (i.e., DNA backlogs) and its actual value in helping to solve crimes—especially homicides (Balding, 2000; Pratt et al., 2006).

DNA Backlogs

The widespread use of DNA in the 1990s spurred the creation of DNA databases by local, state, and federal government agencies, resulting in a centralized network of DNA profiles called the Combined DNA Index System (CODIS; National Institute of Justice [NIJ], 2002). CODIS includes three hierarchical components that separate systems into a local-level DNA Index System (LDIS), a state-level DNA Index System (SDIS), and a national-level DNA Index System (NDIS), which is managed by the Federal Bureau of Investigation under the DNA Identification Act of 1994 (FBI, 2000). Management of LDIS and SDIS varies by state with each level having its own protocols and requirements. The submission of DNA evidence to CODIS is a time- and resource-intensive process that requires collaborative efforts from prosecutors, law enforcement, and forensic laboratories.

Two national surveys of DNA crime laboratories conducted in 1997 and 2000 revealed extensive backlogs of evidence waiting to be tested (Steadman, 2000, 2002). Similarly, a 2002 national census of public crime laboratories reported more than 262,000 backlogged cases and roughly 500,000 backlogged requests for evidence to be tested (Peterson & Hickman, 2005). The census data was updated in 2005, again documenting persistent and growing case backlogs (Durose, 2008).

The U.S. Congress responded to the large backlog in cases by allocating more funds (Strom & Hickman, 2010). In a recent National Institute of Justice (NIJ) report, state and local forensic laboratories reported increases in efficiency of processing and analyzing DNA cases (Lothridge, 2009), but these developments have failed to significantly reduce the existing DNA backlogs (Strom & Hickman, 2010). In another NIJ-funded study, researchers sought to estimate the size of the national backlog of unsolved criminal cases through a survey of a nationally representative sample of local law enforcement agencies (Lovrich et al., 2004; Pratt et al., 2006). The study reported a national estimate of 542,723 unsolved rape, homicide, and property crimes with possible DNA evidence that had not yet been processed (Pratt et al., 2006). More recently, Strom and Hickman (2010) surveyed a nationally representative sample of state and local law enforcement agencies over a five-year period, but included a broader range of forensic evidence. This study confirmed the existence of a substantial backlog of unsolved homicide and rape cases containing forensic evidence.

While both studies cited backlogs in the laboratory as a contributing factor, they also identified several other reasons for the lack of use of DNA evidence. Lovrich and colleagues (2004) found that barriers to processing DNA evidence as reported by the agencies included: no identified suspect, suspect not charged, guilty plea anticipated, lack of funding for DNA analysis, backlog in the laboratory, and analysis is not requested by the prosecution. Strom and Hickman (2010) noted that the inability of crime laboratories to keep pace with submitted evidence was cited as a contributing factor, but respondents more commonly cited other factors to explain the backlog of untested forensic evidence, such as no identified suspect. The authors note that their findings highlight a knowledge gap regarding the potential investigative utility of forensic evidence (Strom & Hickman, 2010).

Assessing the Value of DNA Evidence to Detective Work

A second important question regarding DNA is whether the evidence can improve the effectiveness of the police in terms of solving crimes. A handful of studies have recently sought to explore this question. Briody (2004) examined DNA evidence and case outcomes across a sample of sexual offenses, homicides, serious assaults, and property crimes in Australia, and reported that the presence of DNA evidence increased the likelihood of convictions for all four types of crimes (see also Dunsmuir, Tran, & Weatherburn, 2008). Tully (1998) compared cases from Maryland across three different categories: cases with DNA, historical cases from 1979 to 1986 with biological evidence (pre-DNA), and current cases with biological evidence but no DNA test results. Tully found that the use of DNA was associated with an increased likelihood of positive criminal justice outcomes, especially for conviction in rape cases.

Alternatively, Schroeder and White (2009) examined homicide case files in Manhattan from 1996 to 2003 to explore the actual use of DNA evidence by detectives, as well as how DNA influenced the likelihood of case clearance. The authors classified case files into three different categories, depicted in Table 8.1. Of the 593 cases

Table 8.1 Categories of Homicide Cases in Manhattan, 1996–2003

Year	DNA Not Collected	DNA Collected, Results Not Available	DNA Collected, Results Available
1996	68.1% (94)	26.1% (36)	5.8% (8)
1997	58.8% (57)	34.0% (33)	7.2% (7)
1998	54.4% (31)	43.9% (25)	1.8% (1)
1999	52.6% (41)	35.9% (28)	11.6% (9)
2000	51.5% (34)	43.9% (29)	4.5% (3)
2001	45.3% (24)	50.9% (27)	3.8% (2)
2002	45.1% (23)	45.1% (23)	9.8% (5)
2003	35.8% (19)	54.7% (29)	9.4% (5)
Total	54.5% (323)	38.8% (230)	6.7% (40)
Case Clearance Rate	57.0% (184)	73.9% (170)	27.5% (11)

NOTE: Chi square = 37.319 $(p < .001)$

reviewed, 54.5% of the case investigations did not involve the collection of DNA evidence; 38.8% of the cases involved the collection of DNA evidence, but test results were not available over the course of the investigation; and 6.7% of the cases had DNA evidence that was collected, analyzed, and available to detectives. Moreover, the far-right column in Table 8.1 shows that the use of DNA evidence in homicides changed little over the course of the study period, from 5.8% in 1996 to just 9.4% in 2003. Notably, there are significant changes over time in the other two case categories, as DNA evidence was increasingly collected over time—with results not being available to investigators.

The second part of Schroeder and White's (2009) study examined how DNA evidence affects the likelihood of clearance in those investigations. Table 8.1 (bottom) shows that case clearance rates were highest (73.9%) among the category of cases where DNA evidence was collected but not examined, and lowest (27.5%) among the category of cases where DNA evidence was collected and test results were available to detectives. The authors also ran multivariate models to identify predictors of case clearance, and DNA evidence was strongly and negatively associated with both clearance and time to clearance. These findings led Schroeder and White to conclude that in New York from 1996 to 2003, DNA evidence was a tool of last resort for homicide detectives—a tool that was used only when all else has failed.

Roman et al. (2008) employed a prospective, randomized controlled trial to test the impact of DNA evidence on criminal investigations involving property crimes in five U.S. cities. The study randomly assigned a total of 2,160 residential and commercial burglary cases to two different conditions: immediate DNA testing and delayed DNA testing (60 days). For all five sites, rapid DNA results led to an increase in suspect identification and suspect arrests, and in two sites, led to an increased acceptance for prosecution (in Denver and Los Angeles). Roman et al. also highlighted the challenges associated with increased use of DNA evidence and concluded that "since DNA-led investigations are more costly than business as usual, substantial additional invest-ments will be required to expand the capacity of crime laboratories, police, and pros-ecutors to use this investigative tool efficiently" (p. 6).

Peterson et al. (2010) conducted a multi-site examination of the utility of forensic evidence using crime lab, investigative, and prosecutorial case file information for five crime categories: assault, burglary, homicide, rape, and robbery. Peterson et al. con-cluded,

> While the current study shows that forensic evidence can affect case processing decisions, it is not uniform across all crimes and all evidence types; the effects of evidence vary depending upon criminal offense, variety of forensic evidence, the criminal decision level, and other characteristics of the case. (p. 7)

Peterson et al. also outlined 10 recommendations regarding future research on the util-ity of forensic evidence. Baskin and Sommers (2011) subsequently re-analyzed por-tions of the Peterson et al. (2010) data to investigate the impact of forensic evidence on residential burglary cases in five jurisdictions in the United States. The authors found that forensic evidence was used in a small number of cases and had a minimal impact on arrest, charging, and conviction outcomes. More recently, Peterson et al. (2013) examined the role and impact of forensic evidence on case-processing outcomes in a sample of 4,205 criminal cases. The authors reported that, although forensic evidence was infrequently collected in serious criminal investigations (with the exception of homicide), the evidence "played a consistent and robust role in case-processing deci-sions," including arrest, charges being filed, conviction, and sentence length (p. S78).

In response to the recommendations outlined by Peterson et al. (2010), Schroeder (2011) has been funded by NIJ to track the collection, analysis, and dissemination of forensic evidence for a significant number of criminal cases in the state of Connecticut, from the years 2006 through 2009. This research is currently ongoing and the results will be available in 2015. The study's scope and breadth should provide tangible indica-tions of which types of criminal investigations are better served by the use of DNA evidence, as well as how this type of forensic evidence complemented other types of evidence such as witness statements and suspect confession.

Lastly, Wilson, Weisburd, and McClure (2011) synthesized the existing evidence on the effectiveness of DNA testing for criminal justice outcomes (in a Campbell Collaboration Systematic Review). Wilson and colleagues concluded that for serious crimes, DNA testing is worth the fiscal resources and time, but they noted that this might not always be the case for less serious crimes, such as property and robbery crimes. Although it is time-consuming, and cost-benefit analysis is warranted for dif-ferent types of crime, Wilson et al. concluded that "the possibility that DNA will solve an otherwise unsolvable case in these serious crimes is compelling" (p. 24).

Explanatory Frameworks for Understanding Law Enforcement's Use of DNA Evidence

The previous section highlighted two important findings involving the use of DNA evidence in criminal investigations. First, DNA evidence clearly has great potential in terms of its capacity to identify suspects and solve crimes that would otherwise remain unsolved. Second, despite its great potential, there are significant barriers to its routine use including a significant and persistent backlog of cases with evidence waiting to be tested, and mixed results on its actual utility for criminal investigations.

There are numerous potential explanatory frameworks that can help understand the use of DNA evidence by law enforcement in criminal investigations, especially for serious crimes. Schroeder and White (2009) identified three potential frameworks, drawn from the literature on homicide investigation (see also Simon, 1991; Puckett & Lundman, 2003):

- *Discretionary framework:* Police employ discretion when conducting a homicide investigation, and the level of effort they exert varies based on certain extra-legal characteristics, such as victim race and social class (Black, 1980; Quinney, 1977).

- *Full investigation framework:* All homicides receive aggressive investigative effort regardless of victim characteristics (Klinger, 1997; Wolfgang, 1958).

- *Organizational resistance framework:* Since police departments are complex bureaucracies defined by rigidity, inflexibility, and resistance to change (Perrow, 1972; Wilson, 1989), detectives will resist the infusion of new techniques into their investigative repertoire, choosing instead to rely on more "tried and true" traditional methods.

Schroeder and White (2009) found that each of these frameworks was unable to explain their New York findings. They go on to suggest that the Diffusion of Innovation framework offers an interesting and useful backdrop for examining this question. *Diffusion* refers to the spread of an idea, information, tool, or practice from a source to a larger group (Rogers, 1995). Whether an innovation spreads, as well as the rate of diffusion, is greatly affected by a number of things related to the innovation and those considering its adoption. Wejnert (2002) recently extended the Diffusion of Innovation theory by creating a single conceptual framework that includes three different sets of factors that can influence diffusion—characteristics of the innovation (public and private consequences; costs and benefits), the innovators (nature of the entity, status, and personal characteristics), and the environment (geographic and political conditions, and societal culture)—and by highlighting the interplay across these factors.

DIFFUSION OF INNOVATION: A COMPARISON OF TWO TECHNOLOGIES

Earlier portions of this chapter have demonstrated that a number of factors serve as barriers to the diffusion of DNA evidence, and each of these barriers fit into the Diffusion framework. Alternatively, this framework can also be used to explain why another technology—the TASER—has diffused rapidly in law enforcement. For example, since *TASER International* (TI) introduced their M26 and X26 TASER models in 1999 and 2003, respectively, the diffusion of the weapon in American law enforcement has been quite remarkable. By January 2012, more than 12,000 police departments in the United States have purchased the device (two-thirds of all departments), including departments in 29 of the 33 largest cities (NIJ, 2011; see also http://www.taser.com).

From the Diffusion of Innovation perspective, the widespread and rapid diffusion of the TASER serves as an illustrative counterpoint to the slow diffusion of DNA evidence. The remainder of this chapter is devoted to an examination of each of these technologies across the elements of the Diffusion of Innovation framework.[2]

Characteristics of the Innovation

This component of the framework deals with aspects of the innovation itself that have influenced diffusion, most notably the costs and benefits of adoption. Clearly, those innovations that bring with them more risks than rewards will not diffuse rapidly (or at all), compared to innovations with greater upsides (Klinger, 2003).

DNA Evidence: There are a number of "costs" associated with DNA evidence that have hindered its diffusion, most notably the time required to conduct testing and obtain results. Law enforcement responses to Pratt et al.'s (2006) survey highlight the significance of the time lag issue. For example, one respondent stated that "[the] state laboratory has more than a 4-year wait for processing DNA from property crimes. Therefore, we do not submit it unless the crime is of major significance" (p. 41). Quite simply, detectives do not have the luxury to wait around for months to get DNA test results back—administrative pressures, resources constraints, and public scrutiny require that they clear cases much more quickly. In Wejnert's (2002) terms, there is an incompatibility between the "characteristics of the innovation" and the "needs of the actor" (p. 303).

The "objective feasibility" of DNA evidence may also be limited because, in many cases, detectives do not need DNA evidence. Oftentimes, they can clear the case without DNA evidence (e.g., in Simon's [1991] term, some cases are *dunkers*). Or in other cases, there is no available evidence at the scene that could produce a DNA sample (i.e., a *whodunit* where there is no physical evidence). Moreover, probable cause can be attained through a host of means other than DNA. The authors' anecdotal discussions with detectives as part of their NYPD study highlighted this component of the Diffusion framework, as investigators consistently indicated that they would use DNA evidence when needed; they just did not need it that often.

The TASER: In terms of benefits, the TASER offers a number of advantages over other less-lethal alternatives including its relatively short duration of recovery time among those who are exposed, its reliability from a distance, its compact size and utility, and its perceived effectiveness (White & Ready, 2010). Research has consistently confirmed the efficacy of the device in terms of overcoming suspect resistance and reducing suspect and officer injuries (NIJ, 2011; Smith et al., 2007, 2009; White & Ready, 2007, 2010).

There are also costs or risks associated with the TASER, however. Like any technology, the TASER has direct costs for those considering its adoption. For example, the price of a new X26 TASER device is currently $779.95, with each cartridge costing

---

[2]These technologies are obviously very different. The comparison is made for illustrative purposes to highlight the potential explanatory value of the Diffusion of Innovation framework. Also, given space constraints, the authors are unable to cover all aspects of the Diffusion framework.

about $25.[3] More generally, prior research on police use of the TASER has identified several areas of concern, such as general policy-related questions governing use of the device (e.g., when, against whom, etc.).[4] Another area of concern involves the physiological effects of the TASER, most notably whether it poses an increased risk of death (e.g., approximately 400 people have died subsequent to TASER exposure; see White et al., 2013). Importantly, a large body of research has examined the physiological risks associated with the TASER and concluded that the device is comparatively safe. The National Institute of Justice (2011) recently concluded: "The risk of death in a CED-related use-of-force incident is less than 0.25 percent" (p. viii). In sum, the current research suggests that the risks associated with adoption of the TASER are outweighed by the benefits of the device.

Characteristics of the Innovators

Wejnert (2002) stated that there are also numerous aspects of the innovators or adopters themselves, in this case police departments, which influence the rate of diffusion. One of the most important of these features is familiarity with the innovation. In simple terms, as the novelty of an innovation decreases, its rate of diffusion will tend to increase.

DNA Evidence: Familiarity with the technology surrounding DNA evidence and its collection likely serves as a barrier to its diffusion. The production of a viable DNA test result hinges on a good deal of officer expertise. That is, the crime scene investigator (often a patrol officer in a small department) must identify the evidence, then properly collect, store, and transport it without contamination. Given that more than half of the police departments in the United States are staffed by fewer than 10 officers, it is reasonable to conclude that many police departments across the United States lack the equipment, expertise, and familiarity required to collect evidence likely to yield a DNA sample. Moreover, most law enforcement agencies do not operate their own crime laboratories and must send out evidence for processing. The introduction of factors outside of their control likely serves to inhibit familiarity with DNA evidence and the testing process. Roman et al. (2008) highlighted the complexities surrounding use of DNA evidence, for both police and other stakeholders:

> A gap arises because the capacity of police and labs to identify and collect DNA is limited, crime laboratories are severely constrained in their ability to process biological evidence in volume, and prosecutors have not prepared for the impact of large numbers of cases where DNA evidence is the primary source of offender identification. (p. 6)

---

[3]This is the model (and price) available to law enforcement agencies in January 2013. TASER International has recently developed a new model, called the X2, to replace the older X26. The X2 costs approximately $1,200. Also, a police department's decision to adopt the TASER will likely have other indirect financial costs, such as expenses associated with training, supervision, and changes in policies and procedures.

[4]There are standards and guidelines promulgated by leadership organizations such as the International Association of Chiefs of Police and Police Executive Research Forum.

The TASER: There are a variety of formal and informal networks, advocacy groups, and websites that have served to increase familiarity with the TASER among potential adopters. There are several leadership organizations in law enforcement in the United States (e.g., International Association of Chiefs of Police), and these organizations have offered important information and guidance to local law enforcement on emerging TASER technology. Moreover, there are two additional information sources that have served to increase familiarity with the TASER. The first is the media. For example, from 2002 to 2004, Ready, White, and Fisher (2008) documented a more than 700% increase in the number of news reports about the TASER (see also White & Ready, 2009). Second, *TASER International,* the manufacturer of the most popular Conducted Energy Weapons (M26 and X26), is also an important source of information on the innovation. *TASER International* is very proactive in terms of marketing and advertising, and the company has no doubt played a role in increasing the familiarity (and, as a result, the diffusion) of their device.[5]

Characteristics of the Environment

The Diffusion framework also takes into account the culture or environment of the innovators. Two environmental characteristics are noteworthy when considering the diffusion of technology in policing. The first involves political considerations, and the second involves the police subculture and its traditional resistance to change.

DNA Evidence: Whether it is related to the bureaucratic nature of a police agency or the subcultural norms that govern a department, diffusion of an innovation can be slowed by organizational inertia. Notably, this inertia is perhaps greatest in specialized units, particularly those that investigate serious crimes such as homicide. The investigation of homicide has been romanticized countless times in television and the movies, and these depictions center on "hardened" detectives matching wits with criminals using their intuition, experience, and dedication to solve heinous crimes. Although technological innovation has recently crept into these media depictions (e.g., *CSI*), portrayals are highly unrealistic, and real-life detectives are likely reluctant to adopt new technologies that they deem to be unproven.

The costs associated with DNA testing, and the pressure to solve cases quickly also likely inhibit the widespread diffusion of DNA evidence. For example, the technology required for DNA evidence collection and testing may not be universally available or the cost of it may be prohibitive. For those departments who run their own crime labs, additional costs include equipment, training, and manpower (e.g., see Pratt et al., 2006). Also, there is often significant pressure on detectives to solve homicides, and investigators understand that the likelihood of solving the crime decreases with the passage of time (e.g., the first 48 hours are deemed to be crucial). More generally, clearance rates in homicides are often touted as a departmental performance measure (Simon, 1991), which also increases pressure on detectives to solve cases quickly. In short, both the internal culture of the police and the demands of the external environment may serve to inhibit diffusion of DNA evidence in criminal investigations.

---

[5]The forensics field is similar in that companies are aggressive in the marketing of their products, from evidence seals and labels to fingerprinting equipment and gunshot residue–collection kits.

The TASER: There are several aspects of culture that are especially relevant for examination of the TASER. The first is the court system. The courts play a critical role through examination of use of force incidents on a case-by-case basis to assess reasonableness (i.e., *Graham v. Connor* [1989, 490 U.S. 386]), and courts have recognized and accepted the TASER as a viable and useful less-lethal alternative for police (Smith et al., 2007). The second aspect that is relevant for the TASER discussion is the police culture. Unlike DNA evidence, the traditional inflexibility that defines the police has not inhibited the diffusion of the TASER. This acceptance of the TASER among the organizational culture is likely tied to convergence between courts' acceptance of the device, police departments' goals (overcoming resistance while minimizing injuries and deaths), and the effectiveness of the TASER in terms of achieving those goals.

Table 8.2 summarizes the comparison of the diffusion of DNA evidence and the TASER across the three elements of the Diffusion of Innovation framework. With each element of the framework—characteristics of the innovation, the innovators, and the environment—there is clear evidence explaining why the TASER has diffused rapidly, and why DNA evidence has diffused slowly.

Table 8.2   Using the Diffusion of Innovation Framework to Compare Two Technologies

Framework	DNA Evidence	TASER
Characteristics of the Innovation • "Objective feasibilities" • Costs vs. benefits	• Cost • Time lag • Resource constraints • Equipment, lab access • "Dunkers" (not needed)	• Compact; easy to use • Effectiveness (injuries, resistance) • Quick recovery time • Reduces "hands-on" • Risks? (many resolved)
Characteristics of the Innovators	• Expertise required • Familiarity? (increasing for sure) • Support from professional networks? • Reliance on external sources (crime labs)	• Professional networks support it (IACP, PERF, etc.) • TI—strong marketing • Limited training required • No dependence on others
Environmental Context	• Homicide unit culture ("tried and true" methods) • Skepticism about utility • The first 48 hours . . . • Views changing based on expectations (jurors and the *CSI* effect; prosecutors)	• Acceptance by the courts • Police culture— openness to alternatives in use of force arena

Using the Diffusion Framework to Predict
the Popularity of Emerging Technologies

The authors acknowledge the limitations of comparing the TASER to DNA evidence, though the Diffusion framework clearly offers important insights. The framework can also be used to assess the probable diffusion of emerging technologies such as officer body-worn camera systems and unmanned drones. A quick consideration of on-officer camera systems highlights this point, and perhaps represents a middle ground between the TASER and DNA evidence. A number of companies (e.g., VIEVU, *TASER International*) have begun marketing camera systems that are worn by police officers, either attached to sunglasses or on the officer's uniform. For example, the VIEVU website states that 2,800 law enforcement agencies are currently using their product (http://www.vievu.com). The diffusion of this technology in law enforcement, like the discussion of the other technologies above, will be determined by characteristics of the innovation, the innovators, and the environment. With regard to the innovation, the key questions involve the costs of the technology and its "objective feasibilities." For example, agencies that purchase the cameras must also pay for video storage. Moreover, earlier models of the camera systems were seen by officers as too bulky, and many officers complained of headaches when wearing the sunglass version. Alternatively, the technology offers a number of advantages for police. For example, *TASER International* notes that their AXON product can improve behavior of citizens and police during encounters, reduce false complaints and lawsuits, enhance public trust, and save time and resources (e.g., less report writing; http://www.taser.com/products/on-officer-video). These are clearly important objectives for the police, and the diffusion of the technology will hinge on whether it can deliver on these outcomes.

With regard to characteristics of the innovators, agencies must overcome the skepticism of rank-and-file officers (and their unions), particularly with regard to how the video will be used and monitored by the department leadership (e.g., "big brother," or used by supervisors to "go fishing" against officers). Ultimately, officers' acceptance of the camera systems will be determined by its perceived utility. If officers believe that the camera protects them from false complaints, or that it improves citizen behavior, the technology will be accepted and become more familiar. Last, characteristics of the environment will influence its diffusion as well. Will citizens view the technology as an invasion of their privacy? Or will citizens see the technology as an effort to increase police accountability and thereby enhance police legitimacy?

Conclusion

The two quotes at the beginning of this chapter demonstrate the significant advances that have occurred over the last two decades involving DNA evidence, both with regard to the technology and its use in the criminal justice system. Still, there are significant barriers to widespread use of DNA evidence by police during criminal investigations, and the impact of DNA evidence on arrest, charging, and conviction outcomes remains unclear. The discussion of the Diffusion of Innovation framework, and the rudimentary comparison between DNA evidence and the TASER (and, to a lesser extent, on-officer camera systems), highlight how these barriers have served to limit the emergence of DNA evidence as a routine criminal investigative tool. Moreover, the conclusions of important research studies such as Roman et al. (2008), Peterson et al. (2010, 2013) and Wilson et al. (2011) offer important insights on next steps for research in this area. Clearly, DNA evidence holds great promise as an investigative tool, and as the barriers to its diffusion are overcome through research and technological innovation, that promise will most certainly be realized in the future.

References

Balding, D. J. (2000). Interpreting DNA evidence: Can probability theory help? In J. L. Gastwirth (Ed.), *Statistical science in the courtroom* (pp. 51–70). New York: Springer.

Baskin, D., & Sommers, I. (2011). Solving residential burglaries in the United States: The impact of forensic evidence on case outcomes. *International Journal of Police Science & Management , 13*(1), 70–86.

Black, D. J. (1980). *The manners and customs of the police.* New York: Academic Press.

Briody, M. (2004). *The effects of DNA evidence on the criminal justice process* (Doctoral dissertation, Griffith University). Retrieved from Dissertations and Theses Database (Australian Digital Theses Program).

Bureau of Justice Statistics (BJS). (2002a). *Prosecutors in state courts, 2001.* Washington, DC: U.S. Department of Justice. Retrieved from http://www.ojp.usdoj.gov/bjs/homicide/tables/vsextab.htm

Bureau of Justice Statistics (BJS). (2002b). *Survey of DNA crime laboratories, 2001.* Washington, DC: U.S. Department of Justice. Retrieved from http://www.ojp.usdoj.gov/bjs/homicide/tables/vsextab.htm

Dowler, K., Fleming, T., & Muzzatti, S. L. (2006). Constructing crime: Media, crime, and popular culture. *Canadian Journal of Criminology and Criminal Justice, 48,* 837–850.

Dunsmuir, W. T., Tran, C., & Weatherburn, D. (2008). *Assessing the impact of mandatory DNA testing of prison inmates in NSW on clearance, charge and conviction rates for selected crime categories.* State of New South Wales: Attorney General's Department of NSW.

Durose, M. (2008). *Census of publicly funded forensic crime laboratories, 2005.* Washington, DC: Bureau of Justice Statistics.

Federal Bureau of Investigation (FBI). (2000). Quality assurance standards of forensic DNA testing laboratories, Forensic Science Communications. Retrieved from http://www.fbi.gov/hq/lab/fsc/backissu/july2000/codispre.htm

Fisher, B. A. J. (2000). *Techniques of crime scene investigation* (6th ed.). New York: CRC Press.

Gaines, L. K., & Kappeler, V. E. (2005). *Policing in America* (5th ed.). New York: LexisNexis.

Geberth, V. J. (1996). *Practical homicide investigation.* New York: Elsevier.

Geisser, S. (2000). Statistics, litigation, and conduct unbecoming. In J. L. Gastwirth (Ed.), *Statistical science in the courtroom* (pp. 71–85). New York: Springer.

Gilbert, J. N. (1983). A study of the increased rate of unsolved criminal homicide in San Diego, California, and its relationship to police investigation effectiveness. *American Journal of Police, 2,* 149–166.

Goodman-Delahunty, J., & Tait, D. (2006). DNA and the changing face of justice. *Australian Journal of Forensic Science, 38,* 97–106.

Inman, K., & Rudin, N. (2001). *Principles and practice of criminalistics: The profession of forensic science.* New York: CRC Press.

Klinger, D. A. (1997). Negotiating order in patrol work: An ecological theory of police response to deviance. *Criminology, 35,* 277–306.

Klinger. D. A. (2003). Spreading diffusion in criminology. *Criminology and Public Policy, 2,* 461–468.

Lothridge, K. (2009). Presentation as part of the "Making Sense of the DNA Backlog" panel at the annual National Institute of Justice Research and Evaluation Conference, June 16, 2009, Arlington, VA.

Lovrich, N., Pratt, T., Gaffney, M., Johnson, C., Asplen, C., Hurst, L., et al. (2004). *National forensic DNA study report, final report* (Report No. 203970). Washington, DC: U.S. Department of Justice.

Lyman, M. D. (1999). *Criminal investigation: The art and the science.* Upper Saddle River, NJ: Prentice Hall.

Miller, M. T. (2003). Crime scene investigation. In S. H. James & J. J. Nordby (Eds.), *Forensic science: An introduction to scientific and investigative techniques* (pp. 115–136). New York: CRC Press.

Morton, J. (2001). *Catching the killers: The definitive history of criminal detection.* London: Ebury Press.

National Institute of Justice (NIJ). (2011). *Study of deaths following electro muscular disruption.* Washington, DC: National Institute of Justice.

Perrow, C. (1972). *Complex organizations: A critical essay.* Glenview, IL: Scott, Foresman.

Peterson, J., & Hickman, M. (2005). *Census of publicly funded forensic crime laboratories, 2002.* Washington, DC: U.S. Department of Justice.

Peterson, J., Hickman, M. J., Strom, K. J., & Johnson, D. J. (2013). Effect of forensic evidence on criminal justice processing. *Journal of Forensic Sciences, 58,* S78–S90.

Peterson, J., Sommers, I., Baskin, D., & Johnson, D. (2010). *The role and impact of forensic evidence in the criminal justice process.* Washington, DC: National Institute of Justice. Retrieved from http://www.ncjrs.gov/pdffiles1/nij/grants/231977.pdf

Pratt, T. C., Gaffney, M. J., Lovrich, N. P., & Johnson, C. L. (2006). This isn't *CSI*: Estimating the backlog of forensic DNA cases and the barriers associated with case processing. *Criminal Justice Policy Review, 17,* 32–47.

Puckett, J. L., & Lundman, R. J. (2003). Factors affecting homicide clearances: Multivariate analysis of a more complete conceptual framework. *Journal of Research in Crime and Delinquency, 40,* 171–193.

Quinney, R. (1977). *Class, state and crime.* New York: D. McKay.

Ready, J., White, M. D., & Fisher, C. F. (2008). Shock value: A comparative analysis of news reports and official police records on TASER deployments. *Policing: An International Journal of Police Strategies and Management, 31,* 148–170.

Rogers, E. M. (1995). *Diffusion of innovations* (4th ed.). New York: Free Press.

Roman, J. K., Reid, S., Reid, J., Chalfin, A, Adams, W., & Knight, C. (2008). *The DNA field experiment: Cost-effectiveness analysis of the use of DNA in the investigation of high-volume crimes* (Final Report submitted to the National Institute of Justice). Washington, DC: Urban Institute, Justice Policy Center.

Schroeder, D.A. (2007). DNA and homicide clearance: What's really going on? *Journal of the Institute of Justice & International Studies, 7,* 279–298.

Schroeder, D. A. (2011). The impact of forensic evidence on arrest and prosecution, *Grant Opportunity NIJ-2011-2822; NIJ FY 2011 Social Science Research on Forensic Science*, Awarded November 2011.

Schroeder, D. A., & White, M. D. (2009). Exploring the use of DNA evidence in homicide investigations: Implications for detective work and case clearance. *Police Quarterly*, *12*, 319–342.

Simon, D. (1991). *Homicide: A year on the killing streets.* Boston: Houghton Mifflin.

Smith, M. R., Kaminski, R. J., Alpert, G. P., Fridell, L. A., MacDonald, J., & Kubu, B. (2009). *A multi-method evaluation of police use of force outcomes.* Washington, DC: National Institute of Justice.

Smith, M. R., Kaminski, R. J., Rojek, J., Alpert, G. P., & Mathis, J. (2007). The impact of Conducted Energy Devices and other types of force and resistance on officer and suspect injuries. *Policing: An International Journal of Police Strategies and Management, 30*, 423–446.

Steadman, G. (2000). *Survey of DNA crime laboratories, 1998.* Washington, DC: U.S. Department of Justice.

Steadman, G. (2002). *Survey of DNA crime laboratories, 2001.* Washington, DC: U.S. Department of Justice.

Strom, K. J., & Hickman, M. J. (2010). Unanalyzed evidence in law-enforcement agencies: A national examination of forensic processing in police departments. *Criminology & Public Policy, 9*(2), 381–404.

Tully, L. (1998). *Examination of the use of forensic DNA typing from two perspectives* (Doctoral dissertation). University of Maryland, College Park.

Weir, B. S. (2000). The consequences of defending DNA statistics. In J. L. Gastwirth (Ed.), *Statistical science in the courtroom* (pp. 87–97). New York: Springer.

Wejnert, B. (2002). Integrating models of diffusion of innovations: A conceptual framework. *Annual Review of Sociology, 28*, 297–326.

White, M. D., & Ready, J. (2007). The TASER as a less-lethal force alternative: Findings on use and effectiveness in a large metropolitan police agency. *Police Quarterly, 10*, 170–191.

White, M. D., & Ready, J. (2009). Examining fatal and nonfatal incidents involving the TASER: Identifying predictors of suspect death reported in the media. *Criminology and Public Policy, 8*, 865–891.

White, M. D., & Ready, J. (2010). The impact of the TASER on suspect resistance: Identifying predictors of effectiveness. *Crime and Delinquency, 56*(1), 70–102.

White, M. D., Ready, J., Riggs, C., Dawes, D. M., Hinz, A., & Ho, J. D. (2013). An incident-level profile of TASER device deployments in arrest-related deaths. *Police Quarterly. 16*(1): 85–112.

Wilson, D. B., McClure, D., & Weisburd, D. (2010). Does forensic DNA help to solve crime? The benefit of sophisticated answers to naive questions. *Journal of Contemporary Criminal Justice, 26*(4), 458–469.

Wilson, D. B., Weisburd, D., & McClure, D. (2011). *Use of DNA testing in police investigative work for increasing offender identification, arrest, conviction and case clearance.* Oslo: Campbell Systematic Reviews.

Wilson, J. Q. (1989). *Bureaucracy.* New York: Basic Books.

Wolfgang, M. (1958). *Patterns in criminal homicide.* Philadelphia: University of Pennsylvania.

9

Forensic Science

The Prosecutor's Role

Nina W. Chernoff

Introduction

In August of 2013, police officers pulled over a car in Washington, DC.[1] There were four people in the car, including a 20-year-old college student named Daniel Green. A lawful police search revealed a gun in the car. A police lab fingerprint examiner then compared a latent print recovered from the gun to the prints of all four people in the car and determined that it "matched" Daniel's print. A prosecutor named Paula Smith now has the discretion to decide whether this is sufficient evidence to charge Daniel with possessing the gun—conduct that carries up to a five-year sentence.[2] If Paula does decide to charge Daniel, she must also decide whether and what kind of plea bargain to offer him. If the case goes to trial, Paula must decide whether and how to argue to the judge that the fingerprint evidence is reliable enough to be admitted, how to elicit testimony from the fingerprint analyst about the identification, what information to provide to the defense attorney and the judge about the fingerprint evidence, and what arguments to make to the jury about the reliability and significance of the fingerprint evidence.

Four years before Paula began to make decisions in Daniel Green's case, in August of 2009, a watershed critique of non-DNA forensic evidence—including fingerprint evidence—was issued by the National Research Council (NRC) of the National Academy of Science. The NRC committee had been tasked by Congress with studying forensic science, and included members of the scientific community, forensic practitioners, and legal experts. Their report, *Strengthening Forensic Science in the United States: A Path Forward*, was based on a comprehensive review of studies related to forensic disciplines, independent research, and testimony from experts in the field.

The NRC report reached the unequivocal conclusion that

[w]ith the exception of nuclear DNA analysis . . . *no forensic method* has been rigorously shown to have the capacity to consistently, and with a high degree of certainty, demonstrate a connection between evidence and a specific individual or source.[3]

In other words, no forensic method used in criminal cases can "consistently, and with a high degree of certainty" connect a piece of evidence with a specific criminal defendant. This conclusion was stated even more plainly by the co-chair of the NRC committee, the Honorable Harry T. Edwards, in his testimony before the Senate Committee on the Judiciary.[4] After more than 20 years as a federal judge, Judge Edwards explained that he had assumed that "forensic evidence offered in court is valid and reliable," but "I was surprisingly mistaken."

In particular, the NRC report exposed the "misconception that the forensic discipline of fingerprinting is infallible."[5] The report concluded that the method of evaluating fingerprints, commonly known as "ACE-V,"[6] "is not specific enough to qualify as a validated method," "does not guard against bias; is too broad to ensure repeatability and transparency; and does not guarantee that two analysts following it will obtain the same results."[7] The NRC report cited "a thorough analysis of the ACE-V method" and its "unambiguous" conclusion: "We have reviewed available scientific evidence of the validity of the ACE-V method and *found none.*"[8]

The NRC report was the capstone on the growing scientific recognition that—in sharp contrast to DNA evidence—most traditional forms of forensic science lack a scientific basis and have never been meaningfully tested.[9] After the NRC report was issued, the Supreme Court recognized that "[s]erious deficiencies have been found in the forensic evidence used in criminal trials."[10] The Court specifically cited the NRC report's discussion of the "problems of subjectivity, bias, and unreliability of common forensic tests such as latent fingerprint analysis, pattern/impression analysis, and toolmark and firearms analysis."[11] As the Supreme Court acknowledged, the "legal community now concedes, with varying degrees of urgency, that our system produces erroneous convictions based on discredited forensics."[12]

Indeed, the scientific community's exposé of the unreliability of forensic evidence is consistent with discoveries about the role of flawed forensic evidence in wrongful convictions.[13] A recent comprehensive study revealed that forensic science error was one of the statistically significant causes of wrongful convictions.[14] That error "most often occurred in testimony or interpretation of evidence, rather than in the actual scientific testing."[15] In fact, the "most common forensic error was improper testimony at trial by [the prosecutor's] witness who overstated the precision or inculpatory nature of the results she obtained."[16] The significant role that forensic science errors have played in the wrongful conviction of innocent people—by definition, errors in the *prosecution's* evidence and errors in the testimony of the *prosecution's* witnesses[17]—has been documented in multiple studies.[18]

The scientific conclusions asserted in the NRC report (and underscored by research on wrongful convictions) have far-reaching implications for many players in the criminal justice system.[19] This chapter examines the implications for the most powerful actor in that system—the prosecutor.[20]

The first part of this chapter looks at the rules that govern prosecutor Paula Smith's conduct when she decides whether and how to use the forensic evidence in Daniel's case, decisions that could change Daniel's life forever and affect the safety of the community. Those rules *seem* to require Paula to be open and honest about the unreliability of forensic evidence, both because the prosecutor has a general responsibility to see that justice is done, and because she must comply with specific candor and disclosure requirements. The second part explains why, notwithstanding what the rules appear to demand, there are actually few enforceable *requirements* that Paula be candid with Daniel's attorney, the judge, or any jury about the reliability of the evidence she is using to convict Daniel. The chapter concludes with a description of proposed reforms and a suggestion that the intransigence of the legal system may require members of the scientific community to become "accuracy advocates."

Importantly, this chapter discusses the failure to be honest about forensic evidence by well-meaning prosecutors who are committed to following the rules. Although there is significant evidence that prosecutors routinely engage in willful and egregious violations of the rules (one of the *New York Times'* first editorials of 2014 was a critique of "Rampant Prosecutorial Misconduct"),[21] that is a topic for another forum. This chapter examines only the role of the law-abiding prosecutor in the evaluation and use of forensic evidence; it assumes that the prosecutor Paula Smith will abide by the rules and simply examines what the rules require of her.

The Rules That Govern Prosecutors' Use of Forensic Evidence

There is no single set of rules that regulate prosecutors' evaluation and use of forensic evidence. Instead, the conduct of prosecutors is governed by a combination of state rules of professional responsibility, state and federal statutory rules of procedure for criminal cases, and Supreme Court decisions. When read together, this patchwork of rules imposes six requirements relevant to forensic evidence: Prosecutors are required to

1. evaluate and use forensic evidence consistently with their unique role as a minister of justice;

2. be competent to evaluate and use forensic evidence;

3. consider the reliability of forensic evidence when deciding whether to charge someone with a crime and whether and what plea bargain to offer;

4. disclose certain information about forensic evidence and experts to the defense attorney;

5. be candid with the tribunal about forensic evidence; and

6. refrain from presenting the judge or jury with false forensic evidence or testimony, or arguments that misrepresent that evidence.

These requirements are echoed in three sets of aspirational professional standards that articulate best practices for prosecutors: the ABA's *Criminal Justice Standards* (the CJA Standards), which are "intended to be used as a guide to professional conduct and performance";[22] the National District Attorney's Association's *National Prosecution*

Standards (the NDAA Standards), which are similarly "intended to be an aspirational guide to professional conduct";[23] and, for federal prosecutors, the *U.S. Attorneys' Manual* (the DOJ Standards), which "[provide] only internal Department of Justice guidance."[24] None of the CJA, NDAA, or DOJ standards has an enforcement mechanism or create enforceable rights;[25] they assert what prosecutors *should* do, but not what they *must* do.

This part describes the scope and source of each of the six requirements, identifies the related aspirational standards, and highlights why each should operate to require prosecutors to be honest about the absence of a sound scientific basis for non-DNA forensic evidence. The next part describes the limitations of each.

REQUIREMENT 1: PROSECUTORS ARE REQUIRED TO EVALUATE AND USE FORENSIC EVIDENCE CONSISTENTLY WITH THEIR UNIQUE ROLE AS A MINISTER OF JUSTICE.

Criminal cases are decided though an adversarial system, which is often compared to a sporting event.[26] For example, if a criminal case was roughly analogized to a boxing match, in one corner of the ring, we would see the prosecutor, fighting for the government. In the other corner is the defense attorney, fighting for the person charged with a crime. The judge plays the role of the referee, not available to assist either contestant, but ensuring that the fight is fair. The contest assumes that the boxers are of equivalent strength and skill, and that the exchange of blows will reveal which fighter deserves to win.

Yet, the boxing analogy is ultimately a poor fit for the criminal system for a number of reasons; the most striking distinction is that—unlike any competitor in a boxing match—the prosecutor is charged *both* with fighting in the match as an advocate for the government, *and* with ensuring that "justice is done."[27] This unique and complicated role was most eloquently described by the Supreme Court in 1935, in a passage that has been cited in hundreds of court opinions since:

> [The prosecutor] is the representative not of an ordinary party to a controversy, but of a sovereignty whose obligation to govern impartially is as compelling as its obligation to govern at all; and whose interest, therefore, in a criminal prosecution is not that it shall win a case, but that justice shall be done. As such, he is in a peculiar and very definite sense the servant of the law, the twofold aim of which is that guilt shall not escape or innocence suffer. He may prosecute with earnestness and vigor—indeed, he should do so. But, while he may strike hard blows, he is not at liberty to strike foul ones. It is as much his duty to refrain from improper methods calculated to produce a wrongful conviction as it is to use every legitimate means to bring about a just one.[28]

The Supreme Court's depiction of the prosecutor's role is embodied in the Model Rules for Professional Conduct, promulgated by the American Bar Association (ABA), the preeminent professional association for lawyers. Although the ABA's Model Rules are not themselves enforceable, most states have adopted a version of the Model Rules as their own enforceable professional standards.[29] In particular, Model Rule 3.8, which articulates the "Special Responsibilities of the Prosecutor," has been substantially incorporated into 49 states' professional rules.[30] Because it is part of the professional rules, a prosecutor who does not comply with the rule's requirements could be referred to the state bar and face disciplinary sanctions.[31]

According to the drafters of the Model Rules,

> A prosecutor has the responsibility of a minister of justice and not simply that of an advocate. This responsibility carries with it specific obligations to see that the defendant is accorded procedural justice, [and] that guilt is decided upon the basis of sufficient evidence.[32]

The advisory standards similarly endorse the role of the prosecutor as an "administer of justice,"[33] and reinforce the requirement that prosecutors act to "guard the rights of the accused"[34] and "improve the administration of criminal justice."[35]

The responsibility to seek justice, as prosecutors themselves recognize, "can only be achieved by the representation and presentation of *the truth*."[36] Accordingly, prosecutors can fulfill their unique responsibility only if they use and present forensic evidence in a manner consistent with the *truth*—a truth that includes the fact that, other than DNA, "no forensic method" used in criminal cases can "consistently, and with a high degree of certainty," demonstrate a connection between a piece of evidence and a specific criminal defendant.[37]

What the "Minister of Justice" Requirement Should Mean for the Prosecutor in Daniel Green's Case

If Paula decides to prosecute Daniel Green for gun possession, one piece of evidence on which she will rely is the fingerprint on the gun and the analyst's testimony that it matches Daniel's print. As merely an advocate—a boxer seeking to win the fight—Paula might be allowed to present only an expert who can persuade the jury that fingerprint analysis is an infallible technique that can reliably identify Daniel as the source of the latent print, and who will testify that in his long career as an analyst he has never been "wrong." But Paula's role as a minister of justice would seem to require her to present a more accurate picture of the reliability of fingerprint evidence.[38] Pursuant to her duty to "present[] . . . the truth,"[39] Paula should be required to inform the judge and jury that "the outcome of a friction ridge [fingerprint] analysis is not necessarily repeatable from examiner to examiner,"[40] and that "merely following the steps of ACE-V does not imply that one is proceeding in a scientific manner or producing reliable results,"[41] and that—notwithstanding the examiner's confidence—"claims that [fingerprint] analyses have zero error rates are *not scientifically plausible*."[42]

REQUIREMENT 2: PROSECUTORS ARE REQUIRED TO BE COMPETENT TO EVALUATE AND USE FORENSIC EVIDENCE.

All lawyers—including prosecutors—must provide "competent representation" under ABA Model Rule 1.1, which "requires the legal knowledge, skill, thoroughness and preparation reasonably necessary for the representation." (Model Rule 1.1. has similarly been adopted as an enforceable standard by almost every state.)[43] The comments to the rule highlight that one of these "important legal skills" is "the evaluation of evidence."[44] The comments also make clear that competence is not a static concept and that to "maintain the requisite knowledge and skill, a lawyer should keep abreast of changes in the law and its practice. . . ."[45] Because it is part of the states' professional rules, a prosecutor who is not competent could face disciplinary sanctions from the state bar.[46] The competence requirement has also been recognized by the Supreme Court.[47]

The aspirational standards similarly require a prosecutor to provide competent representation, and observe that this requires continuing education on forensic evidence.[48]

What the Competence Requirement Should Mean for the Prosecutor in Daniel Green's Case

Because the competence requirement requires prosecutors to "keep abreast of changes in the law and its practice" to maintain the legal skill of "evaluating evidence," it would seem that prosecutors are required to keep abreast of new information about the unreliability of forensic evidence.[49] As a result, Paula cannot competently prosecute Daniel's case if she does not have the skill to evaluate fingerprint evidence in light of new revelations that "fingerprint evidence . . . has made its way into the courtroom without empirical validation of the underlying theory and/or its particular application."[50] In addition, Paula cannot competently present the testimony of the fingerprint analyst if she does not know enough about the limitations of the discipline to prevent the analyst from misinterpreting the results or exaggerating the strength of his or her conclusion.

REQUIREMENT 3: PROSECUTORS ARE REQUIRED TO CONSIDER THE RELIABILITY OF FORENSIC EVIDENCE WHEN MAKING DECISIONS ABOUT WHETHER TO CHARGE A PERSON WITH A CRIME, AND WHETHER AND WHAT PLEA BARGAIN TO OFFER.

The decision whether to charge someone with a crime is the most important decision in the criminal justice system. Prosecutors make that decision independently, without input from the court or defense counsel, and "exercise near absolute discretion about what and whom to charge."[51]

Prosecutors "may decline to bring charges, bring only charges they believe they can prove, or 'inflate' the charges by convincing a grand jury to indict a defendant for more and greater charges than they can prove beyond a reasonable doubt at the trial."[52] When describing "the power" the prosecutor wields in that moment, the National District Attorneys' Association observed,

> The prosecutor is making a decision that will have a profound effect on the lives of the person being charged, the person's family, the victim, the victim's family, and the community as a whole. The magnitude of the charging decision does not dictate that it be made timidly, but it does dictate that it should be made wisely with the exercise of sound professional judgment.[53]

Part of that wisdom and professional judgment involves an evaluation of the forensic evidence.[54] First, prosecutors are required to decide whether the evidence in a case meets the threshold requirement of "probable cause," a low standard that asks only if a reasonable person would think the suspect had committed the crime.[55] Under Model Rule 3.8(a), a prosecutor must "refrain from prosecuting a charge that the prosecutor knows is not supported by probable cause." This requirement is an enforceable professional standard in most states.[56] The requirement that prosecutors only file charges in cases where the evidence meets the probable cause threshold is similarly articulated in the CJA,[57] NDAA,[58] and DOJ[59] standards. Therefore, the prosecutor must determine whether the forensic evidence (in conjunction with any other evidence) is reliable enough to establish probable cause.

Second, the professional standards encourage prosecutors to consider whether the evidence is sufficient to meet the significantly higher bar of proof for a conviction at trial—proof beyond a reasonable doubt.[60] As the DOJ Standards explain, the prosecutor "should bear in mind that at trial he/she will have to produce admissible evidence sufficient to obtain and sustain a conviction or else the government will suffer a dismissal."[61] Therefore, the prosecutor should not charge someone with a crime that the prosecutor "cannot reasonably expect to prove beyond a reasonable doubt by legally sufficient evidence at trial."[62] To comply with this higher ethical standard, the prosecutor must scrutinize the forensic evidence even more carefully. For example, the analyst's conclusion that the latent print "matches" Daniel Green might be sufficient to establish probable cause. However, it may not be sufficient to establish proof beyond a reasonable doubt in light of the National Academy of Science's conclusion that fingerprint analysis has not been shown to "consistently, and with a high degree of certainty, demonstrate a connection between evidence and a specific individual."[63] If there is no "high degree of certainty" in the conclusion, that is presumably a reasonable reason to doubt.

Once a prosecutor has decided to charge someone with a crime, the second significant, discretionary decision the prosecutor makes is whether and what plea bargain to offer. Ninety-five percent of all criminal cases are resolved by plea bargain,[64] so in 95% of all cases, it is the prosecutor—and not a judge or jury—who largely controls the outcome of the case.[65] When offering a plea bargain, a prosecutor has discretion to choose to which charges the defendant must plead guilty, which charges should be dismissed, and what sentence is appropriate.[66]

The advisory standards encourage prosecutors to evaluate the evidence when determining what plea to offer. For example, the NDAA Standards advise that "[p]rior to negotiating a plea agreement, the prosecution should consider the . . . [s]ufficiency of admissible evidence to support a verdict,"[67] which should include an evaluation of any forensic evidence. Similarly, one of the factors the DOJ standards advise prosecutors to consider when deciding what plea to offer is the "likelihood of obtaining a conviction at trial"[68]—which requires "weigh[ing] the strength of the government's case . . . bearing in mind legal and evidentiary problems."[69]

Moreover, the professional standards also encourage prosecutors to be truthful when describing the available evidence to the defendant's attorney[70] and to engage in pretrial procedures (including disclosures) that "provide the defendant with sufficient information to make an informed plea."[71]

What the Requirements for Charging and Offering Pleas Should Mean for the Prosecutor in Daniel Green's Case

As Model Rule 3.8 and the aspirational standards make clear, when deciding whether to charge a person with a crime, prosecutors are required to consider the quality of the evidence against the person, including forensic evidence. Thus, Paula is required to evaluate the conclusion of a fingerprint analyst that the latent print on the gun "matches" Daniel's print. In making the decision whether to charge Daniel for gun possession, Paula is required to consider whether fingerprint evidence generally, and this fingerprint analyst in particular, are reliable enough—in combination with any other evidence—to satisfy the probable cause threshold. For example, Paula should give the fingerprint evidence less weight if the first analyst's conclusion has not been replicated by another examiner who was unaware of the first analyst's conclusion. Paula should similarly give the evidence less weight if the examiner was provided with information about the case, such as the fact that the comparison prints were from the four passengers in the car.

Paula should also consider whether the practice of fingerprint matching and the analyst's application of that practice are reliable enough—again, in combination with any other evidence—to provide proof beyond a reasonable doubt that Daniel was the owner of the gun. It is important to Paula to prosecute possession of illegal firearms, but if Daniel is innocent, a conviction will wrongly and irrevocably damage his life,[72] and even just being charged with such a serious crime could harm him.[73] As the NRC report observed,

> The goal of law enforcement actions is to identify those who have committed crimes and to prevent the criminal justice system from erroneously convicting the innocent. So it matters a great deal whether an expert is qualified to testify about forensic evidence and whether the evidence is sufficiently reliable to merit a fact finder's reliance on the truth that it purports to support.[74]

If Paula does decide to charge Daniel with the crime, she should consider the reliability of fingerprint evidence before deciding whether and what kind of plea bargain to offer him.[75] Moreover, if Paula knows that recent studies have gutted the "misconception that the forensic discipline of fingerprinting is infallible,"[76] she should not misrepresent the fingerprint evidence to the defense attorney in plea negotiations as solid or iron clad.[77]

REQUIREMENT 4: PROSECUTORS ARE REQUIRED TO DISCLOSE CERTAIN INFORMATION ABOUT FORENSIC EVIDENCE AND EXPERTS TO THE DEFENSE ATTORNEY.

Prosecutors are required to disclose to defense counsel evidence that would likely make a difference to the judge or jury deciding whether to convict a defendant—an obligation that "flows from the basic duty of the prosecutor to seek justice,"[78] and the criminal defendant's constitutional right to due process of law.

Specifically, pursuant to a constitutional requirement known as the *Brady* doctrine, prosecutors must disclose favorable evidence when "the evidence is material either to guilt or to punishment."[79] Favorable evidence is "material," "if there is a reasonable probability that, had the evidence been disclosed to the defense, the result of the proceeding would have been different."[80] A "reasonable probability" means "only that the likelihood of a different result is great enough to undermine confidence in the outcome of the trial."[81] In other words, unless we are *sure* that jurors would still have reached a guilty verdict—even if they had known of the evidence—then the evidence is "material." If a prosecutor fails to comply with the *Brady* requirement to disclose material evidence, the defendant can seek to have his conviction reversed.[82] Notably, the *Brady* doctrine encompasses both information that exculpates the defendant, and information that impeaches (discredits) any of the prosecution's witnesses.[83]

The *Brady* requirement applies to information in the possession of the prosecutor, as well as information that is "known to the others acting on the government's behalf in the case, including the police."[84] Therefore, in order to comply with the *Brady* disclosure requirements, a prosecutor has the "duty to learn of any favorable evidence" known to others on the prosecution's team.[85]

Model Rule 3.8, as incorporated into most states' professional rules,[86] is broader than the constitutional *Brady* requirement. It requires the prosecutor to "make timely disclosure to the defense of all evidence or information known to the prosecutor that *tends to negate* the guilt of the accused or mitigates the offense. . . ."[87] The Model Rule is broader because it is not limited to "material" evidence, but instead requires disclosure "without regard to the anticipated impact of the evidence or information on a trial's outcome."[88] Thus, a prosecutor has duty under state professional rules to disclose evidence that "tends" to negate the defendant's guilt, even if the evidence would not "undermine confidence in the outcome of the trial." If a prosecutor fails to comply with the professional rules, he or she could face disciplinary sanctions.[89]

The discretionary professional standards similarly instruct prosecutors to disclose, not just material evidence, but any evidence that tends to negate the guilt of the defendant or mitigate the offense.[90] For example, the DOJ Standards require federal prosecutors to

> disclose information that either casts a substantial doubt upon the accuracy of any evidence—including but not limited to witness testimony—the prosecutor intends to rely on to prove an element of any crime charged, or might have a significant bearing on the admissibility of prosecution evidence.[91]

The DOJ Standards join the CJA and NDAA standards in rejecting the materiality requirement and require disclosure of information "regardless of whether it is likely to make the difference between conviction and acquittal of the defendant."[92]

In addition to the duty to disclose favorable material evidence under *Brady* and mitigating evidence under Model Rule 3.8, there is a procedural requirement that the prosecution disclose information about its expert witnesses and scientific test results. Specifically, when the defendant requests it, the prosecutor "must give to the defendant a written summary of any [expert] testimony that the government intends to use . . . during its case-in-chief at trial."[93] The summary "must describe the witness's opinions, the bases and reasons for those opinions, and the witness's qualifications."[94] The purpose of the rule is to allow the defendant to engage in "more complete pretrial preparation" and provide for "a fair opportunity to test the merit of the expert's testimony through focused cross-examination" at trial.[95] In addition, again after a defense request, the prosecution must give the defense access to "the results or reports . . . of any scientific test or experiment" in the government's possession if "the item is material to preparing the defense or the government intends to use the item . . . at trial."[96] If a prosecutor fails to comply with the procedural discovery requirements, the judge has the authority to remedy the problem by ordering discovery, excluding the expert testimony or test results, or any other action "that is just under the circumstances."[97]

What the Disclosure Requirements Should Mean
for the Prosecutor in Daniel Green's Case

Prosecutors are thus required to disclose information they possess[98] about forensic evidence that would "undermine confidence in the outcome of the trial"[99] or tends to negate the guilt of the accused, and should disclose information that "casts a substantial doubt"[100] on the accuracy of any forensic evidence, including the testimony of any forensic experts. Accordingly, the disclosure rules demand that if Paula has in her possession evidence that "[a] 'zero error rate' is a myth in fingerprint analyses and in all other forensic disciplines"[101]—then she should disclose that evidence to Daniel's defense attorney.[102] Similarly, if Paula has in her possession—or if the fingerprint analyst has evidence in his possession—"recent research by [I. E.] Dror [that] has shown that experienced examiners do not necessarily agree with even their own past conclusions when the examination is presented in a different context some time later"[103]—she should disclose that information as well. After all, if the jury had information that the ostensible link between Daniel and gun was based on significantly discredited evidence, it might negate the jury's sense of Daniel's guilt, and could even lead to an acquittal rather than a conviction. Information about the unreliability of the fingerprint evidence could also have a "significant bearing" on the judge's decision whether to admit the fingerprint evidence and allow the analyst to testify.

The rules also require Paula to disclose to Daniel's defense attorney the "bases and reasons" for the fingerprint expert's conclusions, and make available any reports and results of the fingerprint analysis.[104] This disclosure would give Daniel's defense attorney critical information for challenging the reliability of the fingerprint evidence.

REQUIREMENT 5: PROSECUTORS ARE REQUIRED TO BE CANDID WITH THE COURT ABOUT FORENSIC EVIDENCE.

All lawyers, including prosecutors, have a duty of candor to the tribunal. The "tribunal" includes the court that is hearing the criminal case.[105] Under Model Rule 3.3, which most states have incorporated into their professional rules:[106] "A lawyer shall not knowingly . . . make a false statement of fact or law to a tribunal."[107] The comment to Model Rule 3.3 explains that this includes an affirmative duty to "*not allow the tribunal to be misled* by false statements of law or fact or evidence that the lawyer knows to be false."[108] Because it is part of the professional rules a prosecutor who knowingly allows the court to be misled by a false statement of fact or law could face disciplinary sanctions from the state bar.[109]

The Model Rules' requirement to be candid with the court includes a responsibility to inform the court about controlling legal authority adverse to the prosecutor's position.[110] Thus, if a prosecutor is advocating that the court admit ballistics evidence, and the prosecutor knows that the court is bound by a previous case that excluded the same evidence, the prosecutor is required to inform the court about that case—even though it undercuts the prosecutor's argument.

The advisory standards similarly emphasize the prosecutor's duty not to make false statements of law or fact to the court and to disclose contrary binding case law.[111] The standards also highlight the importance of this requirement, one that applies to all lawyers, in the context of the prosecutor's unique role.[112] The rationale for the rule was explained best by the National District Attorneys' Association:

> In order to make just, informed decisions, the court must have the most accurate information available regarding the facts and the law. A prosecutor, in his or her role as a minister of justice, must provide information to the court in an honest and forthright manner.[113]

What the Candor Requirement Should Mean
for the Prosecutor in Daniel Green's Case

Prosecutors are not permitted to make false statements of fact to the court when seeking to admit or using forensic evidence. It is therefore questionable conduct for Paula to assert that the analyst has reliably matched the fingerprint to Daniel, when the NRC has concluded that "there is no scientific evidence that latent fingerprint analysis can consistently and accurately demonstrate a connection between evidence and a specific individual."[114] It also seems inconsistent with the Paula's responsibility to be "honest and forthright" with the court if her presentation of the fingerprint evidence fails to acknowledge that "[m]any of the most basic claims of fingerprint identification have never been tested empirically, and . . . in the strong form in which they usually are presented, those claims in fact are unprovable."[115]

REQUIREMENT 6: PROSECUTORS ARE REQUIRED
TO REFRAIN FROM KNOWINGLY OFFERING FALSE
FORENSIC EVIDENCE OR WITNESS TESTIMONY AT TRIAL.

Pursuant to Model Rule 3.3, "A lawyer shall not knowingly . . . offer evidence that the lawyer knows to be false."[116] This means that lawyers, including prosecutors, cannot present the judge or jury with physical evidence (such as a test result) or witness testimony (such as an analyst's testimony) that the prosecutor knows is false. Because it is part of the professional rules, a prosecutor who knowingly offers false evidence or testimony could face disciplinary sanctions from the state bar.[117] Prosecutors have a related responsibility not make arguments to the jury that mischaracterize the evidence that was presented at the trial.[118]

The advisory standards reiterate the rule that prosecutors may not offer false evidence.[119] The standards also specify other rules designed to ensure that the prosecutor does not mislead the court or jury, recognizing that the "prosecutor is ultimately responsible for evidence that will be used in a criminal case."[120] For example, the standards assert that prosecutors must not use cross-examination as a tool for undermining the testimony of a witness the prosecutor knows is testifying truthfully,[121] and should not "intentionally misstate the evidence or mislead the jury as to the inferences it may draw" from the evidence.[122] In particular, the standards assert that a prosecutor who engages an expert "should respect the independence of the expert and should not seek to dictate the formation of the expert's opinion on the subject."[123] Finally, the standards also direct prosecutors to refrain from mischaracterizing the evidence when making arguments to the jury.[124]

What the Requirement to Refrain From Offering False Evidence Should Mean for the Prosecutor in Daniel Green's Case

The Model Rule establishes that Paula may not knowingly offer false fingerprint evidence or false testimony from the fingerprint analyst, and Paula should also be sure not to dictate the conclusions the fingerprint analyst will reach.[125] In addition, if Daniel's defense attorney presents an expert in forensic evidence generally or fingerprinting specifically, Paula should not try to undermine the expert's testimony with cross-examination if she knows the expert is testifying truthfully. Finally, Paula should not use the closing argument as an opportunity to mislead the jury about the forensic evidence that was presented during the trial.

Why the Rules Do Not Produce Prosecutors Who Are Honest About the Reliability of Forensic Evidence

As the section above explains, there are six requirements that govern the prosecutor's use of forensic evidence. Each one suggests that prosecutors must change the way they are using forensic evidence in light of significant revelations about the unreliability of that evidence. Specifically, as discussed above in the context of Daniel Green's case, the requirements imply that the answer to all of the following six questions is a resounding "No":

1. Can a prosecutor fulfill her role as a minister of justice if she seeks to convict a man with forensic evidence that has exposed as lacking a scientifically sound basis by the National Academy of Science?

2. Can a prosecutor be competent if she is presenting forensic evidence to a jury but does not know that the method used by the "expert" has never been scientifically validated?

3. Can a prosecutor evaluate whether there is enough evidence to charge someone with a crime, or what plea bargain to offer, without considering the current scientific assessment of the reliability of that evidence?

4. Can a prosecutor comply with her discovery obligations if she never discloses to the defense attorney that the evidence against the defendant has been significantly discredited?

5. Can a prosecutor comply with her duty of candor toward the court if she proceeds with a prosecution based on forensic evidence, without ever informing the court that the evidence has been called into question by the most illustrious scientific body in the country?

6. Can a prosecutor avoid presenting false evidence if she permits a forensic expert to testify about a forensic science with a zero error rate?

Yet, though the rules, and basic principles of fairness, suggest that the answer is "No," —in practice, the disturbing reality is that prosecutors can do all of these things without being sanctioned in any way. This part explores the five reasons why the rules described earlier fail to produce a fair and accurate treatment of forensic evidence in criminal trials.

First, some rules are too vague to translate into concrete conduct requirements. Second, other rules are defined too narrowly to encompass prosecutors' use of forensic evidence. Third, even the rules that are both specific and comprehensive enough to address prosecutors' use of forensic evidence are almost never enforced, so they do not serve to correct misconduct or incentivize good conduct. Fourth, the absence of coverage and enforcement leaves most decisions regarding forensic evidence to the discretion of the prosecutor, and for cognitive and structural reasons, this discretion is rarely used to expose problems with forensic evidence. Fifth and finally, the problems with forensic evidence are not ameliorated by either the operation of the adversary system or by the trial judge's authority to exclude forensic evidence from the trial or limit the way it is used.

FIRST PROBLEM: VAGUE REQUIREMENTS

Paula's role as a minister of justice would seem to require her to present a "truthful and forthright"[126] picture of the reliability of fingerprint evidence, including that "surprisingly little conventional science exists to support the claims of the fingerprint examination community."[127] But in practice, the overarching special responsibility of the prosecutor to "seek justice" is a more poetic than concrete requirement. For other than the rules discussed in the section above, the job of ensuring that "justice shall be done" has not been translated into specific, enforceable responsibilities.[128] So while it would be *consistent* with the prosecutor's job to present the judge and jury with the truth about the unreliability of forensic evidence, neither courts nor disciplinary committees have held that the prosecutor's role *requires* such honesty.[129]

Currently, prosecutors do not face disciplinary sanctions for failing to be forthright about the fallibility of forensic evidence even when it is inconsistent with the truth-seeking function.[130] Nor are criminal defendants' convictions reversed when a prosecutor has failed to communicate with the court or defense counsel about the weaknesses of the forensic evidence. Instead, courts have left it to the discretion of prosecutors themselves to decide what conduct will best satisfy their "minister of justice" responsibilities. And for the reasons discussed below, prosecutors rarely use their discretion to illuminate problems with forensic evidence. In short, the Supreme Court language—quoted at the beginning of this chapter—describing the prosecutor's duty to "govern impartially" is "routinely cited but largely ignored."[131]

Similarly, the more modest requirement that a prosecutor be "competent" is ultimately too vague to engender concrete rules for conduct. The competence requirement suggests that Paula cannot competently prosecute Daniel's case if she does not have the skill to evaluate fingerprint evidence in light of new revelations about the absence of a scientific basis for "matching" a person's fingerprint to a print left at a crime scene.[132] But "competence" has not translated into a requirement that prosecutors understand the limits of non-DNA forensic evidence.[133] So while prosecutors have been encouraged to educate themselves about the evidence on which they rely, this requirement has not been used to make that education mandatory.[134] Vague rules make it difficult for prosecutors to determine what conduct is required of them, and for disciplinary boards or courts to sanction prosecutors for violations of those rules.[135]

SECOND PROBLEM: NARROWLY DEFINED REQUIREMENTS

Other rules are specific enough to be enforced, but they are written too narrowly to reach the ways prosecutors use forensic evidence.[136]

The prosecutor's disclosure requirements under *Brady* and Model Rule 3.8, for example, are often interpreted too narrowly to encompass information about the unreliability of forensic evidence. Many courts have concluded that information in the public domain does not fall under *Brady*, concluding that the prosecutor cannot be said to have "possessed" or "suppressed" that information because the courts limit *Brady* to information that is unknown to the defense.[137] And because the information about the unreliability of forensic evidence is in the public domain, those courts would likely conclude that it does not count as information the prosecutor must disclose. Of course, the fact that information is available makes no difference to the fairness of Daniel's trial if neither Daniel's defense attorney nor the judge has accessed that information.[138] If Paula allows the case to proceed without being honest about the weaknesses of the evidence on which she is relying, she indulges in the kind of gamesmanship that is antithetical to the *Brady* rule and the prosecutor's role. And some courts have recognized that the *Brady* disclosure requirement applies to public records if the defendant does not have "enough information to be able to ascertain the supposed *Brady* material on his own."[139] But the narrow reading of *Brady* nonetheless poses a practical barrier to using *Brady* to push prosecutors to be forthright about problems with forensic evidence.[140]

A second limitation on the usefulness of the *Brady* rule is the limitation of the disclosure requirement to "material" evidence. Although the states' professional rules (adopted from Model Rule 3.8) require prosecutors to disclose information that "tends to negate" proof of the defendant's guilt (which would plainly encompass information that tends to undermine the reliability of forensic evidence against the defendant), only "material" information—a higher standard—gives rise to a constitutionally enforceable right. Moreover, it leaves prosecutors with the discretion to determine what is material.[141] This leaves room for Paula to determine that evidence about the unreliability of fingerprint evidence would not change the outcome of the case.[142]

The problem of narrowly defined terms also undermines the efficacy of the prohibition on making false statements of fact to the tribunal and knowingly offering false evidence or testimony. The term *knowingly* is defined narrowly: *knowledge* is defined as "actual knowledge";[143] so if Paula has not complied with the (largely enforceable) requirement to be competent with regard to forensic evidence, she may present forensic testimony without "actual knowledge" that it is unreliable. More importantly, as the comment to Model Rule 3.3 explains, "The prohibition against offering false evidence only applies if the lawyer knows that the evidence is false. A lawyer's reasonable belief that evidence is false does not preclude its presentation to the trier of fact."[144] This definition leaves room for Paula to decide that information about the unreliability of fingerprint evidence does not make the evidence "false," even if it makes the evidence less persuasive.[145] In other words, Paula is permitted to conclude that the fingerprint evidence is only "false" if it has been tampered with or manufactured.

Thus, even if Paula has read the NAS report and reasonably believes fingerprint evidence is unreliable, the rules still permit her to use that evidence in an attempt to convict Daniel. Again, the approach would be incongruous with her role as a minister of justice, but that overarching requirement is vague and unenforced.

THIRD PROBLEM: NO ENFORCEMENT

Even when rules are specific enough to be enforceable and comprehensive enough to reach prosecutors' use of forensic evidence—the open secret of the criminal justice system is that conduct of the most powerful actors in the system is unregulated. The rules governing prosecutors' conduct are simply not enforced.[146] "According to the Center for Prosecutor Integrity, multiple studies over the past 50 years show that courts punished prosecutorial misconduct in less than 2 percent of cases where it occurred."[147]

The lack of transparency is part of the problem, as the prosecutors' "control over and manipulation of the scientific evidence to shape the fact-finder's evaluation of the facts and to persuade the fact-finder of the defendant's guilt usually escapes scrutiny."[148] Most of prosecutors' important decisions never see the light of day because prosecutors make independent, internal decisions about whether to file charges, offer a plea, and how to prepare the forensic expert for trial.[149] When making these decisions, Paula could greatly overestimate the reliability of fingerprint evidence and willfully ignore the conclusions of the NRC report—and no one would ever know. In particular, prosecutors' decisions about what information to disclose are not transparent—the information prosecutors fail to disclose usually remains hidden. It is often only an extraordinary event or accident that reveals information that a prosecutor has failed to disclose.[150] Indeed, prosecutors frequently fail to comply with their obligations under *Brady*,[151] and are almost never penalized for violating the rule.[152]

This reality was recently and sharply critiqued by Federal Judge Alex Kozinski in a dissenting opinion joined by four other federal judges.[153] In describing the conduct of an individual prosecutor, Judge Kozinski wrote,

> I wish I could say that the prosecutor's unprofessionalism here is the exception, that his propensity for shortcuts and indifference to his ethical and legal responsibilities is a rare blemish and source of embarrassment to an otherwise diligent and scrupulous corps of attorneys staffing prosecutors' offices across the country. *But it wouldn't be true.*[154]

In fact, "*Brady* violations have reached epidemic proportions in recent years," yet,

> [i]n the rare event that the suppressed evidence does surface, the consequences usually leave the prosecution no worse than had it complied with *Brady* from the outset. Professional discipline is rare, and violations seldom give rise to liability for money damages. Criminal liability for causing an innocent man to lose decades of his life behind bars is practically unheard of.[155]

Even when prosecutors make unjust decisions that are actually visible, they are almost never referred to the disciplinary committees that enforce state professional standards.[156] This is because disciplinary proceedings are initiated by personal referrals, and defense attorneys may be reluctant to refer prosecutors when they have to return to work with those same prosecutors on a regular basis—and risk retaliatory referrals by angry prosecutors.[157] Judges are similarly reluctant to refer prosecutors to disciplinary boards, even in states where a statute requires judges to make those referrals.[158] Judges may be reluctant because they also feel dependent on the good will of prosecutors,[159] or they trust the adversary system to correct for prosecutorial abuses.[160]

Both defense attorneys and judges may be deterred by the biggest hurdle of all—the fact that disciplinary referrals are usually fruitless.

Indeed, the biggest obstacle to the enforcement of the rules is that disciplinary committees rarely sanction even egregious misconduct by prosecutors.[161] The unwillingness of disciplinary committees to impose sanctions on prosecutors has been documented across multiple jurisdictions.[162] For example:

> In 1999, reporters at the Chicago Tribune examined 381 homicide cases involving prosecutorial misconduct and found that *none* of the prosecutors involved received a public sanction. More recently, in 2003, the Center for Public Integrity examined 2,012 cases in which a conviction was reversed or a sentence was reduced because of prosecutorial misconduct. Of all the cases examined, the prosecutor was brought before state disciplinary authorities in only forty-four, and seven of those cases were dismissed.[163]

In over half of the remaining cases in the Center for Public Integrity's study, the prosecutor's only sanction was a reprimand.[164]

The other potential legal avenues for sanctioning prosecutor misconduct are similarly ineffective. First, prosecutors have absolute immunity from civil liability for misconduct;[165] they are almost never criminally prosecuted (by other prosecutors),[166] or held in contempt (by judges).[167] Second, the appeals process for criminal cases does not contribute much to the regulation of prosecutors, because courts often conclude that even though a prosecutor engaged in misconduct, it was not so egregious to require a reversal of the conviction.[168] This standard is called "harmless error" review and means that even if the prosecutor engaged in misconduct, the reviewing court can decide it was "harmless" if, beyond a reasonable doubt, it "did not *contribute to the verdict* obtained."[169] So the prosecutor may be chastised but the underlying message is that a just outcome was still reached, and prosecutor's conviction record stands.[170]

Finally, the aspirational standards that tend to require the most honest and forthright conduct are not enforceable. For example, the aspirational standards encourage prosecutors to refrain from charging someone with a crime unless the evidence provides proof beyond a reasonable doubt that the suspect is guilty, but only the only *enforceable* requirement is that prosecutors make sure the evidence meets the much lower probable cause standard before charging someone.[171] Similarly, the NDAA Standards define the prosecutor's role as the "representation and presentation of the truth,"[172] but make it clear that "presenting the truth" is not an enforceable rule. In fact, the standards go to great pains to explain that they are not to be used by courts or disciplinary agencies to determine "whether a prosecutor committed error or engaged in improper conduct" or "when passing upon allegations of violations of rules of ethical conduct."[173]

In sum, the few rules specific and comprehensive enough to constitute enforceable requirements are rarely enforced. The near-total absence of enforcement undercuts the requirement to act as a minister of justice, and fails to dis-incentivize the dishonest or unfair use of forensic evidence.[174] Thus, when Paula is making decisions in Daniel's case, she is aware that few of her decisions will ever be scrutinized, and even her mistakes and misconduct will not have any consequences. In fact, Paula has every reason to expect that if she allows the judge and jury to be misled about the reliability of the forensic evidence, and thereby secures a conviction. she will not only avoid any sanctions—she will likely be promoted.[175]

FOURTH PROBLEM: COGNITIVE AND STRUCTURAL OBSTACLES TO THE JUST EXERCISE OF DISCRETION

Because the rules are vague, narrow, and unenforced, much of prosecutors' conduct is governed only by their own discretion.[176] In particular, prosecutors have discretion to determine to what extent—if any, their "minister of justice" responsibilities will actually influence their conduct. For cognitive and structural reasons, prosecutors almost never exercise their discretion in favor of being forthright about the unreliability of forensic evidence.

Prosecutors are unlikely to define the flaws in forensic evidence as an important "truth" that should be shared with the defendant or judge because of cognitive biases that affect their decision making.[177] For example, studies have shown that prosecutors—like police officers—develop confirmation bias in the form of "tunnel vision."[178] In other words, once prosecutors have identified a person as the perpetrator, it is difficult for them to incorporate information that suggests the identified person is *not* the perpetrator.[179] Thus, if Paula concluded early in the investigation that the gun belonged to Daniel, she may have a difficult time incorporating information about the weaknesses of the evidence she will use to prosecute him. As a result, Paula is unlikely to incorporate information about the unreliability of fingerprint evidence when exercising her unreviewable discretion in deciding whether to charge Daniel and offer him a plea, whether to reveal those weaknesses to Daniel's defense attorney or the judge, or whether those weaknesses make the testimony of the fingerprint examiner "false." In addition, prosecutors may resist the conclusions of science to avoid cognitive dissonance.[180] For prosecutors often self-identify as ministers of justice, but their offices have prosecuted untold numbers of people with the evidence that may have produced unjust results.[181] To resolve the cognitive dissonance that results, prosecutors may be inclined to dismiss the scientific conclusion that the evidence is unreliable.[182]

There are also structural reasons that prosecutors are disinclined to incorporate information about the unreliability of forensic evidence into their decisions. Notwithstanding the lofty language of the Supreme Court or the aspirational standards, prosecutors' performance is more often measured by the rates of conviction they obtain.[183] Because introducing or acknowledging the unreliability of forensic evidence could directly threaten those conviction rates, prosecutors are likely to exercise their discretion in favor of ignoring the evidence of unreliability. Not only are promotions and professional success often dependent on conviction rates; there is also evidence that prosecutors' sense of self-worth becomes tied to conviction rates as well.[184] The head prosecutors, whose interests explicitly and implicitly guide internal office policies, may also need high conviction rates to secure re-election and demonstrate their campaign commitments to being "tough on crime."[185]

Importantly, these structural and psychological barriers to being forthright about the unreliability of forensic evidence affect well-meaning prosecutors who are committed to following the rules.[186] Just as a boxer would struggle (and likely fail) if asked to both win the match *and* lose the match if it is the more just result—prosecutors struggle to both obtain convictions and reveal information that could prevent those convictions.[187]

FIFTH PROBLEM: NEITHER JUDGE'S ROLE NOR ADVERSARY SYSTEM ARE ADEQUATE CURE

The rules give prosecutors discretion to decide when—if ever—they need to reveal flaws in forensic evidence to the defense attorney or the judge. And they rarely exercise this discretion in favor of being forthright about those flaws. As a result, criminal charges and trials are often based on grave misconceptions about the reliability of the government's evidence, and neither defense attorneys nor judges are in a position to correct those misconceptions.

Defense attorneys are often ill-equipped to uncover and preset the flaws in forensic evidence because they lack adequate time or funding.[188] Although the adversarial analogy assumes that the boxers are of equivalent strength and skill, defense attorneys are often too overburdened and underfunded to seek out the training that would help them challenge the forensic evidence, effectively cross-examine the prosecution's forensic expert,[189] or hire the experts who could help them explain the unreliability of the evidence to the judge or jury.[190] Moreover, because prosecutors work in conjunction with police, it is prosecutors who have direct access to forensic evidence and work together with the forensic analysts in the police department and lab.[191] The defense, in contrast, "normally has limited access to evidence."[192] As a result, the criminal system is often adversarial in name only when it comes to forensic evidence.[193] On paper, the defense attorney is equipped to highlight the flaws in the prosecutor's evidence, so that—even if the prosecutor is not truthful—the judge or jury ultimately walks away with an accurate picture of the unreliability of the forensic evidence. But the reality is that defense attorneys often fail to challenge the prosecution's forensic evidence, and judges and juries are left with a misleading picture about critical evidence in the case.[194]

Similarly, trial court judges *could* use their authority to exclude unreliable evidence from trials—but frequently judges are not *actually* functioning as a check on prosecutors' discretion. When the prosecution seeks to admit forensic evidence, and the defense attorney challenges the evidence as unreliable, the trial judge has the authority to decide whether the evidence should be admitted, or what limits should be imposed on the expert's testimony. To make the admission decision, most judges are required to employ the *Daubert* test,[195] a standard that requires the judges to play a "gatekeeping role" and closely scrutinize forensic evidence.[196] Specifically, a judge must evaluate whether the method used to produce the forensic conclusion "can be (and has been) tested," "whether the theory or technique has been subjected to peer review and publication," whether the method has a "known or potential rate of error" and what the rate is, and whether the method enjoys "general acceptance" in the relevant expert community.[197]

So, at least on paper, the trial judge is well positioned to limit the introduction of unreliable forensic evidence in light of new information about the lack of scientific bases for most forms of that evidence. Indeed, Judge Edwards, the co-chair of the NRC report committee, predicted that the NRC report would be "'cited authoritatively' by the courts in their assessment of particular cases" because, if the lack of scientific validity of a particular technique had been exposed, "no judge would continue to admit such evidence without considering the new information regarding the scientific validity and reliability of its source."[198]

Yet, judges are not using their power—they are continuing to admit unreliable evidence.[199] As the NRC report concluded,

The bottom line is simple: In a number of forensic science disciplines, forensic science professionals have yet to establish either the validity of their approach or the accuracy of their conclusions, and *the courts have been utterly ineffective in addressing this problem.*[200]

Rather than rigorously scrutinizing the evidence, many judges simply admit any evidence that has been admitted in the past.[201] This reliance on old legal precedent, rather than new scientific conclusions, is problematic because even the least reliable evidence has traditionally been admitted.[202] Judges may resist their gatekeeping role because they feel ill-equipped to make decisions about science,[203] because they trust the adversarial system to expose the flaws in the evidence,[204] or because insisting on evidence of reliability "would likely 'demand more by way of validation than the disciplines can presently offer.'"[205] Judges may also be motivated by antipathy to criminal defendants, a possibility suggested by the evidence that judges routinely admit the evidence proffered by the prosecution, but exclude the evidence when it is proffered by the criminal defendant.[206]

Judges' reluctance to scrutinize evidence offered at trial is compounded by the amount of prosecutorial decision making that occurs outside of the courtroom. Because 95% of criminal cases are decided by a plea, the vast majority of cases do not involve a full trial over which a judge is presiding.[207] Relatedly, many of prosecutors' decisions (when to charge someone, or what evidence to disclose to the judge or the defense attorney) occurs behind the scenes, not in an open court room where the judge can evaluate and influence those decisions.

Although the adversarial model assumes that the judge is like the referee in the boxing match who ensures that the fight is fair, "the legal system is ill-equipped to correct the problems of the forensic science community."[208] As the NRC report recognized, "judicial review, by itself, is not the answer."[209]

The Need for Accuracy Advocates

We now know that the reliability of some of the evidence prosecutors are using to send people to prison has not been scientifically established, and that judges and juries are convicting people without ever being told that the evidence they are evaluating is deeply flawed. A wide range of reforms have been proposed to change the way prosecutors use and present that evidence, now that the problems with that evidence have been exposed. But there is no indication that any of the reforms will be adopted, and instead it appears that unregulated prosecutorial discretion will remain the status quo. As a result, members of the scientific community must not assume that the justice system is incorporating their discoveries, and should instead become more proactive advocates for accuracy.

NUMEROUS PROPOSALS FOR REFORM

One obvious way to improve prosecutors' use of forensic evidence is to change the way we regulate prosecutors' conduct—and the legal scholarship is rich with proposals.[210] One approach is to change the rules that govern prosecutors' use of forensic evidence, including making vague rules more specific,[211] expanding narrowly defined rules to encompass more of prosecutors' behavior,[212] adding new rules to govern the use of scientific evidence[213] and provide for more discovery (including discovery about forensic experts),[214] and creating separate sets of ethical rules for prosecutors.[215] Another approach is to change the way the rules are enforced, by enacting stronger judicial reporting requirements,[216] conducting audits of prosecution offices to expose misuse of forensic evidence,[217] creating separate disciplinary boards for prosecutors,[218] requiring disciplinary boards to be more proactive about investigating misconduct even in the absence of a referral,[219] or just actually enforcing the rules that do exist.[220]

A third approach to changing the conduct of prosecutors is to change the internal operation of prosecutors' offices, including disconnecting performance reviews from conviction rates and providing alternative incentives,[221] educating prosecutors about forensic science[222] and cognitive bias more generally,[223] and introducing internal policies in prosecutors' offices that would provide prosecutors with more guidance than the current rules provide,[224] increase compliance with disclosure obligations,[225] and impose internal sanctions for misconduct.[226]

In addition, defense attorneys and judges could play a more effective role in cabining the misuse of forensic evidence by prosecutors. Defense attorneys should be better informed and better resourced,[227] as training and experts cost money. And defense attorneys should use these resources and education to aggressively litigate challenges to forensic evidence.[228] Members of the criminal defense community have made efforts in this direction,[229] although too many defense attorneys lack the necessary training and funding.[230]

Judges should similarly obtain more training on forensic evidence,[231] refer prosecutors to disciplinary boards more often,[232] and consider using their power to hold an attorney in contempt to sanction prosecutors.[233] Most importantly, judges need to take seriously their gatekeeping role, and scrutinize forensic evidence pursuant to the *Daubert* and *Frye* standards, and apply those tests evenhandedly. As the NRC report warned, "[E]very effort must be made to limit the risk of having the reliability of certain forensic science methodologies judicially certified before the techniques have been properly studied and their accuracy verified."[234] That judicial certification should be a searching inquiry, not a rubber stamp.

RESISTANCE FROM PROSECUTORS

The unfortunate reality is that these proposals have not been adopted by judges, disciplinary committees, rulemaking authorities, or prosecutors. Unregulated prosecutorial discretion continues to be the status quo.[235] The ministers of justice have turned a blind eye to the revelations about the unreliability of forensic science and there are no rules currently being enforced that restrict their discretion to do so. This chapter does not attempt to explain the full range of reasons why reforms have not been adopted, but examines only the role of the prosecutor in that intransigence. For part of the reason that these reforms have not been instituted—though certainly not the only reason—is the active and vocal resistance from prosecutors.[236]

In individual cases, prosecutors not only fail to disclose the truth about forensic evidence; they often actively fight to keep that information away from the judge or jury.[237] Prosecutors resist hearings that would allow the judge to consider whether the forensic evidence is reliable enough to be admitted,[238] they seek to disqualify experts who could help the defense explain the flaws in the evidence to judge or jury,[239] they resist the efforts of defense counsel to limit the testimony of the forensic examiner to results supported by science,[240] they resist the ability of defense counsel to use the NRC report to cross-examine the prosecution's experts,[241] and they resist treating the NRC report as a "learned treatise."[242]

Prosecutors have gone so far as to argue that the NRC report has no implications for criminal cases,[243] notwithstanding the report's inclusion of a chapter "focuse[d] primarily on the forensic science disciplines' capability for providing evidence that can be presented in court."[244] Prosecutors even attempted to support their erroneous claim by misquoting the co-chair of the NRC committee, Judge Harry Edwards. Judge Edwards was forced to publicly denounce the prosecutors' claims:

> I recently had an opportunity to read several briefs filed by various U.S. Attorneys' Offices in which my name has been invoked in support of the government's assertion that the committee's findings should not be taken into account in judicial assessments of the admissibility of certain forensic evidence . . . This is a blatant misstatement of the truth . . . [Such claims] are without basis in fact and utterly absurd.[245]

At the rule-making level, prosecutors have resisted rules that would require them to take action if they had clear and convincing evidence that an innocent person had been convicted.[246] And ironically—given the universal recognition that prosecutors are under-regulated—the National District Attorney's Association and individual prosecutors' offices have resisted the authority of the ABA to establish even the vague, under-inclusive, and unenforced rules that do exist.[247]

ADVOCATING FOR ACCURACY

The NRC report made clear that "forensic science disciplines are supported by little rigorous systematic research to validate the discipline's basic premises and techniques."[248] Rigorous and systematic research is needed to fill that gap. Thus, members of the scientific community can best improve the accuracy and fairness of the criminal system by engaging in "serious research to establish the limits and measures of performance in each discipline."[249] The forensic disciplines that determine the outcome of criminal cases must be improved,[250] and to improve they "must be well connected with the Nation's scientific research base."[251]

One implication of the law's intransigence is that even when the scientific and forensic communities produce rigorous research, they cannot assume that the legal system is incorporating their discoveries. The fact that a forensic practice has been exposed as unreliable, or that a new approach significantly reduces bias, or that research limits the legitimate conclusions an individual analyst can draw—none of these discoveries are making their way into criminal courtrooms. To the extent that members of the scientific community oppose the misrepresentation of science and forensic evidence that is occurring in the legal system, they may need to be more proactive. The importance of the need for "transfer" was highlighted in the NRC report:

The fruits of any advances in the forensic science disciplines should be transferred directly to legal scholars and practitioners (including civil litigators, prosecutors, and criminal defense counsel), federal, state, and local legislators, members of the judiciary, and law enforcement officials, so that appropriate adjustments can be made in criminal and civil laws and procedures, model jury instructions, law enforcement practices, litigation strategies, and judicial decision making.[252]

There are numerous ways that scientists and scholars can facilitate the transfer of scientific knowledge into the legal system. For example, the scientific community can make its research more accessible to the legal community and public by ensuring it is available on educational resource websites used by judges and lawyers.[253] In addition, scientists and scholars can also participating in conferences that bring the scientific and legal communities together,[254] and can seek out or accept opportunities to conduct trainings for judges, defense attorneys, and prosecutors.[255]

Members of the scientific community can also make themselves available as a consultant or a testifying expert in criminal trials.[256] And a scientist or scholar called as an expert by the prosecution should not allow the adversarial system to transform him/her into an advocate for the state. Instead, the expert should be an advocate for accuracy—making sure his/her testimony is not contributing to a trial where the judge or jury is getting an incomplete picture of the science behind forensic evidence. Finally, as informed members of the public, scientists and scholars can also encourage the adoption of proposed reforms in their local area, and seek to hold elected prosecutors accountable for pursuing justice, rather than simply convictions.

Conclusion

When deciding whether and how to use the forensic evidence in Daniel Green's case, Paula has enormous discretion to make choices that will affect the safety of the community, Daniel's life, and the integrity of the criminal justice system. And although Paula has a unique responsibility to see that "justice is done," the current rule structure does not require her to be forthright about the flaws in non-DNA forensic evidence. As a result, Daniel may be convicted by a judge or jury who hears testimony from the prosecution's fingerprint examiner, but never learns of the NRC's conclusion that no forensic method used in criminal cases can connect a piece of evidence with a specific defendant "with a high degree of certainty." The rules recognize "the special role played by the American prosecutor in the search for truth in criminal trials,"[257] but under the current approach to governing prosecutorial conduct, the truth about forensic evidence remains hidden.

Notes

1. This example is based on an actual case, but all names have been changed.
2. D.C. CODE § 22-3204(a).

3. Nat'l Research Council, Nat'l Academy of Science, *Strengthening Forensic Science in the United States: A Path Forward* (2009) [hereinafter 2009 NRC Report] at 7 (emphasis added).

4. Edwards Testimony, March 18, 2009.

5. 2009 NRC Report at 103-04.

6. ACE-V is an acronym which describes the four steps of the fingerprint examination: analysis, comparison, evaluation, and verification. See David R. Ashbaugh, *Quantitative-Qualitative Friction Ridge Analysis: An Introduction to Basic and Advanced Ridgeology*, at 108 (CRC Press, 1999).

7. 2009 NRC Report at 142.

8. *Id.* at 143 (quotation and citation omitted, emphasis added).

9. See, e.g., 4 *Mod. Sci. Evid.* § 32:1 ("Many of the most basic claims of fingerprint identification have never been tested empirically, and . . . in the strong form in which they usually are presented, those claims in fact are unprovable"); see also 2009 NRC Report at Summary, p. 8 ("[T]here is a notable dearth of peer-reviewed, published studies establishing the scientific bases and validity of many forensic methods"); *id.* at 8 n.7 ("Several articles, for example, have noted the lack of scientific validation of fingerprint identification methods").

10. *Melendez-Diaz v. Massachusetts*, 557 U.S. 305, 321 (2009).

11. *Id.*

12. *Id.* at 319 (quoting Pamela R. Metzger, *Cheating the Constitution*, 59 Vand. L. Rev. 475, 491 [2006]).

13. 2009 NRC Report, Summary at 4 (Wrongful convictions have "demonstrated the potential danger of giving undue weight to evidence and testimony derived from imperfect testing and analysis").

14. Jon Gould, Julia Carrano, Richard A. Leo, and Joseph K. Young, *Predicting Erroneous Convictions: A Social Science Approach to Miscarriages of Justice*, Univ. of San Francisco Law Research Paper (March 2013).

15. *Id.* at xix–xx.

16. *Id.* at 77.

17. See Bennett L. Gershman, "Litigating *Brady v. Maryland*: Games Prosecutors Play," 57 *Case W. Res. L. Rev.* 531, 553 (Spring 2007) ("A prosecutor's failure to carefully scrutinize the accuracy and credibility of scientific experts, and to search for evidence that would demonstrate the expert is fabricating or mistaken has been one of the recognized causes of wrongful convictions") (citing Jim Dwyer, Peter Neufeld, and Barry Scheck, *Actual Innocence* at 158–171 [2000]); Jane Campbell Moriarty, "'Misconvictions,' Science, and the Ministers of Justice, 86 *Neb. L. Rev.* 1, 3 (2007) ("[P]rosecutors, by using unreliable forensic evidence and questionable expert witnesses . . . have become part of the mechanism by which misconvictions occur").

18. See, e.g., Brandon L. Garrett and Peter J. Neufeld, "Invalid Forensic Science Testimony and Wrongful Convictions," 95 *Va. L. Rev.* 1 (2009) (Study of exonerated persons found in 60% of trials of innocent defendants "forensic analysts called by the prosecution provided invalid testimony at trial—that is, testimony with conclusions misstating empirical data or wholly unsupported by empirical data"); Craig M. Cooley and Gabriel S. Oberfield, "Increasing Forensic Evidence's Reliability and Minimizing Wrongful

Convictions: Applying Daubert Isn't the Only Problem," 43 *Tulsa L. Rev.* 285, 293 (Winter 2007) ("Chicago Tribune reporters in 2004 conducted an exhaustive investigation on state-funded crime laboratories and determined that more than a quarter of 200 DNA and death row exonerations since 1986 involved 'faulty crime lab work or testimony'") (citing Maurice Possley et al., "Scandal Touches Even Elite Labs: Flawed Work, Resistance to Scrutiny Seen Across U.S.," *Chi. Trib.* at 1 [Oct. 21, 2004]).

19. David A. Harris, *Failed Evidence: Why Law Enforcement Resists Science* at 6 (New York Univ. Press 2012) ("[T]he DNA exoneration cases showed, beyond any doubt, that we simply had to rethink some of our fundamental assumptions about the most basic and common types of evidence used in criminal cases"); Michael J. Saks, "Scientific Evidence and the Ethical Obligations of Attorneys," 49 *Clev. St. L. Rev.* 421, 436–437 (2001) ("[G]rowing societal concerns about flaws in the criminal trial that permit innocent people to be convicted," among other factors "have inevitably changed the responsibilities of both proponents and opponents of expert evidence in criminal trials").

20. Angela J. Davis, *Arbitrary Justice: The Power of the American Prosecutor,* at 5 (Oxford Univ. Press, 2007) ("Prosecutors are the most powerful officials in the criminal justice system"); Bennett L. Gershman "'Hard Strikes and Foul Blows': *Berger v. United States* 75 Years After," 42 *Loy. U. Chi. L.J.* 177, 206 (Fall 2010) (citing "the prosecutor's increasing domination of criminal law, his unilateral control of proof, [and] his virtually unfettered power to charge, bargain, and give immunity").

21. Editorial, *The New York Times,* Jan. 4, 2014. See also, e.g., Gershman, *supra* note 20 at 198, 198 n.113 ("Empirical studies increasingly have documented serious and pervasive misconduct by prosecutors") (citing studies); Davis, *supra* note 20 at 141, ("Prosecutorial misconduct is widespread and unchecked"); *id.* at 125 (describing common forms of misconduct); *id.* at 125 n.3 (providing citations to numerous books and articles about prosecutorial misconduct); Jeffrey L. Kirchmeier and Stephen R. Greenwald with Harold Reynolds and Jonathan Sussman, "Vigilante Justice: Prosecutor Misconduct in Capital Cases", *55 Wayne L. Rev. 1327, 1330–1331* (Fall 2009) (noting that "instances of prosecutor misconduct occur in capital cases around the country" and citing multiple studies showing "that prosecutor misconduct has contributed to innocent defendants being sentenced to death"); see also *Bordenkircher v. Hayes,* 434 U.S. 357, 365 (1978) ("There is no doubt that the breadth of discretion that our country's legal system vests in prosecuting attorneys carries with it the potential for both individual and institutional abuse").

22. CJA Standard 3-1.1; see also CJA Standard 3-1.1 commentary ("These Standards are intended to provide prosecutors with reasoned and appropriate professional advice").

23. NDAA Standards, Introduction.

24. DOJ Standards 1-1.100.

25. See Part II(C) *infra.*

26. Gershman, *supra* note 20 at 197 n.9 (noting that "[m]etaphors of sports and games are often used when describing U.S. litigation").

27. *Connick v. Thompson,* 131 S.Ct. 1350, 1362, 1365 (2011); see also *United States v. Wade,* 388 U.S. 218, 256 (White, J., dissenting) ("Law enforcement officers . . . must be dedicated to making the criminal trial a procedure for the ascertainment of the true facts surrounding the commission of the crime. To this extent, our so-called adversary system is not adversary at all; nor should it be") (footnote omitted).

28. *Berger v. United States*, 295 U.S. 78, 88 (1935).

29. Richard A. Rosen, "Disciplinary Sanctions Against Prosecutors for Brady Violations: A Paper Tiger," 65 *N.C. L. Rev.* 693, 696 (April 1987) ("Every state has adopted Disciplinary Rules, based primarily on models promulgated by the American Bar Association [ABA], that define the ethical standards for lawyers and presumably regulate their conduct") (footnote omitted). And federal prosecutors typically must comply with the state professional standards in the state where they practice. Bruce A. Green and Fred C. Zacharias, "Regulating Federal Prosecutors' Ethics," 55 *Vand. L. Rev.* 381, 390, 400 (March 2002).

30. Brief of the American Bar Association as Amicus Curiae in Support of Petitioner, *Smith v. Cain*, 2011 WL 3739380 (Aug. 19, 2011) ("49 states, as well as the District of Columbia, the United States Virgin Islands, and Guam have adopted ethics rules that include a provision identical or substantially similar to [Model Rule 3.8]").

31. *Connick*, 131 S.Ct. at 1362–63 ("An attorney who violates his or her ethical obligations is subject to professional discipline, including sanctions, suspension, and disbarment"); Rosen, *supra* note 29 at 715 ("Once adopted by a jurisdiction, however, ethical rules have the force of law and serve as the basis for disciplining lawyers within the jurisdiction").

32. Model Rule 3.8 comment 1. The comment also makes clear that the prosecutor's responsibilities as a minister of justice extended post-conviction, "and that special precautions are taken to prevent and to rectify the conviction of innocent persons."

33. See CJA Standard 3-1.2(b) and (c) ("The prosecutor is an administrator of justice, [as well as] an advocate," thus, "[t]he duty of the prosecutor is to seek justice, not merely to convict"); CJA Standard 3-3.11 commentary ("A prosecutor has the responsibility of a minister of justice and not simply that of an advocate. This responsibility carries with it specific obligations to see that the accused is accorded procedural justice and that guilt is decided upon the basis of sufficient evidence, including consideration of exculpatory evidence known to the prosecution") (footnote omitted); NDAA Standard 1-1.1 ("The prosecutor is an independent administrator of justice . . . This responsibility includes, but is not limited to, ensuring that the guilty are held accountable, that the innocent are protected from unwarranted harm, and that the rights of all participants, particularly victims of crime, are respected"); NDAA Standard 2-8.3 ("The prosecutor should cooperate with defense counsel at all stages of the criminal process to ensure the attainment of justice and the most appropriate disposition of each case").

34. CJA Standard 3-1.2 commentary ("Although the prosecutor operates within the adversary system, it is fundamental that the prosecutor's obligation is to protect the innocent as well as to convict the guilty, to guard the rights of the accused as well as to enforce the rights of the public. Thus, the prosecutor has sometimes been described as a 'minister of justice' or as occupying a quasi-judicial position").

35. CJA Standard 3-1.2(d) ("It is an important function of the prosecutor to seek to reform and improve the administration of criminal justice").

36. NDAA Standard 1-1; see also NDAA Part 1.1 commentary ("A prosecutor is the only one in a criminal action who is responsible for the presentation of the truth") (emphasis added); see also *Banks v. Dretke*, 540 U.S. 668, 696 (2004) ("We have several times underscored the special role played by the American prosecutor in the search for *truth* in criminal trials") (internal quotation and citations omitted) (emphasis added).

37. 2009 NRC Report at 7.

38. See Myrna S. Raeder, "See No Evil: Wrongful Convictions and the Prosecutorial Ethics of Offering Testimony by Jailhouse Informants and Dishonest Experts," 76 *Fordham L. Rev.* 1413, 1451 (Dec. 2007) ("[W]hen the particular expertise has been subject to repeated reliability attacks, the prudent prosecutor should use the most reliable scientific evidence at his or her disposal and this should be required by appropriate rule or policy"); Saks, *supra* note 19 at 426 ("It is hard to think of principled reasons why an attorney should not be obligated to acquire a good faith basis for believing either that the proffered expertise is valid or that the specific facts or skills brought to bear on the task-at-hand in the trial are valid as a precondition for ethically offering such expert evidence to a court").

39. NDAA Standard 1-1.

40. 2009 NRC Report at 139.

41. 2009 NRC Report at 142.

42. 2009 NRC Report at 142 (emphasis added).

43. ABA, CPR Policy Implementation Committee, *Variations of the ABA Model Rules of Professional Conduct: Rule 1.1: Competence,* as of Sept. 27, 2012.

44. Model Rule 1.1 at comment 2.

45. *Id.* at comment 8.

46. See note 29, *supra.*

47. *Connick*, 131 S.Ct. at 1362 ("Trial lawyers have a duty to bring to bear such skill and knowledge as will render the trial a reliable adversarial testing process'") (quoting *Strickland v. Washington*, 466 U.S. 668, 688 [1984]).

48. See NDAA Standard 1-5.3 ("At the time they commence their duties and at regular intervals thereafter, prosecutors should participate in formal training and education programs"); NDAA Part 1-5 commentary (An "aspect of training which should be included in each prosecutor's training program is continuing education" on, *inter alia,* "forensic evidence"); see also CJA Standard 3-2.3(a) ("The function of public prosecution requires highly developed professional skills").

49. Fred C. Zacharias and Bruce A. Green, "The Duty to Avoid Wrongful Convictions: A Thought Experiment in the Regulation of Prosecutors," 89 *B.U. L. Rev.* 1, 20 (Feb. 2009) ("[C]ompetent representation of the state arguably requires prosecutors to ascertain the reliability of the evidence before relying on it"); Paul C. Giannelli and Kevin C. McMunigal, "Prosecutors, Ethics, and Expert Witnesses," 76 *Fordham L. Rev.* 1493, 1524 (Dec. 2007) ("[C]ompetence; is the first ethical obligation of an attorney and no criminal practitioner should go into court today without understanding scientific evidence"); *Achieving Justice: Freeing the Innocent, Convicting the Guilty,* Report of the ABA Criminal Justice Section's Ad Hoc Innocence Committee to Ensure the Integrity of the Criminal Process, at 61 (2006) ("No attorney can try criminal cases today without a grounding in scientific evidence").

50. 2009 NRC Report at 102 (quotation and citation omitted).

51. K. Babe Howell, "Prosecutorial Discretion and the Duty to Seek Justice in an Overburdened Criminal Justice System," *Geo. J. Legal Ethics* (forthcoming); see also Davis, *supra* note 20, at 22 ("The charging decision is the most important prosecutorial power and the strongest example of the influence and reach of prosecutorial discretion"); Bennett L. Gershman, "Prosecutorial Decisionmaking and Discretion in the Charging Function," 62 *Hastings L.J.* 1259, 1260 (May 2011) (The "prosecutor's charging decision

involves an enormous exercise of power" and "that power is virtually unreviewable"); Tracey L. Meares, "Rewards for Good Behavior: Influencing Prosecutorial Discretion and Conduct With Financial Incentives," 64 *Fordham L. Rev.* 851, 862 (Dec. 1995) ("The prosecutor's decision to charge an accused is largely subject to the prosecutor's discretion. The prosecutor's charging discretion is, for the most part, unreviewable"); Leslie C. Griffin, "The Prudent Prosecutor," 14 *Geo. J. Legal Ethics* 259, 268 (Winter 2001) ("Prosecutors also have vast discretion to charge" because the probable cause standard "may not be very restrictive in practice"); see also *Bordenkircher v. Hayes*, 434 U.S. 357, 364 (1978) ("In our system, so long as the prosecutor has probable cause to believe that the accused committed an offense defined by statute, the decision whether or not to prosecute, and what charge to file or bring before a grand jury, generally rests entirely in his discretion"); DOJ Standard 9-27.300(B) ("Once it has been determined to initiate prosecution . . . the attorney for the government must determine what charges to file or recommend. When the conduct in question consists of a single criminal act, or when there is only one applicable statute, this is not a difficult task. Typically, however, a defendant will have committed more than one criminal act and his/her conduct may be prosecuted under more than one statute. Moreover, selection of charges may be complicated further by the fact that different statutes have different proof requirements and provide substantially different penalties").

52. Davis, *supra* note 20, at 23.

53. NDAA 4-2 commentary; see also DOJ Standard 9-27.001("The manner in which Federal prosecutors exercise their decision-making authority has far-reaching implications, both in terms of justice and effectiveness in law enforcement and in terms of the consequences for individual citizens").

54. Bennett L. Gershman, "The Prosecutor's Duty to Truth," 14 *Geo. J. Legal Ethics* 309, 337 (Winter 2001) ("Although not articulated in judicial decisions, a prosecutor's duty to truth embraces a duty to make an independent evaluation of . . . the reliability of forensic evidence, and the truth of the defendant's guilt"); Peter A. Joy, "The Relationship Between Prosecutorial Misconduct and Wrongful Convictions: Shaping Remedies for a Broken System," 2006 *Wis. L. Rev.* 399, 407 (2006) ("When prosecutors do not critically examine the evidence against the accused to ensure its trustworthiness . . . rather than act as ministers of justice, they administer injustice").

55. See, e.g., *Rounseville v. Zahl*, 13 F.3d 625, 629-30 (2d Cir. 1994) ("[P]robable cause under New York law is 'the knowledge of facts, actual or apparent, strong enough to justify a reasonable man in the belief that he has lawful grounds for prosecuting the defendant in the manner complained of'") (internal quotation and citation omitted); *Nguyen v. Burgerbusters, Inc.*, 642 S .E.2d 502, 506 (N.C. 2007) (Probable cause "is the existence of such facts and circumstances, known to the defendant at the time, as would induce a reasonable man to commence a prosecution") (internal quotation marks omitted).

56. See note 30, *supra*.

57. CJA Standard 3-3.9(a) ("A prosecutor should not institute, or cause to be instituted, or permit the continued pendency of criminal charges when the prosecutor knows that the charges are not supported by probable cause").

58. NDAA Standard 4-1.3 ("Prosecutors should screen potential charges to eliminate from the criminal justice system those cases where prosecution is not justified or not in the

public interest. Factors that may be considered in this decision include . . . b. Insufficiency of admissible evidence to support a conviction").

59. DOJ Standard 9-27.200.

60. CJA Standard 3-3.9(a) ("A prosecutor should not institute, or cause to be instituted, or permit the continued pendency of criminal charges . . . in the absence of sufficient admissible evidence to support a conviction"); NDAA Standard 4-2.2 ("A prosecutor should file charges that he or she believes adequately encompass the accused's criminal activity and which he or she reasonably believes can be substantiated by admissible evidence at trial"); DOJ Standard 9-27.300(B), 9-27.220(B).

61. DOJ Standard 9-27.300(B).

62. DOJ Standard 9-27.300(B); see also DOJ Standard 9-27.220(B) ("[B]oth as a matter of fundamental fairness and in the interest of the efficient administration of justice, no prosecution should be initiated against any person unless the government believes that the person probably will be found guilty by an unbiased trier of fact"). In fact, "[p]rosecutors routinely engage in overcharging, a practice that involves 'tacking on' additional charges that they know they cannot prove beyond a reasonable doubt or that they can technically prove but are inconsistent with the legislative intent or otherwise inappropriate." Davis, *supra* note 20 at 3.1.

63. 2009 NRC Report at 7.

64. *Padilla v. Kentucky*, 130 S.Ct. 1473, 1485, 1485 n.13 (2010) (citing Dept. of Justice, *Bureau of Justice Statistics, Sourcebook of Criminal Justice Statistics* 2003, p. 418, 450.

65. See Davis, *supra* note 20 at 43 ("Like the charging decision, plea bargaining is controlled entirely by the prosecutor"); Griffin, *supra* note 51, at 271 ("Charging, plea bargaining, and sentencing are interrelated; discretion in each area reinforces discretion in the others . . . Broad charging discretion and the low threshold for charging, however, give prosecutors extensive control over defendants' pleas"). A judge must accept or reject the plea agreement, Fed. R. Crim. Pro. 11(c)(3), but cannot be involved in the plea bargaining process. Fed. R. Crim. Pro. 11(c)(1) ("An attorney for the government and the defendant's attorney, or the defendant when proceeding pro se, may discuss and reach a plea agreement. The court must not participate in these discussions").

66. See Fed. R. Crim Pro. 11(c)(1); DOJ Standard 9-27.400; see also Meares, *supra* note 51, at 863–864 ("Once a prosecution is initiated, the prosecutor can manipulate the offenses on which to charge the accused to control the defendant's exposure to punishment. By controlling the defendant's exposure to punishment, the prosecutor is able to control the dynamics of plea bargaining. That . . . leads inescapably to the conclusion that the prosecutor greatly affects a very important component of the criminal justice system")

67. NDAA Standard 5-3.1.

68. DOJ Standard 9-27.420(A)(6).

69. DOJ Standard 9-27.420(B)(6).

70. NDAA Standard 5-3.3 ("The prosecutor should not knowingly make any false or misleading statements of law or fact to the defense during plea negotiations."); CJA Standard 3-4.1(c) ("A prosecutor should not knowingly make false statements or representations as to fact or law in the course of plea discussions with defense counsel or the accused."); CJA Standard 3-4.1 Commentary ("Although the prosecutor is under no obligation to reveal any evidence to the defense counsel in the course of plea discussions . . .

[t]he prosecutor during plea discussions must also avoid the use of deception in dealing with the evidence").

71. CJA Standard 11.1.1(a)(ii).

72. See *ABA National Inventory of the Collateral Consequences of Conviction*, available at http://www.abacollateralconsequences.org ("Persons convicted of crime are subject to a wide variety of legal and regulatory sanctions and restrictions in addition to the sentence imposed by the court"); see also Joy Radice, "Administering Justice: Removing Statutory Barriers to Reentry," 83 *U. Colo. L. Rev.* 715, 717 (Spring 2012) ("Thousands of civil punishments stand in the way of giving people who served their criminal sentences a true second chance").

73. See, e.g., Rodney Uphoff, "Convicting the Innocent: Aberration or Systemic Problem," 2006 *Wis. L. Rev.* 739, 798 (2006) ("the consequences of pretrial incarceration are often very significant"); Sarah Downey, *Online, you are guilty even after being proven innocent*, The Online Privacy Blog, available at http://www.abine.com/blog/ (May 20, 2011); Brad M. Johnston, "The Media's Presence During the Execution of a Search Warrant: A Per Se Violation of the Fourth Amendment," 58 *Ohio St. L.J.* 1499, 1534 (1997) ("media coverage can be exceptionally harmful to a person's expected personal privacy even if a person is cleared of all criminal charges").

74. 2009 NRC Report at 87.

75. For example, Paula could offer a bargain that requires Daniel to plead guilty to Carrying a Pistol Without a License, D.C. CODE § 22-4504(a), which carries a five-year sentence, or could allow him to plea to Unlawful Possession of a Firearm, D.C. CODE § 7-2502.01(a) which carries up to a one-year sentence, or she could also allow a plea to Attempted Carrying a Pistol Outside of Home or Business, under D.C. Code §§ 22-4504(a) and 22-1803, which carries up to a 180-day sentence and/or a $1,000 fine.

76. 2009 NRC Report at 103-04.

77. Davis, *supra* note 20, at 58 ("The plea bargaining process would be greatly improved if prosecutors were required to provide all of the relevant information that would enable the defendant to make an informed decision. The prosecutor should reveal the weaknesses in her case and inform the defendant of information that is helpful to the defense").

78. CJA Standard 3-3.6, commentary.

79. *Brady v. Maryland*, 373 U.S. 83, 87 (1963).

80. *Kyles v. Whitley*, 514 U.S. 419, 433-34 (1995) (internal quotation and citation omitted).

81. *Smith v. Cain*, 132 S.Ct. 627, 630 (2012) (internal quotation, citation, and modification omitted).

82. *Youngblood v. West Virginia*, 547 U.S. 867, 870 (2006).

83. *United States v. Bagley*, 473 U.S. 667, 676 (1985).

84. *Kyles*, 514 U.S. at 437.

85. *Id.*

86. See note 30 *supra*.

87. Model Rule 3.8(d) (emphasis added).

88. Brief of the American Bar Association as Amicus Curiae in Support of Petitioner, *Smith v. Cain*, 2011 WL 3739380 (Aug. 19, 2011) (quoting ABA Formal Opinion 09454 at 11a).

89. See note 31 *supra*.

90. See CJA Standard 3-3.11(a) ("A prosecutor should not intentionally fail to make timely disclosure to the defense, at the earliest feasible opportunity, of the existence of all evidence or information which tends to negate the guilt of the accused or mitigate the offense charged or which would tend to reduce the punishment of the accused"); NDAA Standard 2-8.4 ("The prosecutor shall make timely disclosure of exculpatory or mitigating evidence, as required by law and/or applicable rules of ethical conduct"); NDAA Part 4-9 commentary ("[I]t is well established that any doubt about whether something is subject to disclosure should be resolved in favor of the defendant, and that disclosure of material exculpatory and impeachment evidence is required"); DOJ Standard 9-5.001C ("Department policy recognizes that a fair trial will often include examination of relevant exculpatory or impeachment information that is significantly probative of the issues before the court but that may not, on its own, result in an acquittal or, as is often colloquially expressed, make the difference between guilt and innocence. As a result, this policy requires disclosure by prosecutors of information beyond that which is "material" to guilt as articulated [in Supreme Court opinions]"). The CJA, NDAA, and DOJ standards make clear that prosecutors should also disclose exculpatory evidence to the grand jury. CJA 3-3.6(b); NDAA 3-3.5(a); NDAA 4-8.2(a); NDAA 4-8.2(g); DOJ 9-11.233.

91. DOJ Standard 9-5.001(C)(2).

92. DOJ Standard 9-5.001(C)(2); see also DOJ Standard 9-5.001 (C)(1) ("A prosecutor must disclose information that is inconsistent with any element of any crime charged against the defendant or that establishes a recognized affirmative defense, regardless of whether the prosecutor believes such information will make the difference between conviction and acquittal of the defendant for a charged crime"); DOJ Standard 9-5.001 (C)(3) ("Unlike the requirements of *Brady* and its progeny, which focus on evidence, the disclosure requirement of this section applies to information regardless of whether the information subject to disclosure would itself constitute admissible evidence"); DOJ Standard 9-5.001(F) ("[T]his policy encourages prosecutors to err on the side of disclosure in close questions of materiality and identifies standards that favor greater disclosure in advance of trial through the production of exculpatory information that is inconsistent with any element of any charged crime and impeachment information that casts a substantial doubt upon either the accuracy of any evidence the government intends to rely on to prove an element of any charged crime or that might have a significant bearing on the admissibility of prosecution evidence").

93. Fed. R. Crim. Pro. 16(a)(1)(G).

94. Fed. R. Crim. Pro. 16(a)(1)(G).

95. Fed. R. Crim. Pro. 16, comments to 1993 Amendment (citing See Eads, "Adjudication by Ambush: Federal Prosecutors' Use of Nonscientific Experts in a System of Limited Criminal Discovery," 67 *N.C. L. Rev.* 577, 622 [1989]).

96. Fed. R. Crim. Pro. 16(a)(1) (F).

97. Fed. R. Crim. Pro. 16(d)(2).

98. As discussed in the next section, issue of what information prosecutors "possesses" is a major limitation.

99. *Cain*, 132 S.Ct. at 630.

100. DOJ Standard 9-5.001(C)(2).

101. Edwards testimony at 3; *id.* (The NRC "committee's report rejects as scientifically implausible any claims that fingerprint analyses have 'zero error rates'").

102. Saks, *supra* note 19 at 430 ("For criminal prosecutors, this probably means that the weaknesses of the proffered science need to be disclosed. If the facts (as to the shakiness of the science) are material to identifying the defendant as the perpetrator and they tend to weaken the identification and negate guilt, then they are adjudicative facts which tend to exculpate and must be disclosed").

103. 2009 NRC Report at 139 (citing I. E. Dror and D. Charlton. 2006. Why experts make errors. Journal of Forensic Identification 56(4):600-616).

104. Fred C. Zacharias, "Structuring the Ethics of Prosecutorial Trial Practice: Can Prosecutors Do Justice?" 44 *Vand. L. Rev.* 45, 83 (Jan. 1991) (A prosecutor's "responsibility to the codes' vision of justice sometimes requires her to provide information or forensic services that discovery rules would not guarantee").

105. Model Rule 1.1 (m).

106. ABA, CPR Policy Implementation Committee, Variations of the ABA Model Rules of Professional Conduct: Rule 3.3: Candor Toward the Tribunal, as of Nov. 1, 2010.

107. Model Rule 3.3(a)(1).

108. Model Rule 3.3, comment 2.

109. See note 31 *supra*.

110. Model Rule 3.3(a)(1) ("A lawyer shall not knowingly . . . fail to disclose to the tribunal legal authority in the controlling jurisdiction known to the lawyer to be directly adverse to the position of the client and not disclosed by opposing counsel").

111. CJA Standard 3-2.8(a)("A prosecutor should not intentionally misrepresent matters of fact or law to the court"); NDAA Standard 6-1.1 ("A prosecutor shall not knowingly make a false statement of fact or law to a court"); CJA Standard 3-2.8(d) ("A prosecutor should not fail to disclose to the tribunal legal authority in the controlling jurisdiction known to the prosecutor to be directly adverse to the prosecutor's position and not disclosed by defense counsel"); NDAA Standard 6-1.2 ("A prosecutor shall inform the court of legal authority in the controlling jurisdiction known to the prosecutor to be directly adverse to his or her position").

112. See CJA Standard 3-2.8, commentary ("It is fundamental that in relations with the court, the prosecutor must be scrupulously candid and truthful in his or her representations in respect to any matter before the court").

113. NDAA Part 6-1 commentary.

114. 2009 NRC Report at 7.

115. 4 Mod. Sci. Evid. § 32:1.

116. Model Rule 3.3(a)(3).

117. See note 31 *supra*.

118. A prosecutor's closing argument can violate the criminal defendant's due process rights "if they 'so infected the trial with unfairness as to make the resulting conviction a denial of due process.'" *Parker v. Matthews*, 132 S.Ct. 2148, 2153 (2012) (quoting *Darden v. Wainwright*, 477 U.S. 168, 181 [1986]).

119. CJA Standard 3-5.6(a) ("A prosecutor should not knowingly offer false evidence, whether by documents, tangible evidence, or the testimony of witnesses, or fail to seek

withdrawal thereof upon discovery of its falsity"); NDAA Standard 6-1.3 ("A prosecutor shall not offer evidence that the prosecutor knows to be false").

120. NDAA Standard 3-1.3.

121. CJA Standard 3-5.7(b) ("A prosecutor should not use the power of cross-examination to discredit or undermine a witness if the prosecutor knows the witness is testifying truthfully"); NDAA Standard 6-1.4 ("A prosecutor should not misuse the power of cross-examination or impeachment to ridicule, discredit, undermine, or hold a fact witness up to contempt, if the prosecutor knows the witness is testifying truthfully").

122. CJA Standard 3-5.8(a).

123. CJA Standard 3-3.3(a) ("To the extent necessary, the prosecutor should explain to the expert his or her role in the trial as an impartial expert called to aid the fact finders and the manner in which the examination of witnesses is conducted").

124. CJA Standard 3-5.8(a) ("In closing argument to the jury, the prosecutor may argue all reasonable inferences from evidence in the record. The prosecutor should not intentionally misstate the evidence or mislead the jury as to the inferences it may draw"); NDAA Standard 6-8.1 ("In closing argument, a prosecutor should be fair and accurate in the discussion of the law, the facts, and the reasonable inferences that may be drawn from the facts").

125. Raeder, *supra* note 38, at 1420 ("[P]rosecutors should be on the lookout for inaccurate or misleading testimony when offering an expert who presents statistics without scientific basis or relies on questionably reliable techniques, such as hair or bite mark analysis").

126. NDAA Part 6-1 commentary.

127. 4 Mod. Sci. Evid. § 32:1.

128. Daniel S. Medwed, "The Prosecutor as Minister of Justice: Preaching to the Unconverted from the Post-Conviction Pulpit," 84 *Wash. L. Rev.* 35, 42 (Feb. 2009) (Observing that "[t]he reliance on 'justice' as a governing principle of prosecutorial behavior is problematic because of the term's inherent vagueness," and noting that the absence of concrete rules "leav[es] the amorphous concept of justice to inform much of prosecutorial behavior"); Zacharias and Green, *supra* note 49, at 13 ("Language . . . exhorting prosecutors to serve justice has been similarly ignored, largely because of the . . . failure to define the meaning of 'justice'"); Zacharias, *supra* note 104, at 48 ("The 'do justice' standard, however, establishes no identifiable norm. Its vagueness leaves prosecutors with only their individual sense of morality to determine just conduct. Some will decide that justice lies in conviction at all cost") (footnotes omitted).

129. Zacharias, *supra* note 104, at 105 ("No prosecutor has ever been sanctioned for failing to do justice at trial"); ABA Formal Opinion 09454 at 4a ("[D]isciplinary authorities rarely proceed against prosecutors in cases that raise interpretive questions under Rule 3.8(d)").

130. See note 146, *infra*.

131. Gershman, *supra* note 20, at 206.

132. For an exploration of the (as yet unrealized) potential to "enforce[e] the general competence standard against prosecutors who fail to exercise reasonable care to prevent false convictions," see Zacharias and Green, *supra* note 49, at 4–5.

133. Gershman, *supra* note 17, at 553 (Spring 2007) ("there are other disturbing examples of prosecutors who appear to be ignorant of their expert's dishonest and incompetent analysis, as well as the expert's use of so-called 'junk testimony,' notwithstanding obvious signs of pervasive and systematic fraud, incompetence, and misconduct by the expert").

134. Zacharias and Green, *supra* note 49, at 16 ("As a practical matter, disciplinary regulators have not implemented rules like Model Rule 1.1 [the competence requirement] against prosecutors").

135. Joy, *supra* note 54, at 400 (Identifying "vague ethics rules that provide ambiguous guidance to prosecutors" as a cause of prosecutorial misconduct); *id*. at 417 ("Commentators writing about prosecutorial misconduct agree that current state ethics rules, principally based on the ABA Model Rules of Professional Conduct, inadequately identify all of the ethical obligations for prosecutors"). Notably, "the ABA Commission on Evaluation of the Rules of Professional Conduct (Ethics 2000 Commission) specifically requested and received a Report on Model Rule 3.8," which "made a series of recommendations for more explicit ethical guidance" for the Rule 3.8. *Id*. at 417–418 (citing Niki Kuckes, Report to the ABA Commission on Evaluation of the Rules of Professional Conduct Concerning Rule 3.8 of the ABA Model Rules of Professional Responsibility: Special Responsibilities of a Prosecutor 1 [1999]). None of those recommendations were implemented. *Id*. at 418.

136. Davis, *supra* note 20, at 150 ("[M]odel Rule 3.8 does not adequately address the conduct and behavior of prosecutors"); Zacharias and Green, *supra* note 49, at 22 ("[T]he existing specific rules do not address much of the conduct that contributes to unjust convictions").

137. Kate Weisburd, "Prosecutors Hide, Defendants Seek: The Erosion of Brady Through the Defendant Due Diligence Rule," 60 *UCLA L. Rev.* 138, 150 (Oct. 2012) (Examining the way lower courts misinterpreted Supreme Court cases and "began to narrow the definition of Brady *evidence* to cover only evidence that is 'unknown'" including "any evidence that is unknowable to the defense with due diligence"); see, e.g., *United States v. LeRoy*, 687 F.2d 610, 618 (2d Cir. 1982) ("Evidence is not suppressed if the defendant either knew, or should have known, of the essential facts permitting him to take advantage of any exculpatory evidence").

138. See Weisburd, *supra* note 137, at 142 (Rule that limits Brady to information the defense could not have discovered though due diligence rule "shifts the burden of disclosure from the government to the defendant, and as a result, less exculpatory evidence is 'fully aired.' In this way, the truth-seeking purpose of criminal trials is undermined").

139. See, e.g., *Milke v. Ryan*, 711 F.3d 998, 1017-18 (9th Cir. 2013) ("That the [relevant documents] were available in the public record doesn't diminish the state's obligation to produce them under *Brady*. In determining whether evidence has been suppressed for purposes of *Brady*, our court has asked whether the defendant has enough information to be able to ascertain the supposed *Brady* material on his own. Where a defendant doesn't have enough information to find the *Brady* material with reasonable diligence, the state's failure to produce the evidence *is* considered suppression") (internal quotation omitted, emphasis in original); *United States v. Payne*, 63 F.3d 1200, 1209 (2d Cir. 1995) (Fact of "document's availability in a public court file" did not obviate prosecutor's duty to disclose the document where there was "no indication that [defense]

counsel was aware of facts that would have required him to discover the [document] through his own diligent investigation").

140. Another example of a related under-inclusive rule is the procedural requirement that the prosecutor disclose the "bases and reasons" of a proposed expert's opinion. This plainly requires the prosecutor to disclose the bases and reasons for the fingerprint examiner's testimony, but does not appear to require disclose of *flaws* in those bases or reasons.

141. See Gershman, *supra* note 17, at 533 (*Brady* standard "is so malleable that it affords prosecutors an extremely broad opportunity to exercise discretion in ways that impede—rather than promote—the search for truth"); Davis, *supra* note 20, at 150 ("Prosecutors and defense attorneys are likely to have very different views of what information this phrase covers").

142. Gershman, *supra* note 17, at 549 ("Although there are many reasons why prosecutors suppress *Brady* evidence, probably the most powerful justification most often relied on is the prosecutor's unilateral conclusion that the evidence is not material").

143. ABA Model Rule 1.1 (f) ("'Knowingly,' 'known,' or 'knows' denotes actual knowledge of the fact in question. A person's knowledge may be inferred from circumstances"); NDAA Definitions ("'Knows,' 'Has Knowledge,' or 'Within the Knowledge of'—Means actual knowledge").

144. Model Rule 3.3 comment 8; see also Zacharias and Green, *supra* note 49, at 22 ("[T]he codes seem to allow prosecutors to offer questionable evidence unless they "know" it to be false, even though exploiting unreliable evidence may lead to an unjust conviction") (footnote omitted); *id.* at 34 ("A prosecutor who offers testimony he reasonably believes, but does not know, to be false cannot be disciplined under Model Rule 3.3(a)").

145. Giannelli and McMunigal, *supra* note 49, at 1526 (observing that a "difficult issue arises when the testimony is accurate in a technical sense and yet misleading").

146. Gershman, *supra* note 20, at 198–199 ("[W]ith a few exceptions, there is little evidence that courts, lawmakers, or professional disciplinary agencies have demonstrated a willingness or capacity to impose sanctions on prosecutors for committing foul blows"); Davis, *supra* note 20, at 8 ("[T]he mechanics of accountability that purport to hold [prosecutors] accountable have proven largely ineffective"); Robert Aronson and Jacqueline McMurtrie, "The Use and Misuse of High-Tech Evidence by Prosecutors: Ethical and Evidentiary Issues", 76 *Fordham L. Rev.* 1453, 1487 (Dec. 2007) ("A prosecutor generally receives relatively light punishment for the unethical use of evidence, leaving little incentive for a prosecutor to change his or her unethical behavior. Although a judge may describe a prosecutor's behavior as 'unforgivable,' 'intolerable,' 'beyond reprehension,' and 'illegal, improper and dishonest,' these attorneys usually face little personal responsibility for their actions and may even advance significantly in their careers. Direct punishment of prosecutors is rare") (footnotes and citations omitted); Kenneth Rosenthal, "Prosecutor Misconduct, Convictions, and Double Jeopardy: Case Studies in an Emerging Jurisprudence," 71 *Temp. L. Rev.* 887, 889 (1998) (noting an "absence of disciplinary sanctions against prosecutors, even in the most egregious cases"); Fred C. Zacharias, "The Professional Discipline of Prosecutors," 79 *N.C. L. Rev.* 721 (2001) (assessing the lack of discipline for prosecutorial misconduct); John F. Terzano, Esq., Joyce A. McGee, Esq., & Alanna D. Holt, "Improving Prosecutorial Accountability: A Policy Review," *The Justice Project*, at 2 (2009) (citing "dangerous and pervasive lack of prosecutorial accountability"); Joaquin Sapien and

Sergio Hernandez, "Who Polices Prosecutors Who Abuse Their Authority? Usually Nobody," ProPublica (April 3, 2013) ("New York's system of attorney oversight is ill-equipped or unwilling to identify, punish and deter prosecutors who abuse their authority"); Bruce A. Green, "Prosecutors and Professional Regulation," 25 *Geo. J. Legal Ethics* 873, 874 (Fall 2012) ("When prosecutors engage in questionable conduct that does implicate professional conduct rules, professional discipline rarely follows"); *id.* at 873 ("Few professional conduct provisions specifically target [prosecutors'] work, and those provisions are mostly undemanding") (footnote omitted); Moriarty, *supra* note 17, at 28 ("As scholars note, prosecutors rarely receive ethical sanctions for their misconduct, even when it leads to wrongful conviction"); Zacharias, *supra* note 104, at 48–49 ("[T]he lack of enforceable ethical standards, together with discipliners' natural hesitation to interfere with governmental actors, has prevented disciplinary bodies from sanctioning prosecutors for violating the professional codes") (footnote omitted).

147. Rampant Prosecutorial Misconduct, *The New York Times*, Jan. 4, 2014 ("And that [punishment] rarely amounted to more than a slap on the wrist, such as making the prosecutor pay for the cost of the disciplinary hearing.").

148. Bennett L. Gershman, "Misuse of Scientific Evidence by Prosecutors," 28 *Okla. City U. L. Rev.* 17, 17 (Spring 2003).

149. Davis, *supra* note 20, at 126 ("Most of the prosecutorial practices that occur behind closed doors, such as charging and plea bargaining decisions and grand jury practices, are never revealed to the public"); Zacharias and Green, *supra* note 49, at 18 ("Prosecutions are not transparent. Only a small amount of prosecutors' work takes place in court. Even when a prosecutor's conduct is on the record, its propriety may depend on related off-the-record conduct. Disciplinary agencies may have difficulty obtaining evidence of a prosecutor's out-of-court misconduct or behavior that would be necessary to evaluate the prosecutor's in-court activities"); John F. Terzano et al., *supra* note 146, at 3 ("The "majority of prosecutorial decisions take place outside the view of the public, the courts, and defense attorneys") (footnotes omitted); Joy, *supra* note 54, at 400 (Identifying "vast discretionary authority with little or no transparency" as a cause of prosecutorial misconduct); Zacharias, *supra* note 104, at 106 ("A prosecutor's ethical breach rarely will appear clearly on the trial record. Often it will be known only to the prosecutor herself") (footnote omitted); Rachel E. Barkow, "Organizational Guidelines for the Prosecutor's Office," 31 *Cardozo L. Rev.* 2089, 2093–2094 (2010) ("[T]here are currently no effective deterrents for prosecutorial misconduct. The biggest problem is that most violations are never discovered in the first place").

150. Barkow, *supra* note 149, at 2093–2094 ("Defendants often have no way of knowing whether a prosecutor is in possession of exculpatory evidence that should be disclosed under *Brady*. In most cases, it is entirely fortuitous that a violation comes to light"); Rosen, *supra* note 29 at 702–703 ("[T]he occasions when defendants do find out about suppressed or falsified evidence usually result from fortuitous circumstances").

151. Gould et al., *supra* note 14, at 19 ("In research on erroneous convictions, the most commonly established transgression is the prosecution's failure to turn over exculpatory evidence"); Barkow, *supra* note 149, at 2090 ("A host of studies have documented prosecutorial misconduct, and one of the most common types of prosecutorial misconduct in these cases involved the suppression of exculpatory evidence in violation of *Brady v. Maryland*")

(footnotes and citations to studies omitted); Ken Armstrong and Maurice Possley, "Trial & Error; How Prosecutors Sacrifice Justice to Win; The Verdict: Dishonor," *Chi. Trib.*, Jan. 10, 1999, § 1, at 1 (reporting on a study that showed that since 1963 "at least 381 defendants nationally have had a homicide conviction thrown out because prosecutors concealed evidence suggesting innocence or presented evidence they knew to be false"), as quoted in Joy, *supra* note 54, at 403 n.20.

152. See Gershman, *supra* note 17, at 565 ("there is virtually no accountability, liability, or punishment for *Brady* violations"); Barkow, *supra* note 149, at 2095 ("even in the relatively rare instances when [Brady] violations come to light, prosecutors are seldom penalized"); Rosen, *supra* note 29, at 697 (Results of study "demonstrate that despite the universal adoption by the states of Disciplinary Rules prohibiting prosecutorial suppression of exculpatory evidence and falsification of evidence, and despite numerous reported cases showing violations of these rules, disciplinary charges have been brought infrequently and meaningful sanctions rarely applied . . . [A]t present insufficient incentive exists for a prosecutor to refrain from *Brady*-type misconduct") (footnotes omitted).

153. *United States v. Olsen*, 737 F.3d 625 (9th Cir. 2013) (Kozinski, J., dissenting).

154. *Id.* at 631 (emphasis added).

155. *Id.* at 630 (citation omitted).

156. See, e.g., California Commission on the Fair Administration of Justice, *Report and Recommendations on Reporting Misconduct*, at 3 (October 18, 2007) ("reliance upon the [California] State Bar as the primary disciplinary authority is seriously hampered by underreporting").

157. Davis, *supra* note 20, at 139 (Bar authorities "seldom receive formal complaints about prosecutors, because the people most likely to discover the misconduct—defense attorneys—fear retaliation from prosecution offices that will continue to wield power and exercise considerable discretion in their client's cases"); Barkow, *supra* note 149, at 2095–2096 ("Defense lawyers may have knowledge of violations, but, as repeat players, they have to be careful not to anger prosecutors and their colleagues who will decide the fate of their clients").

158. For example, one study found that, in 53 cases where the prosecutor engaged in misconduct significant enough to require reversal of the criminal conviction, not one of those prosecutors was referred the state disciplinary committee, even though judges are required by statute to make those referrals. California Commission, *supra* note 156, at 4; Terzano et al., *supra* note 146, at 13 ("Appellate court judges by and large fail to report findings of misconduct to the proper authorities, and oftentimes actively withhold the names of offending prosecutors from their written decisions") (footnote and citation omitted); Sapien and Hernandez, *supra* note 146 ("A ProPublica analysis of more than a decade's worth of state and federal court rulings found more than two dozen instances in which judges explicitly concluded that city prosecutors had committed harmful misconduct. In each instance, these abuses were sufficient to prompt courts to throw out convictions. Yet the same appellate courts did not routinely refer prosecutors for investigation by the state disciplinary committees charged with policing lawyers"); Barkow, *supra* note 149, at 2096 (Judges "have largely failed to call prosecutorial misconduct to the attention of state bar authorities") (footnotes omitted).

159. Zacharias, *supra* note 104, at 63 ("[T]he judge needs the prosecutor's goodwill almost as much as the prosecutor needs his. The court must have the cooperation of the

prosecutor's office to manage the criminal justice system; offending one prosecutor may offend them all"); Ellen Yaroshefsky, "Wrongful Convictions: It Is Time to Take Prosecution Discipline Seriously," 8 *U. D.C. L. Rev.* 275, 292 (Fall 2004) ("On a practical level, many state judges, concerned about career advancement, are loathe to sanction or report lawyers to disciplinary committees because the judge does not want to alienate the powerful prosecutor's office").

160. See, e.g., David E. Bernstein, "Junk Science in the United States and the Commonwealth," 21 *Yale J. Int'l L.* 123, 125 (Winter 1996) (Noting that some "judges were content to rely on the adversarial system to reveal any flaws in tendered scientific evidence").

161. See, e.g., Kevin C. McMunigal, "Prosecutors and Corrupt Science," 36 *Hofstra L. Rev.* 437, 445 (Winter 2007) ("[D]isciplinary or other sanctions . . . are very rarely imposed on prosecutors"); Zacharias and Green, *supra* note 49, at 397 ("the professional codes typically regulate prosecutors with a fairly light touch" and "disciplinary authorities do not appear particularly eager to bring actions against prosecutors except in situations involving unambiguously wrongful conduct").

162. See, e.g., Barkow, *supra* note 149, at 2094 n.27 ("[D]iscovery from a civil rights lawsuit in Queens, New York found that not a single prosecutor was disciplined in the eighty-four cases that involved prosecutorial misconduct resulting in the reversal of a conviction") (citing Brief of Amici Curiae the National Ass'n of Criminal Defense Lawyers et al. in Support of Respondents at 31, *Pottawattamie County v. McGhee*, 547 F.3d 922 [2008] [No. 08-1065], 2009 WL 3022905); *id.* at 2095 ("A nationwide study of all reported cases involving discipline for prosecutorial misconduct found only twenty-seven instances in which prosecutors were disciplined for unethical behavior that compromised the fairness of a trial") (footnotes and citations omitted); Sapien and Hernandez, *supra* note 146 ("A ProPublica analysis of more than a decade's worth of state and federal court rulings" in New York found that only one prosecutor of "the prosecutors who oversaw cases reversed based on misconduct [was] disbarred, suspended, or censured" or was "punished by their superiors in the city's district attorney offices"); Joy, *supra* note 54, at 425–426 ("Studies of wrongful convictions have demonstrated that when prosecutorial misconduct caused or contributed to a wrongful conviction, the prosecutors involved were rarely disciplined, either internally or through external bodies"); Zacharias, *supra* note 146, at 744, 755 (Study of "all reported cases in which prosecutors have been disciplined for violations of professional rules by courts or state disciplinary authorities" found that "prosecutors are disciplined rarely, both in the abstract and relative to private lawyers").

163. Barkow, *supra* note 149, at 2095.

164. California Commission, *supra* note 156, at 13 (Of the 37 remaining cases "twenty [resulted in] in a reprimand or censure, twelve in a suspended license, two in disbarment, twenty-four in a fine, and three in a remand for further proceedings") (citing the Center for Public Integrity, *Harmful Error: Investigating America's Local Prosecutors* [2003]).

165. Prosecutors have absolute immunity for "activities . . . intimately associated with the judicial phase of the criminal process." *Imbler v. Pachtman*, 424 U.S. 409, 430 (1976); Rosen, *supra* note 29, at 704 ("This decision has eliminated potential civil liability as a deterrent"); Joy, *supra* note 54, at 426 n.136 ("Under federal law, prosecutors have absolute immunity from claims for conduct that is associated with the judicial phase of the case, such as initiating the prosecution and pursuing the prosecution in court").

166. Barkow, *supra* note 149, at 2094 ("Although federal prosecutors can bring criminal actions against prosecutors who willfully violate a defendant's constitutional rights under 18 U.S.C. § 242, those actions are almost never brought").

167. Rosen, *supra* note 29, at 703 n.56 ("No cases could be found in which a prosecutor was found in contempt for *Brady*-type misconduct. Professor Alschuler also has found that there does not appear to be a single case in which a prosecutor had been found in contempt for courtroom misconduct") (citing Alschuler, "Courtroom Misconduct by Prosecutors and Trial Judges," 50 *Tex. L. Rev.* 629, 673-74 [1972]).

168. For example, in a study of 2,130 cases in California where the defense claimed the prosecutor engaged in misconduct, the courts "concluded that prosecutorial misconduct did occur in 443 of these cases, or 21%, but in 390 of the 443 cases, 88%, "the court concluded the misconduct was harmless error and affirmed the conviction." California Commission, *supra* note 156, at 3 (citing Cookie Ridolfi, *Prosecutorial Misconduct: A Systemic Review* (July 11, 2007); Raeder, *supra* note 38, at 1433 ("[I]f no prejudice occurs . . . the conviction will be affirmed, even in the presence of the ethical violation. Thus, the answer to whether a freestanding ethical obligation requires a reversal is a resounding no, even when it is clear that a specific obligation, rather than merely an aspirational precept, is violated") (footnote omitted).

169. *Chapman v. California*, 386 U.S. 18, 24 (1967).

170. See, e.g., *Rose v. Clark*, 478 U.S. 570, 588-89 (1986) (Stevens, J., concurring) ("An automatic application of harmless-error review in case after case, and for error after error, can only encourage prosecutors to subordinate the interest in respecting the Constitution to the ever-present and always powerful interest in obtaining a conviction in a particular case"); *United States v. Antonelli Fireworks Co.*, 155 F.2d 631, 661 (2d Cir. 1946) (Frank, J., dissenting) ("This court has several times used vigorous language in denouncing government counsel for such conduct as that of the United States Attorney here. But, each time, it has said that, nevertheless, it would not reverse. Such an attitude of helpless piety is, I think, undesirable. It means actual condonation of counsel's alleged offense, coupled with verbal disapprobation . . . Government counsel, employing such tactics, are the kind who, eager to win victories, will gladly pay the small price of a ritualistic verbal spanking"); Raeder, *supra* note 38, at 1434 ("[I]f the conviction is confirmed, a prosecutor who only cares about winning might view the ethical reproach from the perspective of no harm, no foul—particularly when no disciplinary sanctions are imposed"); Davis, *supra* note 20, at 127 (Oxford, 2007) ("[The harmless error] rule permits, perhaps even encourages, prosecutors to engage in misconduct during trial with the assurance that so long as the evidence of the defendant's guilt is clear, the conviction will be affirmed").

171. Gershman, *supra* note 51, at 1267 ("[A] probable cause standard is an extremely low threshold for bringing charges," and "seems to require so little of a prosecutor that short of venality, it would appear to allow reckless and incompetent charging without any risk of professional oversight"); Meares, *supra* note 51, at 864 (The ABA Model Rules "do not clearly prohibit the prosecutor from deciding to charge an accused with offenses which the prosecutor has probable cause to believe are factually justified but which the prosecutor believes she probably will not be able to prove beyond a reasonable doubt at trial").

172. NDAA Standard 1-1; see also NDAA Part 1.1 commentary ("A prosecutor is the only one in a criminal action who is responsible for the presentation of the truth") (emphasis added).

173. NDAA Standards Introduction ("These standards are not intended to: (a) be used by the judiciary in determining whether a prosecutor committed error or engaged in improper conduct; (b) be used by disciplinary agencies when passing upon allegations of violations of rules of ethical conduct; (c) create any right of action in any person; or (d) alter existing law in any respect"); see also CJA Standard 3-1.1 ("These standards . . . are not intended to be used as criteria for the judicial evaluation of alleged misconduct of the prosecutor to determine the validity of a conviction"); CJA Standard 3-1.1 commentary ("These Standards are not intended, however, to serve as rules to be used as the basis for the imposition of professional discipline . . . Moreover, these Standards are not intended to create substantive or procedural rights that might accrue either to accused or convicted persons"); DOJ Standard 1-1.100 (The Manual "is not intended to, does not, and may not be relied upon to create any rights, substantive or procedural, enforceable at law by any party in any matter civil or criminal. Nor are any limitations hereby placed on otherwise lawful litigative prerogatives of the Department of Justice"); DOJ Standard 9-27.150 ("[This provision] is intended to foreclose efforts to litigate the validity of prosecutorial actions alleged to be at variance with these principles or not in compliance with internal office procedures that may be adopted pursuant hereto").

174. See Zacharias and Green, *supra* note 49, at 11–12 ("[P]rofessional discipline has had little practical effect in constraining prosecutorial behavior that risks faulty convictions"); Joy, *supra* note 54, at 400 (Describing how "inadequate remedies for prosecutorial misconduct . . . create perverse incentives for prosecutors to engage in, rather than refrain from, prosecutorial misconduct").

175. See Sapien and Hernandez, *supra* note 146 ("A ProPublica analysis of more than a decade's worth of state and federal court rulings" in New York found that "several [prosecutors] received promotions and raises soon after courts cited them for abuses"); Ken Armstrong and Maurice Possley, "The Verdict: Dishonor," *Chi. Trib.*, Jan. 10, 1999, at 1 (describing case where the Supreme Court "struck down a conviction of first degree murder because the prosecutor had 'elicited' inaccurate testimony from a key witness with knowledge of its inaccuracy . . . [T]he prosecuting attorney . . . was subsequently recognized as 'Outstanding Texas Prosecutor' by the Texas Law Enforcement Foundation 'in recognition and appreciation of his single and matchless contribution to criminal justice in this state'").

176. Aronson and McMurtrie, *supra* note 146, at 1490 ("Because disciplinary authorities are often unwilling to sanction prosecutorial misconduct, unless it is outrageous, prosecutorial ethics inevitably rely heavily on self-regulation and self-enforcement"); Terzano et al., *supra* note 146, at 5 ("Few jurisdictions have adopted or enforced standards on how prosecutors should appropriately utilize their broad discretionary powers").

177. Alafair S. Burke, "Improving Prosecutorial Decision Making: Some Lessons of Cognitive Science," 47 *Wm. & Mary L. Rev.* 1587, 1593 (March 2006).

178. Alafair S. Burke has identified four types of cognitive bias that affect all humans, including prosecutors, and have an impact on prosecutors' conduct: "confirmation bias, selective information processing, belief perseverance, and the avoidance of cognitive dissonance." Burke, *supra* note 177, at 1605; see also Gould et al., *supra* note 14, at xix ("despite

the weak evidence, the players involved become so committed to proving the defendant's guilt that evidence illustrating the contrary is ignored or discounted"); see also *id.* at xxi; *id.* at 15; *id.* at 86; Medwed, *supra* note 128, at 45–46 (noting that prosecutors may develop tunnel vision through a close working relationship with police).

179. Burke, *supra* note 177, at 1606 (as result of cognitive bias, "The prosecutor will accept at face value any evidence that supports the theory of guilt and will interpret ambiguous evidence in a manner that strengthens her faith in the case").

180. Harris, *supra* note 19, at 80–86. Harris also identifies "group polarization" as a reason for the resistance of prosecutors and police to revelations about traditional forensic science. *Id.* at 86–89.

181. Gershman, *supra* note 148, at 30 ("Prosecutors have also presented as trustworthy the testimony of scientific experts that contained false, exaggerated, and erroneous conclusions that lacked any scientific basis. The records of contemporary criminal trials are replete with instances of so-called 'junk science' finding its way into courtrooms, and championed by prosecutors to win convictions").

182. Burke, *supra* note 177, at 1612–1613 ("[C]ognitive dissonance will further hinder the prosecutor's ability to conduct a neutral evaluation of potentially exculpatory evidence").

183. Medwed, *supra* note 128, at 45 ("[I]nstitutional and professional incentives in most prosecutorial offices are steadfastly aligned with the goal of earning convictions—an ambition that does not invariably dovetail with the minister-of-justice concept"); Daniel S. Medwed, "The Zeal Deal: Prosecutorial Resistance to Post-Conviction Claims of Innocence," 84 *B.U. L. Rev.* 125, 134–135 (2004) ("the highest conviction rates (and, thus, reputations as the best performers) stand the greatest chance for advancement internally"); Aronson and McMurtrie, *supra* note 146, at 1481 ("Incentives at prosecutors' offices for winning, such as career advancement, bonuses, and public posting of individual and office-wide conviction rates, combined with the prosecutors' desire to appear tough on crime to the public, create a conviction-oriented mentality among prosecutors"); Barkow, *supra* note 149, at 2090 ("Prosecutors often feel pressure to obtain convictions to demonstrate their effectiveness, as convictions are the lodestar by which prosecutors tend to be judged"); Zacharias, *supra* note 104, at 108 ("Prosecutors who restrain themselves may convict at a lower rate and thus appear less competent to their superiors").

184. Medwed, *supra* note 128, at 45; Medwed, *supra* note 183, at 128; Aronson and McMurtrie, *supra* note 146, at 1481 (Prosecutors "become emotionally tied to the convictions they win and causes some prosecutors to tie their self-worth to their conviction ratio").

185. Medwed, *supra* note 128, at 45; ("[C]hief prosecutors tend to cite their offices' overall conviction records to justify their budgets to local politicians and to demonstrate, above all, that they are "tough" on crime"); Joy, *supra* note 54, at 405 (citing Robert L. Misner, "Recasting Prosecutorial Discretion," 86 *J. Crim. L. & Criminology* 717, 734 (1996) (stating that more than 95 percent of chief prosecutors on the state and local level are elected).

186. See, e.g., Paul Butler, *Let's Get Free: A Hip-Hop Theory of Justice,* 114 (2009) (Former prosecutor describes how "[e]ven people who go into prosecution with a progressive agenda get derailed [by] . . . the adversarial system, law-and-order culture [of prosecutor offices], and the politics of crime").

187. Zacharias, *supra* note 104, at 104 (One reason the "'do justice' rule may fall short of its goals" is "a theoretical concern: asking prosecutors simultaneously to advocate within a process and assure that the process is fair is inherently contradictory—and perhaps hopeless"); *Olsen*, 737 F.3d at 630 (Kozinski, J., dissenting) (citing "all the incentives prosecutors confront encourage them not to discover or disclose exculpatory evidence").

188. McMunigal, *supra* note 161 at 441 ("inadequate representation by defense counsel, often due to a lack of resources to obtain a defense expert, allows and encourages police and prosecutorial use of corrupt scientific evidence"); NRC Report summary at 12 (Noting that "judges and lawyers . . . generally lack the scientific expertise necessary to comprehend and evaluate forensic evidence in an informed manner").

189. Paul C. Giannelli, "*Ake v. Oklahoma:* The Right to Expert Assistance in a Post-*Daubert,* Post-DNA World," 89 *Cornell L. Rev.* 1305, 1377 (Sept. 2004).

190. McMunigal, *supra* note 161, at 443 ("Many defendants simply do not have the money to hire their own experts to present counter-proof or to provide defense counsel with the information and assistance needed to effectively cross-examine a prosecution expert. Most defense lawyers, without access to an expert, do not, on their own, have the scientific knowledge needed to effectively cross-examine a government expert"); Giannelli, *supra* note 189, at 1307 (citing the pressing concern of "the accessibility of expert assistance for indigent defendants" and observing that "[t]he use of experts is costly, and prosecutors have an overwhelming advantage on this score") (footnote omitted); *Achieving Justice: Freeing the Innocent, Convicting the Guilty*, Report of the ABA Criminal Justice Section's Ad Hoc Innocence Committee to Ensure the Integrity of the Criminal Process, at 59 (2006) ("In many criminal cases, securing the services of experts to examine evidence, to advise counsel, and to testify at trial is critical"). Although defendants have a due process right to expert assistance when necessary, *Ake v. Oklahoma*, 470 U.S. 68, 83 (1985) and there is a statute that provides indigent defendants in federal court with a right to expert assistance when "necessary for adequate representation," 18 U.S.C.A. § 3006A(a), and some states have similar statutes, see Gianelli 89 *Cornell L. Rev.* at 1338, their efficacy is limited by the extremely low monetary limits, see *id.* at 60 ("a number of sources indicate that the lack of defense experts continues to be a problem").

191. Aronson and McMurtrie, *supra* note 146, at 1454 ("The defense usually does not have the means to match police searches for evidence, and, in cases such as FBI laboratories, the 'government has a virtual monopoly on the expert service in question'") (quoting Fred C. Zacharias, "Structuring the Ethics of Prosecutorial Trial Practice: Can Prosecutors Do Justice?" 44 *Vand. L. Rev.* 45, 78 [1991]); Gershman, *supra* note 17, at 532–533 ("Most commentators would agree that the balance of advantage in the criminal justice system tilts heavily to the prosecutor. This is noticeable in every phase of the process, but most notably in the prosecutor's control over the evidence relevant to a defendant's guilt") (footnote omitted); Gershman, *supra* note 148, at 21 ("because of early access to crime scenes and superior investigative and forensic resources, prosecutors usually have exclusive knowledge and control of the scientific evidence"); Rosen, *supra* note 29, at 694 n.2 ("Professor Nakell describes several of the tools that give the prosecutor a decided advantage in obtaining information: (1) because the police often arrive on the scene of a crime promptly, they can begin gathering evidence immediately; (2) the prosecution has available trained and experienced personnel, laboratory and technical facilities, accumulated intelligence, and

cooperation from other law enforcement agents; (3) the prosecution usually has the cooperation of citizens in obtaining evidence and acquiring witnesses; (4) the prosecution can
also use several pretrial procedures to gather information, including grand jury investigations, coronor inquests, and various means of questioning the accused") (citing Nakell,
"Criminal Discovery for the Defense and the Prosecution—the Developing Constitutional
Considerations," 50 *N.C.L. Rev.* 437, 439–442 [1972]). Zacharias, *supra* note 104, at 78
("[T]he defense usually does not have the means to match police searches for evidence . . .
By the same token, the prosecution routinely employs forensic services that defendants
cannot reproduce. This occurs either because the defendants cannot afford competitive
experts or, as in the case of FBI laboratories, because the government has a virtual monopoly
on the expert service in question") (footnote omitted).

192. ABA Formal Opinion 09454 at 9a.

193. Giannelli and McMunigal, *supra* note 49, at 1534 ("Close examination of criminal
cases has revealed what is often in effect an ex parte presentation of scientific evidence by
the prosecution. The defendant and defense counsel are physically present during the presentation of the evidence, but cannot participate in anything other than a pro forma fashion
due to lack of access to the scientific expertise necessary for cross-examination, presentation of counterproof, and addressing evidentiary weaknesses in closing argument").

194. McMunigal, *supra* note 161, at 443 (The . . . typical scenario is that whatever scientific evidence is offered by the prosecution goes without significant challenge to its
accuracy either by defense counsel through cross-examination or by a defense expert"); see
also Jeffrey M. Prottas and Alice A. Noble, "Use of Forensic DNA Evidence in Prosecutors'
Offices," 35 *J.L. Med. & Ethics* 310 (Summer 2007) (in survey of 110 prosecutors' offices,
respondents "reported that they face an admissibility challenge on DNA cases in only 8.5
percent of cases" and "defense attorneys who brought in their own experts to examine DNA
evidence . . . in only six percent of cases"); Giannelli and McMunigal, *supra* note 49, at 1534
("Criminal defendants and their lawyers routinely lack the resources to effectively cross-
examine a prosecution expert, to present competing scientific counterproof, or to point out
weaknesses in that expert's testimony to the fact-finder in closing argument. The lack of an
effective challenge by opposing counsel has the practical impact of nullifying the fact-
finder's ability to distinguish corrupt from valid scientific evidence").

195. *Daubert v. Merrell Dow Pharmaceuticals, Inc.*, 509 U.S. 579, 582 (1993) (Court
"determine[d] the standard for admitting expert scientific testimony in a federal trial"). All
federal judges must use the *Daubert* standard, pursuant to Federal Rule of Evidence 702,
which requires the judge to consider, *inter alia*, whether "the testimony is the product of
reliable principles and methods; and . . . [if] the expert has reliably applied the principles
and methods to the facts of the case." Many state judges do as well. The majority of states
also require judges to apply the *Daubert* standard, but many states use an alternative standard pursuant to *Frye v. United States*, 293 F. 1013, 1014 (D.C.Cir. 1923), which requires
forensic evidence to satisfy only the "general acceptance." See ABA 50 State Survey of
Daubert/Frye Applicability, available at http://apps.americanbar.org/litigation/committees/
trialevidence/daubert-frye-survey.html.

196. *Daubert*, 509 U.S. at 597.

197. *Id.* at 593–594.

198. Harry T. Edwards, "The National Academy of Sciences Report on Forensic Sciences: What It Means for the Bench and Bar," 51 *Jurimetrics* 1, 5 (2010).

199. Moriarty, *supra* note 17, at 19 ("Despite the glaring shortcomings of forensic individualization specialties and the mandate that federal trial courts act as gatekeepers to exclude unreliable evidence, courts have been steadfast in continuing to admit such testimony") (footnote omitted); Cooley and Oberfield, *supra* note 18, at 285 ("[T]he judiciary has failed to apply *Daubert's* 'exacting standards' to forensic evidence offered by the prosecution"); 2009 NRC Report at 106 ("As the reported cases suggest, however, *Daubert* has done little to improve the use of forensic science evidence in criminal cases"); Gould et al., *supra* note 14, at 83 ("[I]n a number of our [study's] cases, the judge failed to use his or her discretionary powers to closely examine the evidence, level the field between prosecution and defense, or otherwise take an active role in protecting the innocent defendant").

200. 2009 NRC Report Summary 53 (emphasis added).

201. See 2009 NRC Report at 107 (Courts often "affirm admissibility citing earlier decisions rather than facts established at a hearing"); Moriarty, *supra* note 17 at 34 ("Many judicial decisions about the admissibility of forensic science, however, assume admissibility as a default position, particularly when there has been a long history of judicial admission of the testimony, as is true with fingerprint or handwriting comparisons").

202. 2009 NRC Report at 107 ("Much forensic evidence—including, for example, bite marks and firearm and toolmark identifications—is introduced in criminal trials without any meaningful scientific validation, determination of error rates, or reliability testing to explain the limits of the discipline") (footnote omitted).

203. 2009 NRC Report at 110 (citing "the common lack of scientific expertise among judges and lawyers who must try to comprehend and evaluate forensic evidence"); Gould et al., *supra* note 14, at 83 ("Judges, like attorneys, appeared [in the cases in study] to lack training and education in new advances in . . . forensic science").

204. See Martin Guggenheim, "The People's Right to a Well-Funded Indigent Defender System," 36 *N.Y.U. Rev. L. & Soc. Change* 395, 421–422 (2012) ("in our system of justice, judges depend on defense counsel to investigate cases and to present any critical issue to the court's attention").

205. NRC Report at 109 (quoting J. Griffin and D. J. LaMagna, "Daubert Challenges to Forensic Evidence: Ballistics Next on the Firing Line," *The Champion*. September–October, at 21 [2002]]).

206. D. Michael Risinger, "Navigating Expert Reliability: Are Criminal Standards of Certainty Being Left on the Dock?" 64 *Alb. L. Rev.* 99, 99 (2000) (Evaluation of over 1,000 cases revealed that "criminal defendants virtually always lose their reliability challenges to government proffers . . . but when criminal defendants' proffers are challenged by the prosecution, the criminal defendants usually lose"); *id.* at 110 (In federal court of appeals cases, "when the government challenged defense proffers, it prevailed two-thirds of the time" and "when the prosecution objected to defense-proffered expertise, the prosecution won two-thirds of the time").

207. Indeed, many plea bargains are resolved before a judge ever has the opportunity to consider the evidence in the case.

208. 2009 NRC Report at 53.

209. *Id.*; see also Edward J. Ungvarsky and Bernadette Mary Donovan, "Strengthening Forensic Science in the Unites States: A Path Forward—or Has It Been a Path Misplaced?" 36 *FEB Champion* 22, 22 (Jan./Feb., 2012) ("the NAS Report's conclusions, including the commonsense notion that lack of validation is peculiarly relevant to admission, have received a mixed reception in court").

210. For an overview, see Kirchmeier et al., *supra* note 21 at 1363–1382.

211. Aronson and McMurtrie, *supra* note 146, at 1491 (recommending "articulating more specific standards" for prosecutors conduct); Raeder, *supra* note 38, at 1439 ("[T]he rules or standards should be modified to provide that a clear pattern of inaccurate laboratory results is adequate to supply knowledge that the testimony in an individual case is likely to be false or misleading").

212. Davis, *supra* note 20, at 183 ("The ABA should also undertake a comprehensive study and review of the Model Rules of Professional Conduct with the specific goal of determining the extent to which the rules fail to address critical aspects of the prosecution function" and "should determine the extent to which the rules might be amended or whether it would be more appropriate to draft a separate code of professional responsibility for prosecutors"); McMunigal, *supra* note 161, at 449 (Recommending an expansion of "the types of culpability required for an ethics violation beyond the knowing use of corrupt scientific evidence to include reckless and negligent prosecutorial use of scientific evidence").

213. Giannelli and McMunigal, *supra* note 49, at 1532 (Suggesting "adding a provision [to Model Rule 3.8] that would make it an ethics violation for a prosecutor to knowingly, recklessly, or negligently offer defective scientific evidence"); *id.* at 1520 (recommending discovery rules that would require prosecutors to disclose all tests and reports related to forensic evidence to the defense); Moriarty, *supra* note 17, at 28 (Proposing adding requirement to Model Rule 3.8 that prosecutor "make reasonable efforts to assure that only reliable expert evidence is admitted into evidence. A prosecutor shall not use evidence that she knows or reasonably should know is unreliable").

214. Joy, *supra* note 54, at 425 ("an open file discovery obligation would help to eliminate one of the major forms of prosecutorial misconduct—the suppression of material evidence, which is a leading cause of wrongful convictions") (footnote omitted).

215. Davis, *supra* note 20, at 161 (Arguing that Bruce Green's suggestion "that the judiciary should consider drafting ethical rules for prosecutors that recognize their unique role as ministers of justice . . . should be seriously considered").

216. California Commission, *supra* note 156, at 10–11.

217. McMunigal, *supra* note 161 at 449.

218. California Commission, *supra* note 156, at 4.

219. Joy, *supra* note 54, at 427 ("Bar disciplinary authorities should implement a system to review reported instances of prosecutorial misconduct and, when they deem it appropriate, conduct investigations or recommend discipline").

220. Davis, *supra* note 20, at 161 (advocating stricter oversight of prosecutors by disciplinary authorities and "[a] separate code of prosecutorial conduct"); *id.* at 180 ("External reform of the prosecution function must include . . . strengthening ethical rules and bar disciplinary proceedings."); *id.* at 181 ("National, state, and local bar associations should begin prosecutorial reform efforts by conducting in-depth investigations and evaluations of state disciplinary proceedings to determine (1) why they have not been effective in

remedying prosecutorial misconduct, and (2) whether and what changes might make the process more effective"); Zacharias and Green, *supra* note 49, at 27 (Proposing "serious disciplinary enforcement of the competence rule"); Moriarty, *supra* note 17, at 28 (Recommending "serious enforcement of the disciplinary rules when the actions of prosecutors contribute to misconvictions").

221. Aronson and McMurtrie, *supra* note 146, at 1490 ("Prosecutors' salaries and other incentives should be based on ethical conduct, and not just on conviction rates"); Meares, *supra* note 51, at 873 (Proposing "a model that financially rewards prosecutors for obtaining convictions either by trial or by plea under the condition that the defendant is convicted on the same charge or charges that the prosecutor pursues at the outset of the case").

222. Gould et al., *supra* note 14, at 99 (one recommendation based on large-scale empirical study of wrongful convictions is that "[p]rosecutors need to be better educated in the techniques of forensic testing and must clarify what results mean if they do not understand a report"); NACDL's *Principles and Recommendations to Strengthen Forensic Evidence and Its Presentation in the Courtroom*, February 27, 2010; Ungvarsky ("Attorneys and judges need significant education and training in the fundamentals of science, statistics, and common forensic practices; and in the limitations of, and potential forms and scope of error associated with, those practices"); Raeder, *supra* note 38, at 1450–1451 ("At a minimum, prosecutors presenting specific expertise would be required to obtain training. A procedure should also be established to have one or more prosecutors with experience in forensic or social science evidence to review the introduction of evidence whose reliability has been questioned"); 2009 NRC Report at 27 ("The fruits of any advances in the forensic science disciplines should be transferred directly to legal scholars and practitioners (including civil litigators, prosecutors, and criminal defense counsel").

223. Burke, *supra* note 177, at 1612–1613.

224. Joy, *supra* note 54, at 424 ("Prosecutors' offices that do not have a written manual or set of guidelines addressing the exercise of discretion would benefit from creating such a document and making it accessible to the public"); Raeder, *supra* note 38, at 1450 ("[E]ach prosecutorial office should be required to adopt written policies governing the introduction of forensic and other expert testimony").

225. Barkow, *supra* note 149, at 2106; Gould et al., *supra* note 14, at 98 (one recommendation based on large-scale empirical study of wrongful convictions is that "[p]rosecutors should pursue a policy of open discovery; the practice might include holding discovery conferences, in particular with forensic evidence presented"); see also Medwed, *supra* note 128, at 57 (proposing that prosecutors set up innocence units for evaluating post-conviction innocence claims).

226. Joy, *supra* note 54, at 427 ("Prosecutors' offices should be required to implement a system of graduated discipline each time there is a finding by a trial judge or appellate court of prosecutorial misconduct"); *id.* at 424 ("Implementing internal policies that value ethical conduct, and implementing and enforcing internal discipline when those norms are violated, would go a long way toward addressing the issue of prosecutorial misconduct").

227. McMunigal, *supra* note 161, at 448 ("[P]erhaps the most obvious remedial step is to assure that defense counsel have access to adequate resources so that the reality of the criminal trial process comes closer to its theoretical view of cross-examination and counter-proof"); NACDL's *Principles and Recommendations to Strengthen Forensic Evidence and*

Its Presentation in the Courtroom, February 27, 2010, at 14 ("Forensic reform should . . . include providing the defense with resources to obtain the assistance of forensic and scientific experts for confidential consultation and testimony, and the use of forensic facilities for independent, confidential testing"); Moriarty, *supra* note 17, at 41 ("courts need to allow defendants to hire experts and allow those defense experts to testify and present contrary evidence").

228. Jennifer Friedman, "A Path Forward: Where Are We Now?" *The Champion*, at 16 (January–February 2012) (encouraging defense attorneys to "familiarize themselves with the NAS Report and work to develop effective strategies for raising these issues in the trial courts" and identifying grounds for legal challenges); Donovan and Ungvarsky, *supra* note 209, at 22 (encouraging "[f]orceful recurring litigation of the need for hearings seeking the exclusion or limitation of the testimony of forensic examiners [to make] clear that defense lawyers will not permit junk science to be grandfathered into the judicial system").

229. See, e.g., NACDL's *Principles and Recommendations to Strengthen Forensic Evidence and Its Presentation in the Courtroom*, February 27, 2010 (Identifying "seven central areas of need: (1) a central, science-based federal agency, (2) a culture of science, (3) a national code of ethics, (4) the prerequisite of research, (5) education, (6) transparency and discovery, and (7) defense resources, particularly for indigent defense services").

230. ABA, *Gideon's Broken Promise: America's Continuing Quest for Equal Justice, A Report on the American Bar Association's Hearings on the Right to Counsel in Criminal Proceedings*, Exec. Summary at iv (2004) ("[R]eport demonstrates [that] defense services in the U.S. are not adequately funded, leading to all kinds of problems. These include a lack of funds to . . . pay for experts, investigative and other support services; cover the cost of training counsel; and reduce excessive caseloads").

231. 2009 NRC Report at Summary 27 ("judges need to be better educated in forensic science methodologies and practices").

232. David Keenan, Deborah Jane Cooper, David Lebowitz, and Tamar Lerer, "The Myth of Prosecutorial Accountability After *Connick v. Thompson*: Why Existing Professional responsibility Measures Cannot Protect Against Prosecutorial Misconduct," 121 *Yale L.J. Online* 203, 244 (Oct. 2011) ("Judges in particular should be compelled to flag an instance of misconduct for review by the grievance committee").

233. Zacharias, *supra* note 104, at 47 n.7 ("[C]ourts might use their supervisory and contempt authority more expansively to deter misconduct"); Note, "The Nature and Consequences of Forensic Misconduct in the Prosecution of a Criminal Case," 54 *Colum. L. Rev.* 946, 981 (June 1954) ("The answer may lie in contempt proceedings which make available a wide range of sanctions from small fines to substantial prison terms, and even indefinite suspension as an attorney") (footnote omitted).

234. 2009 NRC Report at 86.

235. Davis, *supra* note 20, at 179 ("[R]eform will be difficult because there is not widespread belief that it is necessary—either in the prosecution community or the public at large"); Yaroshefsky, *supra* note 159 , at 278 ("[T]here appears to be an implicit agreement that, absent rare circumstances, offending prosecutors should not be subject to sanctions before disciplinary committees. The work of scholars who have studied the issue and offered useful ideas has been met with little response").

236. Yaroshefsky, *supra* note 159, at 292 ("[P]erhaps the most significant reason for the hands off approach to discipline of prosecutors, is their political power and deference to the executive branch").

237. Harris, *supra* note 19, at 8 ("Most . . . . prosecutor's offices have ignored the new science on forensics . . . preferring the status quo. Others have actively resisted change, even fought against it"). Prosecutors also frequently resist post-conviction DNA testing. See Aronson and McMurtrie, *supra* note 146, at 1481; Seth F. Kreimer and David Rudovsky, "Double Helix, Double Bind: Factual Innocence and Postconviction DNA Testing," 151 U. *Pa. L. Rev.* 547, 554 (2002) ("hostility to postconviction [DNA] access typifies an important sector of the prosecutorial community"); Shaila Dewan, "Prosecutors Block Access to DNA Testing for Inmates," *New York Times*, May 18, 2009, at A1 (a study of 225 DNA exonerations "found that prosecutors opposed DNA testing in almost one out of five cases.").

238. See, e.g., *State v. Hull*, 788 N.W.2d 91, 108 (Minn. 2010) (Meyer, J., concurring) (Noting that The State argues that . . . the[*Frye*] test applies only to novel and emerging scientific techniques, and thus the State need *never* meet its burden to show the reliability of fingerprint and handwriting identification methodology").

239. See, e.g., *Smith v. United States*, 27 A.3d 1189, 1196, 1195 (D.C. 2011) (Where defense "sought to present testimony from . . . a fingerprint expert with thirty-five years' experience who had testified 'numerous times' in the trial court and who was familiar with 'MPD methods, resources, and protocols' . . . [who] would provide testimony concerning the quality and adequacy of the government's investigation and the superiority of the available Superglue fuming method in lifting fingerprints," the government objected, arguing that the expert's testimony "would not have aided the jurors, only confused them"); *State v. Sheehan*, 273 P.3d 417, 421 (Utah App. 2012) (objecting to defense request to present expert testimony from Simon A. Cole; "The State . . . argued that . . . [the defendant was not 'entitled to bring in a Ph.D. to talk about the fact that he studied this and there have been mistakes in the past'").

240. See, e.g., *Com. v. Gambora*, 933 N.E.2d 50, 55 (Mass. 2010) and *id*. at 65 (Spina, J., concurring) (Government proffered testimony of expert that "the latent prints had been 'individualized' to the defendant, and that this meant to the exclusion of all others, and that the prints *absolutely* belonged to the defendant," despite defense objection that "latent print could be 'individualized' to a particular person").

241. See, e.g., *Gee v. United States*, 54 A.3d 1249, 1262 (D.C. 2012) ("[D]efense counsel sought leave of court to cross-examine the government's fingerprint expert, Haywood Bennett, by reading or quoting excerpts from the 2009 National Academy of Sciences report . . . The prosecutor objected").

242. See, e.g., *Gee*, 54 A.3d at 1263 (Describing "Government counsel['s] object[ion] to the Report 'being designated as a learned treatise'"). The designation is relevant for the rules of evidence. See Fed. R. Evid. 803(18).

243. Donovan and Ungvarsky, *supra* note 209, at 22 ("prosecutors and the forensic scientists have fought vigorously against defense counsel's invocations of the NAS Report").

244. 2009 NRC Report at 127.

245. Harry T. Edwards, "The National Academy of Sciences Report on Forensic Sciences: What It Means for the Bench and Bar," 51 *Jurimetrics* 1, 6 (2010) (originally

delivered at Conference on the Role of the Court in an Age of Developing Science & Technology, held at Superior Court of the District of Columbia on May 6, 2010).

246. Green, *supra* note 146, at 891 (reporting that "in several . . . states, prosecutors' representatives vigorously opposed the new provisions" that would require prosecutors to take action if they obtain "clear and convincing evidence" that someone has been wrongly convicted).

247. Brief for National District Attorneys Association as Amicus Curiae Supporting Petitioner, *Smith v. Cain*, at 3 (Describing ABA as "a private organization that does not speak for prosecutors"); *id.* at 5 (repeating criticism that ABA has become "a left-wing lobbying group"); *id.* at 10 (Arguing that the "ABA's view in Model Rule 3.8(d) as to what standards prosecutors should follow, going beyond what the law requires, has not been uniformly accepted as the ethical standard"); Yaroshefsky, *supra* note 159, at 292 ("Prosecutors believe that the problem of prosecutorial misconduct is overstated. The President of the National Association of Assistant United States Attorneys testified that federal prosecutors are subject to 'continual and pervasive scrutiny' far beyond that of other lawyers . . . While this view is not readily accepted outside prosecutors' offices, it appears to be sufficiently influential to discourage state disciplinary bodies from asserting their authority") (quoting "The Effects of State Ethics Rules on Federal Law Enforcement." Hearing Before the Subcomm. on Criminal Justice Oversight of the Senate Committee on the Judiciary, 106th Cong. 62–63, 1999) (statement of Richard L. Delonis, President of the National Association of Assistant United States Attorneys); Green, *supra* note 146, at 895 (citing example of District Attorney's Office in Queens County, New York, arguing that "a trial court lacks the institutional competence to investigate and rule on a prosecutor's professional conduct") (citing Memorandum of Law of Richard A. Brown, District Attorney of Queens County, *Brown v. Blumenfeld,* 930 N.Y.S.2d 610 [N.Y. App. Div. 2011], at 24); Davis, *supra* note 20, at 179 ("[P]rosecutors traditionally have resisted even modest efforts at reform"); Zacharias and Green, *supra* note 49, at 397 (citing "perennial complaints by federal prosecutors that state ethics regulation inappropriately ties their hands").

248. 2009 NRC Report at 22.

249. *Id.* at 13.

250. *Id.* at 12 ("The adversarial process relating to the admission and exclusion of scientific evidence is not suited to the task of finding 'scientific truth,'" and there is accordingly a "tremendous need for the forensic science community to improve."").

251. *Id.* at 16.

252. *Id.* at 27.

253. For example, the American Judicature Society Institute of Forensic Science and Public Policy site at http://www.ajs.org/wc/index.asp, and the National Clearinghouse for Science, Technology, & the Law at Stetson University College of Law, at http://www.ncstl .org/, and the George Washington University Forensic Science Resource Center at http:// departments.columbian.gwu.edu/forensicsciences/resources.

254. See, e.g., "Prescription for Criminal Justice Forensics," a conference hosted by the Louis Stein Center for Law and Ethics at Fordham University School of Law and cosponsored by the American Academy of Forensic Sciences, the American Society of Crime Laboratory Directors, John Jay College of Criminal Justice, Innocence Project, Inc., and

Federal Defenders, Inc. (http://www.americanbar.org/content/dam/aba/events/criminal_justice/forensics_2013.authcheckdam.pdf).

255. For example, the National Judicial College (http://www.judges.org/index.html) conducts training for judges, the National Association of Criminal Defense Lawyers (http://www.nacdl.org/meetings/?s=ql) conducts trainings for defense attorneys, and the National District Attorneys Association (http://www.ndaa.org/index.html) conducts trainings for prosecutors. Each state also has a range of training resources. See, e.g., the Arizona Forensic Science Training Academy (conducts joint trainings for prosecutors and defense attorneys).

256. A scientist or scholar can list her/himself in the National Directory of Expert Witnesses (http://national-experts.com/register.html). But experts are typically contacted after an attorney reads an article or study by that expert.

257. *Banks*, 540 U.S. at 696 (internal quotation and citations omitted).

Section IV

Post-Conviction Issues

Forensic evidence serves as a tool that can play an important role in both convicting the guilty and exonerating the innocent. The Innocence Project movement has demonstrated the value of forensic science, particularly DNA analysis, in opening cases and reanalyzing physical evidence using new or enhanced techniques (or simply using techniques that weren't used in the original case) to arrive at a more just outcome. An unfortunate complication is that evidence can of course only be reanalyzed when it is actually retained after the case is closed, and retained using proper storage methods. Yet, laboratory policies regarding evidence retention are varied with regard to how they are implemented and enforced. Some jurisdictions have passed laws requiring evidence retention for particular types of cases (such as homicide) or other special circumstances, and with varying details regarding, for example, the length of time such material must be retained. If only it were so simple. In "The Problems and Challenges of Evidence Retention," John M. Collins Jr. discusses the practical complexities of evidence retention, including having adequately trained personnel, secure facilities with sufficient storage capacity and capability, and suitable record keeping systems. Good communication across stakeholders is the key to success—in this case, communication about priorities, statuses, and anticipated needs. Collins discusses two important communication roles for evidence custodians: as service providers who accept evidence, collect information about the case, and work with investigators to determine what will be tested and what can be packaged and stored; and as customers who transport evidence to the laboratory and provide case information that will help the laboratory to determine the most efficient approach. Collins advocates a jurisdictional approach to case management that integrates information bearing on a case from law enforcement agencies, courts, laboratories, prosecutors' offices, and the defenders' offices. He concludes by reviewing several critical priorities for jurisdictions to incorporate into evidence and property management practices.

Kristen Skogerboe sounds a subtle but important warning bell about confidence in forensic DNA testing: While DNA testing is widely regarded for its individualizing power and has helped to expose the limitations and errors of other forensic disciplines, it is as yet unclear what limitations and errors reside within DNA testing until new technologies, methods, and quality assurance programs are developed and refined. In "Innovation, Success, Error, and Confidence in Forensic DNA Testing," Skogerboe reviews the history of DNA testing and its eventual general acceptance in the courts, drawing on her personal experiences as a chemist serving as an expert witness in *Frye* hearings. The chapter discusses types and sources of error, quality assurance programs, proficiency testing, and research on forensic DNA testing. To build, enhance, and maintain confidence in forensic DNA testing, Skogerboe points to replicate confirmatory testing combined with rigorous quality assurance and blind proficiency testing programs that provide an estimate of error rate (importantly, Skogerboe also suggests that laboratories should provide the public with the results of proficiency testing programs to improve confidence in DNA testing). Collectively, strengthening these aspects of laboratory practice will help ensure that advances in forensic DNA testing are not based in false confidence.

10

The Problems and Challenges of Evidence Retention

John M. Collins Jr.

Introduction

Moviegoers may recall the 1981 blockbuster film *Raiders of the Lost Ark*, which chronicled the adventures of famed archeologist Indiana Jones, who set out to find the biblical ark carrying the stone tablets on which God is said to have etched the Ten Commandments. As Jones' search drew him closer and closer to the ark, colleagues warned him that the ark was "not meant to be disturbed" and that its "unspeakable power" was something not only to respect, but also to fear. In other words, the ark itself was not the true find, but rather what it represented. In one of the most famous scenes in movie history, the ark, having displayed its lethal power to evil onlookers, is rolled in a wooden crate toward its final resting place in what appears to be an endless warehouse of forgotten treasures and other artifacts being kept in government storage. What made this final scene so famous were the special effects that gave the warehouse the appearance of endlessness. But the image can also serve to help readers appreciate the endless accumulation of boxes, bags, envelopes, and other items—large and small—being secured in evidence storage facilities across the United States and around the world. Like Indiana Jones' lost ark, this evidence has meaning, significance, and power. It should be respected and, perhaps to some degree, even feared. When evidence is not treated with the respect it deserves, the consequences can be catastrophic.

To fully appreciate the value of evidence in our 21st-century criminal justice system requires a comprehensive and complete understanding of what evidence *really* is, and the power it wields. Contrary to what might be considered a simpler or traditional view, evidence is not only a physical object or person. Nor is it just a DNA swab or a document bearing a fraudulent signature. Evidence is meaning—a source of context and clarity that helps blend disparate facts and considerations into a unified truth that is both plausible and defensible in a court of law. A judge's or jury's understanding of this truth may then serve as the basis for a subsequent decision of guilt or innocence in a criminal trial. Consider, for example, the bullet holes in the windshield of a victim's automobile. On examination by appropriately qualified personnel, the bullet holes can reveal the location of the shooter, the position of the victim inside the car at the time of the shooting, or perhaps whether or not the victim himself fired any of the shots from inside the vehicle. As evidence, the bullet holes themselves have only incidental value. Ultimately, it is the revelations and logical conclusions drawn by the investigators and the attorneys who will represent the parties in the case that are of any real significance.

It stands to reason, then, that the retention or storage of evidence is influenced by its potential significance—and indeed it is. This may not have been the case, however, in 2007, when a Florida judge declared a mistrial in a capital murder case. According to the Commission on Accreditation for Law Enforcement Agencies, it was determined during the trial that key pieces of evidence, which included audio and video tapes, had been stored in the office desk of an investigator who never logged the evidence into the police department's property room (Latta & Kiley, n.d.). The reported failure of the investigator to protect the integrity and security of the evidence unhinged the basis of the prosecution's case. More recently, in 2011, an angry judge admonished the police department of Lewiston, Maine for losing crime scene photographs in the robbery and battery of a 29-year-old man (Williams, 2011). Prosecutors were made aware of the missing evidence just before trial, which was stopped by the judge as 14 jurors waited in a small room for the trial to commence. According to the *Lewiston-Auburn Sun Journal*, it was discovered just days earlier that the Lewiston Police Department lost a videotape of a confession in another robbery. In that same case, serious discrepancies were also noted in chain of custody records associated with DNA evidence that was to be presented at trial. Justice MaryGay Kennedy implored the police department to clean up its act.

> Something has to give over there and if they have to figure out a new system . . . in terms of how they log in evidence, particularly photographs, tapes, etcetera; and they need to understand that that information is required to be produced to the defendant. It's in the rule. It's in the (U.S.) Constitution. It is imperative that they learn to do their jobs properly.

The problem of mismanaged evidence, however, is not isolated to police. In a 2007 study by Jeffrey Prottas and Alice Noble, 253 local prosecutors were sampled using data from the Bureau of Justice Statistics and surveyed. From the responses, only 41% reported having written policies regarding collection and preservation of biological evidence, despite the fast growing use of DNA in American courtrooms (Prottas & Noble, 2007). Some states have resorted to statutory remedies to address the problem. In Illinois, evidence in murder and sex offenses must be retained for a period of time no less than the total combined time of both incarceration and supervision (Illinois Compiled Statutes, 725 ILCS 5/116–4). Conversely, other statutes significantly limit the lifespan of evidence by setting deadlines after which a defendant cannot be legally prosecuted. Known as *statutes of limitations*, these requirements protect the rights of defendants whose prosecution might otherwise be compromised by the passage of time. Typically, an item of evidence can be properly disposed once this deadline has been expired, a practice that makes room for the storage of new evidence and prevents precious space from being occupied by items that will no longer be needed. Other statutes, however, may also give specific guidance on evidence retention particularly for biological evidence.

One of the most ominous challenges in retaining and disposing of evidence has emerged only recently. The practice of post-conviction litigation, which has resulted in the overturning of hundreds of convictions over the last 20 years, has shattered the sacred notion that judicial verdicts are permanent. Given a sufficient amount of evidence revealing the possible innocence of an imprisoned convict, convictions can be overturned many decades later. If the criminal justice system is forced to accept the legitimacy of post-conviction litigation and the potential for convictions to be erroneous, which it most certainly is, then the importance of physical evidence as a sort of time capsule only magnifies the criticality of its proper storage and preservation. Unfortunately, the long-term storage of evidence can be costly, complicated, and labor intensive. It also requires certain competencies, the absence of which can have grave consequences. In the world of criminal justice, evidence is like money. It must be kept secure and ready for use another day. But as this chapter emphasizes, the enormous volume of evidence managed by our criminal justice system, not to mention the length of time that these items must often be secured, creates challenges for those responsible for ensuring that it is done right. Employees, for example, must be hired and trained to properly manage and store evidence. Facilities must also be adequate to maintain the long-term safety and security of evidence while also protecting the health and safety of evidence custodians. These issues are among those that will be addressed in this chapter.

Personnel

Most criminal evidence is housed in facilities under police control. In some instances, sworn officers are assigned the duty of evidence custodian. But with law enforcement budgets so heavily impacted by the economic turbulence that has marked the early years of the 21st century, commanders are increasingly forced to find new ways to maintain their enforcement presence within their jurisdictions and communities. This can often make civilian employees a better alternative for internal administrative positions such as those tasked with managing a police department's evidence and property inventory.

When a police agency understands the seriousness of evidence and property management (property being those items kept in safe keeping but having no known evidentiary value), close attention will be paid to the training and development of employees assigned to fill this role. Furthermore, the agency will likely have clear expectations and standards of practice for how evidence should be controlled and organized. Ideally, these expectations and standards will have been developed in partnership with other interested parties working in the jurisdiction, such as prosecutors, public defenders, and judges. This concept of agency interdependence will be discussed later in this chapter, but it should be noted that the evidence custodian's job description and training plan must encourage the development of competencies that allow for effective communication and collaboration with professionals throughout the jurisdiction's criminal justice system. Communication becomes critical when decisions must be made about the current status of evidence and its preparedness for disposal or other change in its current disposition.

In *Understanding Police Culture*, John Crank (1998) aptly explains an unfortunate reality facing many police organizations that will ultimately impact how evidence and property facilities are staffed. According to Crank, one of the strongest unifying themes of police work and police culture is bravery. In fact, it is not only a cultural theme; circumstances frequently make bravery a requirement of the position—sometimes when it is least expected. "Bravery is an important element of the cultural ethos of police officers because fear is profoundly debilitating," writes Crank, "yet officers occasionally have to place themselves in harms way" (p. 233). In considering the importance of bravery to the police culture, one may perceive stark contrasts between police work that requires bravery and police work that does not. It is quite possible, then, that types of police work not requiring demonstrations of bravery will never be fully accepted by the predominant police culture.

This poses a problem for human resource management experts in police agencies because the profession of policing relies heavily on critical services that are not viewed as being part of the traditional police culture. Certainly, this includes a function such as the management of evidence and property. Yet, in the coming decades, the importance of physical evidence, particularly those items that will be tested by a forensic science laboratory, will likely grow by orders of magnitude. This will require HR specialists to ensure that the right people with the right skills are hired to manage evidence 24 hours a day, 7 days a week. Although the investment of scarce fiscal resources in evidence custodial positions may be painful for police commanders who would understandably prefer to invest in their enforcement capacity, any serious errors or missteps in the management of evidence by unqualified personnel can have disastrous and expensive consequences.

In 1993, an important development occurred. An association titled the International Association for Property and Evidence (IAPE) was formed as a way to elevate perceptions of the practice of properly managing evidence and property. This organization also serves as a conduit through which educational materials and guidelines can be brought to personnel whose responsibility it is to keep and secure physical evidence. Among IAPE's most enduring contributions has been the creation and administration of a certification program for Property and Evidence Specialists (CPES) that "indicates that the holder is a professional who has completed requirements in training; has worked in the field for a required period of time; and has demonstrated their knowledge of professional standards through a written test." (IAPE, n.d.). The potential for this certification program to advance the management of evidence and property as a bona fide profession is an encouraging and important priority for those in this line of work.

Safe and Secure Facilities

In 2012, the Colorado Springs Police Department found itself with an unexpected problem that came with a price tag of over $93,000. Employees at the department were exposed to the *Aspergillus* mold, a dangerous but common problem in facilities where large quantities of marijuana are stored. Symptoms included "headaches, breathing problems and rashes." In previous years, Colorado Springs spent tens of thousands of dollars in an attempt to deal with the mold and make room for the increasing quantity of marijuana evidence (Koen, 2012). In light of the complaints raised by concerned employees, the police department was forced to take action. In 2007, the DuPage County Sheriff's Office, located just west of Chicago, faced a different sort of problem. One of its senior officers responsible for managing evidence and property was indicted on two counts of theft and three counts of official misconduct following his arrest for allegedly stealing cash from evidence storage. The indictments were announced in a DuPage County (2007) press release, which noted that the amount of cash stolen exceeded $300. Incidents such as these are not common, but they serve to illustrate the importance of controlling the safety and security of both the evidence and the people responsible for managing it.

The long-term storage of evidence creates a number of challenges for police departments despite the fact that the overwhelming majority of evidence items will never see the inside of a courtroom. According to the Bureau of Justice Statistics (n.d.), only 5% of all felony cases go to trial; 95% end in a plea agreement. Consequently, courts play a negligible role in the long-term management of evidence. The responsibility to properly secure, store, and dispose of evidence—and deal with all the challenges associated therewith—falls squarely on the police. In meeting this responsibility, police officials are likely to have success when they mitigate the most serious risks by focusing on some basic objectives:

- Store evidence in facilities having controlled, documented, and limited access
- Enforce best practices in the sealing and marking of evidence containers and items
- Prohibit employees from accessing cash, jewelry, or other high-value evidence without being accompanied by a witness or "spotter"
- Maintain adequate ventilation
- Keep drug evidence in well-sealed, opaque envelopes that will minimize the temptation of an employee who may be dealing with a substance abuse problem
- Keep biological evidence at proper temperature and humidity
- Inventory all items in a secure, reliable database designed specifically for evidence
- Encourage (demand if necessary) the involvement of prosecutors and courts in the management and disposal of evidence
- Conduct full audits of all evidence annually; conduct spot checks of randomly selected evidence items on a weekly basis

The practice of managing evidence has become such a serious, high-stakes business that police departments should not go it alone. The assembly of an *evidence management committee* that includes police evidence custodians, prosecutors, defenders, and facility engineers—to name a few—can help retain a coalition of professionals within a jurisdiction whose responsibility it is to put in place effective procedures and policies governing the management of evidence and ensure that they are followed. Such a committee can also convene to resolve other unforeseen challenges when they arise. Whatever solutions are employed, they must involve effective communication.

Inventory and Disposition

Record keeping in the criminal justice system centers on individual offenses, or cases, most of which have a known victim or complainant. Unique identification numbers, often called *complaint numbers* or *case numbers*, are assigned by police departments to aid in organizing and filing all records associated with an offense. Each evidence item collected and packaged for storage or possible transport to a crime laboratory is marked with the police complaint number and a supplemental identifier that distinguishes it from all other evidence in the case. Unlike years before, when evidence was logged by hand into a ledger, today's evidence is increasingly stored in robust, electronic database systems designed to facilitate the efficient inventory, auditing, storage, and disposal of evidence. Small or rural police departments that don't store large quantities of evidence may function effectively with less. But it is safe to say that large metropolitan police organizations will not be able to survive in today's legal and judicial environments without well-structured evidence databases.

More advanced databases are also able to track the statutory limitations of cases, which marks the point in time when evidence may be legally disposed. The importance of this feature cannot be overstated when one considers how fast evidence can pile up in an evidence vault, particularly in a major city with considerable rates of crime. The ability to quickly identify and dispose of expired evidence makes room for new evidence in new cases. Some systems will automatically flag expired evidence and even produce computer-generated notices of disposal that can be signed and filed with other case records. Once evidence is flagged for disposal, the evidence custodian must simply retrieve the evidence from its storage location, which should be recorded in the inventory, and dispose of the evidence in compliance with applicable laws and policies. Although this may seem simple enough, it is not.

Complicating matters related to the storage of evidence in almost every jurisdiction in the United States is the fact that most police evidence systems do not communicate effectively with other systems utilized by prosecutors, crime laboratories, and courthouses. The judicial status of cases can sometimes change without police evidence custodians being made aware of it, or perhaps case circumstances dictate that an item of evidence may also be important to an entirely different case. A serial rapist, for example, may be convicted and imprisoned for 15 years, at which point his DNA is matched to an unsolved rape that occurred 20 years ago—five years before his conviction. Said another way, only prosecutors and the courts can confirm with 100% certainty that an item of evidence has exceeded its statutory limitation and may be disposed. But it is rarely practical for police departments to seek immediate permission for the disposal of every item of expired evidence. For seized property, public notices of some sort are typically released to the public to provide a sufficient amount of time for rightful owners to claim their property prior to disposal or public auction. For evidence collected or used to support the adjudication of a criminal case, however, interagency communication of some sort must take place to ensure that evidence disposal is performed properly and legally. This communication must occur within the framework of a collaborative system of reviewing the status of evidence that has been marked for disposal, thus introducing the concept of jurisdictional case management as a way to increase efficiency and improve the quality of interagency communications regarding evidence.

Forensic Testing

This chapter commenced with a brief discussion about evidence items as the holders of meaning and significance for our criminal justice system. Frequently, however, the retention of evidence must take into account any possible forensic testing to be conducted by a crime laboratory on items of scientific value to the courts. Physical objects, of course, do not speak for themselves, so they require properly trained and qualified people to speak for them. Evidence custodians, trial attorneys, and crime scene technicians are some examples of professionals who are relied on to give evidence a voice and ensure that it is heard. Few professionals in our criminal justice system, however, occupy a more specialized and solemn role in communicating the meaning of physical evidence than the forensic scientists who work in whatever crime laboratory happens to be serving a particular jurisdiction. It is often solely in the laboratory that scientists can evaluate the properties of evidence that remain invisible to the rest of us. The work is highly sensitive, tedious, and technically demanding. Moreover, when evidence arrives at the crime laboratory for analysis, scientists cannot always predict whether the requested work will take five hours, five days, or five weeks to complete. Unlike a clinical laboratory with which many people are familiar due their necessity in diagnosing common health ailments such as high cholesterol or hyperthyroidism, for example, the forensic science environment is highly variable and even unpredictable due to the equally variable and unpredictable nature of the evidence that is tested there.

Perhaps it makes sense, then, that the symptoms of a jurisdiction's failure to properly and collaboratively manage its cases and evidence would tend to emerge in the most sensitive of environments—the crime laboratory. The laboratory may be a state-operated, multijurisdictional forensic services provider or a county-based laboratory that serves only one jurisdiction. If that jurisdiction has demonstrated itself to be incompetent in the prioritization of its cases and the control of its evidence, the resulting dysfunction will eventually find its way to the crime laboratory. And indeed, a decade's worth of news reporting has confirmed just how serious the problem has become. On a national scale, crime laboratory backlogs have reached epidemic proportions. In 2013, for example, the forensic backlogs of the North Carolina State Bureau of Investigation reached such alarming numbers that officials in the City of Durham and Durham County considered the establishment of their own crime laboratory (Gibbs, 2013). Drug cases, which require faster completion due to the fast pace of the courts in dealing with such cases, were taking up to six months to complete, causing a crippling bottleneck for prosecutors and the courts.

North Carolina is not alone. The problem of forensic backlogs is now a national phenomenon. Unfortunately, social scientists have yet to comprehensively study forensic backlogs as a symptom of jurisdictional dysfunction related to the overall management of evidence rather than a simple problem of staffing and funding in the crime laboratory. It is likely, though, that this will change soon. In states such as Florida, Ohio, Michigan, and Wisconsin, improved interagency communications and decision making with regard to evidence have shown themselves to successfully resolve the problem of forensic evidence backlogs.

To understand how critical good communication is to the effective management of evidence and its eventual testing at the crime laboratory, we can look to a business model familiar to anyone who owns an automobile. The front desk of an automotive service center is an example where customers must reliably convey their needs to a technician who will record the information before using it to guide their diagnosis and correction of the problem. Particularly when the problem with a vehicle is not obvious, the owner will be asked to describe the problem, noises, vibrations, or other mechanical oddities experienced while driving. This allows the technician to immediately suspect likely causes while ruling out others. The result is a more efficient and less costly repair of the vehicle. But imagine a situation where a difficult customer brings a vehicle to the service center and refuses to share any information with the technician. "I don't know what's wrong, just fix it," the customer barks before turning and walking out the door. Depending on the situation, the time and cost of the technician's work could be enormous—even if the technician is never able to diagnose what is wrong, if anything, with the car. In the absence of good information from the customer, the service center is unable to follow an efficient business process to deliver its services reliably and promptly. And if other customers behaved in a similar fashion, the work of the service center would come to a halt—leading frustrated customers to take their business elsewhere.

The absurdity of this scenario plays out daily in many of America's crime laboratories. Poor communication among agencies serving within a criminal jurisdiction, often exacerbated by a lack of proper training and education, causes three critical failures that impede the functioning of its crime laboratory:

- Inability to efficiently prioritize evidence for analysis

- Clogging of the laboratory intake system with evidence that is redundant or of no real probative value

- The demoralization of crime laboratory employees and customers, which further decreases the efficiency and productivity of the laboratory

Critics may argue that these kinds of communications with forensic science personnel create biases that inappropriately favor one party or another. While not an unreasonable concern, it can be easily managed through training, education, and strong internal policies. That being said, any criminal jurisdiction wishing to experience the tremendous benefits of a well-functioning forensic science system must design and adhere to a robust system of multi-agency communications that are built around reasonable policies and practices governing the forensic testing of evidence. Judges, prosecutors, defenders, police investigators, and crime laboratory scientists must collaborate in the development of these policies and practices so that they address both the legal and scientific nuances of all evidence. One of the more progressive recommendations offered in this regard came from the National District Attorneys Association in 2004 in a publication titled *DNA Evidence Policy Considerations for the Prosecutor*, which described how multidisciplinary teams can be of value in prioritizing forensic evidence. "In evaluating every case, prosecutors, police and forensic scientists . . . should determine what evidence is probative of the defendant's guilt," the report states. "This evidentiary or case review should be a collaborative process" (Kreeger & Weiss, 2004, p. 3). Because the legal and technical aspects of evidence can be so complex, the idea of multidisciplinary collaboration, when needed, seems to have considerable value.

In a jurisdiction that demonstrates effective communication in matters pertaining to the scientific value and testing of evidence, evidence custodians take on a combination of two critical roles—that of customer and service provider. As a service provider, evidence custodians accept evidence from investigators and collect critical information regarding case circumstances. In this role, custodians often work directly with investigators to determine what items of evidence require testing and what items can be packaged and placed in storage. On the other hand, as a customer, the custodian may transport the evidence to the crime laboratory where he or she will be responsible for relaying relevant case information to the laboratory. This helps the laboratory maximize its efficiency during the evaluation and testing of the evidence, just as it would an automotive service center. If there is a breakdown in communication, or if there is any challenge surrounding the ability of the custodian to function effectively in those two roles, the entire jurisdiction will be adversely impacted. This necessarily requires all relevant parties in a jurisdiction to take seriously the role of evidence custodian and the policies and practices governing the management, forensic testing, and storage of evidence.

Jurisdictional Case Management

Law enforcement agencies don't store evidence and property for the fun of it. To the contrary, it is a difficult and risky responsibility that allows our criminal justice system to function as it does. The loss of a single package or paper bag can quickly turn into a nightmare if it happens to be associated with a major investigation or criminal trial. But this important responsibility of caring for items and packages is not unique. We need look only to companies such as FedEx, Walmart, or the U.S. Postal Service for examples of organizations that have mastered the ability to protect and track an enormous number of items at any one time. FedEx, for instance, can immediately identify the location of any item in its custody. It can also provide a history of where the item has been since the customer entrusted its care to FedEx. Mistakes will happen from time to time, but overall the ability of companies to manage and care for large inventories is impressive to say the least.

This would not be possible, however, without modern-day computer systems and the ability to give any item a unique identity that can be entered and tracked in a reliable database. To the extent, therefore, that police departments struggle to manage their evidence and property in a systematic way, more likely than not it can be attributed to a significant deficiency in its information management capabilities and the segregation of individual police agencies in their tracking of evidence. Even within a single county or criminal jurisdiction, there may be several disparate evidence tracking systems that do not communicate with each other. One can easily project just how complicated and inefficient the situation can become when considering that prosecutors, courts, and crime laboratories usually operate their own disparate systems as well.

A 2007 study commissioned by the National Institute of Justice noted that "[t]he use of information systems can enhance the ability of police agencies to manage, track, and monitor forensic evidence associated with criminal cases. This could include identifying cases that are in need of additional analysis" (Strom et al., 2009, p. 3-11). Yet, the same study found that only 43% of reporting law enforcement agencies had a computerized system capable of tracking forensic evidence inventory. The study also found that "larger police agencies were more likely to report having an information system that contained information on forensic evidence in place. Nearly three in four agencies with 100 or more sworn officers reported having such a system."

Time will tell how quickly various agencies within a jurisdiction may be able to consolidate or interoperate information management systems. For jurisdictions that function at the county level, for example, we may witness sheriffs playing an increasingly important role in the management of evidence and property for all law enforcement agencies in the county. Perhaps one day we could even see court administrators take responsibility for the management of evidence, which makes sense as courts can so often require possession of evidence on a moment's notice—not to mention that courts are also the high authorities that set statutes of limitations on cases, at which time evidence may be disposed.

Whatever the problems or solutions, there is one difficult truth that must be confronted. A single criminal case can require access to information and data under the control of a police department, a courtroom, a crime laboratory, a prosecutor's office, and a defender's office. The complexity and cost of developing the kind of solution that could bring these disparate data sets into a single, well-functioning information management system is probably more than any one agency or jurisdiction could bear. This, essentially, becomes a problem of scale. With the resources needed to manage cases, forensic laboratory results, and evidence spread over so many independent, sovereign agencies, the kinds of systems that are really needed to meet the needs of individual jurisdictions are cost prohibitive. But if we can think differently about how our criminal justice system could work, and how the right kinds of information management systems could be designed and utilized, the potential for our criminal justice system to function more efficiently and reliably is exciting to ponder.

Conclusion

It is encouraging to recognize that contemporary best practices in the management of property and evidence are, in fact, being put into practice. In Washington, DC, for example, the Metropolitan Police Department began preparations to move its property, evidence, and custodial staff into a new $20 million, 30,000-square-foot warehouse facility. According to a report by the *Washington Post*, "the move has enabled the District to do a comprehensive inventory of evidence it has on hand by assigning bar codes in preparation for the new cataloguing system" (Flaherty, 2011). The report also noted that the new facility provides "much better working conditions" for employees tasked with managing large quantities of property and evidence. But it is important to note that the facility was envisioned after a 2008 report by the District of Columbia Office of the Inspector General found that the previous facility, originally constructed in 1962, was overcome with serious structural and environmental problems such as "inadequate heating, ventilation, and air conditioning (HVAC) system, a poor electrical system, leaky pipes and roof, severe overcrowding in storage areas, and poor physical security." A new facility would not only help to correct these conditions, it would also reduce the risk of "theft, misuse, or loss of evidence, which may compromise the District's ability to successfully prosecute criminal cases."

Many jurisdictions do not have access to $20 million for the construction of a new facility. For those that do, it may still take many years to build or renovate a facility worthy of housing criminal evidence and other forms of retained property. Therefore, the following is a brief recap of the critical priorities that every jurisdiction must incorporate into its evidence and property management practices:

1. *Encourage respect for the function of property and evidence management and its importance to criminal justice.* Without reliable evidence, the rest of the criminal justice system cannot do its job.

2. *Hire and train the right personnel to manage the inventory.* It is a specialized function requiring specialized skills.

3. *Ensure safe and secure facilities.* Lost evidence and sick employees can be much more tragic, expensive, and embarrassing than the cost of fixing existing problems.

4. *Use effective inventory management systems.* The 21st century will require property and evidence to be managed with the same level of accountability as money in a bank.

5. *Pay close attention to evidence requiring forensic testing.* When requests for laboratory tests are made, it is a sure sign that the evidence is of particular importance.

6. *Be effective in managing individual cases and related information.* Evidence is much more than simple objects; it has meaning that must be considered within the larger context of individual cases. The information that allows this context to be considered must be managed as well as the evidence itself.

No agency can overcome the challenges associated with the storage and retention of evidence if it is not made a priority, both culturally and in written policy. If it is not a priority, even the best recommendations or ideas will fall short of success. Plenty of news reports are available to highlight the damage done when evidence is not taken seriously. Hopefully these examples of catastrophe can motivate even the most stubborn administrators to change their cultures and place an added emphasis on this important specialty. The investment of resources and attention are worth the effort. One day, we may even see the management of evidence and property rise to a level of importance that is on par with the management of banks or jewelry retailers. Because evidence can have life or death consequences for defendants, this comparison is entirely appropriate.

References

Bureau of Justice Statistics. (n.d.). *FAQ.* Retrieved from http://www.bjs.gov/index .cfm?ty=qa&iid=405

Crank, J. (1998). *Understanding police culture.* Cincinnati, OH: Anderson.

District of Columbia Office of the Inspector General. (2008, January 4). *Office of the Inspector General's observations at the Metropolitan Police Department's evidence control branch* (OIG No. 07-1-21(a)). Washington, DC: Author. Retrieved from http:// www.scribd.com/doc/14554884/DC-Audit-of-Evidence-Control-Branch-2008

DuPage County, IL. (2007, September 13). *Former sheriff's office employee charged with theft* [Press release]. Retrieved from http://www.dupageco.org/Content.aspx?id=30457

Flaherty, M. P. (2011, March 16). D.C. police open new evidence warehouse. *Washington Post*. Retrieved from http://www.washingtonpost.com/blogs/crime-scene/post/dc-police-open-new-evidence-warehouse/2011/03/16/ABOPWJe_blog.html

Gibbs, T. (2013, January 11). Durham considering its own crime lab. *ABC News*. Retrieved from http://abclocal.go.com/wtvd/story?section=news/local&id=8950470

Illinois Compiled Statutes. 725 ILCS 5/116–4. Retrieved from http://www.ilga.gov/legislation/ilcs/fulltext.asp?DocName=072500050K116-4

International Association for Property and Evidence. (n.d.). *Certified Property and Evidence Specialist (CPES) and Corporate Certified Property and Evidence Specialist (CCPES)*. Retrieved from http://iapevideo.com/cart_certification

Koen, A. (2012, November 19). Storing seized marijuana costs police and taxpayers. *KOAA*. Retrieved from http://www.koaa.com/news/storing-seized-marijuana-costs-police-and-taxpayers

Kreeger, L. R., & Weiss, D. M. (2004). *DNA evidence policy considerations for the prosecutor*. Alexandria, VA: American Prosecutors Research Institute. Retrieved from http://www.ndaa.org/pdf/dna_evidence_policy_considerations_2004.pdf

Latta, J. T., & Kiley, W. P. (n.d.). Commission on Accreditation for Law Enforcement Agencies. (n.d.). Property and evidence control—the hidden (and ticking) time bomb. *CALEA Update Magazine, 94*. Retrieved from http://www.calea.org/calea-update-magazine/issue-94/property-and-evidence-control-hidden-and-ticking-time-bomb

Prottas, J., & Noble, A. (2007). Use of forensic DNA evidence in prosecutors' offices. *Journal of Law, Medicine & Ethics, 35*, 310–315.

Strom, K., Ropero-Miller, J., Jones, S., Sikes, N., Pope, M., & Horstmann, N. (2009, October). *The 2007 survey of law enforcement forensic evidence processing: Final report* (NCJ 228415). Washington, DC: National Institute of Justice. Retrieved from https://www.ncjrs.gov/pdffiles1/nij/grants/228415.pdf

Williams, C. (2011, October 23). Justice reprimands Lewiston police for losing evidence; says "sloppiness" hurt cases. *Lewiston-Auburn Sun Journal*. Retrieved from http://www.sunjournal.com/comment/86144

11

Innovation, Success, Error, and Confidence in Forensic DNA Testing

Kristen Skogerboe

Introduction

Since 1985, the adoption of DNA testing for forensic evidence has provided for a significant change in the landscape of forensic science and criminal justice. The individualizing power of DNA testing has placed it into routine use in forensic science and correspondingly has awarded it significant confidence in its power to inform. While professional and public confidence with DNA testing has grown, the technology has revealed problems and issues with other areas of forensic science. Eyewitness identification, serology, and hair analysis are examples of methods that have a diminished level of confidence because DNA testing has revealed problems or comparative limitations (Saks & Koehler, 2005). Hence the criminal justice system now has a lesser degree of confidence for various methods, as DNA is typically considered the "gold standard" of forensic methods. The value of DNA testing to the criminal justice community has elevated the public's general awareness of forensic science, and, correspondingly, the field has been subject to increased public and professional scrutiny. In 2009, the National Research Council (NRC) issued a National Academy of Science report focused on improving forensic sciences in the United States. This report provides an extensive list of recommendations for innovation, quality assurance, and professional oversight that illuminates many of the challenges in the modern practice of forensic science.

This chapter, offered from a chemist's perspective, focuses on issues of confidence in DNA testing in revealing challenges with other forensic methods as well as the intricacies inherent to placing such confidence in DNA testing. The history of DNA testing is provided, with a particular focus on the road to general acceptance of DNA testing in courtrooms around the country. Included in this section is a personal account of serving as an expert witness in the early phase of DNA testing. This experience and some of the impediments to the adoption of DNA evidence offer insight as to how the path forward for forensic science in this country can be travelled with increased confidence. Written for non-scientists, this chapter identifies issues related to error, quality assurance, research, and success in forensic DNA testing. Finally, the chapter offers a summary of what is required to build and maintain confidence in the rapidly changing field of forensic science. If the criminal justice, legal, and scientific communities, as well as the general public, operate under the illusion that there is no basis for concern related to continued and improved oversight of DNA testing, then there is a false confidence that has the potential to create a spreading uncertainty that would need to be addressed.

While DNA offers a window into limitations and errors of other forensic methods, identifying what, if any, of these are present in a DNA test is yet to be determined until new technologies, and improved methods and comprehensive quality assurance programs are developed, implemented and improved upon. Certainly, the widespread reliance on DNA testing is an indication of its usefulness as a forensic science technique. It is difficult to imagine that any single event, or series of legal decisions, could arise that would significantly undermine the continued use of routine DNA testing. However, it is conceivable that situations could arise where diminished confidence in DNA testing could cause major concern in the administration of justice for current cases and those that might be appealed. Analogous problems such as occurred in Washington State with the set-aside of convictions based on quality-control issues associated with blood alcohol testing in the state crime lab (Vosk, 2008) would certainly increase concerns about the reliability of forensic testing. The multitude of other various problems in forensic DNA testing including the closure of the Houston Crime lab detailed by Thompson (2006) go further to mar the public confidence in forensic DNA testing.

History of DNA and Its Application in Criminal Justice

Since the discovery of DNA as the primary genetic material of a cell, testing has always been of interest to scientists. From medical genetics to biotechnology, DNA has provided information for unlocking a variety of scientific questions and producing biomaterials relevant to pharmaceuticals and agriculture. The DNA research emanating in 1985 from Sir Alec Jeffrey's university labs unleashed a multitude of applications, including the evaluation of forensic evidence (Jeffreys, Wilson, & Thein, 1985). The first adoption of DNA testing to crime scene evidence occurred in England and was soon applied to criminal proceedings in the United States when it was used to prosecute Tommie Lee Andrews, the first American convicted by DNA evidence in 1987 (Ahlers, 1988). That same year, in *New York v. Castro*, a serious challenge to the admissibility of DNA testing, revealed that, while powerful as a forensic tool, there was a lack of confidence that the technique was ready for routine use (Patton, 1990). Correspondingly, this invigorated the research and forensic laboratory science communities to evaluate the limitations of DNA testing and develop programs to promote quality. Even as this assessment was underway, DNA analysis was simultaneously being used in cases where there was sufficient biologic material to conduct the test.

There were many prosecutions and convictions during the next 10 years where serologic rather than DNA testing was performed on crime scene evidence. This transition period occurred as DNA methods were being developed, and the results were presented for acceptance in courtrooms according to general rules, such as a *Frye* or *Daubert* test. Simultaneously, local, state, and federal crime laboratories and technology vendors were building expertise and capacity for DNA testing, a process that took about a decade. One prominent case during this time period was the prosecution of Kirk Bloodsworth for the 1984 murder of a young girl (Junkin, 2004). In the Bloodsworth case, there was biologic evidence but the quantity of evidentiary DNA was insufficient for informative testing. Unfortunately, this was the situation for many criminal cases during this time period, so DNA testing was only useful for analysis of evidence where there was a significant amount of DNA present in/on a sample. This typically meant that there needed to be a large amount of biologic material (usually blood or semen) and that the cells in the material had to be well preserved and not environmentally degraded so the DNA would be intact. These limits provided stringency to the types of evidence that could be evaluated and impacted the broad applicability of DNA testing.

These boundaries were shortly overcome by the 1985 invention of the Polymerase Chain Reaction (PCR) (Saiki et al., 1985), which was soon applied to evaluate forensic evidence. The technique was first used forensically in 1986 in Pennsylvania to establish the origin of autopsy samples (*Commonwealth v. Pestinikas*, 1986). Shortly thereafter, scientists at the FBI laboratories reported on the forensic use of the technology (Comey & Budowle, 1991), with more extensive evaluation following two years later (Comey et al., 1993). Because PCR allowed for genetic profiling of extremely small amounts of DNA, even samples with only a drop of blood, saliva, or semen could be tested, and courts across the country were ruling on the admissibility of PCR testing. In 1993, after serving eight years in prison awaiting execution, Kirk Bloodsworth became the first man to be exonerated from death row because of DNA testing (Junkin, 2004). Through 2012, Bloodsworth was joined by 302 other individuals exonerated by DNA testing (see the Innocence Project, www.innocenceproject.org).

Methods to apply PCR to forensic testing continued to be developed, and soon PCR testing of Short Tandem Repeats (STR) became the most common mode of forensic testing. A standard grouping of STR tests was adopted as the basis for the Combined DNA Index System (CODIS), a database of individual DNA profiles which by 2012 included over 9,700,000 individuals in the United States (FBI, 2012). CODIS serves as a powerful platform for individualizing forensic evidence, and the established infrastructure for testing and database management effectively institutionalize the system for the foreseeable future.

Even though CODIS is expected to be the cornerstone of forensic DNA testing, its future is not without challenges. The CODIS system is a hierarchy of DNA Index Systems (DIS), which include national (NDIS), state (SDIS), and local (LDIS) levels (Cass, 2010). DNA profiles can be entered at any of the levels and compared nationally to find linkage between individuals and crime scene evidence. A 2006 U.S. Department of Justice (DOJ) audit has evaluated the system, finding that while meeting the primary objectives of the program, there are a number of administrative and technical challenges. The audit revealed that administratively, the CODIS system had not always implemented uniformly by all hierarchies. Of further concern are reports that even when a match identifies a potential suspect, there are examples where it was not acted on by law enforcement in a timely fashion to protect the public safety and prevent further harm (Willing, 2006). One technical concern over CODIS is how the system deals with partial DNA matches. A partial match is one where there are significant similarities between two profiles, but they are not exactly the same. Partial DNA matching in the CODIS system may arise for a number of reasons, including random luck, mixtures of DNA, or a biologic relationship between the true perpetrator of the crime and other individuals whose DNA is in the database. Understanding the statistical likelihood of any of these possibilities would illuminate the best way to use and improve CODIS but would require more interaction with the database than is currently possible given that CODIS data has not been widely released for scientific study. A number of forensic scientists have requested access to the database to evaluate efficacy and risk of error, and to develop strategies for strengthening the program (Krane et al., 2009).

The Role of DNA in Highlighting Limitations in Other Forensic Disciplines

The exoneration of the innocent through the power of DNA testing has offered a window into types of errors and problems that are typical in the criminal justice arena. DNA testing is highly informative because of its ability to individualize the source of forensic evidence. Compared to serology, a methodology that narrows the source of a biologic sample to perhaps one in a few thousand individuals, DNA profiling has the ability to increase the probability that a suspect contributed the DNA to well over a million to one. In this manner, when there is full confidence in DNA testing, the result acts as an agent of retrospective quality assurance, revealing limitations, areas of concern, and errors that are present in other forensic techniques. The factors associated with 86 wrongful convictions are summarized by Saks and Koehler (2005), indicating a large fraction of these are attributable to eyewitness errors and other non-technical issues such as misconduct by police, prosecutors, or forensic scientists. This retrospective information confirms that the criminal justice system must continue to assess issues outside of errors that arise in the analytical laboratory domain. Forensic science testing errors and problems associated with erroneous expert witness testimony significantly contributed to wrongful conviction, combining as contributing factors in well over half of the 86 cases. DNA testing has revealed astonishingly high error rates (ranging from 35% to 100%) of other forensic methodologies, especially in bitemarks, handwriting analysis, voice identification, and hair and fiber analysis.

Estimation of these large error rates for non-DNA forensic methods involves a leap of faith relative to the reliability of DNA testing (Derksen, 2000). This leap is scientifically justifiable but not absolute because the samples being tested are unknowns, and the true values can only be estimated but not definitively established with 100% certainty. It can never be absolutely known if there is positive or negative error associated with the results. For example, to be revealed as a retrospective error, a false confidence in hair analysis (combined with other case facts) is revealed because the conclusion drawn from such evidence was at one time sufficient, beyond a reasonable doubt, to warrant a conviction. The relevance of this is summarized by Lynch (2003): "What should not be forgotten, however, is that the DNA revolution in criminal justice was initially mapped on to an older forensic technology, and it was framed and legitimated through the ancient institution of the courts" (p. 97). As science is progressive, so is the need to study, assess, and improve forensic science in this country. Certainly, the exoneration of the wrongfully convicted indicates that complete confidence in any forensic science methodology, both retrospective and prospective, is not warranted.

The Intersection of Success, Innovation, and Risk of Error in DNA Testing

The move from evaluation of biologic evidence by serologic methods to DNA was exciting to many and worrisome to others (Imwinkelried & Kaye, 2001; Thompson, 1993). Was the testing reliable? What was the error rate? Was there a sufficient program of quality assurance to proceed to court? These questions, standard to the process of allowing the science to be used in court, were the basis of many *Frye* and *Daubert* proceedings across the United States. The early years of forensic DNA testing were a very interesting time because most of the traditional forensic scientists or crime lab technicians working in the profession lacked expertise in DNA testing. Conversely, most of the research scientists working on DNA testing research had little to no forensic testing expertise. Of concern was the fact that quality assurance programs for DNA testing did not fully exist while testing was concurrently being relied on for court decisions. Assessing the reliability of forensic DNA testing required an evaluation of errors, methodology, and quality assurance—terms that are defined in Table 11.1.

Table 11.1 Selected Terms in Establishing the Reliability of Forensic DNA Testing

Term	Definition
Quality assurance	The systematic actions necessary to demonstrate that a product or service meets specified requirements for quality (FBI, 2000)
Laboratory accreditation	Results from a successful completion of an inspection or audit by an accrediting body such as ASCLD (American Society of Crime Laboratory Directors) (Butler, 2012, p. 173)
Proficiency testing	A quality-assurance measure used to monitor performance and identify areas in which improvement may be needed
External proficiency test	One which is obtained from a second agency not the lab conducting the test
Blind external proficiency test	An external test where the conducting laboratory is not aware that the test is for the purposes of determining proficiency as it appears to involve routine evidence from a real case
Contamination	The inadvertent addition of an individual's DNA during or after collection of the sample as evidence (Rudin & Inman, 2002)
Degradation	A process by which DNA breaks down into smaller fragments influenced by factors such as sunlight, heat, humidity, and age of the sample

(Continued)

Table 11.1   (Continued)

Term	Definition
Analytical error	An error in the testing/analytical phase of sample evaluation that includes all laboratory steps between preparing the sample and interpretation and reporting of results
Pre-analytical error	An error that occurs before the analysis phase of testing; this common error is typically a specimen transportation, identification, or labeling mistake
False positive error	An association between two items when they actually came from different sources (Koehler, 2008)
False negative error	A forensic exclusion between two items when they came from the same source (Koehler, 2008)
Overall error rate	The number of errors found in the total testing process across all laboratories involved
Specific error rate	An error rate that takes into account the specific sample, lab, methodology, analyst performing the analysis (Jabbar, 2010)

To understand the potential for error in forensic DNA testing, scientists have looked to studies of error rates in other types of complex laboratory testing such as what occurs in a clinical chemistry lab. Clinical labs handle millions of samples every year and, as a discipline, laboratory medicine is remarkably adept at tracking quality and recording errors. A 1996 Department of Justice commissioned review of quality assurance in forensic labs discusses the relevance of clinical lab error rates to forensic testing, concluding that the quality assurance and proficiency testing programs of accredited labs are a good starting point for translating programs that might be used to predict error in forensic science (Peterson et al., 2003).

Laboratory testing can traditionally be segregated into three phases: analytical, pre-analytical, and post-analytical. Several reviews describe the types and number of errors that have been uncovered by accredited clinical labs, where the operational culture is to improve quality by monitoring errors and making adjustments (Hammerling, 2012; Plebani, 2006). Compiled reported error rates from accredited clinical labs reveal an overall error rate ranging between 0.1% and 3.0%, with most of these coming in the pre-analytical phases. On average, mistakes in the analytical phase typically account for about 10% of the overall clinical laboratory testing error rate (Hammerling, 2012).

The culture of clinical laboratory medicine is to use the information gathered by powerful quality-assurance programs not only to uncover errors but to improve clinical outcomes (Plebani, 2007). While decreasing errors is important to both clinical and forensic laboratories, the use of error tracking and reporting as a means of quality assurance may be discordant with forensic labs where the mission is not to improve health but to promote justice.

While a basic definition of forensic error is offered in Table 11.1, the scientific and legal definition of error rate in DNA testing is still being debated. The fact that there are seven different types of errors listed in Table 11.1 provides a glimpse at why categorizing error is a challenge in the forensic arena. First, it is unclear if each category of error holds equal relevance in criminal justice. For example, false positive errors would tend to contribute to false convictions, while false negative errors could trigger the release of a guilty defendant (Jabbar, 2010). Second, calculation of an overall error rate would include all errors, both positive and negative, caused by all types of errors across all labs performing DNA testing. Many professionals involved in forensic DNA testing contend that estimation of errors within a single lab, only using data from samples representative of those being tested in a given case—for example, a specific error rate is more relevant to establishing a baseline estimate for laboratory mistakes (Budowle, Bottrell, et al., 2009).

The controversy of error rate in forensic science is illuminated by the writing of Mnookin et al. (2011), who calls for a stronger culture of research in the practice of forensic science, which includes studying the kinds of errors that occur. In a response to the call for error rate estimation, Bono (2011), president of the American Academy of Forensic Sciences, reflected on how creating a research culture benefits the criminal justice community and what is gained from knowing a generalized error rate for DNA testing, suggesting that "discerning why and when errors occur is more important than attempting to quantify how often errors occur" (p. 785). The perspective on forensic error reflected in this commentary certainly reveals some differences in thinking between the criminal justice and scientific communities. First, it is impossible to discern why and when errors occur without having some estimate of the error rate. Errors revealed by random sampling of forensic results do not fully inform the laboratory testing community as to how and why an error occurred and whether there is a justifiable basis for correcting the error. While it is possible that measuring an error rate may have restricted meaning in any particular legal context, it is unrealistic to propose that forensic testing can be improved without having a baseline estimate of error rate.

Topics in quality assurance, proficiency testing, and error rates have been at the forefront in the criminal justice, legal, and scientific communities since the advent of the forensic DNA era. The first hurdle to gaining and retaining this confidence is for the evidence to be admissible in court as judged by a *Frye* or *Daubert* hearing. The central question in such hearings is whether DNA testing is generally accepted by the scientific community. In the advent of new DNA testing, this became a difficult question, because it was asking whether something was accepted as an application of the original scientific advance that was itself still being evaluated by the research community. Whether DNA testing is generally accepted by the scientific community is altogether a different question than whether DNA testing of forensic evidence is generally accepted by the scientific community. The subtlety of this question as it relates to the adoption of new scientific advances to the evaluation of crime scene evidence is still very much an issue today.

The Road to Testing and Exonerations: DNA From a Chemist's Perspective

In 1988, I was a fellow in molecular genetics and laboratory medicine, working on clinical applications of DNA testing to the diagnosis of disease. I had experience with PCR analysis of DNA from all different kinds of clinical samples via my work in a clinical environment, as well as the establishment and implementation of quality-control programs to track and minimize laboratory errors. This background, combined with my experience as a laboratory accreditation inspector, resulted in my being approached to serve as *Frye* hearing defense consultant in a murder case. I was reluctant to do so, thinking that the defense should find a "forensic scientist" to do this job. Like many scientists, I came from, and still reside in, a place of professional uncertainty. From my seat in the lab, I did know a few things: (1) There are always random errors; (2) there are interferences and biases in laboratory testing that may not be predictable given the uniqueness of each sample; and (3) mistakes happen. Forensic DNA testing was not my specific area of expertise, and agreeing to become part of the legal proceedings via a *Frye* hearing was not something I was eager to do. However, given my background in clinical genetics testing, and because I generally knew the power of laboratory inspection and quality assurance in establishing and maintaining high standards of excellence in clinical testing, I agreed to serve as a consultant.

I traveled to the DNA testing laboratory and observed the analytical evaluation of biologic evidence in the case. Certainly, I did not observe any obvious errors during the analysis of the blood evidence. However, because there were so few labs performing DNA testing on crime scene evidence, quality-assurance and proficiency-testing programs were hardly robust. Thus, there was really no way to estimate the reliability in the form of an error rate. Correspondingly, the evidence was not tested by duplicate, separate day, or second lab analysis, practices I knew to be useful in revealing errors in the complex process of DNA testing.

Within weeks of returning from observing the DNA testing in this case, the suspect pled guilty to the crime, and there was no *Frye* hearing and no trial. But there was continued need for experts to help with admissibility of DNA evidence from other cases, and over the next few years, I observed the analysis of DNA in several cases and also testified. In 1992, the NRC published a review of the challenges and limitations of forensic DNA testing, highlighting many of my concerns related to the rapid adoption of DNA testing: "Before a method can be accepted as valid for forensic use, it must be rigorously characterized in both research and forensic settings to determine the circumstances under which it will and will not yield reliable results" (pp. 51–52). The report went on to conclude that PCR testing had not met the standard for acceptance: "PCR analysis is extremely powerful in medical technology, but it has not yet achieved full acceptance in the forensic setting" (p. 69).

One particular case in which I was involved highlighted the controversies surrounding DNA testing described in the NRC report. The case included a *Frye* hearing associated with the use of PCR testing in a 1991 murder case that had relied on its use for testing a vaginal swab and carpeting recovered from an automobile (*State v. Russell*, 1994). At the time, only one forensic lab in the country was performing PCR testing, there were limited articles published about the technique applied to crime scene evidence, and a lack of proficiency testing to evaluate the error rate. I testified for the defense expressing my concerns about whether PCR testing was generally accepted in the scientific community and the deficiencies of the voluntary quality assurance programs being adopted by the lab. Ultimately, the judge decided that the results of PCR testing were admissible, and the defendant was found guilty of two counts of aggravated first-degree murder and one count of first-degree murder, a verdict that was affirmed on appeal.

Three years later, opinions from the *Russell* case were issued when the case was appealed to the Washington State Supreme Court. The appeal centered on the idea that the *Frye* decision to allow DNA results to be admitted was in error, and that PCR analysis had not had the extended period of use and testing necessary to meet the general acceptance criteria of *Frye*. While the conviction was ultimately upheld in a split decision, there were affirmative and dissenting statements from the justices describing the positions that provided a unique window into the judicial scope and thought processes involved in the case. Often, scientific experts know little about the collective evidence or specific outcomes of a case. It was interesting to read that several of the justices felt that the *Frye* standard had not been met. The dissenting opinion outlined sections of controversy discussed in the 1992 NRC report, especially highlighting laboratory certification, proficiency, and quality assurance program as areas of concern. Justice C. J. Anderson summarized his concern with PCR in his dissent:

I wish to reiterate that we are not here considering the expertise or proficiency of one high-quality laboratory or one exceptionally well qualified forensic scientist or the reliability of one PCR kit; we are deciding for all laboratories whether DNA PCR testing should be admissible to prove guilt or demonstrate innocence in a criminal trial in this state. Until there is general acceptance in the scientific community that PCR analysis is valid and reliable when used on crime scene evidence, to my view, we are acting prematurely to admit this powerful and often determinative evidence. I have no doubt that this kind of evidence, in some form, is the wave of the future—at the present moment in scientific history, however, that is where it belongs—in the future (*State v. Russell*, p. 45).

The controversy of the admissibility of DNA testing in an environment with less than optimal validation and oversight that was revealed by the split decision in *State v. Russell* continued in many courtrooms around the country. Most states approved DNA testing, but there were successful *Frye* challenges to the admissibility of PCR testing. One example that reveals the controversy is the Colorado case of *State v. Shreck* (2001), where the version of PCR testing used in 1999 was first ruled inadmissible, a decision later reversed by the state supreme court. Interestingly, Pennsylvania, the state that allowed the first use of PCR testing in a criminal case, also mounted a successful prosecutorial challenge to a defense request to allow PCR testing on a piece of forensic evidence on the grounds that it was not reliable (*Commonwealth v. Francis*, 1990). This outcome indicates that each case is different, involving unique circumstances, samples, testing methods, and laboratories. Thus, even though seemingly related testing has already passed an admissibility challenge, each case should be considered separately.

Innovation, Challenges, and Emerging Issues in Forensic DNA Testing

The identification of errors that may be present in modern DNA testing methods is a challenge because confirmatory testing happens via the same technology. In this environment, the only way to detect an error is do replicate testing, compare results with other labs, and participate in a comprehensive proficiency-testing program that looks at the most challenging types of samples. To what extent is this happening in forensic labs today? The answer to this question is not especially clear, as the public is not privy to extensive information about proficiency testing programs, and there is not an open repository of errors to evaluate. Labs do not reveal the errors unless subpoenas or severe problems with proficiency or accreditation warrant public disclosure. Providers of forensic DNA proficiency-testing programs generally do not support the use of program-testing data for the calculation of error rates. For example, every proficiency report from Collaborative Testing Services, Inc. (2010), a major proficiency testing provider, states that "the results compiled in the Summary Report are not intended to be an overview of the quality of work performed in the profession and cannot be interpreted as such" (p. 1). Using data from 2002, Peterson and Hickman (2005) looked at this issue and found that while 97% of publicly funded forensic labs reported some type of proficiency testing program, only about a quarter of them reported using blind proficiency testing (p. 11). A follow-up census in 2009 showed that blind proficiency testing dropped to only 10% of labs (Durose, Walsh, & Burch, 2012). This is a concerning development at a time when the NRC report (2009) recommends strengthening the quality-assurance programs of forensics laboratories. Unfortunately, at present, there is not a readily transparent approach for estimation of error rate in DNA forensic testing using existing programs.

In 2004 the Washington State crime lab took a bold step and revealed a roster of errors uncovered in the DNA section of the lab, by publishing these in the newspaper ("DNA Testing Mistakes," 2004). This type of transparency is unique because the enterprise of forensic science does not generally disclose errors as doing so has the potential to have the results used out of context and undermine the general public confidence. Conversely, recognizing that testing is intricate and acknowledging that errors happen satisfies the public's basic understanding that DNA testing is complex. When the public learns of fairly large-scale problems with forensic testing, there is certain to be a loss of confidence. Even so, there continues to be controversy as to how the forensic science community should respond to the NRC (2009) call for the establishment of error rates in forensic testing. Leading forensic scientists propose that each case is unique and that "reanalysis by a qualified examiner would be more meaningful and less costly than entertaining experts espousing hypothetical errors and error rates" (Budowle, Bottrell, et al., 2009, p. 802). Certainly, this statement reflects the culture of scientists engaged in research and data collection. Reproducibility, as assessed by independent, replicate data, is a key factor in the confidence a scientist has in drawing a conclusion. Whenever possible, forensic analysis should be repeated and confirmed. However, the circumstances surrounding some cases do not allow for replicate analysis, and retesting may not reveal all possible errors (e.g., contamination or pre-analytical errors such as mislabeling). Thus, to enhance confidence in DNA testing, there needs to be replicate confirmatory testing combined with excellent quality-assurance and proficiency-testing programs that provide an estimate of error rate.

One of the continuing major concerns with analytical reliability of forensic DNA testing is the possibility of contamination, which is the inadvertent addition of DNA to a forensic sample. The errors reported at the Washington State Crime Laboratory ("DNA Testing Mistakes," 2004) reveal that contamination can happen anywhere, and its impacts can be very important in the continuing confidence in DNA testing.

Scientists describing the potential for problems with contamination for the law enforcement community reveal the following concern:

> Contamination occurs when the evidence comes in contact with another individual's body fluids through actions, such as sneezing, coughing, or touching . . . But, the PCR process cannot distinguish between DNA from a suspect and another source. Therefore, any substantial contamination to the DNA material will result in a confusing result. (Smialek, Word, & Westveer, 2000, pp. 18, 19)

Monitoring, tracking, and preventing contamination presents significant challenges for forensic science. There is essentially no magic test that will identify whether contamination has occurred and, if it did, at what step. This is because extraneous DNA can contaminate a sample at collection, at processing, or at analysis. The extent of the contamination depends on the analytical methodology, the amount of extraneous DNA added, as well as the quantity and source of DNA initially in the sample. The confusion in interpretation of results invoked by contamination is generally higher when the forensic samples are smaller and contain trace amounts of DNA. Just about the only way to recognize if a sample has been contaminated at collection is to have other samples (known as blanks and controls and replicates) to piece together the puzzle. This assumes certain aspects of the various samples that are impossible to verify, and it is conceivable that the true DNA composition of a forensic sample will never be known with certainty. Each individual case is different and will carry with it more or less uncertainty depending on the number and types of samples tested and the ability to retest to confirm results (Budowle, Bottrell, et al., 2009). Numerous methods to lessen the chance of contamination, to test for PCR-product contamination, and even authenticate the sample as genomic DNA have been reported (Frumkin et al., 2010). While important in helping to minimize the chance of a false result, the fact remains that for any forensic DNA analysis, there is no way to be entirely certain that contamination at some level did not occur. Thus, contamination is a concurrent byproduct of DNA testing and imparts a level of uncertainty and possible error into every conclusion drawn from forensic DNA analysis.

Current analytical methods allow for the analysis of extremely small amounts of DNA, known as *touch DNA* (Goray et al., 2010; Wickenheiser, 2002). Touch DNA is transferred to a surface (e.g., wood, skin, glass, paper, etc.) as a person comes into contact with it, and is often gathered by swabbing a surface. Touch DNA analysis is especially prone to contamination by extraneous DNA (either at collection of the sample or during the analysis) because the swabs typically do not contain much DNA, and a cell or two from a contaminating source can easily become the predominant DNA profile in the sample.

Besides contamination, touch DNA samples are also likely to contain DNA from more than one individual. "Mixed DNA" samples are different than "contaminated DNA" samples, as the mixture is not a result of extraneous DNA. Mixed DNA samples are created prior to sample collection and reflect DNA contributed by people who have been in the proximity of, or who have come in physical contact with, the object being investigated. Any forensic sample representing a mixture of DNA from different sources is a challenge for a variety of technical reasons. Samples containing trace levels of DNA are especially difficult because possible contamination adds to the challenge of interpreting the results of the mixture itself. Concerns and guidelines for measuring and interpreting trace DNA have been raised (Budowle, Onorato, et al., 2009; Kruger, 2012), and correspondingly, only a fraction of DNA forensic labs perform analysis when the DNA recovered in the sample is below an established threshold (Raymond et al., 2008). While the overall error rate in standard DNA profiling is still not known, certainly the error in touch DNA analysis is expected to be larger. Several studies indicate the extent of this possible error (Buckleton, Curran, & Gill, 2007; Paoletti et al., 2005). Paoletti and colleagues report that as many as 70% of mixed DNA samples yielded improper conclusions as to how many individuals contributed DNA to the swab. The potential for problems and errors in this domain is further illuminated by research looking at the presence of touch DNA on swabbed skin of laboratory volunteers. This study revealed finding touch DNA on one quarter of all volunteers, and 5% of these had DNA from at least three other individuals on their skin (Graham & Rutty, 2008). It is reasonable to expect that any case centered around touch DNA could still expect a significant admissibility challenge under *Frye* or *Daubert* because the techniques may not have been "rigorously characterized in both research and forensic settings to determine the circumstances under which it will and will not yield reliable results" (NRC, 1992, pp. 51–52).

Television shows depicting crime scene investigation and forensic DNA testing tend to mislead the general public about the general timeframe necessary for DNA testing (see chapter 2, this volume). It is not typically a rapid process yielding a DNA profile within minutes of the sample arriving at the lab. In actuality, DNA results take days to weeks to produce, even in expedited cases. However, there are new research developments in STR methodology, termed *rapid DNA,* that can shorten the testing turnaround time to a few hours (Hopwood et al., 2010; Yeung et al., 2008). Methodological improvements offer an exciting advancement in technology and opportunities for law enforcement to benefit from rapid DNA profile matching. This has the potential to quickly identify suspects and allow detectives to pursue leads before the trail becomes cold. The excitement about this prospect is understandable, but application of rapid DNA testing will face similar, and perhaps greater, challenges regarding confidence and reliability in the testing. It is likely to expect that contamination may impact the reliability of rapid DNA differently than standard CODIS testing. The location and staffing of rapid DNA–testing laboratories bring another level of uncertainty and potential for error as this testing is implemented. Finally, it is not clear how rapid DNA reporting and database inclusion in CODIS will impact the challenges already identified in the DOJ audit (U.S. Department of Justice, 2006).

Achieving and Maintaining Confidence With a Research Mentality and Quality Assurance

Maintaining the utmost confidence in DNA testing requires the full attention of the forensic science community to the National Academy of Science recommendations (NRC, 2009). Among these, having independent review of forensic lab performance is critical (Koppl, 2005). This oversight should not be intertwined with law enforcement or forensic laboratory management. The simultaneous work of scientists at the FBI to provide leadership in validating methodologies, creating progressive quality-assurance programs, and providing technical guidance on best practices in DNA analysis to crime labs around the country, while simultaneously conducting forensic casework, does not demonstrate the independence suggested by the NRC report. The American Society of Crime Laboratory Directors (ASCLD) is an organization created by directors of the laboratories that also offers the industry's major accreditation program. Based solely on the name, one is not confident in the independent nature of the program as it allows the interpretation that the program serves crime lab directors rather than the public. Recently, the federal government announced the formation of an independent forensic science commission, an excellent step in addressing an important recommendation of the 2009 NRC report (Federal Register, 2013).

Improving the accreditation and quality-assurance programs of laboratories is also important for enhancing and maintaining confidence in DNA testing. Few scientists would argue with Giannelli's (2008) statement regarding quality assurance, "If proficiency programs are not rigorous, they provide only an illusion of reliability. Indeed, by bestowing an undeserved imprimatur, they are affirmatively misleading" (p. 217).

Quality-assurance practices must be placed under an independent microscope, be proactive in addressing trends in forensic science, and work to track errors and improve outcomes. An obvious approach to creating rigorous quality assurance is to require that labs engage in blind proficiency testing (Koehler, 2013). Such a program has frequently been suggested, and the feasibility has been studied. While it was determined to be feasible, blind external proficiency testing is not yet a standard practice owing to implementation and budgetary considerations (Peterson et al., 2003). This is unfortunate, given what is known about un-blinded testing in a forensic arena. Studies of biases that arise when the circumstances of the case are known to the laboratorian (known as the *sharpshooter effect*) provide a strong rationale for blind testing of all kinds (Thompson, 2009).

Other recommendations for improving confidence in DNA testing are to provide the interested public details of proficiency-testing programs and create blind proficiency-testing programs that emulate challenging forensic specimens. Prior criticism of forensic proficiency programs are that the samples may not adequately represent the most challenging cases handled by the labs, such as complex mixtures or touch DNA. Labs and proficiency-testing agencies should be free from the worry that the provision and subsequent testing of challenging samples will be used to discredit overall capabilities as an accredited lab or proficiency test provider. In this environment, cutting-edge proficiency-testing programs can be used to gather information and improve the overall testing process in an iterative way.

Since there is not another technology that can be used to verify the reliability of DNA profiling, the only way to reveal possible intrinsic errors in the testing process is by proficiency and replicate testing. From this chemist's perspective, it is not acceptable that only 10% of publically funded DNA labs participate in blind proficiency testing. Advances in new technology such as touch and rapid DNA cannot be placed into confidence until blind testing is adopted and other quality assurance programs are strengthened. Oversight of labs must be made independent and errors studied, tallied, and reported to the general public. Database information that is held in the NDIS should be released for evaluation by independent scientists, and an independent forensic science commission should carefully review all the recommendations of the NRC (2009) and develop a plan for implementing and assessing a clear path toward moving ahead with the highest quality possible. This must be carried forward in the way that will impart the most confidence in the testing process so that the criminal justice system can assuredly rely on the technology in the years to come. External oversight and a research mentality to find, correct, and report errors must be adopted knowing that some new technology will inevitably be invented and validated that will shed light on the random and intrinsic errors that occur in the current practice of DNA testing.

References

Ahlers, M. (1988, February 6). Rapist convicted on DNA match. *New York Times.* Retrieved from http://www.nytimes.com/1988/02/06/us/rapist-convicted-on-dna-match .html

Bono, J. P. (2011). Commentary on the need for a research culture in the forensic sciences. *UCLA Law Review, 58,* 781–787.

Buckleton, J. S., Curran, J. M., & Gill, P. (2007). Towards understanding the effect of uncertainty in the number of contributors to DNA stains. *Forensic Science International: Genetics, 1*(1), 20–28.

Budowle, B., Bottrell, M. C., Bunch, S. G., Fram, R., Harrison, D., Meagher, S., et al. (2009). A perspective on errors, bias, and interpretation in the forensic sciences and direction for continuing advancement. *Journal of Forensic Sciences, 54*(4), 798–809.

Budowle, B., Onorato, A. J., Callaghan, T. F., Manna, A. D., Gross, A. M., Guerrieri, R. A., et al. (2009). Mixture interpretation: Defining the relevant features for guidelines for the assessment of mixed DNA profiles in forensic casework. *Journal of Forensic Sciences, 54*(4), 810–821.

Butler, J. M. (2012). *Advanced topics in forensic DNA typing: Methodology.* Waltham, MA: Academic Press.

Cass, J. (2010, March 23). The cost of making crime not pay: Obama, CODIS and forensix DNA [Web blog message]. Retrieved from http://www.genomicslawreport.com/index .php/2010/03/23/the-cost-of-making-crime-not-pay-obama-codis-and-forensic-dna

Collaborative Testing Services, Inc. (CTS). (2010, March 30). *CTS statement on the use of proficiency testing data for error rate determinations.* Retrieved from http://www .ctsforensics.com/assets/news/CTSErrorRateStatement.pdf

Comey, C., & Budowle, B. (1991). Validation studies of the analysis of the HLA DQalpha locus using the Polymerase Chain Reaction. *Journal of Forensic Sciences, 36*(6), 1633–1648.

Comey, C., Budowle, B., Adams, D., Baumstark, A., Lindsey, J., & Presley, L. (1993). PCR amplification and typing of the HLA DQalpha gene in forensic samples. *Journal of Forensic Sciences, 38*(2), 239–249.

Commonwealth v. Pestinikas, 617 A. 2d 1339 (Pennsylvania 1986)

Commonwealth v. Francis, no. 86–11015 (Pennsylvania 1990)

Derksen, L. (2000). Towards sociology of measurement: The meaning of measurement error in the case of DNA profiling. *Social Studies of Science, 30*(6), 803–845.

DNA testing mistakes at the State Patrol crime labs. (2004, July 21). *Seattle Post Intelligencer.* Retrieved from http://www.seattlepi.com/local/article/DNA-testing-mistakes-at-the-State-Patrol-crime-1149846.php

Durose, M. R., Walsh, K. A., & Burch, A. M. (2012) Census of publicly funded forensic crime laboratories, 2009. *Bureau of Justice Statistics Bulletin,* 1–13. Retrieved from http://bjs.gov/content/pub/pdf/cpffcl09.pdf

Federal Bureau of Investigation (FBI). (2000). *Quality assurance standrads for forensic DNA testing laboratories.* Retrieved from http://www.cstl.nist.gov/strbase/dabqas.htm

Federal Bureau of Investigation (FBI). (2012). *CODIS brochure.* Retrieved from www.fbi .gov/about-us/lab/biometric-analysis/codis/codis_brochure

Federal Register. (2013, February 22). Notice of establishment of the National Commission on Forensic Science and solicitation of applications for commission membership (FR Doc. 2013-04140). Washington, DC: Government Printing Office. Retrieved from https:// www.federalregister.gov/articles/2013/02/22/2013-04140/notice-of-establishment-of-the-national-commission-on-forensic-science-and-solicitation-of

Frumkin, D., Wasserstrom, A., Davidson, A., & Grafit, A. (2010). Authentication of forensic DNA samples. *Forensic Science International: Genetics, 4*(2), 95–103.

Giannelli, P. C. (2008). Wrongful convictions and forensic science: The need to regulate crime labs. *North Carolina Law Review, 86,* 163–235.

Goray, M., Eken, E., Mitchell, R. J., & van Oorschot, R. A. (2010). Secondary DNA transfer of biological substances under varying test conditions. *Forensic Science International: Genetics, 4*(2), 62–67.

Graham, E. A. M., & Rutty, G. N. (2008). Investigation into "normal" background DNA on adult necks: implications for DNA profiling of manual strangulation victims. *Journal of Forensic Sciences, 53*(5), 1074–1082.

Hammerling, J. A. (2012). A review of medical errors in laboratory diagnostic and where we are today. *LabMedicine, 43*(2), 41–44.

Hopwood, A. J., Hurth, C., Yang, J., Cai, Z., Moran, N., Lee-Edghill, J. G., et al. (2010). Integrated microfluidic system for rapid forensic DNA analysis: sample collection to DNA profile. *Analytical chemistry, 82*(16), 6991–6999.

Imwinkelried, E. J., & Kaye, D. H. (2001). DNA typing: Emerging or neglected issues. *Washington Law Review, 76*(2), 413–414.

Jabbar, M. (2010). Overcoming *Daubert's* shortcomings in criminal trials: Making the error rate the primary factor in *Daubert's* validity inquiry. *NYU Law Review, 85,* 2034.

Jeffreys, A., Wilson, V., & Thein, S. (1985). Hypervariable "minisatellite" regions in human DNA. *Nature, 314*(6006), 67–73.

Junkin, T. (2004). *Bloodsworth: The true story of the first death row inmate exonerated by DNA.* Chapel Hill, NC: Shannon Ravenel Books/Algonquin Books of Chapel Hill.

Koehler, J. J. (2008). Fingerprint error rates and proficiency tests: What they are and why they matter. *Hastings Law Journal, 59*(5), 1077–1100.

Koehler, J. J. (2013). Proficiency tests to estimate error rates in the forensic sciences. *Law, Probability and Risk, 12*(1), 89–98.

Koppl, R. (2005). How to improve forensic science. *European Journal of Law and Economics, 3,* 255–286.

Krane, D. E., Bahn, V., Balding, D., Barlow, B., Cash, H., Desportes, B. L., et al. (2009). Time for DNA disclosure. *Science, 326,* 1631–1632.

Kruger, E. (2012). Visualizing uncertainty: Anomalous images in science and law. *Interdisciplinary Science Reviews, 37*(1), 19–35.

Lynch, M. (2003). God's signature: DNA profiling, the new gold standard in forensic science. *Endeavour, 27*(2), 93–97.

Mnookin, J. L., Cole, S. A., Dror, I. E., Fisher, B. A., Houck, M. M., Inman, K., et al. (2011). Need for a research culture in the forensic sciences, *The UCLA Law Review, 58,* 725–780.

National Research Council (NRC). (1992). *DNA technology in forensic science.* Washington, DC: National Academies Press.

National Research Council (NRC). (2009). *Strengthening forensic science in the United States: A path forward.* Washington, DC: National Academies Press.

Paoletti, D. R., Doom, T. E., Krane, C. M., Raymer, M. L., & Krane, D. E. (2005). Empirical analysis of the STR profiles resulting from conceptual mixtures. *Journal of Forensic Sciences, 50*(6), 1361–1366.

Patton, S. M. (1990). DNA fingerprinting: The Castro case. *Harvard Journal of Law & Technology, 3,* 223–259.

Peterson, J. L., & Hickman, M. J. (2005). Census of publicly funded forensic crime laboratories, 2002. *Bureau of Justice Statistics Bulletin,* 1–16. Retrieved from http://bjs.gov/content/pub/pdf/cpffcl02.pdf

Peterson, J. L., Lin, G., Ho, M., Chen, Y., & Gaensslen, R. E. (2003). The feasibility of external blind DNA proficiency testing. I. Background and findings. *Journal of forensic sciences, 48*(1), 21–31.

Plebani, M. (2006). Errors in clinical laboratories or errors in laboratory medicine? *Clinical Chemical Laboratory Medicine, 44*(6), 750–759.

Plebani, M. (2007). Errors in laboratory medicine and patient safety: The road ahead. *Clinical Chemical Laboratory Medicine, 45*(6), 700–707.

Raymond, J. J., van Oorschot, R. A., Walsh, S. J., & Roux, C. (2008). Trace DNA analysis: Do you know what your neighbour is doing? A multi-jurisdictional survey. *Forensic Science International: Genetics, 2*(1), 19–28.

Rudin, N., & Inman, K. (2002). *An introduction to forensic DNA analysis* . Boca Raton, FL: CRC Press.

Saiki, R., Scharf, S., Faloona, F., Mullis, K., Horn, G., Erlich, H., et al. (1985). Enzymatic amplification of B-globin genomic sequences and restriction site analysis for diagnosis of sickle cell anemia. *Science, 230*(4732), 1350–1354.

Saks, M. J., & Koehler, J. J. (2005) The coming paradigm shift in forensic identification science. *Science, 309*(5736), 892–895.

Smialek, J., Word, C., & Westveer, A. E. (2000, November). The microscopic slide: A potential DNA reservoir. *FBI Law Enforcement Bull,* 18–22. Retrieved from http://www.fbi.gov/stats-services/publications/law-enforcement-bulletin/2000-pdfs/nov00leb.pdf

State v. Russell, 125 Wn.2d 24 (Washington 1994).

State v. Shreck, 22 P.3d 68 (Colorado 2001).

Thompson, W. C. (1993). Evaluating the admissibility of new genetic identification tests: Lessons from the "DNA war." *Journal of Criminal Law & Criminology, 84,* 22–104.

Thompson, W. C. (2006). Tarnish on the "gold standard": Understanding recent problems in forensic DNA testing. *The Champion, 30*(1), 10–16. Retrieved from http://www.bioforensics.com/articles/Thompson_Champion_Tarnish.pdf

Thompson, W. C. (2009). Painting the target around the matching profile: The Texas sharpshooter fallacy in forensic DNA interpretation. *Law, Probability and Risk, 8*(3), 257–276.

U.S. Department of Justice, Office of the Inspector General. (2006). *Combined DNA index system operational and laboratory vulnerabilities* (DOJ Audit Report 06–32). Retrieved from http://www.justice.gov/oig/reports/FBI/a0632/final.pdf

Vosk, T. (2008). Chaos reigning: Breath testing and the Washington state toxicology lab. *The Champion* (May–June), 56–62. Retrieved from http://www.truthinjustice.org/ChampionToxLab.pdf

Wickenheiser, R. A. (2002). Trace DNA: A review, discussion of theory, and application of the transfer of trace quantities of DNA through skin contact. *Journal of Forensic Sciences, 47*(3), 442–450.

Willing, R. (2006, November 21). Many DNA matches aren't acted on. *USA Today.* Retrieved from http://www. usatoday30.usatoday.com/news/nation/2006–11–20-dna-matches_x .htm

Yeung, S. H., Liu, P., Del Bueno, N., Greenspoon, S. A., & Mathies, R. A. (2008). Integrated sample cleanup—capillary electrophoresis microchip for high-performance short tandem repeat genetic analysis. *Analytical Chemistry, 81*(1), 210–217.

Section V

The Future Role of Forensic Science in the Administration of Justice

We close out this text with three readings that provide outlooks on what the future might hold for forensic science and how we may come to better understand its role in the justice process. First, Max M. Houck and Paul J. Speaker discuss how the adoption of a systems-level, business model approach may lead to more rational assessments of laboratory efficiency and effectiveness, and, as a result, improved decision making about the optimal provision of forensic services. In "Developing New Business Models for Forensic Laboratories," Houck and Speaker suggest that the forensic community needs to explore a concept of operations (CONOPS) that would articulate the goals, strategies, policies, responsibilities, operational processes, and other organizational parameters. Critical to developing a CONOPS is data about the costs and benefits of forensic services, values that can be elusive given that forensic services are largely within the public sector. Drawing from their experience with Project FORESIGHT, Houck and Speaker explore some of the laboratory metrics (such as cost per case, by investigative area) that may be useful in aggregate form to help inform and evaluate different business models. Importantly, the authors also argue that the development of a CONOPS would be intimately tied to many of the recommendations contained in the NAS report.

Next, the editors provide a chapter exploring the interface of forensic services with the larger criminal justice process. In "Rethinking the Role of the Crime Laboratory in Criminal Justice Decision Making," Strom and Hickman argue that the role of the forensic system in the administration of justice has evolved to the point where crime laboratory personnel should be properly recognized as criminal justice decision makers who exercise discretion (e.g., about what types of evidence to accept, what analyses to perform, and with what priority), and can substantively influence decision making at other criminal justice decision stages by other actors. Strom and Hickman suggest that it may be time to consider incorporating forensic services in the classic flowchart of the criminal justice system developed by the 1967 President's Commission on the Administration of Justice, and last revised by the Bureau of Justice Statistics in 1997. No longer simply ancillary justice services, forensic laboratories and their personnel are key decision makers who can have a significant impact on the administration of justice and who must be considered as a key partner within the forensic process.

Finally, Walter F. Rowe examines where forensic science might be in the next 20 to 30 years. In "The Future of Forensic Science," Rowe begins by identifying some of the scientific and administrative challenges that need to be resolved within that timeframe. These include improving the scientific status of the identification sciences (fingerprints, firearms, and toolmarks, etc.); the development of new analytical instrumentation (and validation of new analytical methods) to extract more information, faster, with lower detection limits, and at less cost; and the separation of laboratories from law enforcement agencies and prosecutor's offices. Rowe thoroughly dissects the forensic community and walks the reader through technological developments in crime scene investigation, medico-legal death investigation, and forensic nursing; drug chemistry; trace evidence; forensic biology; forensic pathology; digital evidence; and forensic databases. Next, Rowe tackles the scientific issues facing the identification sciences, and focuses on handwriting identification, fingerprinting, and firearm/toolmark analysis. Finally, administrative changes in the forensic sciences, such as regulation (standards and accreditation), management, standardized reporting, examiner certification, ethics, independence, legislative activity, and forensic science education are taken up. Although the broad range of challenges discussed might feel overwhelming and perhaps even insurmountable, the chapter leaves the reader with a sense of optimism about the future of forensic science. We also hope that the text as a whole, by exploring the broad and exciting range of social science research on the forensic science, contributes to that optimism.

12

Developing New Business Models for Forensic Laboratories

Max M. Houck and Paul J. Speaker

Forensic service providers inhabit a unique, central place in the criminal justice system. Stakeholders in the forensic enterprise abound, from law enforcement to attorneys to the courts and even the public they all serve. The public orientation of these services and stakeholders necessitates that forensic managers rely on providing sound performance at a reasonable cost. Certainly, the laboratory's jurisdiction will judge performance on criteria such as accuracy, timeliness, and cost. Too much emphasis on quantitative outcomes, however, can create an imbalance that ignores longer-term issues, such as quality and value. Thus, efficiency, the extent to which time and effort are used to produce the desired outcome, can be mistaken for effectiveness, the attainment of that desired outcome, but they are intimately connected. A sports car is an effective method for getting to the market but hardly an efficient one, for example; if it is your sole means of transportation, however, efficiency may hardly matter. Benchmarking of services can help with assessments of efficiency. From efficient benchmarks strategies may be developed to promote better effectiveness.

Immediate criteria such as timeliness and cost beg the question of a larger business model for the provision of forensic services. Various models exist, at least implicitly, but few are proposed or evaluated explicitly. A concept of operations (CONOPS) provides a narrative, how the system operates to achieve the desired goals through stated methodologies and generally includes the following (IEEE Standards Board, 1998):

- Stated goals
- Strategies, tactics, policies, and constraints of the system

221

- Organizations, activities, and relationships among stakeholders
- Clear responsibilities and authorities
- Specific operational processes
- Processes for initiating, developing, executing, maintaining, and retiring the system

The CONOPS of the provision of forensic science services can be thought of as an enterprise of nonprofit, production-oriented organizations staffed by knowledge workers. Forensic scientists convert physical items and data (evidence) into knowledge using (forensic) science, in the form of reports and testimony; this is their manufacturing function and their product, respectively. They specialize in these conversions, occupying a specific and necessary space as translators of complex scientific information, simplifying it into a format suitable for consumption by non-scientists. Moreover, with forensic scientists occupying this space, investigators and attorneys do not need to find numerous individuals to conduct the specific examinations separately required for a case; the forensic organization provides a coherent and convenient source of valued service to stakeholders.

Simply, forensic service providers can be thought of in three ways: as public good providers, private entities, or as mixed providers. Based on the current knowledge about the industry (Durose, Walsh, & Burch, 2012), the vast majority of forensic providers are governmental and are funded directly or indirectly through public funds derived from a relevant population. Like police officers and fire fighters, the services are available more-or-less uniformly to everyone in a given jurisdiction. Private forensic providers are for-profit businesses and charge customers for the services. Mixed providers are just that: They have some aspects of a public laboratory and some of a private one. An interesting example of a mixed model is the Crown Research Institute, Environmental Science & Research (ESR) in New Zealand, a public lab set up with a for-profit mandate. Another is the Netherlands Forensic Institute, which is funded by their government to work on in-country cases but can also work on external cases for a fee, even through contractual agreements for volume work.[1]

For historical and political reasons, most forensic service providers are administratively part of law enforcement agencies. Being within a para-military organization brackets the forensic service provider's relationships with their parent agency and related agencies; it also frames the externalities the organization must weather to perform adequately or succeed. Recently, this paradigm has been challenged by the National Academy of Sciences' (NAS) 2009 report on the forensic sciences, which recommended that forensic service providers be administratively or financially independent of law enforcement-based parent agencies.

Successful independence requires a greater sense of self-awareness and an objective analysis of the organization's CONOPS or model, process, and performance (Collins, 2005). Absent a business model or CONOPS, the forensic enterprise will have a difficult time applying "lessons learned" through the evaluation of other provider systems. Without a framework or narrative in which to fit what works and what doesn't, testable improvement of service delivery—like data observations without hypotheses—will be

---

[1]http://www.forensicinstitute.nl/products_and_services

out of context and lack meaning. This chapter explores baseline metrics that can be aggregated to assist in evaluating models and concepts for forensic enterprises through global examples of ways for laboratories to analyze and assess their work.

Economic Foundations

The global economic climate has made it necessary for justice systems, among other segments of the public sector, to reconsider what constitutes the best service model to meet their mandates. An investigation into what is the best model invites a series of questions about what *best* means. Is "best" about a process or is it a result of organizational form? Is it a question of public versus private or a combination of the two? Is customer satisfaction at the heart of the question or is it a question of size? Or is the "best model" the result of some combination of analytical processes, leadership, human resource development, sound financial management, and distribution of resources?

Several authors have bemoaned the application of business principles to forensic science laboratories. Leslie (2010) intimates that a business analytical approach to the question of best forensic science model commoditizes forensic sciences. Referencing the UK's Forensic Science Service (FSS), another author suggests that "the market approach to forensic science services is flawed in principle . . . the language of market exchange irrevocably distorts and debases the pursuit of criminal justice" (Roberts, 1996, p. 37). And others suggest that questions surrounding the measurement of the value of services may lead to a reduction in the delivery of justice:

> Many concerns have already been expressed within the law and forensic sectors about the potential tensions between commercial imperatives and judicial concerns . . . Precisely what do the processes of the future constructions of science and liberalization hold for the delivery of justice? (Lawless, 2010, p. 19)

At the other extreme, free market economists have suggested that privatization of forensic laboratories is necessary for justice to be served (Koppl, 2005).[2] "Under competitive self regulation, each jurisdiction would have several competing forensic labs. Evidence would be divided and sent to one, two, or three separate labs" (p. 275). However, in an examination of the performance of public laboratories with an eye toward economies of scale, McAndrew (2012) suggests that privatization would offer an improvement only if public sector laboratories were inherently inefficient.

Microeconomic theory offers insight into the foundation from which to assess questions regarding the best business model for an industry. While most of the economics literature references a business in the for-profit industry, the basic tenets may be easily applied to forensic laboratories in the for-profit, not-for-profit, or public sector. Whichever sector applies to a given laboratory, the determination of best model begins

---

[2]Koppl's argument suggests the elimination or minimization of error via provision of laboratory services through the private sector, but stories of errors are as rampant in private provision as they are in public laboratories (e.g., "Rape Case Reopened," 2012).

with an examination of the objective of the organization. In the case of the for-profit laboratory, the sector identification reveals the objective. That is, the assessment of best business model begins with the specification that a laboratory makes its decisions to maximize the discounted value of all future profits, where profit is the excess of revenues over expenses.

For the other sectors, there is no interest in profit, but the objectives instead center on one of the elements of profit, either revenue or expenses. A not-for-profit enterprise will focus on revenue generation and attempts to acquire as much funding as possible to achieve the most "good" associated with its mission that revenues will support. They are revenue maximizers. The public enterprise, on the other hand, concentrates on the other end of the profit measure as it attempts to achieve as much good as possible for a given budget, essentially minimizing expenses.

Any determination of the best model for forensic laboratories must be made relative to the mission and objectives of the justice system and the revenue allocation that the justice system makes to the forensic laboratory. That determination requires the ability to measure the good and connect that output with the inputs, processes, and distributions of scarce resources toward the production of that good.

Metrics and Measurement

The European QUADRUPOL project (European Network of Forensic Sciences, 2003) offered a strong opening to the concept of consistent measurement of the performance of forensic laboratories. Four national laboratories developed a standard for consistent measures and collected data for budgets, personnel, and expenses to enable comparisons for a consideration of efficiencies. This necessary first step set the stage for a broader application of analysis through project FORESIGHT (Houck et al., 2009). Project FORESIGHT adopted the standards established in QUADRUPOL and refined definitions and expanded the detail of the collected data. While originally a North American study with a group of 17 laboratories from the United States and Canada, the study has grown to include a large group of laboratories from across the globe. Participation includes national, provincial, metropolitan, and other local jurisdictions, as well as modest participation from private laboratories.

The initial level of comparison from the QUADRUPOL and FORESIGHT project data involves a review of key performance metrics related to the mission of the forensic laboratory (Speaker, 2009a). Which metrics to select for comparison depends on the objectives for a forensic science laboratory.[3] If the objective of the justice system calls for laboratories to maximize the amount of good[4] for a given budget, then the

---

[3] Certainly, a discussion of objectives should be broader than merely the objectives of the laboratory and should extend to a discussion of the goals of the justice system. Peterson et al. (2010) consider the contribution of forensics laboratories to the justice system, but limit measures to convictions and ignore other intended outputs. Doleac (2013) suggests a much broader measure of objectives (including exoneration), but uniform data collection at the laboratory level has yet to include the breadth of those broader outcomes.

[4] The term *good* is used to represent the intended outcome of a not-for-profit organization or a government entity. For the forensic laboratory, *good* may be interpreted as a correctly processed case or other outcome tied to the mission of the laboratory.

evaluation of laboratories can be centered in the efficiency and effectiveness as measured through cost minimization metrics (Speaker, 2009b). Using basic financial management techniques, the performance metrics may be reduced to a series of measures that are representative of efficiency, quality, analytical process, and market conditions. The joint metrics generated by this decomposition allow a laboratory to target those areas in need of process improvement, strategic changes, or other alternations to lower the average cost of its investigations (Kobus et al., 2011).

Table 12.1 presents the summary statistics of the cost per case for the voluntary sample of 65 forensic laboratories for 2011.[5] With common measures across laboratories and ratios connected to the stated goals of the organizations, the data offer a point of reference for any laboratory to assess performance against industry standards.

Through the decomposition of those metrics into other ratios representing analytical process, risk, efficiency, and market conditions, the laboratory can then begin to establish strategic plans to address any issues and to monitor performance (Newman, Dawley, & Speaker, 2011). This includes an implementation of a balanced scorecard approach to a variety of projects as well as attention to the budgetary process and reallocation of resources within the laboratory for maximum effectiveness (Speaker & Fleming, 2009, 2010).

Table 12.1   Cost/Case Summary Statistics Project FORESIGHT 2011

Investigative Area	Mean	Median	Std. Dev.
Blood Alcohol	$255	$124	$389
Digital Evidence	$10,851	$2,789	$15,225
DNA Casework	$2,255	$2,186	$637
DNA Database	$283	$75	$650
Document Examination	$2,756	$2,281	$1,658
Drugs—Controlled Substances	$274	$240	$162
Explosives	$9,117	$6,550	$9,445
Fingerprint Identification	$528	$435	$295
Fire Analysis	$2,465	$1,567	$2,795
Firearms and Ballistics	$1,150	$816	$785
Gun Shot Residue	$2,105	$1,648	$1,795
Marks and Impressions	$5,010	$2,612	$5,570
Serology/Biology	$663	$568	$516
Toxicology Ante Mortem	$663	$489	$806
Toxicology Post Mortem	$875	$652	$946
Trace Evidence	$5,528	$4,412	$5,442

[5]Because the sample includes laboratories from across the globe, all currencies were converted to U.S. dollars using closing exchange rates on December 31 of the sample year.

A Balanced View

The attention to average cost and other ratio metrics only offers a first glimpse of the performance story. As Leslie (2010) and others note, a pure attention to short-term cost metrics ignores one of the other mandates of laboratories: research and development. Houck et al. (2012) note that a balanced scorecard approach "ensures an appropriate mix of performance metrics from across the organization to achieve operational excellence; thereby the balanced scorecard ensures that no single or limited group of metrics dominates the assessment process, possibly leading to long-term inferior performance" (p. 209). The performance metrics occasionally raise a red flag, signaling that the average cost in an investigation falls outside the normal bounds. But the red flag is a signal to look deeper into the reason behind the anomaly, rather than a signal to act without forethought.

Many of the other concerns in a laboratory's balanced scorecard are related to issues of human resources, including staffing, retention, and employee satisfaction. The so-called "*CSI* effect" (see Chapter 2, this volume) has placed significant pressures to perform as demand for laboratory services increases in an era of stagnant or shrinking budgets (Houck, 2006). Dale and Becker (2003) offer an early look into the staffing needs for the industry and the need for long-term planning to educate new scientists and to address the needs of the forensic sciences. The rising demand for services requires new and innovative models for the analysis of forensic evidence. Heames and Heames (2011) note that a continual retooling and review of processes is required to allow productivity to rise along with increased demands for services. Schade (2009) shows how such examinations can turn a seeming budgetary crisis into an opportunity through reviews of processes and responding with innovations that are efficient and cost-effective.

As a new generation is attracted to the forensic sciences as a career choice, there are some significant benefits to forensic laboratories as the forensic sciences offer an opportunity for women in the sciences (Houck, 2009). The characteristics of this new generation of scientists differ from the characteristics of prior generations of scientists, and this has introduced some tension into many laboratories and their ability to perform. The newer scientists from Generation Y bring a different focus toward work than prior generations. Further complicating the connection between this technology-focused generation and prior generations is the gender difference between the generations with laboratory workers from Generation Y being majority female and prior generations dominated by male workers. Combine these differences with generational differences in the form of education and training and laboratory productivity often suffers. Dawley and Munyon (2012) examine the connection between laboratory job satisfaction, determining characteristics of satisfaction, and the performance of the laboratory. They measure the significant effect of job satisfaction and the implications for laboratory directors and managers to effect higher performance through nurturing their human resources effectively.

Efficiency and Cost-Effectiveness

While Koppl (2005) calls for a market solution[6] for improvements in the provision of forensic science services, it is unclear that a market solution is the only viable

---

[6]*A market solution* refers to a competitive situation as is typically found in a private sector allocation of scarce resources with the determination of price and output from the interaction of buyers and sellers of goods or services.

answer to a question of the best model for forensic laboratories. It is true that competition eventually eliminates inferior quality and high-cost providers as market forces push such providers out of business. But that market reality does not condemn public provision of forensic science services to be a second-best solution. Indeed, private sector provision incurs a cost that is not found in the public laboratories—the risk-adjusted rate of return (i.e., profit) that must be earned to justify activity. The public sector can be more cost-effective than the privatized laboratory through the adoption of the appropriate analytical techniques for the best scale and scope of operations.

The question of the right scale of operations introduces an additional dimension to the metrics found in Table 12.1. *Economy of scale* refers to levels of output that experience a lower average cost as the provision of goods or services are increased. Perfect economies of scale are achieved at that level of production where average costs are minimized. Across a broad spectrum of possible production levels, the average cost curve is a U-shaped curve, and the bottom of that curve is the level of output that best addresses the economic problem for the optimal allocation of scarce resources.

In the private sector, competition guides businesses to this "right size," and we only get to observe the survivors who are competing at the optimal size. Occasionally, we are able to observe the U-shaped cost curve in the public sector, when we are able to uniformly measure the public sector output. One such example involves the public provision of crematoria services in the United Kingdom (Knapp, 1982). A second example is found with private contracts for cleaning public schools (Christoffersen, Paldam, & Wurtz, 2007). Project FORESIGHT data has permitted the display of these U-shaped curves and a sense of the optimal level of operations for forensic laboratories (Witt & Speaker, 2012).

The search for new models, or the best model among those currently in operation, requires that attention be paid to both efficiency and cost-effectiveness. Maguire, Houck, and Speaker (2012) show that the vast majority of forensic laboratories in the FORESIGHT sample are operationally efficient. That is, most public laboratories are operating along the U-shaped average cost curve and are applying their trade following analytical techniques and productivity at the low cost for their level of casework. However, these efficient operations are not always cost-effective because their level of casework is insufficient to bring them to the perfect economies of scale level of production. To recognize the greatest gains, alternatives such as in-sourcing, out-sourcing, privatization, or cross-jurisdictional cooperation may be needed.

Identifying the Best Business Models for Forensic Laboratories

Houck et al. (2011) offer a round-table discussion on forensic science in Australia that offers many of the key questions in the examination of best model globally. While most public laboratories are stitched together from similar cloth, there are a number of more recent constructs that bear examination. The evolution (Roberts, 1996) and dissolution (Budowle, Kayser, & Sanjantila, 2011) of the FSS in the United Kingdom serves as an example of what might be done, or what might be done better (House of Commons, 2013). A rush to a decision may be more costly than doing nothing at all. Rincon (2013) suggests that the closure of the FSS may have cost more than the cost in perpetuity of keeping the FSS unchanged. In the United States, other "experiments" with novel

CONOPS include public-joint ventures, like the Northeastern Illinois Regional Crime Laboratory, located in Vernon Hills, IL, which services 950,000 residents from the northern boundary of Chicago to the Wisconsin state border. Thirty-five law enforcement agencies fund and govern its operation.[7] Regionalization like this may offer jurisdictions the opportunity to leverage budgets into cooperative models of greater benefit than individual solutions.

Generating less attention is the model offered in New Zealand by the Crown Research Institute, Environmental Science & Research (ESR). Bedford (2011) describes the formation of this public laboratory that operates under a for-profit mandate. It is quite successful in its operations and offers a glimpse at how the benefits of competition may influence public sector provision of forensic laboratory services. Those lessons are not limited to the mandate of the Crown Research Institute or its ilk, but may be replicated in a variety of forms. However, the decision to depoliticize management decisions is found throughout Bedford's description of the operations of ESR. Speaker (2013) examines the decisions and finds that the decisions made under the ESR have been a strong response to economic signals and have further benefited by a scale of operations that permits New Zealand to take great advantage of economies of scale in its operations. Of particular interest in the ESR case is the commentary over the years in the annual report (e.g., Institute of Environmental Science and Research, 2009), where there is some regret expressed over the decline in the demand for certain services, such as trace evidence. However, this is the nature of the market model where suppliers and consumers interact to decide on highest valued uses of resources. On a topical level, regionalization again may offer some hope of continued service: Laboratories could parse case types, like trace, by expertise or instrumentation, thereby distributing the load and maximizing resources. More work is needed to determine if this CONOPS would be operationally and financially feasible.

Other business model questions include issues of economies of scope—the proper mix of areas of investigation for any laboratory. At this point, there has been little research into questions of scope. However, some interesting questions are being raised. That includes Roman et al. (2008) on the use of DNA. More recently, Doleac (2013) speculates on the potential return from a more intensive use of DNA technology and offers a cost-benefit analysis that suggests great gains from an expansion of DNA databases. Given the attention that backlogs continue to receive (e.g., Twohey, 2011), a closer look into the cost-benefit of such changes is warranted.

Regardless of the model alternative considered, adaptation to any jurisdiction must be reconsidered in terms of the local legal, cultural, and political environment. What works in one country may be prohibited in another country. Even within a single country, local and regional restrictions may make the direct application of a perceived better model prohibited. For example, in discussions with several FORESIGHT laboratories that neighbored each other, the potentially significant savings that could have been realized by sharing resources through centralized testing of cases (all trace cases going to one laboratory) were not possible because the jurisdictions had no mechanism for exchanging funds between extra-state agencies. Another example is the adversarial nature of the U.S. courts, which makes certain demands on expert witnesses' reports, testimony, and appearances.

---

[7]www.nircl.org

Conclusion

Why bother with a model for forensic service? What is the benefit of having a CONOPS? Along with the enterprise architecture (fundamental organization of a complex program) and governance structure (management principles and decision making) (Giachetti, 2010), a CONOPS provides a holistic framework for establishing and evaluating forensic service providers. On its own, a CONOPS can provide these benefits:

- Sets context for measuring system efficiency and effectiveness

- Provides a logic trail of capability

- Creates a basis for communication between stakeholders (who now have a common vocabulary)

- Illustrates how the system should function

- Sets the "as is" and bridges the "to be" states

- Helps scope the situation and proposed solutions (Frittman & Edson, 2010)

Of the 13 main recommendations made by the NAS (2009) committee on forensic science, most relate to the establishment of a CONOPS, although not in so many words. Highly paraphrased, the 13 recommendations are as follows:

1. Create a National Institute of Forensic Science

2. Standardize terminology and reports

3. Research the accuracy, reliability, and validity of forensic science disciplines

4. Forensic science laboratories should be independent of law enforcement

5. Research human error and bias in forensic examinations

6. Create standards for forensic examinations

7. Accreditation and certification should be mandatory

8. Quality assurance and quality control procedures should be established

9. A national code of ethics in forensic science should be established

10. Improve forensic science educational programs

11. Improve death investigations and convert the nation to a medical examiner system

12. AFIS should be interoperable

13. Forensic science needs to play a role in homeland security

Reviewing the list of benefits of a CONOPS, recommendations 2, 3, 5–8, 11, and 13 can be directly tied in with the creation of a CONOPS. While the other recommendations are sufficient to contribute to a CONOPS, they are not necessary for one.

Table 12.2 maps out suggested correlations between the NAS recommendations and the three system-level requirements.

Because forensic science has no historical or traditional enterprise or strategic models from which to work, it has rarely if ever seen itself at a systems or enterprise level (Houck et al., 2009). This blinkered view is not only systemic but also structural. Arguably, small laboratories have access to the same resources as larger laboratories; some of these are free (such as the publications from government agencies and sponsored working groups like the SWGs), and some are at market cost (consumables, capital investments, salaries, benefits, among others). Nevertheless,

> There are great disparities among existing forensic science operations in federal, state, and local law enforcement jurisdictions and agencies. This is true with respect to funding, access to analytical instrumentation, the availability of skilled and well-trained personnel, certification, accreditation, and oversight . . . any approach to overhauling the existing system needs to address and help minimize the community's current fragmentation and inconsistent practices. (NAS, 2009, pp. 5–6)

The enterprise architecture and the governance structure need to ensure that agencies or jurisdictions are not disadvantaged by the system. And disadvantages are not only financial: Ignorance of community standards, obsolete processes, or what constitutes proper service delivery can disadvantage a jurisdiction as much as a lack of money. The contribution of forensic services to the U.S justice system must be uniform

Table 12.2   Mapping the NAS 2009 Recommendations to a Systems-Level Approach for Forensic Science

NAS Recommendation	Enterprise Architecture	Governance Structure	CONOPS
1		X	
2			X
3			X
4	X	X	
5			X
6		X	X
7	X	X	X
8		X	X
9		X	
10	X		
11	X	X	X
12		X	
13	X		X

and balanced; oversight with checks and balances—and consequences for falling short—are necessary for the system to work.

The question remains, however, how the community moves forward to evaluate and implement any new or adjusted business model. The need for strategic leadership in forensic science is critical, and, again, the lack of a historical systems-level view (or any view, really) has hampered the development of strong strategic leadership. Professional organizations can help through supporting initiatives but the creation and championing of those initiatives must come from the community itself. Forensic service providers, traditionally subsumed under law enforcement agencies, have had few opportunities to have a collective, distinctive political voice. Leaders must emerge to effect change: Without them, no progress will be made. Whether the change is evolutionary or revolutionary remains to be seen; "the true measure of a successful revolution is the realization there is no going back" (Davis, 2013, p. 11).

This chapter argues the need for the exploration and systematic examination of CONOPS or business models in forensic service provision. Data from programs like FORESIGHT offer badly needed infrastructure on which to build or even outline a CONOPS with the goal of enterprise-level definition. In light of the critical and significant role the forensic industry plays in criminal justice and national security, a clearer analysis of the services, costs, and benefits of forensic service provision is desperately needed.

References

Bedford, K. (2011). Forensic science service provider models—is there a "best" option? *Australian Journal of Forensic Sciences, 43*(2–3), 147–156.

Budowle, B., Kayser, M., & Sanjantila, A. (2011). The demise of the United Kingdom's Forensic Science Service (FSS): Loss of the world's leading engine of innovation and development in the forensic sciences. *Investigative Genetics, 2*(4), 1–2.

Christoffersen, H., Paldam, M., & Wurtz, A. H. (2007). Public versus private production and economies of scale. *Public Choice, 130,* 311–328.

Collins, J. (2005). *Good to great and the social sectors.* Boulder, CO: Author.

Dale, W. M., & Becker, W. S. (2003). Strategy for staffing forensic scientists. *Journal of Forensic Sciences, 48*(2), 465–466.

Davis, W. (2013) Revolution. *Smithsonian Magazine* (May), 11–12.

Dawley, D. D., & Munyon, T. P. (2012). Enhancing employee outcomes in crime labs: Test of a model. *Forensic Science Policy & Management: An International Journal, 3*(3), 105–112.

Doleac, J. (2013, January). *The effects of DNA databases on crime* (Faculty Working Papers). Charlottesville, VA: Frank Batten School of Leadership and Public Policy, University of Virginia.

Durose, M. R., Walsh, K. A., & Burch, A. M. (2012). *Census of publicly funded fornesic crime laboratories, 2009.* Washington, DC: U.S. Department of Justice, Bureau of Justice Statistics.

European Network of Forensic Sciences. (2003). *QUADRUPOL.* European Network of Forensic Sciences.

Frittman, J., & Edson, R. (2010). *Illustrating the Concept of Operations (CONOPs) continuum and its relationship to the acquisition lifecycle.* Excerpt from the Proceedings of the 7th Annual Acquisition Research Symposium. Monterey, CA: Naval Postgraduate School.

Giachetti, R. E. (2010). *Design of enterprise systems: Theory, architecture, and methods.* Boca Raton, FL: CRC Press.

Heames, J. T., & Heames, J. T. (2011). Forensic science staffing: Creating a working formula. *Forensic Science Policy & Management: An International Journal, 2*(1), 5–10.

Houck, M. M. (2006). CSI: Reality. *Scientific American, 295,* 84–89.

Houck, M. M. (2009). Is forensic science a gateway for women in science? *Forensic Science Policy & Management: An International Journal, 1*(1), 65–69.

Houck, M. M., Riley, R. A., Speaker, P. J., & Fleming, A. S. (2012). Balanced scorecard approach. *Science and Justice, 52*(4), 209–216.

Houck, M. M., Riley, R. A., Speaker, P. J., & Witt, T. S. (2009). FORESIGHT: A business approach to improving forensic science services. *Forensic Science Policy & Management: An International Journal, 1*(2), 85–95.

Houck, M. M., Robertson, J., Found, B., Kobus, H., Lewis, S., Raymond, M., et al. (2011). A round table discussion on forensic science in Australia. *Forensic Science Policy & Management: An International Journal, 2*(1), 44–54.

House of Commons, Science and Technology Committee (UK). (2013, January 24). *Forensic science: Second report of session 2013–14.* Retrieved from http://www.parliament.uk/ business/committees/committees-a-z/commons-select/science-and-technology- committee/inquiries/parliament-2010/fss-follow-up/

IEEE Standards Board. (1998). *IEEE Standard 1362-1998, IEEE Guide for Information Technology-System Definition-Concept of Operations (ConOps) Document.* New York: Institute of Electric and Electronics Engineers, Inc.

Institute of Environmental Science and Research. (2009). *Annual report.* Porirua, New Zealand: Institute of Environmental Science and Research.

Knapp, M. (1982). Economies of scale in local public services: The case of British crematoria. *Applied Economics, 14,* 447–453.

Kobus, H., Houck, M. M., Speaker, P. J., & Witt, T. S. (2011). Managing performance in the forensic sciences: Expectations in light of limited budgets. *Forensic Science Policy & Management: An International Journal, 2*(1), 36–43.

Koppl, R. (2005). How to improve forensic science. *European Journal of Law and Economics, 20,* 255–286.

Lawless, C. (2010). *A curious reconstruction? The shaping of "marketized" forensic science.* London: Centre for Analysis of Risk and Regulation, London School of Economics and Political Science. Retrieved from http://eprints.lse.ac.uk/36544/1/Disspaper63.pdf

Leslie, M. (2010). Quality assured science: Managerialism in forensic biology. *Science, Technology, & Human Values, 35*(3), 283–306.

Maguire, C., Houck, M., & Speaker, P. (2012). Cost effectiveness in the forensic sciences: In-sourcing, out-sourcing, and privatization. *Forensic Science Policy & Management: An International Journal, 3*(2), 62–69.

McAndrew, W. (2012). Is privatization inevitable for forensic science laboratories? *Forensic Science Policy & Management: An International Journal, 3*(1), 42–52.

National Academies of Science (NAS). (2009). *Strengthening forensic science in the United States: A path forward.* Washington, DC: National Academies Press.

Newman, J., Dawley, D., & Speaker, P. J. (2011). Strategic management of forensic laboratory resources: From Project FORESIGHT metrics to the development of action plans. *Forensic Science Policy & Management: An International Journal, 2*(4), 164–174.

Peterson, J., Sommers, I., Baskin, D., & Johnson, D. (2010). *The role and impact of forensic evidence in the criminal justice process.* Washington, DC: U.S. Department of Justice.

Rape case reopened after DNA forensics blunder. (2012, March 9). *BBC News.* Retrieved March 10, 2012 from http://www.bbc.co.uk/news/uk-england-manchester-17311101

Rincon, P. (2013, January 29). "Higher cost" of forensic science service closure. *BBC News Science & Environment.* Retrieved January 30, 2013 from http://www.bbc.co.uk/news/science-environment-21251162

Roberts, P. (1996). What price a free market in forensic science services? The organization and regulation of science in the criminal process. *British Journal of Criminology, 36,* 37–60.

Roman, J. K., Reid, S., Reid, J., Chalfin, A., Adams, W., & Knight, C. (2008). *The DNA field experiment: Cost-effectiveness analysis of the use of DNA in the investigation of high-volume crimes.* Washington, DC: Urban Institute, Justice Policy Center.

Schade, W. (2009). Budget crisis or management opportunity. *Forensic Science Policy & Management: An International Journal, 1*(1), 57–61.

Speaker, P. J. (2009a). Key performance indicators and managerial analysis for forensic laboratories. *Forensic Science Policy & Management: An International Journal, 1*(1), 32–42.

Speaker, P. J. (2009b). The decomposition of return on investment for forensic laboratories. *Forensic Science Policy & Management: An International Journal, 1*(2), 96–102.

Speaker, P. J. (2013). Forensic science service provider models: Data-driven support for better delivery options. *Australian Journal of Forensic Sciences, 45*(4), 398–406.

Speaker, P. J., & Fleming, A. S. (2009). Monitoring financial performance: An approach for forensic crime labs. *The CPA Journal, 79*(8), 60–65.

Speaker, P. J., & Fleming, A. S. (2010). Benchmarking and budgeting techniques for improved forensic laboratory management. *Forensic Science Policy & Management: An International Journal, 1*(4), 199–208.

Twohey, M. (2011, February 11). State crime lab reports more than 4,000 untested rape kits. *Chicago Tribune.* Retrieved from http://articles.chicagotribune.com/2011-02-17/news/ct-met-dna-backlog-20110217_1_crime-lab-crime-evidence-orchid-cellmark

Witt, T. S., & Speaker, P. J. (2012, April 10). The power of information. *Forensic Magazine,* 1–6.

13

Rethinking the Role of the Crime Laboratory in Criminal Justice Decision Making

Kevin J. Strom and Matthew J. Hickman

Introduction

The criminal justice system has been described as a series of organized parts that represent decision stages, with key stakeholders exercising discretion at each stage. Police officer's decisions to arrest, prosecutor's decisions to charge, and judge's sentencing decisions are common examples. The classic "flowchart" of criminal justice, which was first presented in the 1967 report from the President's Commission on Law Enforcement and Administration of Justice, illustrates the key decision points along the justice process and delineates the police, the courts, and corrections as major stages (see Figure 13.1). The president's task force also called for the increased use of scientific evidence in crime investigations and highlighted the important role of crime laboratory personnel and forensic technicians in processing crime scenes, collecting evidence, and supporting investigations.

In the more than four decades since these foundational reports were published, the role and relevance of crime laboratories within the criminal justice system has grown considerably. The amount of physical evidence collected and submitted for analysis has increased, as have the number of state and local laboratories and their technical and scientific capacity for examining and interpreting physical evidence. Yet, despite the more prominent role of forensic laboratories, criminal justice *services*, such as those provided by crime laboratories, are still not commonly thought of as key decision stage within the criminal justice process. Laboratory analysts, managers, and administrators are not often viewed as exercising discretion or even as being part of the criminal justice process *per se*. More importantly, crime laboratory staff too often are absent from any discussions of critical decision making, including their role and the role of other key stakeholders in shaping more efficient and equitable justice outcomes.

Figure 13.1 The Classic "Flowchart" of the Criminal Justice System

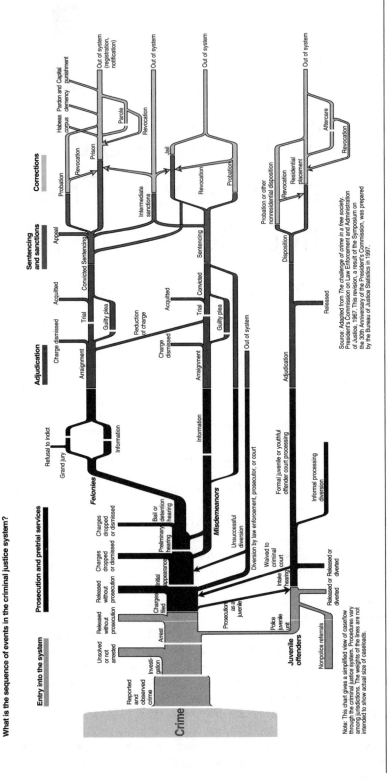

What is the sequence of events in the criminal justice system?

SOURCE: U.S. Department of Justice.

We argue that, due to the increasing use of forensic services in criminal justice decision making by other actors (such as police and prosecutors) and the associated demands and constraints on laboratory resources, crime laboratories are of necessity becoming (or already have become) a significant part of the criminal justice decision-making process. Insofar as laboratory decisions and policies concerning the processing of evidence impacts the work and decision making of police and prosecutors, laboratory personnel constitute classic criminal justice decision makers, who exercise discretion and impact the justice process. As such, it is critical to understand the nature of the relationships between police, prosecutors, and crime laboratories, and how the decisions of laboratory personnel may influence criminal justice outcomes.

The past decade has seen a steadily increasing focus of social science research on the forensic sciences, including an examination of the policies and practices, costs and resources, and decision making and discretion used in prioritizing evidence analyzed in cases. This chapter discusses the role of the crime laboratory in criminal justice case processing. As part of this review, we examine the role of crime laboratories as well as how that role has changed over time. We also discuss critical issues for the forensic sciences and for crime laboratories moving forward, including policies and practices that can result in the more efficient use of laboratory resources, improved information sharing, and improved procedures for collecting, prioritizing, submitting, and analyzing forensic evidence.

The Changing Role of the Crime Laboratory

Crime laboratories have historically been an outgrowth of law enforcement agencies. From the very first U.S. crime laboratories, established at the local level by the Los Angeles Police Department in 1923, and at the national level by the Federal Bureau of Investigation in 1932, to the more than 400 public crime laboratories enumerated in the latest Bureau of Justice Statistics census of crime laboratories (Durose, Walsh, & Burch, 2012), the scope of public forensic services has broadened across federal, state, and local governments as well as regional jurisdictions. The crime laboratory's historic roots as an extension of law enforcement have undoubtedly influenced laboratory resources, caseloads, and the overall approach to the evaluation of scientific evidence. Police and prosecutors have traditionally made decisions and exercised control over what types of evidence will be collected, submitted, and examined, and laboratories have historically been thought of as service providers to the justice system.

At the same time, the demand for laboratory services has increased substantially in concert with increased reliance on forensic evidence in a variety of domains, laboratory capacity issues, popular media effects, and unrealistic expectations about the utility of forensic analyses (see Chapters 1–3, this volume). The nation's 411 public crime laboratories received more than 4 million analytic requests for services in 2009, representing more than a 50% increase since 2002 (see Durose et al., 2012; Peterson & Hickman, 2005). The bulk of the requests were in the areas of DNA analysis (including CODIS requests) (34%), controlled substances (33%), and toxicology (15%). The running backlog (though see Chapter 3, this volume) is about 1 million requests, most of which is in the area of forensic biology, followed by controlled substances.

The primary goal of the crime laboratory is to provide scientific analyses in support of the investigative and adjudicative processes that may ultimately lead to the arrest, conviction, or exoneration of an accused individual. However, the crime laboratory does not necessarily "work for" the prosecution or the police. This pervasive misconception has led many to call for greater independence of laboratories, in terms of both administrative and physical separation (e.g., National Academy of Sciences [NAS], 2009). The crime laboratory is ideally an independent entity that must make decisions about how to achieve its goals optimally (i.e., efficiently, effectively, and in support of justice), and these decisions may or may not favor the primary users of their services. To be fair, laboratories operating within law enforcement organizations often have procedures in place to ensure that laboratory analysts can perform independently, but the independence of crime laboratories has received considerable attention in recent years (NAS, 2009; see also Chapters 5–6, this volume).

Crime laboratories remain very much in the middle of the investigation and "case building" process between the police and prosecutors. As the frontline agents of the criminal justice system, the police are the initial point of entry for evidence into the criminal process. Police make critical decisions that determine the types and volume of cases presented to prosecutors as well as the potential demands placed on crime laboratories. Peterson (1974) described this flow and attrition in physical evidence as a funnel-like process.

The prosecutor must then decide whether and how to charge defendants. In some jurisdictions, guilty plea agreements may be reached on the basis of presumptive field tests. Criminal charges may also be filed on the basis of presumptive tests, but confirmatory analyses will be required for trial-bound cases. As the second major decision stage in the criminal justice process, this is an example of how prosecutors can also serve as an important filter in determining whether and what laboratory resources will be required. Requests may be made for the laboratory to initiate analyses, even though the results may later be unnecessary because of un-communicated changes in prosecutorial strategy or priority.

Effective communication is a critical link among these three principal actors (police, prosecutor, and crime laboratory). Prosecutors must communicate with police about prosecutorial priorities, as well as the legal constraints and thresholds related to evidence collection. When the police act as an informed filter, the cases presented for prosecution are more likely to be an efficient use of prosecutorial resources. In the other direction, effective communication about case dispositions can help the police with issues such as evidence storage. Likewise, communication between prosecutors and crime laboratories will help ensure effective decision making about whether and how to charge, and updates on case progress and outcomes may make analysis unnecessary (i.e., minimizing unnecessary submissions to the laboratory). Finally, communication between police and crime laboratories is critical in regard to how the evidence is collected and submitted.

Laboratory Decision Making

With regard to decision making, crime laboratories can have policies in place that dictate how, when, and why they will analyze cases submitted to them by partnering agencies. Some alternatives for the crime laboratory include the outright rejection of cases or requests submitted for analysis, suggesting other types of analyses, (de)prioritizing cases or requests, and outsourcing of requests. The primary decision problem however, is whether to provide the requested analysis. Some of the information used by crime laboratories to guide their selection among alternatives includes their present workload, backlog, the appropriateness of requested analyses, and, importantly, the outcomes of prior cases. In the decision-making context, information is defined as "data that reduce uncertainty (that is, provide guidance as to the probabilities) of achievement of desired decision objectives" (Gottfredson & Gottfredson, 1988, p. 4). This is to say, information that bears directly on the laboratory goal of optimally supporting investigative and adjudicative processes. Information should help the crime laboratory answer the question, What is the likely outcome once the decision to reject analytic requests—either individually or as a standing policy—has been made?

Adequate information is thought to be the key to improved rationality in criminal justice decision making (Gottfredson & Gottfredson, 1988). In the absence of adequate information, decision makers must rely on anecdote, belief, or gut instinct, and their resulting decisions are not likely to achieve the decision goals in optimal fashion. Empirical research has tended to underscore three common criminal justice correlates, including the seriousness of the offense, prior criminal conduct of the offender, and the personal relationship between victim and offender. Is it reasonable to expect laboratory decision making might also mirror these correlates? Insofar as police and prosecutor decision making is guided by these correlates, any discretionary laboratory decision making would be an additional filtration beyond that discretion already exercised. We would expect to see greater laboratory discretion being exercised for evidence stemming from less serious offenses, for example.

As an illustration, laboratory decision making concerning how controlled substance cases are received and prioritized remains an important topic. The analysis of drug evidence has historically represented a substantial share of typical laboratory caseloads (Durose et al., 2012). Decisions and policies on how a laboratory intends to handle drug evidence can impact not only laboratory resources across all forensic disciplines, but also the resources of other criminal justice actors and, in some instances, the case outcomes of drug investigations.

Moving forward, the absence of feedback—specifically information about the ultimate outcomes or consequences of laboratory decision making—is perhaps the most important hurdle to be overcome. If laboratory decision making is not informed by knowledge of ultimate case outcomes, it would be difficult to argue that such decisions had a rational basis (provided the goal is to support investigative and adjudicative processes). Instead, such decisions would only serve the administrative needs of the laboratory itself.

Given the basic information and feedback needs outlined above, it is logical to ask, What can be done to help structure laboratory processes with the goal of improving rationality in decision making, supporting the changing role of the crime laboratory, and ensuring that justice is optimally served?

Promising Examples of Crime Laboratory Decision-Making Policies

LABORATORY CASE MANAGEMENT POLICIES

Forensic laboratories need to implement effective and well-constructed laboratory submission guidelines that establish clear rules outlining what evidence will be accepted for analysis. These rules are most effective when they are developed based on research regarding the types of cases that would benefit most from testing. For example, prioritizing the types of cases (e.g., highest statute exhibits within a case) that are most likely to be used by prosecutors. Prior studies have found support for significant reductions in laboratory case workload and turnaround time, both in drug chemistry and in other laboratory sections, after the implementation of laboratory acceptance policies (Strom et al., 2011). Furthermore, it is critical that submitting agencies, prosecutors, and defense attorneys be consulted and involved early on in the development of these guidelines after initial drafting by the laboratory. Submission policies also need to be revisited by all stakeholders on a regular basis. Staff attrition and changes in policies and practices create the potential for practice to deviate from policy over time.

During the Strom et al. (2011) study, which involved stakeholder interviews in ten U.S. jurisdictions, it was observed that most law enforcement officers were only marginally aware of submission policies. However, laboratory personnel in the same jurisdiction would immediately point to a complete document of explicit submission policies when this issue was raised in interviews with these staff. The appearance was that policies had been communicated during initial implementation training by the laboratory, but were not regularly revisited leaving new law enforcement personnel to learn from senior law enforcement officers rather than laboratory staff. While this on-the-job training is certainly beneficial, it must also be reinforced with regular training on standards and policies for evidence collection and submission to ensure that practice does not deviate from policy.

In the area of controlled substances analysis, one of the most significant effects of laboratory submission guidelines can be to limit the number of misdemeanor drug cases submitted to the laboratory. Misdemeanor cases handled in Magistrate Court (or the "lower courts") not only require more resources in terms of volume, but the judicial process is also time-consuming and can place a heavy burden on officers who have to testify. Limits appear to be very effective for the laboratory, but establishing effective limits requires the input of prosecution and law enforcement. Again, these policies need regular, recurrent input to allow for all personnel to continually understand the needs and capabilities of each stakeholder.

ROUTINE TWO-WAY COMMUNICATION

Frequent and routine communication between submitting law enforcement agencies, laboratories, and prosecutors is essential toward promoting both the efficient and effective use of evidence. This, while respecting the need to maintain an "arm's length" relationship in terms of scientific processes and the type of independence called for in the 2009 NAS report. Prosecutor communication with laboratories in particular has been documented as a significant problem in many U.S. jurisdictions (Strom & Hickman, 2010; Strom et al., 2011). For instance, in the Strom et al. (2011) study, prosecutors were found to rarely contact laboratories to provide updates on drug cases and, in most instances, did not have a standard practice of informing laboratories of cases resolved due to a guilty plea or dismissal. Study participants estimated that 50% to 75% of the drug case "backlog" represented cases that had already been pled out or dismissed. Laboratory staff in at least three sites spent considerable time comparing their active cases to online systems that would allow them to see which cases had been removed from the active court dockets.

Improving basic procedures for communications is a natural first step. These improvements may include protocols and training that clearly define roles and expectations for closing out cases. For example, protocols that state a prosecutor's role in a case is not complete until a phone call or email from the prosecutor's office has been placed to the laboratory when a case is pled out or dismissed. A continuous system of communication also benefits law enforcement by providing information on the status of cases so that evidence can be destroyed in a timely manner, and so law enforcement can close their active cases.

CASE TRACKING

All jurisdictions should provide cross-agency information sharing systems to their partnering agencies, including laboratory staff, prosecutors, defense attorneys, and submitting police agency personnel (or in the cases where systems already exist, provide electronic access to case tracking). The idea is to develop systems that link information across systems, using barcodes and other unique identifiers, to track critical information as it moves from one stage of case processing to the next. One of the essential factors for success is the development of a single case identifier used to track evidence across agencies. More short-term approaches toward case reporting include web-based Laboratory Information Management Systems (LIMS), which provide a secure means for online communication as well as timely updates on laboratory case results (including the ability to print laboratory reports remotely and access to electronic laboratory result litigation packets), and the promotion and use of court-based systems that provide updates on cases.

TRAINING

A better understanding of the responsibilities, roles, and policies of each stakeholder is a critical need. This should include training for prosecutors, law enforcement, and laboratory staff on the judicial system processing including how they charge suspects and conduct plea negotiations. In addition, prosecutors and defense attorneys must educate law enforcement officers about the importance of submitting evidence in a timely fashion to laboratories. Laboratory staff must routinely train law enforcement officers about how the laboratory functions, the appropriate submission process, and the reasons and importance behind particular submission policies. Part of this training could be accomplished as part of the police academy curriculum, but could also be provided in booster sessions as a regular web-based training, or at least documented on a website for convenient reference. As is the case with the Field Investigation Drug Officer (FIDO) program, laboratory staff can also be instrumental in certifying officers to field test for particular drugs, which will ultimately streamline the number of cases submitted to the laboratory and provide prosecutors with more assurance of the field testing process.

For their parts, laboratory staff should be educated about the issues and needs of the law enforcement officers and for the prosecution. This is especially critical in jurisdictions where there is fragmented communication, a lack of case acceptance policies, and where laboratory staff faces backlogs. In these jurisdictions, it is not uncommon for laboratory staff to receive cases for re-analysis that they had already processed and for cases to be routinely submitted as rushed requests.

Lastly, prosecutors and law enforcement alike should have a minimal understanding of the capabilities and limitations of forensic science disciplines. Without proper training or mentorship, new prosecutors will not fully understand the laboratory process, the necessity of certain procedures, and the nature of and reasons behind a growing evidence backlog. Prosecutors and law enforcement officers need to be aware of the limitations of certain types of evidence (e.g., latent fingerprints or touch DNA in controlled substances cases) and the time and resource burdens these types of requests place on the laboratory.

LABORATORY CASE BACKLOG REDUCTION

It should be emphasized that there is no "one size fits all" solution to ending laboratory backlogs, but we believe there are a number of strategies bear mentioning as potential solutions to mitigate laboratory backlogs. Among crime laboratory personnel, there has been a general consensus that when a backlog does exist, it can be extraordinarily difficult for the laboratory staff to get caught up with cases in the absence of receiving resources such as additional staff, funding, or equipment (Strom et al., 2011). To address the immediate backlog problem, laboratories may be able to secure funding for overtime pay or outsource backlogged cases in favor of its own staff processing incoming, current cases. Yet, these solutions should also be implemented concurrently with a prioritized case management policy, which can greatly reduce the volume of incoming cases such that laboratory staff could more effectively manage their caseload once their backlog was resolved.

Increased laboratory funding should also look at providing key administrative staffing. Laboratories have identified key operating efficiencies when there were coordinating staff who were dedicated to managing court subpoenas and testimony, monitoring evidence submissions to ensure quality, communicating with submitting officers when there were issues, and weeding out from the lab's active cases those that were terminated by guilty plea or dismissal. Ideally, these positions would serve as a communications hub for all three agencies. This type of administrative staffing can free up technical and scientific laboratory personnel to focus on analytic tasks.

Developing effective policies for retaining qualified staff within the crime laboratories should also be a major goal moving forward. For instance, within a crime lab, the drug section can be a "revolving door" for analysts who use the laboratories as a training ground for more lucrative careers in the private sector or in other states. Increasing salaries to make these positions more attractive would be one way to resolve the problem of staff attrition. Criminal justice systems are also affected when laboratory staff attrition is high to the extent that prosecutors may need to pay the expenses for the analyst to testify after they have left their position.

Lastly, in recent years, the funding for forensics has been earmarked for DNA equipment and training. Yet, the reality is that the majority of cases submitted to the laboratories are for other forms of forensic evidence including controlled substances evidence. Broadening the funding streams so that some of the forensic spending can support needed equipment will be important, in addition to allowing for the financial support of temporary positions that would allow particular laboratories to augment their capacity to reduce any backlogs.

Conclusion

As the criminal justice process becomes more reliant on the services of crime laboratories, laboratory personnel are increasingly taking on a role as decision makers within the processing of criminal justice cases. The crime laboratory can be conceived of as a decision stage in which discretion is exercised with regard to the types of cases that will be accepted for analysis, the types of evidence that will be processed (and how it will be processed), and the priority assigned to submitted cases. These decisions ultimately impact the justice process. In some jurisdictions, these are negotiated decisions made in consultation with police or prosecutors. In other jurisdictions, written policies are established spelling out the criteria for case acceptance and processing (although with varying levels of conformity).

Research has shown that the crime laboratory can take on a proactive role in developing processes that facilitate the decision-making and information-sharing process. This is best achieved by implementing case acceptance and analysis protocols that improve efficiencies throughout the system. For example, case acceptance policies that are developed in consultation with law enforcement, prosecution, and defense partners. Yet, laboratory staff must be careful to ensure that these do not only serve the needs of the laboratory, but rather address the broader goal of optimally providing scientific analysis in support of investigative and adjudicative processes. In addition, these decisions should not be made in the absence of systematic information and feedback regarding the ultimate outcomes of these decisions.

Results demonstrate that other criminal justice actors, namely, the police and prosecutors, have important and necessary roles in shaping forensic case processing as well as the overall efficiency of the system. For instance, the failure of law enforcement personnel to adhere to field testing protocols or case submission protocols can impact subsequent stages. In particular, the inability to communicate can have major repercussions on system-wide efficiencies. This is evident in the sizable proportion of laboratory backlogged cases estimated to represent dismissed or plead out cases, and also demonstrated in the failure to view labs as equal partners and not simply as "service" providers. Processes and systems that facilitate communication can have numerous and extended benefits and result in increased efficiencies, improved quality of justice, and conserved resources. Moving forward, there is a clear need to better articulate the role of the crime laboratory and to improve communication and coordination among police, prosecutors, and laboratory personnel.

In sum, we believe the available evidence shows that crime laboratories are not simply passive actors in the criminal justice process. Rather, the ability of crime laboratories to operate efficiently and effectively (and with integrity) can have a critical impact on the outcomes of criminal cases. The failure to do so can have adverse effects in the form of case processing delays and case dismissals, but also more significantly on reduced confidence among other criminal justice partners such as the police and prosecutors. The police, prosecutors, and crime laboratories must universally endorse the view that there are not endless resources for the collection and analysis of physical evidence. All stakeholders must appreciate their shared responsibilities for creating an efficient system that also achieves the dual goals of protecting the innocent and convicting the guilty.

Looking ahead, it may be time to incorporate forensic laboratories into the classic flowchart of the criminal justice system developed by the 1967 President's Commission on the Administration of Justice, and last revised by the Bureau of Justice Statistics on the 30th anniversary of the Commission's reports in 1997 (see Figure 13.1). We challenge the reader to consider where and how the forensic system interacts with this classic depiction of the justice process, and how one might restructure and elaborate the classic flowchart to recognize and accommodate the crime laboratory. In considering the future role of forensic science in the administration of justice, we can no longer think of forensic laboratories as simply ancillary justice services; rather, forensic laboratories and their personnel have evolved to the point that they are more properly conceived of as decision-makers who can have a significant impact on the administration of justice. Such recognition may change the way we approach questions of resource allocation, how we approach the problem of caseload management and, perhaps most importantly, the manner in which we view the scientific evaluation of physical evidence. In the wake of the 2009 NAS report, and at the outset of a new National Commission on Forensic Science, anything that can help to improve both the substance and perception of the "science" of forensic science cannot be disregarded. Recognizing the changing role of the crime laboratory and the importance of improving rationality in criminal justice decision making are essential steps for the future of the field.

Authors' Note: This chapter is based on earlier work by the authors (Strom, Hickman, Smiley-MacDonald, et al., 2011).

References

Durose, M., Walsh, K., & Burch, A. (2012). *Census of publicly funded forensic crime laboratories, 2009*. Washington, DC: U.S. Department of Justice, Office of Justice Programs, Bureau of Justice Statistics.

Gottfredson, M. R., & Gottfredson, D. M. (1988). *Decision making in criminal justice*. New York: Plenum.

National Academy of Sciences (NAS). (2009). *Strengthening forensic science in the United States: A path forward*. Washington, DC: National Academies Press.

Peterson, J. (1974). *Utilization of criminalistics services by the police: An analysis of the physical evidence recovery process* (NCJ 010310). Washington, DC: Government Printing Office.

Peterson, J., & Hickman, M. (2005). *Census of publicly funded forensic crime laboratories, 2002*. Washington, DC: U.S. Department of Justice, Office of Justice Programs, Bureau of Justice Statistics.

Strom, K., & Hickman, M. (2010). Unanalyzed evidence in law enforcement agencies: A national examination of forensic processing in police departments. *Criminology & Public Policy, 9*(2), 381–404.

Strom, K., Hickman, M., Smiley-MacDonald, H., Ropero-Miller, J., & Stout, P. (2011). Crime laboratory personnel as criminal justice decision makers: A study of controlled substance processing in ten jurisdictions. *Forensic Science Policy & Management, 2*(2), 57–69.

14

The Future of Forensic Science

Walter F. Rowe

The human race, to which so many of my readers belong, has been playing at children's games from the beginning, and will probably do it till the end, which is a nuisance for the few people who grow up. And one of the games to which it is most attached is called "Keep to-morrow dark," and which is also named (by the rustics in Shropshire, I have no doubt) "Cheat the Prophet." The players listen very carefully and respectfully to all that the clever men have to say about what is to happen in the next generation. The players then wait until all the clever men are dead, and bury them nicely. They then go and do something else. That is all. For a race of simple tastes, however, it is great fun.

—G. K. Chesterton, *The Napoleon of Notting Hill*

[T]here can be no prediction of the course of human history by scientific or any other rational methods.

—Karl Popper, *The Poverty of Historicism*

This may be the most important proposition revealed by history: "At the time, no one knew what was coming."

—Haruki Murakami, *1Q84*

Introduction

Over the last two decades, there has been a spate of books and articles examining future trends in forensic science (Denmark & Mount, 2013; Mennell, 2006; Mennell & Shaw, 2006; Mount & Hackman, 2012, 2013; Palenik, 2001; Robertson, 2008; Schiro,

2000; Tjin-A-Tsoi, 2013; Ubelaker, 2013). Predicting the development of forensic science over the next two to three decades is a daunting task. Who, when looking at the first transistor, would have predicted integrated circuits, personal computers, or the Internet (along with commercial enterprises such as Amazon, Google, or Facebook)? In the field of forensic science, who in the mid-1980s would have predicted that DNA profiling would attain the importance that it currently enjoys? When DNA profiling was first used in court, it was a cumbersome and time-consuming process. Sample sizes required for DNA analysis were large. And the Combined DNA Index System (CODIS) did not exist. Now, methods based on the polymerase chain reaction (PCR) allow an analyst to profile reliably picogram quantities of "touch DNA" in one to two days (Tjin-A-Tsoi, 2013). A query of CODIS may solve an unknown subject rape case in just a few hours.

DNA profiling led indirectly to other major changes in the practice of forensic science. Twenty years ago, the forensic science field as a whole suffered from a lack of standardization. American Society for Testing and Material Committee e30 existed but had produced only a handful of standards. There were no technical or scientific working groups. Now a new scientific working group seems to crop up every day, with standards for the education and training of practitioners, for performing examinations and interpreting results. Proficiency testing of examiners was confined to on-the-job training programs; it typically occurred before an examiner was cleared to do casework but was not repeated thereafter (despite the suspicion that examiner performance could deteriorate over time). Proficiency testing is now built into the laboratory accreditation process (American Society of Crime Laboratory Directors Laboratory Accreditation Board, 2010).

Part of the future of forensic science will be growth: Forensic science laboratories will grow in size, in capabilities, and in the number of examinations performed (Tjin-A-Tsoi, 2013). Growth in size and in capabilities will be required to cope with a growing backlog of requests for examinations. The U.S. Department of Justice reported that in 2009 (the last year for which data were available) publicly funded forensic science laboratories had an aggregate backlog of 1,144,900 pending requests for services (Burch, Durose, & Walsh, 2012). This represents a 1% increase over the previous year. There was a 12% increase in the casework backlog in forensic biology, indicating increased demands for DNA profiling. Forensic science is also in transition: It is moving from its traditional role of support for investigations and prosecutions to one in which its tools drive investigations (Mennell & Shaw, 2006; Ribaux, Walsh, & Margot, 2006; Tjin-A-Tsoi, 2013). In the words of Dr. T. B. P. M. Tjin-A-Tsoi, chief executive officer of the Netherlands Forensic Institute,

> [T]he role of forensic science is changing. Whereas before it was cast in a supporting role, it is now set to become the playmaker in many types of investigation, providing quick and reliable information on scenarios and suspects and thus, in a sense, directing the efforts of investigators. (p. 2)

A number of difficulties will have to be surmounted for this transition to take place.

In 1900, mathematician David Hilbert proposed a list of 23 problems that he felt mathematicians needed to solve in the 20th century (Bottazzini, 2011). This set of problems proved to be very influential in the development of mathematics in the 20th century. In the same spirit, I will discuss a list of problems that I think forensic science needs solve in the next 20 years, if not sooner. Some of these problems are scientific or technical in nature, but others are administrative. Some problems (such as the growing backlog of requests for DNA profiling) may require both technological innovation and administrative changes.

The most pressing scientific problem in the forensic sciences in my view is the status of the so-called "identification sciences": fingerprints, firearm, and toolmark identification, handwriting comparison, and shoe and tire impressions identification and comparison. These are quintessential forensic examinations. They are crucial for placing a suspect at the scene a crime, or determining the source of fired bullets and cartridge cases, or determining who wrote a particular document; consequently, they have played major roles in criminal investigations and prosecutions. The identification sciences require the analysis of patterns for class characteristics (features or attributes that define a group of objects, such as brands of tires) and for individual characteristics (features or attributes unique to a particular object). The identification sciences have been challenged in court due in part to changes in federal standards for the admission of scientific evidence (Page, Taylor, & Blenkin, 2011a, 2011b) and also in part due to the fall-out from the admission of DNA profiling (Saks & Koehler, 2005).

In other areas of forensic science (e.g., DNA profiling, trace evidence and drug chemistry), the scientific challenge is to extract more information faster with lower detection limits and at lower cost. New analytical instrumentation coming online will meet this challenge. However, the new instrumentation will require new analytical methods. These methods will require careful validation. As forensic scientists are able to analyze smaller and smaller amounts of material, they will need to know more and more about the trace contaminants routinely present at scenes of crimes and on items of evidence. Only by understanding this "background" can forensic scientists focus on the forensically meaningful traces. An example drawn from the detection of ignitable liquids will illustrate this point. When ignitable liquid residues were collected by steam distillation of fire debris, no one worried about the possible presence of hydrocarbons in the substrate materials. Now with more advanced methods of trapping and analyzing ignitable liquids, analysts must be aware of the large number of common materials that contain hydrocarbons (Stauffer, Dolan, & Newman, 2008). In a similar way, as the detection limits for DNA are lowered, it may become more difficult when a "touch DNA" analysis is preformed to distinguish the forensically significant DNA from pre-existing DNA contamination.

The scientific challenges facing forensic science are likely to prove more tractable than the administrative challenges. Improving the science in forensic science is not likely to face opposition: It requires only appropriately focused research funding. However, it is increasingly clear that forensic science as an institution is facing an existential crisis. A number of high-profile scandals involving forensic scientists such as Fred Zain (Giannelli & McMunigal, 2007; Pyrek, 2007), Joyce Gilchrist (Giannelli & McMunigal, 2007; Pyrek, 2007), Arnold Melnikoff (Pyrek, 2007), and, most recently, Annie Dookhan (Jacobs, 2013) have raised serious questions about the competence and objectivity of forensic examiners. The recent National Research Council report *Strengthening Forensic Science in the United States: A Path Forward* (National Research Council, 2009) was particularly critical of the perceived bias of forensic examiners arising from forensic science laboratories being part of law enforcement agencies and recommended removing all publically funded forensic science laboratories from the control of law enforcement agencies and prosecutor's offices.

Technological Developments

CRIME SCENE INVESTIGATION, MEDICO-LEGAL DEATH INVESTIGATION, AND FORENSIC NURSING

In the science fiction movie *Gattaca*, a crime scene investigator brings a small portable device to the scene of a homicide. The investigator's little black box sucks in dust and dander and tells the investigator who had been at the murder scene. Crime scene investigation has not quite reached this level of sophistication; however, the processing of crime scene and evidence collection generally will undergo significant changes in the future.

Crime scene processing remains the Achilles' heel of forensic science. If physical evidence is not collected or is not properly documented, or is collected in insufficient quantities or is not protected from contamination or spoilage, it really does not matter how good the forensic scientists in the laboratory are or how sophisticated their instrumentation is. Currently, there is a lack of standardization in the fields of crime scene and medico-legal death investigation, both in the protocols used at scenes and in the qualifications of investigators. The future will see greater standardization of crime scene processing, with standard protocols for handling the most frequently encountered types of evidence. As will be discussed later, there is a growing recognition that crime scene investigators and medico-legal death investigators should be certified (Howe et al., 2013).

More attention needs to be paid to the collection of forensic evidence from the living, particularly the victims of crimes. Much of this evidence collection takes place in hospital emergency rooms and is carried out by emergency room physicians and nurses. Because of the growing understanding of the importance of evidence collection by healthcare professionals, forensic nursing has emerged as a nursing specialty. While forensic nursing has tended to focus on victims of sexual assault, the future role of forensic nurses will expand from examination of victims of sexual assault to victims of domestic violence, child abuse and neglect, and elder abuse and neglect. More schools of nursing will include forensic nursing among the recognized nursing specialties (Howe et al., 2013).

As forensic instrumentation advances, new types of evidence will start to play roles in investigations. Crime scene investigators, medico-legal death investigators, and forensic nurses will need to keep abreast of these developments through continuing education (e.g., workshops and professional meetings). Optimizing the recognition and collection of physical evidence will require close liaison between these investigators and the forensic analysts in the laboratory who will ultimately examine the evidence.

Documentation of crime scenes is a critical part of crime scene processing. Historically, documentation has taken the form of notes, sketches, and photographs. Crime scene investigators now have access to high-quality digital cameras that can record both still images and video. The resolution of these cameras is rapidly approaching that of film. However, the ISO equivalent speed ratings of digital cameras need to be increased without degradation of image quality so that high quality "stop motion" photographs can be taken. Special cameras have been developed that are capable of capturing panoramic images of scenes; computer software can then convert the image into a crime scene sketch. Tablet computers with built-in cameras are already being marketed that can capture multiple images of a crime scene, upload them to a remote computer with software that can stitch the images together to provide a "virtual" crime scene that can be viewed from any angle. While such cameras and their specialized computer software are currently too expensive for most law enforcement agencies, a number of software packages exist that can perform photogrammetry on crime scene photos and generate data for crime scene sketches. High-quality aerial images of outdoor crime scenes can now be obtained by relatively inexpensive unmanned aerial vehicles (UAVs, also called *drones*). The end of forensic photography as a discipline requiring extensive specialized training will come when a camera combines three capabilities: great depth of focus, high dynamic range, and 180° field of view. Virtually no training would be required to operate such a camera (Edward Robinson, personal communication, April 18, 2013).

Western societies will remain under threat of terrorist attack for the foreseeable future. First responders (police, fire personnel, and emergency medical personnel) will continue to confront potentially life-threatening situations as they respond to emergency calls. Inexpensive high-level personal protection equipment (PPE) needs to be developed for their use. They also need means of analyzing a wide range of potentially lethal materials. Is there an explosive device in this building? Is the white powder that spilled out of an envelope in an office mailroom anthrax or some hoax substance? What is that residue in the glassware on the workbench in a clandestine laboratory? Crime scene processing will require smaller, field-deployable versions of many of the instrumentation now used in forensic laboratories. In addition to being smaller and lighter than the instruments used in the laboratory, these field-deployable instruments should also require little or no sample preparation and produce high-quality analytical results in a short period of time. It should be possible for the data files to be transmitted immediately to the laboratory for interpretation. Some of this field-deployable instrumentation already exists: ion mobility spectrometers (IMS), hand-held attenuated total reflectance Fourier transform infrared (ATR FTIR) spectrometers, and hand-held laser Raman spectrometers.

Some field-deployable devices are under development, most notably DNA laboratories on chips. These devices will permit crime scene personnel to sample DNA at the scene, profile it, and transmit the results to a laboratory facility where the profile can be submitted to CODIS. These laboratories on chips would also permit law enforcement personnel to sample an arrestee's DNA, profile it in a short period of time, and transmit that profile to state or national DNA databases to search for matches. Proponents of DNA profiling on arrest liken it to the accepted practice of taking arrestees' fingerprints to confirm identity and to search for outstanding warrants. Critics of this type of DNA profiling have alleged that such sample collection is motivated by a desire on the part of law enforcement to expand DNA databases (Murphy, 2013). However, the potential for apprehending perpetrators justifies DNA collection and profiling at the point of arrest. In a split 5–4 decision, the U.S. Supreme Court held the Maryland DNA Collection Act, under which the defendant's DNA was taken on booking and later matched to DNA in a rape case, did not violate the Fourth Amendment (*Maryland v. King*, 133 S. Ct. 1958; 186 L. Ed. 2d 1; 2013 U.S. LEXIS 4165; 81 U.S.L.W. 4343; 24 Fla. L. Weekly Fed. S 234). Critics have also expressed concern over the potential for invasion of privacy. However, solution of several high-profile cold cases would go far to sway public and political opinion in favor of DNA sample collection at point of arrest.

Placing analytical instrumentation at crime scenes will require more rigorous training of crime scene investigators. Another argument for rigorous training of crime scene investigators is the growing importance of digital evidence. Crime scene investigators need to be able to recognize the presence of digital evidence (Baker et al., 2013). Digital evidence is to be found not only in computers but also in devices such as cameras, mobile telephones, and global positioning systems. Investigators need to know the appropriate ways to collect and preserve such evidence.

The increasingly technical nature of crime scene investigation, with growing requirements for on-scene evidence analysis, is another argument in favor of civilianizing crime scene processing. Just as the management culture of law enforcement agencies does not lend itself to the effective management of forensic science laboratories, that same culture is not compatible with the need for the meticulous and objective recognition, documentation, and collection of evidence. Senior police officials are rarely conversant in science, nor are they likely to understand the necessity of objective, dispassionate assessment of what evidence at the scene of a crime should be collected and how. As has been noted with regard to scientific experts (Giannelli, 1997), it is all too easy for those in the police chain of command to develop a prosecutorial bias. Such bias often manifests itself as confirmation bias: Evidence against an individual is focused on, while exculpatory evidence is downplayed or completely ignored.

FUTURE FORENSIC SCIENCE IN THE LABORATORY

Before discussing possible new forensic science instrumentation, it would be useful to outline the features desirable in such instrumentation. First of all, little or no sample preparation should be required. The instruments should produce their results quickly. They should have low detection limits. Ideally, they should be non-destructive or consume so little sample as to be effectively non-destructive. Forensic samples are often very limited in size. Tests that consume little to no sample permit more tests to be run on samples. Ideally, the test methods used in forensic science should be highly discriminating, able to distinguish samples of similar type from one another. This is important when the analyst is attempting to determine possible sources of a piece of evidence. Connected with this desirable attribute is the attribute of providing usable investigative leads. Instruments should also be versatile; they should be applicable to the analyses of a number of types of forensic evidence. For example, GC/MS can be used to analyze drugs (both from dosage forms and from tissues and body fluids), explosives, and ignitable liquid residues. Micro-FTIR and micro-Raman spectroscopy can be applied to man-made fibers, dosage forms of drugs, explosive residues, inks, and papers. Finally, analytical instruments should be cheap. Accurate mass or exact mass time-of-flight mass spectrometry is a newer analytical technology that has a very wide range of potential forensic applications, including drugs, ignitable liquids, energetic materials, and trace evidence.

FORENSIC DRUG CHEMISTRY

Forensic chemistry is one the areas in which major changes can be expected (Tjin-A-Tsoi, 2013). Forensic chemists typically work in one of two areas: forensic drug chemistry or trace evidence analysis. Forensic drug chemistry deals with the analysis of dosage forms of drugs (plant material, powders, liquids, tablets, capsules, and the like).

Some changes are in store for forensic drug chemists. There will be more research on the optimal sampling of large quantities of seized drugs (Ballou et al., 2013). There has been discussion of using DNA technology to genetically track marijuana samples. While genetic profiling of cannabis might facilitate the prosecution of some drug-trafficking conspiracy cases, the cost of such profiling will probably outweigh the benefits. For many years, marijuana cases made up the majority of drug cases handled by the chemistry sections of state and local crime laboratories. It is clear that marijuana will soon be decriminalized in the United States. In such a case, analysis of marijuana samples will become an issue only when possession or use of this drug becomes an issue in an investigation of some other type of incident, such as a motor vehicle death. More to the point, crime laboratories are not equipped to extract plant DNA and such analyses require special reagents.

Clandestine drug laboratories will continue to produce the old standbys such as methamphetamine. Production of methamphetamine will continue to be attractive in the chronically economically depressed areas of the United States, while its psychomimetic properties will continue to make it an attractive drug of abuse. Drug entrepreneurs will continue to look for new designer drugs to circumvent the Controlled Substances Act. Illicit drug chemists will continue to mine the patent literature and the peer-reviewed scientific literature for the syntheses of psychoactive materials that are not yet listed as controlled substances. The synthetic cannabinoids offer a case illustrating this point: Cannabimimetic indole compounds were first synthesized in the early 1990s; some of these compounds began to appear in herbal mixtures about 10 years later; and five of these compounds were placed in Schedule I in 2011 (Wiley et al., 2011). Illicit drug chemists may even create completely new drugs by modifying the molecular structures of existing drugs. In addition to the issue of scheduling, newly synthesized drugs will present forensic drug chemists with the problem of developing validated analytical procedures for their analysis. Validated analytical methods require reference samples of the drugs in question (Scientific Working Group for the Analysis of Seized Drugs, 2011). Emerging drugs of abuse will require greater communication between law enforcement agencies and forensic laboratories about trends in drug abuse. Some of the new analytical technologies (e.g., exact mass time-of-flight mass spectrometers) may facilitate the early identification of new drugs of abuse.

TRACE EVIDENCE

One of the negative impacts of forensic DNA profiling has been the cutbacks in the trace sections of many laboratories (Ballou et al., 2013). Laboratory administrators are often forced to choose between funding of DNA units and funding trace sections. Unfortunately, once the trace sections are gone, laboratories will have lost the ability to analyze unknown particles. One type of trace evidence examination was directly destroyed by DNA profiling. Microscopical comparisons of human hair were shown to have unacceptable error rates.

The Federal Bureau of Investigation (FBI) conducted a retrospective study of the microscopical hair comparisons conducted in its laboratory (Houck & Budowle, 2002). Eighty positive hair associations were identified and the known and questioned hairs subjected to mitochondrial DNA (mtDNA) sequencing. In nine instances, the mtDNA sequences of the questioned and known hairs did not match, indicating that the hairs did not come from the same source. Even without this direct demonstration of the limitations of microscopical hair comparisons, doubts about the competence of many forensic hair examiners emerged in a series of high-profile cases (Pyrek, 2007). Microscopical hair comparisons retain some value for screening evidentiary hairs prior to mtDNA sequencing. However, few forensic laboratories are likely to see the need to have hair examiners or the specialized microscopes they require.

FORENSIC BIOLOGY

When the Combined DNA Index System (CODIS) shifted from the use of restriction fragment length polymorphisms (RFLPs) to polymerase chain reaction (PCR) amplification, DNA analysis times were substantially shortened. PCR-based DNA profiles based on short tandem repeats (STRs) have become the standard approach for forensic profiling of nuclear DNA. Because of the very large number of STR profiles in CODIS, it is unlikely that STRs will be abandoned for other markers in the near future. Instead, research will focus on gaining economies of time and scale in DNA analysis through an expanded use of laboratory robotics. The development of microfluidic devices (DNA laboratories on chips) will further shorten analysis times while moving some analyses out of the laboratory to crime scenes or police stations. DNA samples can be taken at the point of arrest and DNA profiles quickly generated for uploading to CODIS (Ballou et al., 2013).

The development of DNA profiling methods based on PCR has permitted DNA profiling on an almost industrial scale. Because PCR has made DNA profiling cheaper and faster, DNA laboratories may have additional capacity to allocate to cold cases. Increasingly, DNA laboratory resources have been refocused on cases that have gone unsolved for many years. If even traces of DNA remain on the case evidence, it may be possible to produce a DNA profile and find a match in CODIS. The case of Alfredo Prieto provides an example (Green, 2012). After he was convicted of a rape/murder in California, his DNA profile was placed in CODIS in 2005. DNA profiles from two unsolved rape/murders in Northern Virginia were matched to Prieto. The Northern Virginia cases had occurred in 1988, and the biological evidence was not processed for DNA until 1999.

When there is no suspect in a case or when a DNA profile produced from the case evidence does not result in a CODIS match, DNA laboratories can still aid investigations. DNA laboratories may use single nucleotide polymorphisms (SNPs) to provide phenotype information (e.g., eye, skin, and hair color) (Sturm, 2009). Ancestry-informative SNPs can provide information about the population ancestry of the source of the DNA (Sampson et al., 2011).

In the future, the fingerprint and DNA databases will be merged with other information to create forensic biometric databases (Tjin-A-Tsoi, 2013). These will likely include 2D or 3D high-resolution images of faces (from arrest records or civil identification such as drivers licenses and passports), anthropometric data (such as height and various body proportions), along with fingerprint patterns and DNA profiles. Other biometric modalities may not be incorporated into forensic biometric databases: iris patterns, retinal blood vessel patterns, gait, or facial thermography. These modalities are unlikely to result in crime scene traces, except under highly unusual circumstances, although they will have value in the security area.

The analysis of microbial DNA will become more significant. The threat of terrorism will not diminish in the near future; consequently, laboratories may have to identify biological warfare agents (Budowle, Murch, & Chakraborty, 2005). The human micro-biome (the population of micro-organisms on human skin and in human body fluids) has great potential for forensic applications. New DNA technologies can determine the species of micro-organisms in a sample and their abundance. The specific populations of micro-organisms on human skin are unique to a particular person (Fierer et al., 2010). Human biological fluids (e.g., blood, saliva, and vaginal secretions) also have distinctive patterns (Benschop et al., 2012; Donaldson et al., 2010). Microbial RNA may also prove useful in the identification of body fluids (Akutsu et al., 2012).

Epigenetics is an expanding area of research and some forensic applications have already been investigated. For example, human biological fluids can be differentiated by differences in DNA methylation patterns (An et al., 2013; Madi et al., 2012). Monozygotic twins may show different methylation patterns in their DNA, allowing the DNA of monozygotic twins to be distinguished (Bell & Spector, 2011). In no-mother paternity cases, DNA methylation patterns could be used to distinguish paternal alleles from maternal alleles (Zhao et al., 2005). Because methylation of DNA increases with age, epigenetics may provide an additional method for determining the age of human remains (Bocklandt et al., 2011).

FORENSIC PATHOLOGY

Forensic pathologists are making increasing use of what has been termed *molecular testing*. For example, DNA testing can reveal the presence of cardiomyopathies or electrolyte channelopathies that could have caused or contributed to a sudden, unexplained death. The genomics of drug metabolism, drug transporters, and drug receptors can also aid in the interpretation of postmortem toxicological findings. Some individuals metabolize drugs poorly and thus may be in danger of drug overdoses; they may also not respond well to drug therapies in which the therapeutic agent has to be metabolized to an active form. Finally, molecular biology has provided a number of tests for a number of pathogens (Gill et al., 2013).

As the number of hospital autopsies continues to decrease, the autopsy has increasingly become the exclusive province of forensic pathologists. The next new thing in forensic pathology is the "virtual autopsy" or "virtopsy" (Honigsbaum, 2013; McKenna, 2012; Wecht, 2012). The virtospy originated in Switzerland, but has yet to be widely adopted in the United States. It relies heavily on imaging technologies already in widespread use for medical diagnostics. The virtopsy usually involves (1) 3D photogrammetry of the body surface, (2) computed tomography (CT), and (3) magnetic resonance imaging (MRI) scans of the entire body. The 3D photogrammetry of the body surface documents injuries such as stab wounds, lacerations, and bullet entrance and exit wounds. The CT x-ray scans "cut" the body into thousands of slices. These slices can be used to follow wound tracks through the body. Contrast media can be injected into blood vessels for CT angiography. Surface markers placed on the body permit alignment of the 3D surface scans and the CT and MRI scans of the skeleton and internal organs. A robotic sampling arm is being developed to work in conjunction with the CT and MRI imaging to take tissue samples from precisely defined locations. The expensive imaging equipment required for a virtual autopsy is already available because it is widely used in other medical specialties. The virtual autopsy has a number of advantages over conventional autopsy methods. First of all, it can find evidence like bullet fragments that might elude a forensic pathologist using only a scalpel and his naked eyes. The virtual autopsy also produces a mass of detailed data that can be reviewed by other forensic pathologists or presented in court. Virtual autopsies can be used to document unidentified remains, which could then be buried rather than being stored indefinitely. Finally, because virtual autopsies are not invasive, they can be used when the deceased's family objects to a conventional autopsy on religious or other grounds. The medical community's experience with the interpretation of CT scans and MRI has almost exclusively been with living individuals. Research will have to be done to assess the impact of postmortem changes on CT scans and MRIs.

DIGITAL EVIDENCE

Digital evidence continues to grow in importance. Digital devices may contain evidence material to investigations; they may be the target of criminal activities. Forensic scientists in this vital field face a number of challenges. First of all, they must cope with an increasing volume of digital evidence. They must also keep abreast of the rapid technological innovations affecting everything from integrated circuits to data storage devices. New digital devices seem to appear every few months. These devices often incorporate specialized software and data-handling protocols with which forensic scientist must be familiar. Advanced data hiding and data protection techniques are evolving: These greatly complicate the collection of digital evidence. Because of the Internet and the networking of digital devices within governmental and industrial organizations, many digital devices can be remotely accessed. This provides greater opportunities for the theft of data. Unauthorized persons may be able to seize control of critical control devices (e.g., those controlling regional or national power grids). The growth of cloud computing presents significant problems for digital investigators. Cloud resources may disappear, leaving little or no trace. Even if traces or artifacts of cloud computing are recoverable, associating them with particular individuals or groups may be impossible (Baker et al., 2013).

Modern societies have increasingly become surveillance societies. Police traffic cameras monitor intersections for light runners and keep track of traffic flow on major arteries. Banks, ATMs, stores, and gas stations routinely record activity on surveillance cameras. Many citizens carry digital cameras with still image and video capabilities. Most mobile telephones now have digital image capabilities. All sorts of crimes may be caught on these digital devices. The beating of Rodney King by Los Angeles police officers was recorded by a concerned citizen. The Ryder rental truck filled with explosive that was parked in front of the Alfred P. Murrah Federal Building in Oklahoma City, Oklahoma, can be seen in a bank security camera video. The recent investigation of the bombing of the Boston Marathon resulted in investigators critically examining thousands of digital still images and digital videos. Faster and even more effective computer algorithms will need to be developed to cope with this enormous volume of digital evidence.

FORENSIC DATABASES

Forensic scientists have access to databases for a number of different types of physical evidence: fingerprints (the Integrated Automated Fingerprint Identification System maintained by the FBI, http://www.fbi.gov/about-us/cjis/fingerprints_biometrics/iafis/iafis), DNA profiles (the Combined DNA Index System, also maintained by the FBI, http://www.fbi.gov/about-us/lab/biometric-analysis/codis), bullets and cartridge cases (the Integrated Ballistic Identifications System, maintained by the Bureau of Alcohol, Tobacco and Firearms, http://www.nibin.gov), tire tracks (commercial products TreadMark™, http://www.treadmark.biz; and TreadMate, http://www.fosterfreeman .com/index.php?option=com_content&view=article&id=30&Itemid=64), shoe impressions (the commercial database SoleMate, http://www.fosterfreeman.com/index .php?option=com_content&view=article&id=4&Itemid=22), handwriting (the Forensic Information System for Handwriting, maintained by the U.S. Secret Service, http://www.secretservice.gov/forensics.shtml), inks (the International Ink Library, maintained by the U.S. Secret Service, http://www.secretservice.gov/forensics.shtml), paint (the FBI's National Automotive Paint File [Bowen & Schneider, 2007] and the Royal Canadian Mounted Police's Paint Data Query [Royal Canadian Mounted Police, 2013]), ignitable liquids (the Ignitable Liquid Reference Collection, maintained by the National Center for Forensic Science, http://ilrc.ucf.edu), smokeless powders (http:// www.ilrc.ucf.edu/powders), glass (the Glass Evidence Reference Database, maintained by the Technical Support Working Group, an interagency working group of the U.S. State Department and the U.S. Department of Defense [Bowen & Schneider, 2007]), and drugs and trace evidence (commercial mass spectral, FTIR, and Raman libraries for drugs, polymers, and explosives). The creation and maintenance of these databases requires commitment of laboratory assets, such as analysts and equipment. Not all laboratories have been able to sustain the upkeep of their databases. There also need to be more forensic databases: for example, a database of the morphology, physical properties, and visible spectra of man-made textile fibers. The creation and maintenance of forensic databases could be one mission undertaken by the National Institute of Forensic Science proposed by the National Research Council (2009).

The more objective information available to forensic scientists in forensic databases, the more rapidly crimes can be solved and the guilty brought to justice. The innocent are more likely to be eliminated early from police inquiries. It is, however, necessary to raise a note of caution. Most of the databases discussed above do not involve the collection or retention of personal information. Obviously, biometric databases such as those for DNA and fingerprints do require collection and retention of personal information. Special safeguards are required to prevent unauthorized access to these databases and the unauthorized release of information about individuals from these databases. Biometric databases require strict policies to insure compliance with confidentiality and privacy requirements. Certain uses of databases may be viewed by the general public as abuses. "Familial" DNA searching has the potential for directing police inquiries at persons whose only "crime" is the possible sharing of parts of a DNA profile with the perpetrator of a crime. Policies for the investigative uses of forensic databases need to be carefully developed.

"IDENTIFICATION SCIENCES"

As I indicated earlier, one of the most significant scientific problems confronting forensic science at the beginning of the 21st century is the scientific status of the so-called "identification sciences" (handwriting identification and comparison, fingerprint identification, firearm and toolmark identification, shoe and tire impressions, and handwriting). The 1993 Supreme Court decision in the case of *Daubert v. Merrell Dow Pharmaceuticals, Inc.*, 509 U.S. 579, provided criteria for the admissibility of scientific evidence:

- Can the theory or technique be tested? Has the theory or technique been tested?

- Has it been subject to peer review and published?

- Are there standards for performing the technique?

- What is the error rate?

- Is the theory or technique generally accepted in the field to which it belongs?

Since *Daubert*, challenges have been mounted against the admission of results of forensic document examinations, fingerprint identification and firearm identification (Page et al., 2011a). While the majority of the challenges have failed, there have been a number of instances where the evidence was excluded outright or the scope of the testimony of the forensic experts was limited. Almost half of the exclusions resulted from a perceived lack of reliability (Page et al., 2011b).

HANDWRITING IDENTIFICATION

Handwriting identification is a key component of forensic document examination. According to Riordan et al. (2013), "[T]he comparison and identification of handwriting and hand printing still comprises the majority of examinations performed by forensic document examiners" (p. 247). The comparison and identification of handwriting is based on the principle that no two people write in exactly the same way. Testimony based on this principle has been accepted by courts in the United States for nearly a century. However, in 1995, the defendants in *United States v. Starzecpyzel* (880 F. Supp. 1027; 1995 U.S. Dist. LEXIS 4216; 42 Fed. R. Evid. Serv. (Callaghan) 247) challenged the admissibility of handwriting identification. The prosecution in this case alleged that the defendants had forged the signature of the victim of their fraud on two documents. The Court granted the defendant's *Daubert* hearing at the conclusion of which the Court ruled that the evidence of the forensic document examiner did not meet the criteria of expert scientific evidence; it could, however, be admitted as technical or specialized knowledge. In its decision the Court made the following comment:

> The Daubert hearing established that forensic document examination, which clothes itself with the trappings of science, does not rest on carefully articulated postulates, does not employ rigorous methodology, and has not convincingly documented the accuracy of its determinations.

The Court went on to liken forensic document examiners to harbor pilots.

Although handwriting identification has continued to be admitted into courts in the United States, the community of forensic document examiners has come to recognize the need for further research in their discipline. Research in this field has focused in two areas: (1) Demonstrating that forensic document examiners do better than laypersons at handwriting identification and (2) examining the frequency of handwriting features in large data sets. Computers are increasingly used to search and compare handwriting samples. The Forensic Information System for Handwriting has already been mentioned. Two others are the Cedar Forensic Examination (CEDAR-FOX) and the Forensic Language-Independent Automated System for Handwriting Identification (FLASH ID) (Riordan et al., 2013). The CEDAR-FOX software was developed at the

Center of Excellence for Document Analysis and Recognition at the University at Buffalo and is available for download (Center of Excellence for Document Analysis and Recognition, 2013). FLASH ID was developed by the FBI for the comparison of handwriting in foreign languages. Hopefully, these new research efforts will establish the scientific stature of forensic handwriting comparison.

FINGERPRINTS

Fingerprint identification is one of the examinations that most laypersons think of when they encounter the phrase "forensic science" (another being DNA profiling). Great technical strides have been made in the development of latent fingerprints; automated fingerprint identification systems (AFIS) have vastly sped up the process of searching fingerprint databases for matches for crime scene fingerprints. Given these facts, most laypersons would consider fingerprinting virtually bulletproof as far as challenges to the claim that matching a latent print to an inked reference print means that the source of the latent print has been absolutely determined. However, the admission of fingerprint identification into courts of law in the United States predated the first pronouncement of a criterion for the admission of scientific evidence in the 1923 *Frye* decision (*Frye v. United States*, 293 F. 1013 (D.C. Cir 1923)). Fingerprint identification was in effect "grandfathered" in. Even now, courts are reluctant to exclude fingerprint evidence even while they acknowledge the problematic basis of fingerprint identification (Page et al., 2011b). For years, agencies conducting fingerprint comparisons (either comparisons of inked fingerprints on 10 cards or comparisons of crime scene fingerprints with inked fingerprints) used administratively established guidelines for the number of ridge characteristics (Galton features or minutiae) that needed to be matched to declare an identification. One agency might require matching 12 ridge characteristics in a single print; another might require 16 (Kirk & Thornton, 1974; Walls, 1974). Such numbers were not based on empirical tests but rested instead on the plausible but never demonstrated claim that fingerprint patterns are unique. In 1973, the International Association for Identification (IAI) Standardization Committee stated that "no valid basis exists at this time for requiring that a pre-determined minimum number of friction ridge characteristics must be present in two impressions in order to establish positive identification" (International Association for Identification Standardization Committee II, 2010, p. 3). The IAI Standardization Committee II offered a modified statement in 2010: "There currently exists no scientific basis for requiring a minimum amount of corresponding friction ridge detail information between two impressions to arrive at an opinion of single source attribution" (p. 3). This leaves fingerprint identification in the unsatisfactory position of lacking a threshold level of ridge detail information for making a source attribution for a fingerprint. The IAI Standardization Committee II called for research to remedy this deficiency:

> The Committee recommends that the IAI support the pursuit of research in an attempt to establish a measurable threshold requirement for identification of latent prints, with the intent of achieving a standard. The Committee recognizes the difficulty or potential impossibility of this endeavor. (p. 4)

This research would involve the development and application of probability models for fingerprint ridge details and the testing of these models against large collections of fingerprints. Fingerprint identification is too important a method of personal identification to be left in scientific limbo, and eventually, fingerprint examiners around the world will employ a common methodology for fingerprint comparison and apply a common set of criteria for declaring a source attribution. Eventually, fingerprints, DNA profiles, and other data will be combined in biometric databases.

FIREARM AND TOOLMARK IDENTIFICATION

Firearm examiners attempt to make source attributions of fired bullets and cartridge cases by comparing markings such as striation patterns on the surfaces of bullets and firing pin impressions and breechblock markings on cartridge cases. Toolmark examiners attempt to make source attribution of toolmarks by comparing microscopic features of evidentiary toolmarks with test toolmarks made with suspect tools. For many years, firearm and toolmark examiners were willing to make source attributions with absolute certainty. However, claims of absolute certainty in the identification sciences have no scientific basis (Rowe, 2005).

After *Daubert*, defense counsels have mounted a series of attacks on the admission of the results of firearm and toolmark examinations with a limited degree of success (Page et al., 2011a, 2011b). The National Research Council (2009) made the following comment about firearm and tool mark examinations: "Because not enough is known about the variabilities among individual tools and guns, we are not able to specify how many points of similarity are necessary for a given level of confidence in the result" (pp. 5–21). Firearm and toolmark examinations have heretofore involved the comparison of two-dimensional images (Rowe, 2005). Newer approaches that use surface profiles (Bachrach, 2002; Banno, Masuda & Ikeuchi, 2004; Chu et al., 2010; De Kinder & Bonfanti, 1999) will be able to provide more objective match criteria and allow firearm and toolmark examiners to provide courts with realistic error rates.

All of the identification sciences have problems with source attribution. In light of the *Daubert* decision, it would be desirable to be able to give estimates of the error rates associated with these examinations. However, estimates of error rates presupposes the existence of numerical assessments of similarity and empirical research on the application of the numerical assessments of similarity to a population of samples (be it handwritings, striation patterns on bullets, firing pin impressions, or accidental characteristics on shoe soles or tire treads). As the National Research Council (2009) noted,

> [T]here is no consensus regarding the number of individual characteristics needed to make a positive identification, and the committee is not aware of any data about the variability of class or individual characteristics or about the validity or reliability of the method. Without such population studies, it is impossible to assess the number of characteristics that must match in order to have any particular degree of confidence about the source of the impression. (pp. 5–17)

Administrative Changes in Forensic Science

The National Research Council (2009) identified a number of factors affecting the status and stature of forensic science in the United States: lack of resources (resulting in case backlogs); the ascendency of DNA profiling (with its attendant shift of resources from more traditional forensic examinations); the revelation (primarily from post-conviction DNA testing) that some well-accepted forensic science examinations lacked adequate scientific bases; errors or outright fabrication of evidence (again, primarily revealed by post-conviction DNA testing); the so-called "*CSI* effect" (see Chapter 2, this volume); a fragmented and inconsistent system of medico-legal death investigation; incompatible automated fingerprint identification systems; growing importance of forensic science to homeland security; and the close ties of forensic science with the justice system. The National Research Council made a number of recommendations to improve the status and stature of forensic science. While the focus of the National Research Council was on forensic science in the United States, many of the recommendations apply in Europe as well (Tjin-A-Tsoi, 2013).

FORENSIC LABORATORY ACCREDITATION

In the next 20 years, forensic science will become a regulated industry, in much the same way that healthcare is presently a regulated industry. The first recommendation of the National Research Council (2009) called for the establishment of a National Institute of Forensic Science (NIFS) which should focus on "establishing standards for the mandatory accreditation of forensic science laboratories and the mandatory certification of forensic scientists and medical examiners/forensic pathologists" (p. S-14). The intent of forensic laboratory accreditation is to insure that the work product of the laboratory meets a certain standard. According to the Bureau of Justice Statistics (Burch et al., 2012), in 2009 (the most recent year for which data are available), most public forensic laboratories are already accredited by some professional body such as the American Society of Crime Laboratory Directors Laboratory Accreditation Board (ASCLD-LAB), the American Board of Forensic Toxicology (ABFT), and the National Association of Medical Examiners (NAME). Eighty-three percent of all publically funded forensic laboratories were accredited by a professional forensic science organization. State-level laboratories had the highest level of accreditation (92%), and municipal laboratories the lowest (62%). More forensic science laboratories in the United States will also become ISO/IEC 17025 compliant.

An important component of laboratory accreditation is the adoption of a laboratory quality management system (Tilstone, 2011). Such systems have been widely used in private industrial laboratories and in non-forensic governmental laboratories for many years. The purpose of quality management systems is to insure that the product of the laboratories (i.e., their analytical results) meet some defined levels of trueness (the new term that has displaced accuracy) and precision. At minimum, quality management systems require validated analytical procedures, detailed laboratory protocols for the performance of analyses, for the interpretation of analytical results, and for reporting of the precision of the results. When applied to forensic science laboratories, quality management systems lay out the physical attributes of the facilities, including security (to insure the integrity of evidentiary chains of custody); the equipment required to conduct analyses; the required educational backgrounds of laboratory examiners; and detailed protocols for the reception of evidence, for its analysis, and for the reporting of results. There are also requirements for ongoing proficiency testing of laboratory examiners.

As forensic science becomes a regulated industry, there will be standardization of many laboratory procedures. There will also be standardization of report writing. There is a clear need for standardization. The National Research Council (2009) report made the following recommendation:

> The National Institute of Forensic Science (NIFS), after reviewing established standards such as ISO 17025, and in consultation with its advisory board, should establish standard terminology to be used in reporting on and testifying about the results of forensic science investigations. Similarly, it should establish model laboratory reports for different forensic science disciplines and specify the minimum information that should be included. As part of the accreditation and certification processes, laboratories and forensic scientists should be required to utilize model laboratory reports when summarizing the results of their analyses. (p. S-13)

CERTIFICATION OF FORENSIC LABORATORY EXAMINERS

The intent of certification of forensic laboratory examiners is to insure that examiners reach a certain standard of competence. Because of the diverse nature of the forensic sciences, there cannot be a general certification of forensic science examiners. Instead, forensic examiners become certified in a forensic science specialty. The situation is analogous to that of physicians. Physicians are licensed to practice medicine but become board-certified in one or more specialties. Certification of forensic laboratory examiners has not advanced as far as the accreditation of forensic science laboratories. At present, the American Board of Criminalistics (http://criminalistics.com/) offers diplomate status to forensic scientists or forensic educators who have a bachelor's degree in natural science, two years' experience in a forensic laboratory, or two years' experience teaching forensic science, and who pass an examination in one of ABC certifying examinations: Comprehensive Criminalistics Examination (CCE), Drug Analysis (DA), Molecular Biology (MB), Fire Debris Analysis (FD), Trace Evidence—Hairs and Fibers (THF) and Trace Evidence—Paints and Polymers (TPP). Diplomates of the ABC may become fellows of the ABC by passing a proficiency test in a forensic specialty and by performing examinations in that specialty for two years. The specialty areas in which one may become a fellow are Molecular Biology, Drug Analysis, Fire Debris Analysis and Trace Evidence—Hairs and Fibers, and Trace Evidence—Paint and Polymers.

Other professional organizations offer certifications of forensic laboratory examiners. The American Board of Forensic Toxicology (http://abft.org) offers two levels of certification: diplomates, who hold a doctoral degree and have the equivalent of three years' full-time professional experience in forensic toxicology (practice, research, teaching, or administration); and specialists, who have the same experiential credentials as diplomates and have bachelor's degrees in natural science, The Association of Firearm and Tool Mark Examiners (http://afte.org) offers certification in three areas: firearm evidence examination and identification, toolmark evidence examination and identification, and gunshot residue evidence examination and identification.

CODES OF ETHICS

The crisis that currently confronts forensic science in the United States has been brought on in part by the unethical behavior of a small number of forensic scientists.

A number of forensic science professional organizations have codes of ethics (see the American Academy of Forensic Sciences, 2013; Association of Firearm and Tool Mark Examiners, 2013; the California Association of Criminalists, 2010; and the Society of Forensic Toxicologists, 2012). These range from cursory to highly detailed. However, these codes of ethics have one thing in common: They are only enforceable against members of these organizations. Moreover, the strongest action the professional organizations can take against errant members is expulsion. If a forensic scientist declines to join a professional organization (as many do), his or her unethical conduct may go without any meaningful sanction. The National Research Council (2009) made the following recommendation:

> The National Institute of Forensic Science (NIFS), in consultation with its advisory board, should establish a national code of ethics for all forensic science disciplines and encourage individual societies to incorporate this national code as part of their professional code of ethics. Additionally, NIFS should explore mechanisms of enforcement for those forensic scientists who commit serious ethical violations. Such a code could be enforced through a certification process for forensic scientists. (p. S-19)

The Forensic Education Program Accreditation Commission (2012) requires the incorporation of ethics into the curricula of forensic science education programs.

CONTROL OF FORENSIC SCIENCE LABORATORIES

One of the most far-reaching recommendations made by the National Research Council (2009) was Recommendation 4:

> To improve the scientific bases of forensic science examinations and to maximize independence from or autonomy within the law enforcement community, Congress should authorize and appropriate incentive funds to the National Institute of Forensic Science (NIFS) for allocation to state and local jurisdictions for the purpose of removing all public forensic laboratories and facilities from the administrative control of law enforcement agencies or prosecutors' offices. (p. S-17)

Historically, forensic science laboratories have been part of law enforcement agencies. In many cases, the laboratory examiners have been sworn officers. The potential for pro-prosecution bias with such an administrative structure is obvious. It is difficult for forensic scientists to be accorded the stature of other scientists when they are regarded as merely the police or prosecutor's "tame scientists." This is not a theoretical discussion: Examples of biased forensic science are numerous. One need only think of the scandals attached to the names of Fred Zain (Giannelli & McMunigal, 2007; Pyrek, 2007), Joyce Gilchrist (Giannelli & McMunigal, 2007; Pyrek, 2007) and Arnold Melnikoff (Pyrek, 2007) to see how forensic scientists can be motivated to slant their results to favor law enforcement and prosecutors.

While the removal of forensic science laboratories from the control law enforcement agencies may be a necessary condition to insure unbiased analyses and interpretation, it is not a sufficient condition. Virginia's Department of Forensic Sciences has always existed free from law enforcement oversight. The case of Karl Michael Roush is instructive. In 1997, one of the department's hair and fiber examiners claimed to have matched fibers from a victim of a rape/murder to a van belonging to Karl Michael Roush; however, the FBI laboratory re-examined the fibers and concluded that the fibers found on the victim did not come from Roush's vehicle. The Virginia hair and fiber expert resigned, and her body of case work had to be reviewed (Neuberger, 1997). The gross misconduct of Annie Dookhan, forensic drug chemist at the William A. Hinton State Laboratory Institute in Boston (a part of the Massachusetts Department of Public Health), resulted in her drug laboratory being closed. Of particular concern in this case is the close personal relationship Dookhan developed with one of the prosecutors for whom she frequently testified (Jacobs, 2013).

PROPOSED FEDERAL LEGISLATION

In 2011 and 2012, legislation was introduced in the U.S. Senate (Senate bills S.132 and S.3378) to implement many of the recommendations of the National Research Council. Bill S.132, Criminal Justice and Forensic Science Reform Act of 2011, would establish an Office of Forensic Science and a Forensic Science Board. The Office of Forensic Science would collaborate with the National Institute of Standards and Technology (NIST) and with the National Science Foundation. The Forensic Science Board would act in an advisory capacity to the Office of Forensic Science. The director of the Office of Forensic Science would have to certify that a forensic science laboratory was accredited for the laboratory to receive federal funds. The Forensic Science Board would be charged with developing accreditation standards for forensic science laboratories. Federal funding would also be denied to forensic science laboratories if any laboratory examiners were not certified. Certification requirements for each forensic science discipline would be established by the Forensic Science Board. The Office of Forensic Science would be able to give grants and technical assistance to forensic science laboratories to aid them in meeting the accreditation and certification requirements. The Forensic Science Board would develop a comprehensive research program for the forensic sciences. The Director of the NIST would have the authority to make grants for forensic science research projects consistent with the research program developed by the Forensic Science Board. Senate bill S.132 would also require the Forensic Science Board to come up with standards and best practices for each forensic science discipline; the Office of Forensic Science would then publish these standards and best practices. Finally, the bill charges the Office of Forensic Science with plans for the education and training of judges, lawyers, and law enforcement personnel in the proper use of forensic science; the Office of Forensic Science would also support the development of undergraduate and graduate education in forensic science.

Senate bill S.3378, the Forensic Science and Standards Act Of 2012, makes the National Science Foundation responsible for developing and funding a forensic science research program; NIST would develop forensic science standards. The bill also establishes a Forensic Science Advisory Committee (chaired jointly by the director of NIST and the attorney general of the United States) which would make recommendations on the adoption of standards. The attorney general would require the adoption of the standards in the federal forensic science laboratories.

As of this writing, both of the Senate bills are still in committee. In 2013, the Department of Justice and NIST announced the creation of a National Commission on

Forensic Science, which will make policy recommendations to the attorney general regarding best forensic practices, codes of professional responsibility, training, and certification (NIST, 2013). Clearly, the National Commission on Forensic Science will be able to address some of the issues raised by the National Research Council (2009).

Forensic Science Education

In light of the major technological and administrative changes that can be expected in forensic science, forensic science education will become even more important as we move forward. Many of the scientific working groups in forensic science disciplines have promulgated basic educational standards for practitioners in their fields, as well as adopting requirements for continuing education. While a degree in a natural science such as physics, chemistry, or biology would be a *sine qua non* for entry into disciplines such as forensic chemistry, forensic molecular biology, or forensic toxicology, degrees in natural science by themselves do not provide adequate grounding in forensic science. The number of forensic science degree programs at the undergraduate and graduate levels will grow in response to the increasing need for forensic examiners due to the increasing demand for forensic testing. As the number of forensic scientists grows the demand for forensic science training will also grow.

In the coming decades, academic institutions will provide workshops and short training programs in addition to their course offerings in their forensic science degree programs. Many if not most of the academic institutions' courses will follow a growing trend and be offered online. The same will be true of the workshops and short training programs. Online offerings will likely be less expensive than residential programs. Even if such is not the case, online workshops and training courses will be attractive to forensic science laboratories because there would be no travel expenses, and training could take place with only limited diversion of personnel from casework. In the forensic science degree programs, the conventional academic offering of lecture, recitation, and laboratory work will be replaced by integrated online problem-solving scenarios in which forensic casework is presented realistically through virtual reality. Students would advance through a series of increasingly challenging scenarios in which they identify relevant evidence, analyze it, interpret analytical data, prepare reports, and even provide expert testimony. Similar approaches will be adopted with respect to continuing education.

Current approaches to continuing education do not provide the deliberate practice that Ericsson and others have shown to be required to reach high levels of performance (Clark, 2008; Ericsson, 2009; Ericsson & Charness, 1994; Ericsson, Krampe, & Tesch-Römer, 1993: Ericsson, Nandagopal, & Roring, 2009). Based on studies of high-performing individuals in sports, music, and science, Ericsson came up with a rule of thumb: 10 years or 10,000 hours of deliberate practice are required to become an expert. Even counting the four years spent studying for a bachelor's degree (not all of which are spent studying science) and one to two years pursuing a master's degree, the typical neophyte forensic scientist is still four years from achieving Ericsson's 10-year benchmark. Developing programs of deliberate practice for forensic experts has not been attempted before. *Deliberate practice*, as the term is used by Ericsson, has a number of critical components: Deliberate practice pushes the envelope of the performer's capabilities; it is frequent; and it involves immediate evaluation and feedback. In the forensic sciences, deliberate practice should involve the full range of functions that forensic experts carry out: analysis of evidence, interpretation of results, report writing, and courtroom testimony. Deliberate practice exercises could involve complete analyses of mock cases (like existing proficiency tests, but in greater depth). Mock cases could be done online, with the examiner specifying tests to be performed on evidence, being presented with test results, analyzing the results, writing a report, and perhaps even responding to cross-examination questions. The mock-case approach would obviously be very demanding of the forensic examiner's time. Other approaches to deliberate practice could involve within-laboratory mentoring over extended periods of time, regular detailed review of completed case work (in greater depth than currently practiced technical peer review), regular consultation with fellow examiners, or periodic internships in other laboratories. Because deliberate practice involves pushing the limits of performance, it involves—requires—opportunities for failure. Given the potential for the results of deliberate practice exercises such as mock cases being used by opposing counsel to impeach the testimony of a forensic expert, deliberate practice for forensic experts would have to be conducted under conditions of anonymity. The widespread adoption of deliberate practice in the field of forensic science would require changes in the management culture of most forensic laboratories. Few laboratories encourage or facilitate their personnel taking workshops or attending forensic science meetings. When forensic laboratory budgets are cut, funds for training are the first to go.

Conclusion

A theme that runs through this chapter is the centrality of computers to the field of forensic science. The advanced imaging technologies coming into use in crime scene investigation and forensic pathology depend on the computational power of new generations of computers. The utility of the proliferating forensic databases stems from the existence of the Internet and modern high-speed computers. Computers will also allow the tracking of evidence from the crime scene through the forensic laboratory to the courtroom. Computers will allow this tracking within agencies and across agencies. Anyone with access to the computer system will be able to locate an item of evidence and call up images of it, reports of analyses, and the underlying analytical data. In this way, agencies will be able to insure that the results of an analysis (such as a DNA match) are followed up on. In many areas of forensic science, new science and technology will make it possible for forensic scientists to extract more information from smaller evidentiary samples in a shorter period of time. Research programs focusing on the "identification sciences" will alleviate many of the problems facing these fields and give them more scientific credibility.

In addition, forensic science will become a regulated industry with mandatory laboratory accreditation and mandatory forensic examiner certification. Even if the recommendations of the National Research Council (2009) are only partially implemented, forensic science will have to create stronger codes of ethics to prevent future scandals. Because of the increasing demand for forensic science services, forensic laboratories will have to prioritize their case work and focus their efforts on the most serious cases.

Finally, there will be major changes in the delivery of forensic science education and training, with greater emphasis on deliberate practice to develop higher levels of expertise among forensic examiners.

References

Akutsu, T., Motani, H., Watanoabe, K., Iwase, H., & Sakurada, K. (2012). Detection of bacterial 16S ribosomal RNA genes for forensic identification of vaginal fluid. *Legal Medicine, 14*(2), 160–162.

American Academy of Forensic Sciences. (2013). *American Academy of Forensic Sciences bylaws*. Retrieved April 26, 2013 from http://aafs.org/aafs-bylaws

American Society of Crime Laboratory Directors Laboratory Accreditation Board. (2010). *ASCLD/LAB-International program overview, 2010 edition*. Retrieved April 24, 2013 from http://www.ascld-lab.org/programs/intl_testing_overview.html

An, J., Choi, A., Shin, K., Yang, W., & Lee, H. (2013). DNA methylation-specific multiplex assays for body fluid identification. *International Journal of Legal Medicine, 127*(1), 35–43. doi:10.1007/s00414-012-0719-1

Association of Firearm and Tool Mark Examiners. (2013). *AFTE code of ethics*. Retrieved April 26, 2013 from http://www.afte.org/AssociationInfo/a_codeofethics.htm

Bachrach, B. (2002). Development of a 3D-based automated firearms evidence comparison system. *Journal of Forensic Sciences, 47*(6), 1253–1265.

Baker, D. W., Brothers, S. I., Geradts, Z. J., Lacey, D. S., Nance, K. L., Ryan, D. J., et al. (2013). Digital evolution: History, challenges and future directions for the digital and multimedia sciences section. In D. H. Ubelaker (Ed.), *Forensic science: Current issues, future directions* (pp. 252–291). Chichester, UK: Wiley-Blackwell.

Ballou, S., Houck, M., Siegal, J. A., Crouse, C. A., Lentini, J. J., & Palenik, S. (2013). Criminalistics: the bedrock of forensic science. In D. H. Ubelaker (Ed.), *Forensic science: Current issues, future directions* (pp. 29–101). Chichester, UK: Wiley-Blackwell.

Banno, A., Masuda, T., & Ikeuchi, K. (2004). Three dimensional visualization and comparison of impressions on fired bullets. *Forensic Science International, 140*(2–3), 233–240. doi:10.1016/j.forsciint.2003.11.025

Bell, J., & Spector, T. (2011). A twin approach to unraveling epigenetics. *Trends in Genetics, 27*(3), 116–125. doi:10.1016/j.tig.2010.12.005

Benschop, C., Quaak, F., Boon, M., Sijen, T., & Kuiper, I. (2012). Vaginal microbial flora analysis by next generation sequencing and microarrays; can microbes indicate vaginal origin in a forensic context? *International Journal of Legal Medicine, 126*(2), 303–310. doi:10.1007/s00414-011-0660-8

Bocklandt, S., Lin, W., Sehl, M., Sanchez, F., Sinsheimer, J., Horvath, S., et al. (2011). Epigeneitic predictor of age. *PLoS One, 6*(6), e14821. doi:10.1371/journal.pone.0014821

Bottazzini, U. (2011). Hilbert's problems: A research program for "future generations." In C. Bartocci, R. Betti, A. Guerragio, & R. Luchetti (Eds.), *Mathematical lives: Protagonists of the twentieth century from Hilbert to Wiles* (pp. 1–10). Heidelberg, Germany: Springer.

Bowen, R., & Schneider, J. (2007). Forensic databases: Paint, shoe prints, and beyond. *NIJ Journal, 258,* 34–28.

Budowle, B., Murch, R., & Chakraborty, R. (2005). Microbial forensics: The next forensic challenge. *International Journal of Legal Medicine, 119,* 317–330. doi 10.1007/ s00414-005-0535-y

Burch, A., Durose, M., & Walsh, K. (2012). Census of publicly funded forensic crime laboratories, 2009. Washington, DC: U.S. Department of Justice, Office of Justice Programs, Bureau of Justice Statistics. Retrieved April 24, 2013 from http://www.bjs.gov/index .cfm?ty=pbdetail&iid=4412

California Association of Criminalists. (2010). *Code of ethics of the California Association of Criminalists.* Retrieved on April 26, 2013 from http://www.cacnews.org/ membership/handbook.shtml

Center of Excellence for Document Analysis and Recognition. (2013). *Forensic/questioned document examination: Research to validate individuality in handwriting & develop computer assisted procedures for handwriting comparison.* Retrieved on April 21, 2013 from http://www.cedar.buffalo.edu/NIJ/

Chu, W., Song, J., Vorburger, T., Yen, J., Ballou, S., & Bachrach, B. (2010). Pilot study of automated bullet signature identification based on topography measurements and correlations. *Journal of Forensic Sciences, 55*(2), 314–347. doi:10.1111/ j.1556–4029.2009.01276.x

Clark, R. (2008). *Building expertise: Cognitive methods for training and performance* (3rd ed.). San Francisco: Pfeiffer.

De Kinder, J., & Bonfanti, M. (1999). Automated comparisons of bullet striations based on 3D topography. *Forensic Science International, 101,* 85–93. doi:10.10016/S0379-0738(98)00212-6

Denmark, A., & Mount, M. (2013). Forensic laboratory—investigation activities. *Forensic Magazine.* Retrieved April 16, 2013 from http://www.forensicmag.com/article/forensic-laboratory-2030-investigation-activities

Donaldson, A., Taylor, M., Cordiner, S., & Lamont, I. (2010). Using oral microbial DNA analysis to identify expirated bloodspatter. *International Journal of Legal Medicine, 124,* 569–576. doi:10.1007/s00414-010-0426-8

Ericsson, K. A. (Ed.) (2009). *Development of professional expertise.* Cambridge: Cambridge University Press.

Ericsson, K. A., & Charness, N. (1994). Expert performance: Its structure and acquisition. *American Psychologist, 49*(8), 725–747.

Ericsson, K. A., Krampe, R., & Tesch-Römer, C. (1993). Deliberate practice in the acquisition of expert performance. *Psychological Review, 100*(3), 363–406.

Ericsson, K. A., Nandagopal, K., & Roring, R. (2009). Toward a science of exceptional achievement: Attaining superior performance through deliberate practice. *Annals of the New York Academy of Science, 1172,* 119–217. doi:10.1196/annals.1393.001

Fierer, N., Lauber, C., Zhou, N., McDonald, D., Costello, E., & Knight, R. (2010). Forensic identification using skin bacterial communities. *Proceedings of the National Academy of Sciences, 107*(14), 6477–6481.

Forensic Education Program Accreditation Commission. (2012). *Forensic Education Program Accreditation Commission (FEPAC) accreditation standards.* Retrieved April 26, 2013 from http://fepac-edu.org/accreditation

Giannelli, P. (1997). The abuse of scientific evidence in criminal cases: The need for independent crime laboratories. *Virginia Journal of Social Policy and the Law, 4,* 439–478.

Giannelli, P., & McMunigal, K. (2007). Prosecutors, ethics and expert witnesses. *Fordham Law Review, 76,* 1493–1537.

Gill, J. R., Tang, Y., Davis, G. G., Harcke, H. T., & Mazuchowski, E. L. (2013). Forensic pathology—the roles of molecular diagnostics and radiology at autopsy. In D. H. Ubelaker (Ed.), *Forensic science: Current issues, future directions* (pp. 102–130). Chichester, UK: Wiley-Blackwell.

Green, F. (2012, December 31). Virginia death row: Alfredo R. Prieto. *Richmond Times-Dispatch.* Retrieved April 28, 2013 from http://www.timesdispatch.com/archive/virginia-s-death-row-alfredo-r-prieto/article_f64fa3e8–431a-5638-abd9-bb990ef94c76.html

Honigsbaum, M. (2013, February 23). Virtual autopsy: Does it spell the end of the scalpel? *The Observer.* Retrieved April 21, 2013 from http://www.guardian.co.uk/science/2013/feb/23/virtual-autopsy-virtopsy-forensic-science/print

Houck, M., & Budowle, B. (2002). Correlation of microscopic and mitochondrial DNA hair comparisons. *Journal of Forensic Sciences, 47*(5), 964–967. doi:10.1520/JFS15515J

Howe, J., Duval, J., Shepard, C., & Gaffney, R. (2013). General forensics—no one else starts until we finish. In D. H. Ubelaker (Ed.), *Forensic science: Current issues, future directions* (pp. 6–28). Chichester, UK: Wiley-Blackwell.

International Association for Identification Standardization Committee II. (2010). *The report of the International Association for Identification, Standardization II Committee.* Retrieved April 29, 2013 from https://www.ncjrs.gov/pdffiles1/nij/grants/233980.pdf

Jacobs, S. (2013, February 3). Annie Dookhan pursued renown along a path of lies. *Boston Globe.* Retrieved April 27, 2013 from http://www.bostonglobe.com/metro/2013/02/03/chasing-renown-path-paved-with-lies/Axw3AxwmD33lRwXatSvMCL/story.html

Kirk, P., & Thornton, J. (1974). *Crime investigation* (2nd ed.). Malabar, FL: Krieger Publishing Company.

Madi, T., Balamurugan, K., Bombardi, R., Duncan, G., & McCord, B. (2012). The Determination of tissue-specific DNA methylation patterns in forensic biofluids using bisulfite modification and pyrosequencing. *Electrophoresis, 33*(12), 1736–1745. doi:10.1002/elps.201100711

McKenna, M. (2012). The virtues of the virtual autopsy. *Scientific American, 307*(11), 30–32. doi:10.1038/scientificamerican1112-30

Mennell, J. (2006). The future of forensic and crime scene science: Part II. A UK perspective on forensic science education. *Forensic Science International, 157S,* S13–S20. doi:10.1016/j.forsciint.205.12.023

Mennell, J., & Shaw, I. (2006). The future of forensic and crime scene science: Part I. A UK forensic science user and provider perspective. *Forensic Science International, 157,* S7–S12. doi:10.1016/j.forsciint.205.12.002

Mount, M., & Hackman, S. (2012). Forensic laboratory 2030: Scientific environment. *Forensic Magazine.* Retrieved April 16, 2013 from http://www.forensicmag.com/print/7230

Mount, M., & Hackman, S. (2013). Forensic laboratory 2030: Physical environment. *Forensic Magazine.* Retrieved April 16, 2013 from http://www.forensicmag.com/article/forensic-laboratory-2030-physical-environment

Murphy, E. (2013). The government wants your DNA. *Scientific American, 308,* 72–77. doi:10.1038/scientificamerican0313-72

National Institute of Standards and Technology (NIST). (2013). *Department of Justice and National Institute of Standards and Technology announce launch of National Commission on Forensic Science* [Press release]. Retrieved on April 30, 2013 from http://www.nist.gov/oles/doj-nist-forensic-science021513.cfm

National Research Council. (2009). *Strengthening forensic science in the United States: A path forward.* Washington, DC: National Academies Press.

Neuberger, C. (1997, June 11). Scientist who erred in Silva case resigns; officials are dropping charges against suspect. *Richmond Times-Dispatch,* p. A-1.

Page, M., Taylor, J., & Blenkin, M. (2011a). Forensic identification science evidence since *Daubert*: Part I—a quantitative analysis of the exclusion of forensic identification science evidence. *Journal of Forensic Sciences, 56*(5), 1180–1184. doi:10.1111/j.1556-4029.2011.0777.x

Page, M., Taylor, J., & Blenkin, M. (2011b). Forensic identification science evidence since *Daubert*: Part II—judicial reasoning in decisions to exclude forensic identification evidence on grounds of reliability. *Journal of Forensic Sciences, 56*(4), 913–917. doi:10.1111/j.1556-4029.2011.01776.x

Palenik, C. (2001). *The role of the forensic scientist in the new millennium.* Retrieved April 16, 2013 from http://yfsf.aafs.org/content/role-forensic-scientist-new-millennium-christopher-s-palenik

Pyrek, K. (2007). *Forensic science under siege: The challenges of forensic laboratories and the medico-legal investigation system.* Burlington, MA: Academic Press.

Ribaux, O., Walsh, S., & Margot, P. (2006). The contribution of forensic science to crime analysis and investigation: Forensic intelligence. *Forensic Science International, 156,* 171–181. doi:10.1016/j.forsciint.204.12.028

Riordan, W. M., Gustafson, J. A., Fitzgerald, M. P., & Lewis, J. A. (2013). Forensic document examination. In D. H. Ubelaker (Ed.), *Forensic science: Current issues, future directions* (pp. 224–251). Chichester, UK: Wiley-Blackwell.

Robertson, J. (2008). Science futures. *Australian Journal of Forensic Sciences, 40*(1), 17–24. doi:10.1080/00450610802051012

Rowe, W. (2005). Firearms identification. In R. Saferstein (Ed.), *Forensic science handbook* (Vol. 2, pp. 401–486). Upper Saddle River, NJ: Prentice-Hall.

Royal Canadian Mounted Police. (2013). *Royal Canadian Mounted Police forensic laboratory services—paint data query.* Retrieved April 28, 2013 from http://www.rcmp-grc.gc.ca/fs-fd/pdfs/pdq-eng.pdf

Saks, M., & Koehler, J. (2005). The coming paradigm shift forensic identification science. *Science, 309,* 892–895.

Sampson, J., Kidd, K., Kidd, J., & Zhao, H. (2011). Selecting SNPs to identify ancestry. *Annals of Human Genetics, 75*(4), 539–553. doi:10.1111/j.1469–1809.2011.00656.x

Schiro, G. (2000). *Forensic science and crime scene investigation: Past, present and future.* Retrieved March 19, 2013 from http://www.forensicscienceresources.com/CSIPPF.htm

Scientific Working Group for the Analysis of Seized Drugs. (2011). *Scientific Working Group for the Analysis of Seized Drugs (SWGDRUG) recommendations.* Retrieved April 27, 2013 from http://swgdrug.org/approved.htm

Society of Forensic Toxicologists. (2012). Over view of ethics procedures. Retrieved April 26, 2013 from http://soft-tox.org/files/SOFT_ethics_procedures.pdf

Stauffer, E., Dolan, J., & Newman, R. (2008). *Fire debris analysis.* Boston: Academic Press.

Sturm, R. (2009). Molecular genetics of human pigmentation diversity. *Human Molecular Genetics, 18*(Review Issue 1), R9–R17. doi:10.1093/hmg/ddp003

Tilstone, W. (2011). Quality in the forensic science laboratory. In A. Mozayani & C. Noziglia (Eds.), *The forensic laboratory handbook: Procedures and practice* (2nd ed., pp. 335–368). New York: Humana Press

Tjin-A-Tsoi, T. (2013). *Trends, challenges and strategy in the forensic science sector.* Retrieved April 16, 2013 from http://www.nist.gov/oles/forensics-2012.cfm

Ubelaker, D. H. (Ed.). (2013). *Forensic science: Current trends, future directions.* Chichester, UK: Wiley-Blackwell.

Walls, H. (1974). *Forensic science: an introduction to scientific crime investigation.* New York: Praeger.

Wecht, C. (2012). Virtual autopsy. *Forensic Examiner, 22*(1), 72–80.

Wiley, J., Marusich, J., Huffman, J., Balster, R., & Thomas, B. (2011). *Hijacking of basic research: The case of synthetic cannabinoids* (RTI Press publication OP-0007–1111). Retrieved October 13, 2013 from http://www.rti.org/pubs/op-0007-1111-wiley.pdf

Zhao, G., Yang, Q., Huang, D., Yu, C., Yang, R., Chen, H., et al. (2005). Study on the application of parent-of-origin specific DNA methylation markers to forensic genetics. *Forensic Science International, 154*(2–3), 122–127. doi:10.1016/j.forsciint.2004.09.123

Index

About the Editors

Kevin J. Strom is a senior scientist at RTI International where his research activity is focused on the impact of forensic science on the criminal justice system, law enforcement responses to community violence and terrorism, and crime- and forensic data–reporting systems. His work has been published in peer-reviewed journals that include *Criminology & Public Policy, Journal of Forensic Sciences, Journal of Quantitative Criminology*, and *Crime & Delinquency*. Dr. Strom has led numerous law enforcement– and forensic-related studies, including projects that have developed recommendations for increasing efficiency in forensic evidence processing. This research has included assessing how forensic evidence is collected, processed, used, and retained across law enforcement, crime laboratories, and prosecutors' offices. Dr. Strom has been an active member of the International Association of Chiefs of Police Research Advisory Committee since 2009. Before joining RTI, he was employed by the U.S. Department of Justice's Bureau of Justice Statistics. He received his Ph.D. in criminology from the University of Maryland, College Park.

Matthew J. Hickman is an associate professor in the Department of Criminal Justice at Seattle University. He received his Ph.D. in criminal justice from Temple University. He previously worked for the Bureau of Justice Statistics, U.S. Department of Justice (2000–2007), where he specialized in national data collections relating to law enforcement agencies, forensic laboratory operations, and medicolegal death investigation systems in the United States. At Seattle University, he has an active research agenda focused primarily on issues in policing, quantitative research methodology, and the impact of forensic sciences on the administration of justice. His work has been published in numerous peer-reviewed journals including *Criminology, Criminology & Public Policy, Journal of Quantitative Criminology, Journal of Forensic Sciences, Sociological Methods and Research, Crime & Delinquency, Police Quarterly*, and *Policing*. Dr. Hickman is a member of the American Society of Criminology, the American Academy of Forensic Sciences, and the International Association of Crime Analysts.

About the Contributors

Charles E. H. Berger is principal scientist at the Netherlands Forensic Institute (NFI) and professor of criminalistics at Leiden University. He specializes in criminalistics and specifically in subjects such as forensic interpretation and inference. At NFI, he is active in a number of areas such as education and research and development, about which he publishes internationally. He also supports the NFI experts, advises the institute's direction, and monitors scientific quality. He is currently involved in promoting logically correct reasoning and interpretation, through education, research, and international cooperation and standards. He enjoys the challenge of working at the interface of science, policing, and the law.

Andrea R. Borrego is a third-year doctoral student in the Criminology and Criminal Justice Department at Arizona State University. She received her B.A. in psychology from the University of Notre Dame in 2009 and her M.S. in Criminology and Criminal Justice from Arizona State University in 2011. For her master's thesis, Andrea examined arrest-related deaths in the United States using information from the Bureau of Justice Statistics and media reports. Her research interests include neighborhoods, policing, the intersection of these two topics, and LGBT victimization.

Nina W. Chernoff is an associate professor at the City University of New York (CUNY) School of Law. Prior to joining CUNY's faculty, Nina was a staff attorney in the Special Litigation Division of the Public Defender Service (PDS) for the District of Columbia. In that capacity, she litigated systemic criminal justice issues, including prosecutorial misconduct, jury representation, and the reliability of forensic evidence. Prior to PDS, she was a staff attorney and Zubrow Fellow at the Juvenile Law Center, and served as a law clerk for the Honorable Thomas L. Ambro, U.S. Court of Appeals for the Third Circuit. Nina graduated from Georgetown University Law Center magna cum laude in 2003, and received her B.A. in sociology from Bryn Mawr College in 1997, and her M.S. with distinction in justice, law, and society from the School of Public Affairs at American University in 2000.

John M. Collins Jr. is a forensic science policy and management advisor at RTI International. With over 20 years in forensic science, he has worked in federal, state, and local crime laboratories, and is the former director of forensic science for the Michigan State Police, where he led its seven laboratories to their first-ever international accreditation. Collins is a 1992 graduate of the Michigan State University forensic science program, earned his M.A. degree in organizational management in 2006, and became formally certified as a Senior Professional in Human Resources through the Human Resource Certification Institute in 2008. Collins is an active writer and speaker on forensic science policies and practices. He has spoken to thousands of scientists, attorneys, investigators, and students about contemporary forensic science issues. In 2007, Collins testified before the special committee on forensic science convened by the National Academy of Sciences. His published work was also cited in the committee's final report in 2009. He currently resides near Lansing, Michigan.

Rachel Dioso-Villa is an assistant professor at the School of Criminology and Criminal Justice at Griffith University. She received her Ph.D. in criminology, law, and society from the University of California, Irvine, and her M.A. in criminology from the University of Toronto. Her broad research interests include the study of forensic science, law, and society. She examines the admissibility of forensic evidence in court, representations of crime and forensic science in the media, jury studies, and miscarriages of justice and wrongful convictions. Dr. Dioso-Villa recently completed a comparative study on the admission of expert evidence in criminal and civil cases in the United States. She is also working on research in the area of forensic science and its role in wrongful convictions. Dr. Dioso-Villa has received grants and fellowships from the Social Science and Humanities Research Council of Canada, the American Society of Criminology, and the Canadian Foundation of University Women. Her work has appeared in the *Stanford Law Review*, *Canadian Journal of Criminology*, *Law Probability and Risk*, and the *Wall Street Journal*.

Dr. Itiel E. Dror is a cognitive neuroscientist. Interested in how the brain and cognitive system perceives and interprets information, he got a Ph.D. at Harvard University in 1994. Dr. Dror's work focuses on the cognitive architecture that underpins expertise. He researches expert performance in the real world, examining medical surgeons, military fighter pilots, frontline police, and forensic analysts. Dr. Dror's research provides insights into the inherent trade-offs of being an expert. In the forensic domain, he has demonstrated how contextual information can influence the judgments and decision making of experts; he has shown that even fingerprint and DNA experts can reach different conclusions when the same evidence is presented within different extraneous contexts. He has published over 100 research articles and has been extensively cited in the American National Academy of Science Report on Forensic Science. He currently is working on a number of major research projects aimed at providing a better understanding of forensic experts and finding ways to make their judgments more reliable. Dr. Dror has been working with numerous police forces and agencies to implement cognitive best practices in evaluating forensic evidence. More information is available at www.cci-hq.com.

Barry A. J. Fisher served as the crime laboratory director for the Los Angeles County Sheriff's Department from 1987 to 2009, and began his career at the lab in 1969. He is a distinguished fellow and former president of the American Academy of Forensic Sciences; a past president of the International Association of Forensic Sciences; a past president of the American Society of Crime Laboratory Directors; and a past chair of the American Society of Crime Laboratory Directors–Laboratory Accreditation Board. Fisher is co-author of three texts: *Techniques of Crime Scene Investigation* (2012, 8th ed.), *Introduction to Criminalistics: The Foundation of Forensic Science* (2009), and *Forensics*

Demystified (2007). He holds a B.S. degree in chemistry from the City College of New York, a M.S. degree in chemistry from Purdue University, and an M.B.A. from California State University, Northridge.

Robert Hayes is research manager (crime scene) at the Victoria Police Forensic Service Department in Victoria, Australia. Robert has qualifications in chemistry/pharmacology and business management. He has operational experience as a forensic scientist in the drug analysis, pharmacology, and chemical trace evidence disciplines coupled with business/strategic services in risk management, quality, strategic planning, research management, and training/education. Outside of the forensic sector, Robert has considerable experience in the chemical industry, including research, product development, laboratory management, process re-engineering/improvement, field quality, and production. Robert was a Partner Investigator on the Australian Research Council (ARC) Linkage Grant–funded project, "The Effectiveness of Forensic Science in the Criminal Justice System" with the University of Tasmania/Tasmanian Institute of Law Enforcement Studies, University of Technology Sydney, University of Canberra, and University of Lausanne, and plays a similar role in the ARC Linkage Grant–funded project, "Universal Immunogenic Reagents for the Detection of Latent Fingermarks" with University of Technology Sydney, University of Canberra, Northern Illinois University, and Flinders University. Robert is a member of the Australian Academy of Forensic Sciences and the Australian and New Zealand Forensic Society.

Dr. Max M. Houck is an internationally recognized forensic scientist who has worked for the FBI Laboratory, at a medical examiner's office, in the private sector, and in academia. His casework includes the Branch Davidian Investigation, the September 11 attacks on the Pentagon, the D. B. Cooper case, and the West Memphis Three case, among hundreds of others. He served for six years as the chair of the Forensic Science Educational Program Accreditation Commission and serves on other committees, including for Interpol. Dr. Houck has published widely in books and journals. He is a founding editor of the journal *Forensic Science Policy and Management* and has also co-authored a textbook with Dr. Jay Siegel, *Fundamentals of Forensic Science* (2010, 2nd ed.). In 2012, he was in the top 1% of connected professionals on LinkedIn. Dr. Houck lives and works in Washington, DC as the Director of the DC Department of Forensic Sciences (www.dfs.dc.gov).

Roberta Julian, Ph.D., is associate professor and director of the Tasmanian Institute of Law Enforcement Studies at the University of Tasmania, Australia, where she conducts research in policing and criminology. She also held this position as the inaugural director from 2003 to 2009. She is a sociologist with a particular interest in forensic science. Between 2002 and 2005, she was chief investigator for a series of projects (funded by the National Institute of Forensic Science) that examined knowledge and awareness of forensic science among police in three states in Australia: Tasmania, South Australia, and Victoria. She is currently the lead chief investigator in a five-year Australian Research Council Linkage Grant with Victoria Police, the Australian Federal Police (AFP), and the National Institute of Forensic Science (NIFS) that began in 2009. This project is examining the effectiveness of forensic science in the criminal justice system with a focus on police investigations and court outcomes. She is supervisor of two Ph.D. students within this project whose research focuses on "Lawyers and DNA:

Understanding and Challenging the Evidence" and "Measuring the Impact of Forensic Science on Police Investigations and Court Trials." Prof. Julian is also a chief investigator on a NIFS-funded project on "The Interfaces Between Science, Medicine and Law Enforcement" and a supervisor for an AFP-funded Ph.D. candidate whose project is on "Communicating Scientific Expert Opinion: What Do Forensic Scientists Say and What Do Police, Lawyers and the Jury Hear?" Prof. Julian is an editorial board member of the *Australian and New Zealand Journal of Criminology*, a member of the Board of Studies of the Australian Institute of Police Management, an associate investigator with the Centre of Excellence in Policing and Security, a member of the Committee of Management of the Australian and New Zealand Society of Criminology, and a past president of the Australian Sociological Association.

Dr. Sally Kelty is an applied social and behavioral scientist with a management background. For the past 20 years, she has worked in research and program development within the health, disability, and criminal justice areas. She has worked in private industry, in university research centers, and in government departments. Her program work includes the development and evaluation of prison-based programs, programs for people with mild cognitive impairment, independent community living programs for adults with cognitive impairments, and the development of psychological test batteries in recruitment and criminal justice settings. Sally has worked on several longitudinal health projects with high-risk adolescent mothers and their children. Sally joined the Tasmanian Institute of Law Enforcement Studies (TILES) in July 2009 as a research fellow working on a five-year project mapping the effective use of forensic science and expertise by policing and legal agencies in criminal investigations and court outcomes. In this project, Sally works with several police jurisdictions and has completed several applied projects including identifying the key attributes of Australia's top-performing crime scene examiners. More recently, she has been the lead program developer for a recruitment strategy and career-advancement program for forensic scientists within police agencies. Sally was the chief investigator on a National Institute of Forensic Science project exploring "The Interfaces between Science, Medicine and Law Enforcement," which examined inter–justice agency communication and working relationships between four professions/professional groups (law enforcement, forensic medicine and health, forensic science, law). Sally supervises five Ph.D. students at TILES in the forensic studies research area. She is the inaugural president of the Tasmanian Branch of the Association of Psychiatry, Psychology and Law.

Wim Kerkhoff is a forensic firearms examiner. He joined the Netherlands Forensic Institute (NFI) in 1990 and worked on firearms-related casework almost continuously. This casework often involves bullet and cartridge case comparison, which is largely a "manual," non-automated forensic field. Mr. Kerkhoff is convinced that, apart from developing more objective techniques, effectively dealing with contextual information is a big and needed step forward in forensic science. Interested in developing the field of forensic firearms examination, he both initiated and assisted in a number of research projects at the NFI's Firearms Section.

Erwin J. A. T. Mattijssen works as a forensic firearms examiner at the Netherlands Forensic Institute since 2010. After receiving a B.Sc. degree in biology at Leiden University (2007), he received a M.Sc. degree in forensic science at the University of

Amsterdam (2009) and in teaching biology at Leiden University (2010). Since 2013, he also works as a lecturer for the course "Observer Based Techniques" within the master's forensic science program at the University of Amsterdam.

Joseph L. Peterson, D.Crim., is a retired professor in the School of Criminal Justice and Criminalistics at California State University, Los Angeles. Over the past 40 years, Peterson's research and publications have monitored the evolution of the forensic sciences, documenting its growing potential as well as its shortcomings. His research has focused on the uses and effects of scientific evidence at key decision points in the judicial process (arrest, charging, determination of guilt or innocence, and sentencing). His work has also explored the quality of crime laboratory results via proficiency testing of examiners, problems associated with the location of crime laboratories within law enforcement agencies, and ethical dilemmas faced by forensic scientists practicing in an adversarial justice system. Peterson's 2002 and 2005 *Census(es) of Publicly Funded Forensic Crime Laboratories* for the Bureau of Justice Statistics have documented high caseloads, long backlogs, and severe budgetary and personnel needs. He recently completed two National Institute of Justice studies examining the role and impact of scientific evidence in the criminal justice process, and the results of DNA tests and their impact on sexual assault kits backlogged in the LASD and LAPD crime laboratories. Peterson received the Distinguished Fellow Award from the American Academy of Forensic Sciences in 2008.

Walter F. Rowe is professor of Forensic Sciences at The George Washington University. He has been a member of the faculty of the Department of Forensic Sciences since 1975. Dr. Rowe's forensic experience includes service in the U.S. Army Criminal Investigation laboratory as a forensic drug chemist and as a forensic serologist. He has a B.S. with highest honors in chemistry from Emory University and an A.M. and Ph.D. in chemistry from Harvard University. Dr. Rowe is a fellow in the Criminalistics Section of the American Academy of Forensic Sciences. He is also a member of ASTM Committee e30. Dr. Rowe is the author of more than 50 articles and book chapters dealing with forensic science.

David A. Schroeder is an assistant professor in the Criminal Justice Department, and an assistant dean in the Henry C. Lee College of Criminal Justice and Forensic Sciences at the University of New Haven. Dr. Schroeder began his career as a private investigator in Orange County, California, where he specialized in death penalty defense investigations. Dr. Schroeder also served as an investigator for the Orange County Alternate Defender's Office, specializing in homicide investigations. Dr. Schroeder completed his doctorate in 2007 from the CUNY Graduate School through John Jay College of Criminal Justice. Dr. Schroeder's other research interests include aberrant/episodic homicide, defense investigation, tolerance issues in law enforcement, and hostage negotiations. Dr. Schroeder has published in *Police Quarterly* and in the *Journal of the Institute of Justice and International Studies*.

Jay Siegel holds a Ph.D. in analytical chemistry from The George Washington University. He worked for three years at the Virginia Bureau of Forensic Sciences, analyzing drugs, fire residues, and trace evidence. He was then professor of chemistry and forensic science at Metropolitan State College for three years. From 1980 to 2004, he was professor of forensic chemistry and director of the forensic science program at Michigan State University in the School of Criminal Justice. In 2004, he moved to Indiana University–Purdue University Indianapolis (IUPUI) to become director of the forensic and investigative sciences program, a position which he held until August of 2011. In 2008, he also became chair of the Department of Chemistry and Chemical Biology at IUPUI. He retired from IUPUI in 2012 and is now a consultant in forensic science. Dr. Siegel has testified over 200 times as an expert witness in 12 states, federal court, and military court. He is editor-in-chief of the *Encyclopedia of Forensic Sciences* and has over 30 publications in forensic science journals. He has co-authored a college textbook titled *Fundamentals of Forensic Science* (2010) for Elsevier and a high school forensic science textbook, *Forensic Science: The Basics* (2010), published by CRC. Both are in their second editions. His newest book, *Forensic Science: A Beginner's Guide*, came out in 2008. In February 2009, he was named distinguished fellow by the American Academy of Forensic Sciences. In April 2009, he was given the Distinguished Alumni Scholar Award by his alma mater, the George Washington University.

Kristen Skogerboe is a professor of chemistry at Seattle University. She holds a B.S. from Colorado State University (1982) and a Ph.D. from Iowa State University (1986). From 1986 to 1990, she held fellowships in laboratory medicine and molecular medical genetics at the University of Washington School of Medicine, and was board certified in clinical chemistry (DABCC) and molecular genetics (DABMG). She served as a clinical pathology laboratory director, establishing a molecular diagnostic program for viral, prenatal, and genetic disease diagnosis, and founding an AABB-accredited paternity testing laboratory. Since 1995, she has been a faculty member at Seattle University, teaching chemistry and forensic science, and serving as the chairperson of the chemistry department from 2002 to 2012. She is interested in the analysis of biomolecules and has numerous reports and professional publications. She has consulted with attorneys and law enforcement agencies related to forensic evidence, and has worked closely with the Seattle University Law School.

Paul J. Speaker is a faculty member of the West Virginia University Department of Finance in the College of Business and Economics. He holds an M.S. and Ph.D. in economics from Purdue University, and a B.A. in economics from LaSalle College. Dr. Speaker also holds the position of chief executive officer of Forensic Science Management Consultants LLC, a firm that specializes in the business of forensics using the forensics of business. He serves as principal investigator for Project FORESIGHT, a National Institute of Justice–funded effort to provide a business approach to improve forensic laboratory efficiency and cost effectiveness. Dr. Speaker's research activity is concentrated in economic modeling, including regulated industries, business valuation, the role of not-for-profit institutions, and the business of forensics. His teaching areas include corporate finance, managerial economics, business valuation, and financial management.

Reinoud D. Stoel was trained as a psychologist and received his doctorate in psychometrics in 2003. After obtaining his Ph.D., he had a position as assistant professor methods and statistics at the University of Amsterdam, and in 2008, he started as a forensic statistician. He is currently team leader of the statistics group of the Netherlands Forensic Institute. He has developed into a psychometrician and statistician with broad practical experience in both teaching and research (from psychology and behavioral genetics to forensics), with many publications in peer-reviewed international journals. In his current position, he provides teaching in statistics (interpretation of evidence) to experts, police officers, judges, and lawyers, as well as statistical consultancy in both forensic casework and research. His current main research interests are the development of methods that minimize cognitive bias and context effects in forensic casework, and conceptual issues in the interpretation of forensic evidence.

Michael D. White is an associate professor in the School of Criminology and Criminal Justice at Arizona State University (ASU), and is associate director of ASU's Center for Violence Prevention and Community Safety. He received his Ph.D. in criminal justice from Temple University in 1999. Prior to entering academia, Dr. White worked as a deputy sheriff in Pennsylvania. Dr. White's primary research interests involve the police, including use of force, training, and misconduct. His recent work has been published in *Justice Quarterly*, *Criminology and Public Policy*, *Crime and Delinquency*, and *Criminal Justice and Behavior*.

ⓈSAGE research**methods**

The essential online tool for researchers from the world's leading methods publisher

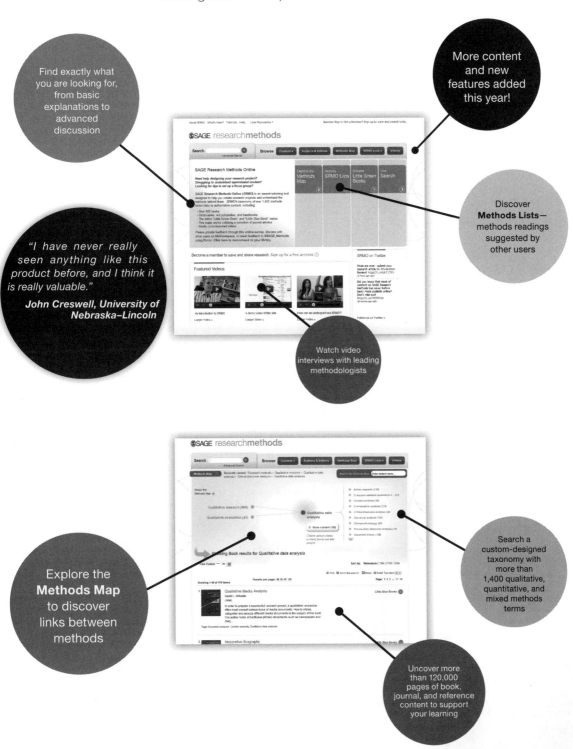

Find exactly what you are looking for, from basic explanations to advanced discussion

More content and new features added this year!

"I have never really seen anything like this product before, and I think it is really valuable."

John Creswell, University of Nebraska–Lincoln

Discover **Methods Lists**— methods readings suggested by other users

Watch video interviews with leading methodologists

Explore the **Methods Map** to discover links between methods

Search a custom-designed taxonomy with more than 1,400 qualitative, quantitative, and mixed methods terms

Uncover more than 120,000 pages of book, journal, and reference content to support your learning

Find out more at
www.sageresearchmethods.com